Pioneers and Partisans

Pioneers and Partisans

An Oral History of Nazi Genocide in Belorussia

ANIKA WALKE

UNIVERSITY PRESS

Oxford University Press is a department of the University of Oxford. It furthers
the University's objective of excellence in research, scholarship, and education
by publishing worldwide. Oxford is a registered trade mark of Oxford University
Press in the UK and certain other countries.

Published in the United States of America by Oxford University Press
198 Madison Avenue, New York, NY 10016, United States of America

© Oxford University Press 2015

First issued as an Oxford University Press paperback, 2018

All rights reserved. No part of this publication may be reproduced, stored in
a retrieval system, or transmitted, in any form or by any means, without the
prior permission in writing of Oxford University Press, or as expressly permitted
by law, by license, or under terms agreed with the appropriate reproduction
rights organization. Inquiries concerning reproduction outside the scope of the
above should be sent to the Rights Department, Oxford University Press, at the
address above.

You must not circulate this work in any other form
and you must impose this same condition on any acquirer.

Library of Congress Cataloging-in-Publication Data
Walke, Anika, author.
Pioneers and partisans : an oral history of Nazi genocide in Belorussia / Anika Walke.
pages cm—(Oxford oral history series)
ISBN 978-0-19-933553-4 (hardback : alk.); 978-0-19-088883-1 (paperback : alk.)
1. Jews—Belarus—Biography.   2. Jews—Belarus—Biography—History and criticism.
3. Holocaust, Jewish (1939-1945)—Belarus—Biography—History and criticism.
4. Jews, Soviet—Biography.   5. Oral history—Belarus.   6. Belarus—Ethnic relations.
I. Title.
DS135.B383A188 2015
940.53′180922478—dc23
2014047219

Contents

Preface vii
Acknowledgments xi
Note on Transliteration and Geopolitical Terminology xv
Maps xvii

INTRODUCTION 1

1 **ON METHODOLOGY:** Oral History and the Nazi Genocide 23

2 **BETWEEN TRADITION AND TRANSFORMATION:** Soviet Jews in the 1930s 37

3 **THE END OF CHILDHOOD:** Young Soviet Jews in the Minsk Ghetto 67

4 **SUFFERING AND SURVIVAL:** The Destruction of Jewish Communities in Eastern Belorussia 103

5 **FIGHTING FOR LIFE AND VICTORY:** Refugees from the Ghettos and the Soviet Partisan Movement 131

6 **OF REFUGE AND RESISTANCE:** Labor for Survival in the "Zorin Family Unit" 164

CONCLUSION: Soviet Internationalism, Judaism, and the Nazi Genocide in Oral Histories 204

Notes 233
Sources 285
Index 309

Preface

On a bright and sunny day in St. Petersburg, eight of us, six women, one man, and I, were enjoying an outing into the Primorskii Park Pobedy (Maritime Victory Park) on the west side of the Russian city's Krestovskii Ostrov (Cross Island), a setting of lush green lawns, bushes, and trees. The majority of my hosts had survived the Nazi genocide committed in the Soviet Union, primarily in Belorussia, and now they were all members of the Association of Former Prisoners of Nazi Ghettos and Concentration Camps, St. Petersburg Branch. The women had invited me to a picnic in the park after collecting a monthly payment from the Jewish Claims Conference, a payment that increased the meager pensions of survivors of the Nazi genocide residing in Eastern Europe.

We chatted, standing around a bench, drinking vodka, munching on *zakuski*, the inevitable, mostly savory, accompaniments of drinking in Russia: marinated cucumbers, caviar, cheese, and bread. As the women were offering me more and more food, along with more and more drinks, they spoke about the other Germans in their lives, those that had taken away and killed their parents, relatives, friends, and neighbors. One of the women began to sing a German song she had picked up in the concentration camp. This moment, conjuring up militant occupants' actions and their imprint on individuals' memory, is a compelling invitation to think across time and space about genocide and its repercussions, and to note the connections between relationships situated in 1941 Nazi-occupied Europe and 2008 post-Soviet St. Petersburg.

As I break bread with these elderly people, reflecting on the tradition of *cum panis*, we are establishing companionship. At the same time it is clear that we all were aware of the cracks in this companionship, of the past that continues to affect the lives of these elderly people in Russia and my life in Germany and as a German, albeit in different ways. Raisa Soboleva, the association's bookkeeper and the only other non-Jewish person in the group, gives words to my thoughts: "I look at these people, I see them every day, they are happy and have a good life. But one thing you should never forget: they are all orphans. When I had problems, I could always rely on my parents, my mother, but they had nobody; all their relatives were gone." Although the park had grown green where, at the end of World War II, corpses and bomb craters gave witness to the 900-day siege of Leningrad by German troops, the remnants of the past are still present. They are often invisible, yet undeniable. The lives of Frida Ped'ko, Elena Drapkina, Pavel Rubinchik, and their friends who were with me in the park had been forever marked by the experience of violence, survival, and the reconstruction of lives left in ruins after the war.

This book shows how Soviet Jews, born between the mid-1920s and the early 1930s, experienced the Nazi occupation and genocide in Belorussia, and how they remember it. This portrayal of the history and memory of systematic violence necessitates looking at the ways in which people learned to perceive and understand their lives, before, during, and after the war. Only such an integrated perspective allows us to decode how representations of the past emerge, why specific aspects are left out, and why others are emphasized. Notably, policies and debates on nationality, gender, and war determined how Soviet Jewish youths related to their society and other individuals. The breakdown of the Soviet project, and its policies' prospects and promises, as a result of the Nazi occupation is a central element of Soviet Jews' experience of the Nazi genocide.

This portrayal of survival under the Nazi genocide in eastern Belorussia is based on personal narratives. It is not only a critique and rectification of a postwar history in which many Soviet Jewish survivors were discriminated against, it also highlights how the ideological and cultural framework of Soviet society molded both how young Soviet Jews experienced the Nazi genocide and how they, as elderly women and men, represent it after the Soviet Union has ceased to exist. A collective biography of young Soviet Jews who endured Nazi persecution and often barely escaped mass murder, this book shows that surviving the Nazi genocide in German-occupied Soviet territories affected people's lives far beyond the hunger, violence, and lethal danger during the war. The Nazi regime destroyed people and places, but it also invalidated the lived reality of a prewar world where social equality and peaceful interethnic cohabitation seemed possible.

Tracking these women's and men's lives in light of broader historical and cultural tendencies set in motion by first Soviet, then Nazi, and then again Soviet rulers, the following pages reveal the shift in perspective that Soviet Jewish children and adolescents had to undergo, from a privileged position as builders of a new society to a position at the bottom of society, as bodies that could be exploited for work and then targeted for extinction. They introduce the experiences, and in later years memories, of a generation of Jews that lived through a series of upheavals, that saw the hopes inspired by Soviet prewar internationalism collapse with the German invasion, that managed to survive the Nazi extermination project, and that finally re-entered and remained in Soviet society after the war.

The story is one of repeated transformations of identity, from Soviet citizen in the prewar years to a target of genocidal violence during the war to barely accepted national minority in the postwar Soviet Union. The story is also one of multiple forms of violation piled on top of each other, beginning with Soviet nationality policies obstructing the cultural and religious framework of traditional Jewish identity, continuing to the Nazi annihilation policy eradicating Jewish people and their culture, and followed by the systematic omission of Soviet Jews' wartime experience from the official portrayal of the war within and beyond the Soviet Union.

At its core, this book is a rumination about how we can live in the present with an unbearably violent past. It is a book of memory for the women and men I met in St. Petersburg and Minsk, and for their friends, relatives, and neighbors who confronted Nazi racism and its repercussions, often left to do so on their own. Remembering this isolation cannot undo it, but it may pose important questions and suggest answers on how to live ethically with the aftermath of systematic violence and with those who suffered from it.

Acknowledgments

This book marks a preliminary end to work that began in earnest in April 2001 when I conducted my first interviews with survivors of the Nazi genocide in St. Petersburg, Russia. The selection of material, its assembly, and the views and interpretations offered in this book are my responsibility, yet my efforts to account for these people's history and memory benefited from the support and assistance of many people and institutions, in many places and over a long time. I am offering my sincerest gratitude to those in Russia, Belarus, Germany, and the United States who have made this book possible.

Research such as mine would be impossible without the many women and men who agreed to speak to me about their lives, or those who volunteered their narration for other interview projects. I thank all of them for their sincerity, generosity, and patience as they spoke to interviewers like me who were often unaware of the full scope and weight of a life lived under duress and after. I identify these personal encounters and other interview sources in a full list at the end of this volume, but they ought to be named here.

Raisa Soboleva, the late Tatiana Litvinova, and Pavel Rubinchik of the Association of Former Prisoners of Ghettos and Concentration Camps, St. Petersburg, offered valuable support in contacting interviewees in St. Petersburg, always listened to my concerns, and, over several years, prepared numerous cups of tea during my visits. Mikhail Treister, from the Minsk branch of the Association, and Frida Reisman and Maia Krapina of the Hesed Rakhamim Welfare Organization, also in Minsk, provided helpful guidance during my research trips to the capital of Belarus. Elena Bogdanova, the late Ingrid Oswald, Viktor Voronkov, and their colleagues from the Centre for Independent Social Research generously supported my endeavors in St. Petersburg, as scholars and as friends. Ute Weinmann and

Vlad Tupikin opened their home and minds and made research visits to Moscow enjoyable.

While my research led me, first of all, into many people's homes, it also utilized a number of archival sources. The following people offered crucial help in identifying and accessing these sources: Natalia Iatskevich (National Archives of Belarus, Minsk), Leonid Terushkin and Il'ia Al'tman (Russian Research and Educational Holocaust Center, Moscow, Russia), Vadim Altskan (Archives of the US Holocaust Memorial Museum), Martin Dean (Jack, Joseph and Morton Mandel Center for Advanced Holocaust Studies at the US Holocaust Memorial Museum), Vincent Slatt and Ronald Coleman (Library of the US Holocaust Memorial Museum), and Crispin Brooks (USC Shoah Foundation Institute).

The research for this book required substantial institutional and financial support. I benefited from scholarships and research grants of the DAAD (German Academic Exchange Service), a doctoral fellowship of the Rosa Luxemburg Foundation, Berlin (Germany), and travel grants of the Center for Women's and Gender Studies at Carl von Ossietzky University of Oldenburg, Germany, and the DFG (German Research Council) when conducting research in Russia and Belarus. Further research was made possible by a fellowship of the Miles Lerman Center for the Study of Jewish Resistance at the Jack, Joseph and Morton Mandel Center for Advanced Holocaust Studies of the United States Holocaust Memorial Museum. Crucial periods of writing were supported by the Chancellor's Dissertation-Year Fellowship at University of California at Santa Cruz and a Thesis Fellowship of the Fondation pour la Mémoire de la Shoah, Paris (France). Final extensions and revisions were completed during a postdoctoral fellowship in International and Area Studies at Washington University in St. Louis.

Research like mine develops through several stages; its multinational dimension adds a layer of complexity encoded in personal, academic, and administrative challenges that deserve special appreciation. Ronald Sperling, Lydia Potts, and Ahlrich Meyer, at the time all based in Oldenburg, Germany, offered crucial advice and encouragement when I conducted the first interviews with survivors and embarked on a journey that would last several years; without their support this project would not have come to fruition. Discussions with members of the colloquium "Nationalsozialismus und Zeitgeschichte" at the Carl von Ossietzky University of Oldenburg and the advocacy group for the compensation of former forced laborers paved the way for my analysis. In particular, Stefan Kanke was instrumental for my first forays into conducting oral history interviews.

I continue to be in astonishment at the level of support I received at UC Santa Cruz. Barbara Epstein is a mentor whose support is stimulating at all times, critical when called for, and never in question. She shepherded my thinking and writing through its various stages and continues to do so long after she signed off on my dissertation. Bettina Aptheker, Gail Hershatter, Peter Kenez, and Angela Davis were generous readers, encouraging much-needed confidence and conciseness as I wrote the dissertation that is at the core of this book. Ahlrich Meyer and Lydia Potts, at Carl von Ossietzky University of Oldenburg, were attentive and responsive throughout my doctoral work and in its final stages.

Anjali Arondekar, Donna Haraway, and David Marriott taught me to ask different questions and thus shaped my perspective on oral history in crucial ways. I thank my peers, in seminars, as fellow teaching assistants at UC Santa Cruz, during my fellowship at the US Holocaust Memorial Museum, at conferences, and during workshops for important criticism and insightful discussions. Nicole Archer, Adam Hefty, and Jürgen Matthäus were careful and helpful readers of early drafts. Wendy Goldman, Lisa Kirschenbaum, Harriet Murav, Jean Allman, and Tim Parsons pushed me to strengthen my argument and offered valuable advice as I strove to bring this work into book shape.

I am grateful for the guidance and assistance in bureaucratic matters that I received from Sheila Peuse, Anne Spalliero, Kris West, Ingeborg Gerdes-Wiehebrink, Kathy Daniel, Toni Loomis, Sheryl Peltz, and Margaret Williams.

Nancy Toff and Kathy Nasstrom of Oxford University Press provided invaluable insight and advice at crucial junctures of this book's completion. Two outside readers deserve appreciation and thanks for their suggestions. I am immensely grateful to James Warren for his thorough and excellent editing at a critical moment. Steve Dodson was a wonderful copy editor for the final manuscript. Kate Nunn, who saw the book through production, was a pleasure to work with. Steven Feldman and the Emerging Scholars Program at the Mandel Center for Advanced Holocaust Studies supported the preparation of the manuscript and of the book proposal. Jacqueline Voluz produced excellent maps and rescued me from committing typical errors of lay cartographers. I thank Galina Levina (Scientific Director of the

Memorial to the Victims of the Holocaust in Minsk at the "Iama", Pit) and sculptor Aleksandr Finskii for the generous permission to use a photo of the late Leonid Levin's work on the cover of this book.

I am fortunate to share distinct periods and realms of life with people who, each in their own way, have sustained me in my ambitious endeavor. The unwavering support of my parents Marianne and Willibald Walke, as well as the curiosity and encouragement offered by my siblings Tobias, Sabine, and Dorit and my niece Julia, throughout different periods and across thousands of miles have been vital for my transnational endeavors. Karla and Dwight Sangrey have helped in many and much-appreciated ways. The (now transatlantic) friendship of Jette and Peter Schulte, Marion Fittje, and Wolle Bruch, as well as the more recent companionship provided by Nicole Archer, Apryl Berney, Adam Bush, and Sowande' Mustakeem, have been invaluable in many respects. I am grateful for the distractions offered by the Family Dinner group, 5G, and my fellow Frontrunners.

I am deeply indebted to my partner Trevor Joy Sangrey, who is a fine writing coach, always available to process ideas and insecurities, and has accompanied me gracefully during the ups and downs of representing violence and its aftermath.

An earlier version of chapter 2 appeared as "Memories of an Unfulfilled Promise: Internationalism and Patriotism in Post-Soviet Oral Histories of Jewish Survivors of the Nazi genocide," *Oral History Review* 40, no. 2 (2013): 271–279, and a previous, much shorter iteration of chapter 3 was published as "Jewish Youth in the Minsk Ghetto: How Age and Gender Mattered," *Kritika–Explorations in Russian and Eurasian History* 15, no. 3 (2014): 535–562.

Note on Transliteration and Geopolitical Terminology

A modified Library of Congress transliteration system is used throughout the text. The Russian endings ий and ый appear as ii and yi; except for the Russian soft (') and hard (") signs, all diacritics are omitted. Names and toponyms are given in their non-anglicized form except for famous personalities or when authors chose differently in their own publications. Russian, Yiddish, and German terms are italicized and translated the first time they are used.

Belorussia

This book develops an inside perspective on the lives of Jewish children and adolescents during the Nazi occupation of Belorussia. In 1941, the Belorussian Soviet Socialist Republic (BSSR) included territories roughly to the east of, and including, Minsk, which had been part of the USSR since 1922, and formerly Polish territories in the west that had been annexed by the Soviet regime and incorporated into the BSSR in 1939. People who lived in the eastern territories, often called Soviet Belorussia, and in Minsk before World War II are at the center of this book. To refer to this region, I use "eastern Belorussia" throughout, because that terminology reflects the republic's status at the beginning of the German occupation in 1941. I use "Belorussia" or "BSSR" when referring to the whole republic during and after the war, and "Belarus" when addressing developments following the breakup of the Soviet Union in 1991, when the BSSR acquired national sovereignty as the Republic of Belarus.

Maps

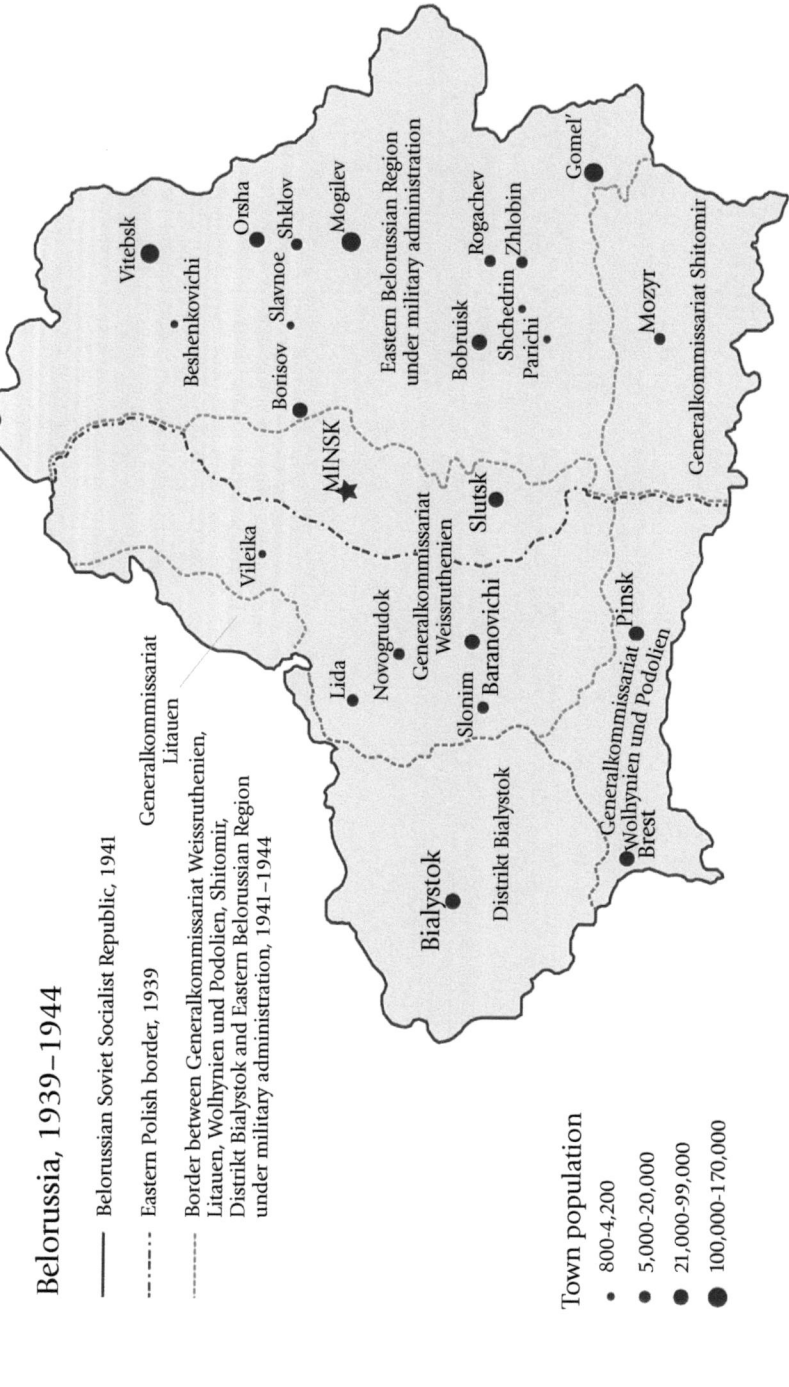

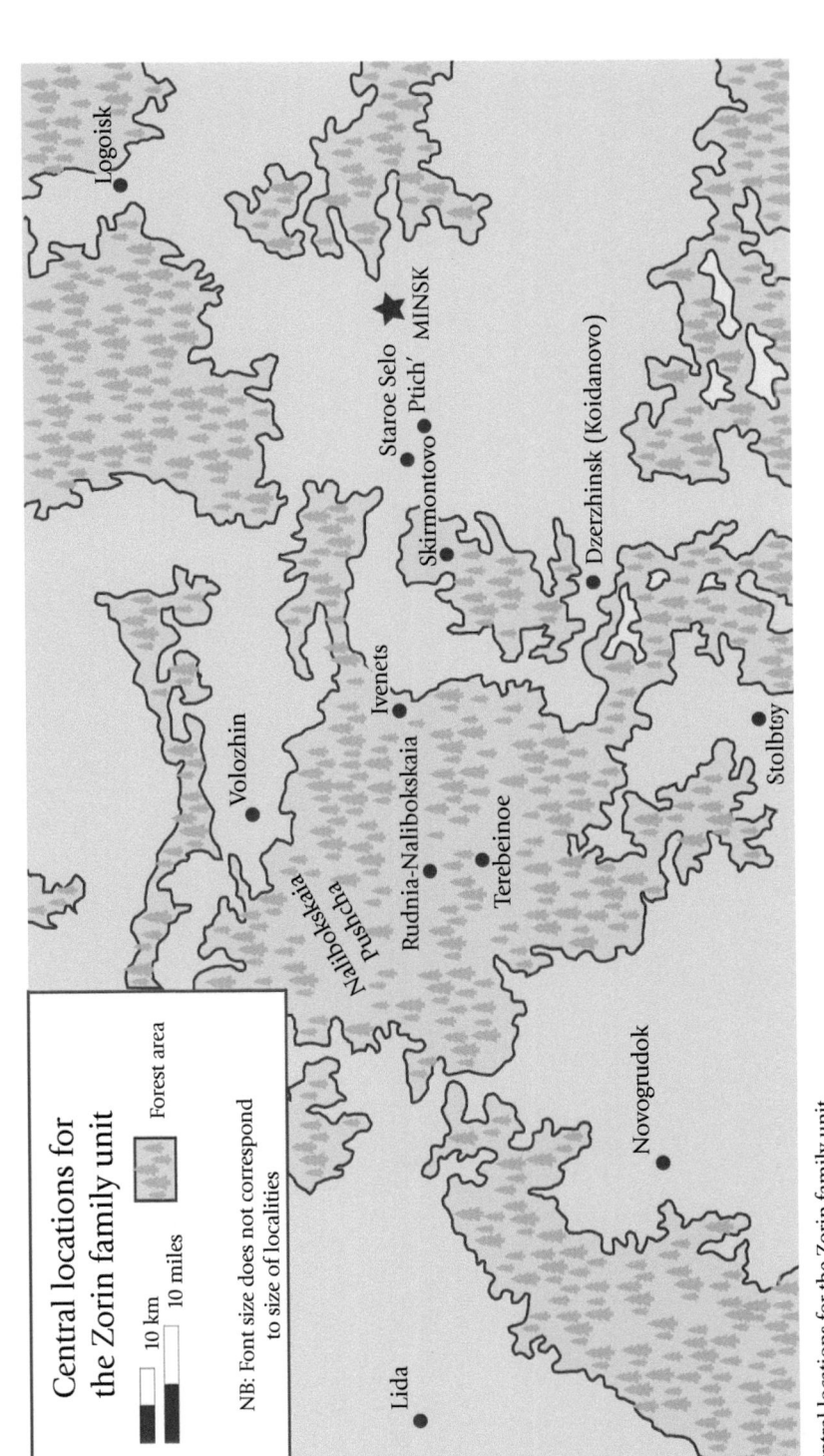

Central locations for the Zorin family unit

Pioneers and Partisans

Introduction

Frida Ped'ko has a vivid memory of the day the Jews of Slavnoe, a small town near Vitebsk, Belorussia, were killed. On the morning of March 16, 1942, Jewish women and men, adults alongside adolescents and children, were lined up and led to an execution site near the town. Asked whether she, then seven years old, understood what was happening, Ped'ko says,

> I didn't really understand, when they took us and told me, "We're going to mama." I had understood that she was shot and that that was terrible, but I didn't understand that that was forever. I thought she is somewhere ... But when my sister said, "They'll shoot us," I was terrified, asked, "What do you mean, they will shoot at me? That will hurt and will make me bleed!"[1]

A few minutes before the column of people, lined up in rows of three or four, reached the borders of the town, someone pushed Frida and her sister Elena into the arms of an onlooker. Piotr I. Stasevich took the children and placed the seven- and ten-year-olds in the house of Vera and Vania Nastiporenko. Afraid that German troops would find out about the hidden Jewish children, the family asked Stasevich to move them a few days later. This he did, hiding the sisters in a hut he built in the woods outside of the small settlement. Stasevich thus rescued the two children from sure death: as many as 150 Jews residing in Slavnoe were shot on March 16, 1942, in a ditch near the village of Gliniki.[2]

For two and a half years, Frida and Elena scraped by in their hideout in the woods. They lived on mushrooms, berries, herbs, and whatever else they could find. Piotr Stasevich also brought food and sometimes demanded that Mrs. Nastiporenko help the children as well. In addition, Frida Ped'ko says that she and her sister sometimes snuck into the Nastiporenko family's pigsty and grabbed food from the feeding troughs. Joining a partisan unit, a formation of guerilla fighters that emerged in the forests and swamps of this Soviet republic, as many other ghetto refugees were able to do, was not an option:

> Nobody took us, children were of no use to them. That would have been an additional burden. When my sister asked them, they said that they would take her; but me, being seven years old, they couldn't take me. But she couldn't abandon me and leave me behind on my own.[3]

In the summer of 1944, the two children were too exhausted to imagine themselves still alive the following spring. They had already survived two harsh winters, suffering illness as a result of eating poisonous mushrooms, and fearing wild animals roaming the forest at night. "We decided to go to the local commander and ask him to kill us. We were so wasted, there was no real food."[4]

During our interview, Frida Ped'ko was aware that these thoughts must appear disturbing: "It is strange, how calmly we spoke about this, that we would somehow make it through the summer, but that, if the country would not be liberated by the winter, we would surrender. We remember this often nowadays, it was so horrible."[5] Luckily, on a trip to find food, the older sister, Elena, noticed Soviet troops in the area and, in June 1944, found out that the region had been liberated. The two sisters could safely leave their hideout in the forest and ask for help in the nearby village.

At the time of our first encounter in 2000, Frida Ped'ko was filing paperwork for material compensation allocated by the German government to survivors of Nazi ghettos. She was also applying for social benefits that the Russian state granted to veterans of the war. In both instances, the claims were initially denied for lack of evidence and because Frida was considered too young to have suffered substantive damage. The loss of a mother—shot in June 1941 for being Jewish and for being a Communist Party official in the local granary—and the postwar struggle of an orphan coping with the emotional and physical traumas of surviving undernourished and exposed to the elements were insufficient grounds for her claims.[6] Instead, bureaucrats in the local administration insulted her, arguing that "living in a ghetto wasn't that bad."[7]

Frida Ped'ko is acutely aware of how her Jewish nationality marked her as a specific target of ignorance, discrimination, and violence, compounding the suffering and loss she experienced as a child. On the other hand, she very clearly recognizes that she shares her difficulties and many of her memories with her non-Jewish compatriots, and thus she identifies herself as part of a larger, Soviet collective:

> In Belorussia, who was it who died there—everyone. It is of course a different story that almost all Jews died, but the Belorussians lost every fourth too. And if you look at the old women from my hometown who saw everything and who mourned with us—if you see how they live today, nobody helps them at all. That is why I think that everything should be distributed equally. Everybody should live well. I am an internationalist.

Remembering her life before, during, and after the war, Ped'ko emphasizes when she was singled out, but also places herself within the framework of Soviet society more generally and insists on people's equality. "Internationalism," understood here as a form of interethnic solidarity, was an important tenet of Soviet ideology.[8] Throughout her life she actively participated in building a society based on this ideology, supporting, for instance, the local *Komsomol*, the Communist Party's youth organization, whenever possible.[9] And she joined the Communist Party, explaining it by saying "I was thankful that the Soviet Army rescued us."

Frida Ped'ko's story exemplifies the lives of thousands of other men and women who, as children and adolescents, survived the Nazi occupation of Belorussia and the genocide that targeted them for being Jewish. Some of them survived in hiding, like Frida and her sister; others joined or were admitted into partisan units. Small numbers were evacuated to the Soviet rear when the opportunity arose, but not before they too had witnessed murder and starvation and pondered the effects of systematic physical violence.

Shocking in their frankness, young Frida's thoughts on what it means to be shot crystallize the terror and disbelief with which residents of the former Jewish Pale of Settlement—roughly comprising present-day Lithuania, Belarus, Poland, Moldova, Ukraine, and parts of western Russia—confronted the onslaught of German troops in the summer of 1941. What we call the Holocaust, the murder of European Jewry, in this area happened very quickly, and very publicly. Most of the Jews in eastern Belorussia were killed by March 1942, usually falling victim to mass shootings at trenches, ravines, or pits near or in their hometowns.[10] Overall, an estimated 800,000 Jewish civilians, roughly 80 percent of the prewar population, were murdered by the Nazi regime in Belorussia.[11] Exact numbers and percentages are difficult to establish, because it is unclear how many Jews were physically located within Belorussian borders when German troops began the murder campaign there.[12] An influx of refugees from Poland from the beginning of the war in 1939, mass escapes and evacuations organized by the Soviet government in the summer of 1941, deportations of Jews from Germany, Austria, Hungary, and elsewhere to Belorussia by the Nazi regime, and finally the exodus of surviving Jews after the war make it impossible to say precisely how many Jews died during the occupation.

The speed and brutality of the Nazi campaign of extermination in eastern Belorussia is remarkable when compared to these campaigns elsewhere in Europe. The internal life of the ghettos in eastern Belorussia deserves attention because the role and purpose of these ghettos in the process of the so-called "final solution of the Jewish question" differed markedly from those of the ghettos in Poland and other Eastern European countries. In the Soviet territories, ghettos did not serve as transitional spaces of internment from which inmates were deported to extermination camps. Rather, they were themselves, or were in close proximity to, sites of mass murder. For the most part, they were holding pens in preparation for genocide.[13] Stories about life in the ghettos of Slavnoe—Frida Ped'ko's hometown—or elsewhere in eastern Belorussia and in Minsk are thus not merely "untold" stories to be added to the literature on the Holocaust: Frida Ped'ko and other Jews in eastern Belorussia witnessed, experienced, and responded to extermination campaigns differently than Jews elsewhere. In part this is, because prior to the German occupation, Jews residing in this region did not necessarily perceive themselves as members of a specific and identifiable community. This was especially true of a young generation of Jews who did not view their lives as distinct from those of their non-Jewish compatriots; a religiously or nationally defined Jewish community did not previously provide an important framework for their daily lives.[14]

Granted, a sense of integration, even assimilation, was widely shared among Jews across Europe. Throughout the nineteenth century, more and more Jews—in France, Germany, Italy, and elsewhere—had sought to become full members of the societies in which they lived. They limited the practice of their Jewish faith to the home, intermarried, and otherwise followed the trend to secularize their public lives.[15] Albeit hampered by the upsurge of racial antisemitism that denied Jews, for instance in Germany, the possibility of ever becoming proper German citizens, because supposedly they were different "by blood," many European Jews were able to build a life in the midst of their non-Jewish contemporaries.[16]

Though Soviet Jews shared this experience, their assimilation was unique, the result of a state project that included the abolition of religious Judaism. Void of its spiritual and ritual core, "being Jewish" in the Soviet context was increasingly limited to a legal category, especially for a younger generation who had not been taught Hebrew or how to read the Torah. They were Jewish by nationality, a concept used to describe the different ethnic groups of the Soviet Union.[17] In this system of thought, Russian, Ukrainian, German, Jewish, Tatar, and other nationalities were distinguished by their common heritage and shared linguistic and cultural traditions, including religious beliefs. Religious frameworks for national cultures were increasingly dismantled, however, in the 1920s and 1930s. A drive toward secularization was motivated by the hope that all Soviet citizens would adopt the ideas and values of communism, viewing themselves as members of the proletariat, makers of their own fate, and builders of a revolutionary state.[18]

For Frida and many of her contemporaries, the Soviet state had taken on the capacity to give meaning to an individual's life and to determine daily and weekly schedules. In addition, it provided a frame for people to live together despite national differences between them. In this environment, "Jewish community" refers to a group of people who share the same nationality, but not to a tightly knit group that is identifiable because they perform the same rituals, visit the synagogue, or observe the Shabbat. Soviet Jews, in sum, were increasingly recognizable only by their passport, where, since 1932, each Soviet citizen's nationality was listed as one of many identifiers.[19] For young citizens like Frida, even that was irrelevant, as they would not receive a passport until they were sixteen years old. They saw themselves as Soviet children, had friends who were Belorussians or Russians, and did not conceive of themselves as people who would warrant any kind of special treatment, positively or negatively. This framework, the idea that different nationalities can live together, broke down when Germans began to kill Jews en masse and some Soviet citizens supported them.

Frida Ped'ko's overall account echoes other survivors' experiences and perceptions, moving from descriptions of a promising prewar life of peace, interethnic friendships with other adolescents, and her mother's social and economic mobility to the shock of Nazi violence and the small, if pivotal, moment of narrowly escaping execution. She further addresses postwar disappointments at state antisemitism that hindered her personal career and obstructed respectful treatment. Like many others, she balances this account by placing her wartime losses within those suffered by the Soviet population as a whole and by affirming her commitment to the Soviet state. Ped'ko's evocative memory of her and her sister's planning to have themselves killed, along with her recognition of the difficulty of grasping this decision in the present, is a powerful reminder that there is a difference between what then, during the war, seemed inevitable and how we may think about it now. What she tells us and how she narrates her story is based on a movement between the past and the present.

As a whole, life stories such as Frida Ped'ko's show how people make sense of violence and how they remember it. Rather than studying accounts exclusively focused on wartime experience, this book is based on oral histories spanning the course of a life to detect the dynamics of this sense-making and remembering.[20] My inquiry draws on scholarship suggesting the role of social and cultural frames for how individuals construct their memory.[21] Narrations about personal experiences not only bring narrators' minds close to events and actions in the past, but also remind them of social rules and limits to what could be said publicly at the time of the remembered events.[22] These restrictions resurface when people recall their past, as evidenced by the use of specific terms or refusal to describe intimate experiences such as sexual violence or other themes that are considered taboo. Considering these dynamics is important in order to understand the effects of social change on individual lives and how, in turn, individuals make sense of these changes or particular events and periods of their lives.

Hannah Arendt posited that it is the task of the historian to detect new elements of human history by recognizing that an "event cannot but appear as an end of [a] newly discovered beginning."[23] The study of the German occupation and Nazi genocide in the USSR (as an event) is here the catalyst to reveal "an unexpected landscape of human deeds, sufferings, and new possibilities" that preceded the event and, in doing so, exposes its destructive impact more fully.[24] Considering the unexpected landscape of the prewar period, which originally was not at the center of inquiry, produces a reevaluation of Soviet nationality policies, especially toward Jews, that suggests that internationalism was a partially lived reality that held great promise for the future. Teasing out that this lived reality is a point of comparison for elderly Jews in the former Soviet Union—to its breakdown with the German invasion, and later on the dissolution of the USSR in 1991—this book develops a new way of looking at Holocaust-related accounts coming out of the post-Soviet context. The oral history–driven approach to understanding the Nazi genocide in the Soviet territories reveals the meaning of the Soviet project for individuals as a sincere attempt to create a society that overcomes national (racial) discrimination, and that in the 1930s it seemed possible to establish such a society. The devastation wrought by the Nazi regime turned these hopes into memories of a bright, yet forever unfulfilled, future of friendship and equality.

This book offers an inside perspective on the life of Jewish children and adolescents during the Nazi occupation of Belorussia. This is, of course, a partial account. The ongoing war, competition between various administrative bodies, and the arbitrariness with which individual soldiers, members of the SS, and collaborators treated Soviet citizens under occupation generated a highly complex and often contradictory environment that was not apparent in its entirety to individuals and groups who were trying to survive. While subjective and reflecting diverse personal experiences, the portrayal advances three major insights. Firstly, age and gender are crucial factors for experiencing, surviving, and remembering the Nazi genocide in Soviet territories. Secondly, survivors' memories in the post-Soviet context reflect a flexible sense of self, oscillating between identifying as Jewish, Soviet, or both. Lastly, the shared trauma of war and genocide in Nazi-occupied Belorussia facilitated new, and revived previously established, interpersonal bonds among Jews and between Jews and Gentiles.

These three analytical dimensions—age and gender, identity and memory, trauma and community—are deeply intertwined, yet it is helpful to tease out their specificities individually to highlight their significance. Outlining how these factors mold historical experiences and their memory and how they have been previously treated by scholars provides important background information for the stories this book seeks to tell.

Age, gender, violence

Among the 800,000 Belorussian Jews killed by Germans and their collaborators were parents, grandparents, and other relatives of thousands of young Jews who survived the war. The young Jews—girls, boys, some teenagers, some younger—thus became orphans and struggled for survival on their own. This situation, however, is often not acknowledged in studies of the Nazi ghettos, where the people who populate descriptions of ghetto life appear ageless. Only a few monographs attend specifically to the lives of children in the Nazi ghettos.[25] Mostly, children and adolescents come into the picture when museums try to reach younger audiences.[26] This omission or relegation of age-specific portrayals to largely pedagogical purposes is problematic. Age did matter for everyday life within ghettos, in hiding places, or within partisan units. More importantly, scholarship on the Holocaust and Jewish responses in the Nazi-occupied Soviet Union must be aware of this, since most of its source material reflects the perspective of young survivors.

The study of how Soviet Jewry in the former Pale of Settlement experienced occupation and extermination relies in large part on utilizing personal testimonies by survivors. The narratives fill a critical gap, because the study of Nazi genocide in Soviet territories can hardly make use of documentation produced during or immediately after the war. Wartime documents of German provenience can be used to trace the occupation authorities' decision-making processes regarding the treatment of Soviet Jewry, but they provide few insights into how ghetto inmates themselves responded to deprivation and violence.[27] Conditions in the ghettos rarely allowed people to keep diaries, write letters, or otherwise record and describe their experiences.[28] Much of the extermination of Soviet Jews took place without ever being recorded; especially in the early stages of the war, Jewish residents were summarily rounded up and shot. And even if there were such documents, the situation of Jews in the ghettos, how prisoners perceived their experiences, what they thought or how they made decisions, could not be discerned from these materials.[29]

Immediately after the war, Jewish historical commissions and psychologists began to collect testimonies, especially from children, in several European countries, but no such efforts were made in the Soviet territories.[30] In the USSR, statements recorded immediately after the war, primarily by the Soviet Extraordinary State Commission for Ascertaining and Investigating Crimes Perpetrated by the German-Fascist Invaders and Their Accomplices, list human and material losses and German crimes but rarely include descriptions of how Soviet citizens, let alone Jews, *lived* under the occupation.[31] The famous *Black Book of Russian Jewry* unquestionably fills some of these gaps, yet these accounts pertain to multiple locales and do not provide a comprehensive view of how individuals survived under conditions of violence, forced labor, and trauma.³² To complement the few accounts of ghetto life that were offered in the immediate postwar period, it is therefore necessary to analyze recently available personal narratives.³³

This book examines the individual and communal experience of ghettoization and destruction in ghettos such as Minsk, Slavnoe, Shklov-Ryshkovichi, Shchedrin, and Zhlobin. The account is largely based on more than a hundred interviews and video testimonies produced since the late 1990s, but also uses recently published memoirs and secondary scholarship. For the most part, these are interviews, testimonies, and memoirs by women and men who stayed to live in the USSR after the war, a deliberate limitation that helps understand the dynamics of remembering and identity formation in the specific context of the Soviet Union and its successor states.

The interviews I conducted, as well as other testimonies and memoirs in use here, are largely products of the breakdown of the Soviet Union in 1991. Prior to that, censorship and indifference condemned both survivors and scholars to silence about the history of Soviet Jews' suffering and survival during, and resistance against, the Nazi regime. Many survivors thus never managed to speak about their survival and postwar lives before they passed away. The majority of recently collected or published testimonies or memoirs are consequently accounts by people who, during the war, were children and teenagers and took on a distinct role within, and perspective on, life in the ghetto. While one may see these narratives as questionable sources due to their belated recording, they ought to be taken seriously. Descriptions of everyday life under conditions of occupation and genocide were hardly the subject of governmental censorship in Soviet postwar society, precisely because the genocide itself was largely omitted from the official portrayals.³⁴ Moreover, essential episodes of wartime experience remain largely intact in child survivors' memories despite the passage of time.³⁵ Thus, though chronicled several decades after the war, the oral histories and testimonies that this book weaves together allow us to grasp the perspective of adolescents who confronted the abrupt end of a world of relative normalcy and official equality and were largely left to fend for themselves in the Nazi ghettos.

Children and youth were at once the most vulnerable and the most resourceful group in the ghettos in Belorussia. They were vulnerable because they were easy targets during roundups and killing actions, and many died of starvation in a context where only workers received the minimal food rations. They were, however, also highly mobile within and beyond the ghetto, and could rely on friendships and relationships built before the war, and not subject to racial ideology, to navigate the ghetto's dangers. Strong bonds with peers provided youth with emotional stability and crucial access to information and essential resources. Furthermore, they could often count on adults both within and outside the ghetto who strove to save children from the ghettos.

For Jewish children and teenagers, rescue from the genocide more often than not consisted of escaping the reach of the German regime—in other words, disappearing from public view.[36] In eastern Belorussia, refugees from the ghettos either survived in hiding, as Frida Ped'ko did, or they became part of one of the many partisan formations based in swamps and forests. The struggle for survival thus included a negotiation of different environments and often complicated relationships with adults or peers of the same age. Jewish life in these circumstances was structured by the Nazi regime, which placed Jews at the bottom of society. In addition, prewar Soviet policies and perceptions regarding national difference had a lasting impact on relationships within the occupied society. Some Soviet citizens had welcomed the campaigns to eradicate national hatred and saw their Jewish neighbors or classmates as equals, which encouraged them to support persecuted Jewish women and men during the German occupation. Others disagreed with the campaigns of the 1930s or harbored deep anti-Jewish resentment; many of them were willing to help the Nazi regime identify Jews and actively supported the genocide.

The children's and teenagers' experiences of ghetto and destruction were also determined by gender; gender significantly shaped the available opportunities, dangers, and perceptions.[37] In the ghettos such as those in Minsk or Bobruisk, a gendered division of labor that placed men and women in distinct economic spheres also influenced chances for survival. Men were often employed in the production of war equipment or infrastructure and women in domestic and service work, including cooking and cleaning; subsequently, skilled workers, mostly men, were favored in selections, whereas auxiliary, unskilled workers were condemned to death. At the same time, circumstances in the ghetto and especially within partisan units allowed for traditional gender roles to be disrupted; for instance, young women were involved in underground or military operations and young men in household and care work. Moreover, sexual violence—that is, sexual harassment, rape, forced castration, and other forms of violation that targeted women or men's sexuality, genitals, or reproductive capabilities—also shaped people's experiences inside and outside of the ghetto.[38] Whereas both women and men were targeted by this violence, its meaning and extent varied depending on the victim's gender.

Sexual violence, especially rape, functioned as a direct attack on women, but also as a "means of communication" and to establish and confirm relationships of power. For one thing, it showed the women, but also their female and male relatives and community members, that they were powerless against the perpetrator and served to create the impression of mastery.[39] Secondly, women's bodies took on symbolic value as the sites of the family's and the national community's biological reproduction. Therefore, when women's bodies are destroyed or humiliated, the continuity of the family or community is in danger too.[40] Some scholars argue that sexual violence was an extreme form of seeking pleasure and distraction from the difficult everyday life of a German soldier or local collaborator.[41] The everyday labor of occupying police and SS consisted largely in military violence against the local population, especially ghetto prisoners; the violence accompanying the rapes and torture was thus a continuation of everyday violence, not a distraction. The assault on the reproductive ability of the Jewish community points to the shared and mutually enforcing vulnerability and the symbolic and real role of children, youth, and women in the context of the Nazi genocide. The destruction in the present was to deny Soviet Jews their future, both as individuals and as a community, a destruction that is most starkly articulated in the image of Soviet Jewish women who had small children in their arms while they were killed.

In Soviet postwar portrayals of the war, shifting gender roles and sexual violence have largely been omitted. The denial of public recognition for individuals who were engaged in labor for survival has sidelined gendered experiences of the war. Continuing taboos, for instance, against the public discussion of sexual violence—whether committed by Germans, collaborators, or Soviet partisans—make it difficult for women and men to relate such experiences.[42] Allusions to rape or harassment in oral histories suggest that underneath the shared experiences of starvation, forced labor, and killing actions is a layer of uncommon experience determined by gender and the possibility of sexual violence. While it is obvious that speaking does not necessarily provide relief or a cure for difficult memories and ongoing pain, it is important to note when and why violence is being committed. Survivor accounts are often scrutinized for silences, for the incapacity to speak about deeply troubling experiences, and scholars diagnose a "sanctuary of silence."[43] This form of protection may indeed be relevant here, but as in the case of sexual violence, silence is often a result of shame or the speaker's assumption that no one wants to hear them. Rather than focusing solely on the trauma that may inform the silence, we may do better to trace and dissect the deliberate deafness toward survivors of violence.

The silencing at work here results, in part, from modes of communication typical for Soviet and post-Soviet societies, where intimate experiences, positive and negative, are considered inappropriate for public discussion.[44] Several times I was asked to turn off my recording device because interviewees wanted to share something with me, but not with a larger audience, such as intimate relationships among partisans or experiences of sexual violence, but also criticism of the Russian government. Such moments are reminders that oral history interviews are designed to reach an audience beyond the narrator and the researcher. In addition, they alert us to the aftereffects of restrictions on public speech during Soviet times when opinions or statements critical of the party leadership or of the economic, social, or political conditions were actively silenced or confined to private conversations. When interviewees regulate their memory, we understand that individual memories are anchored in a collective history with specific limitations. These restrictions, here visible in people's hesitance to speak on the record about emotions or intimate encounters, define what information can become publicly known and what should remain private. Paying attention to these moments, where age, gender, and sexuality shape historical experiences and remembering it for others, helps us to comprehend the social history of Soviet Jewish communities and individuals during and after the Nazi occupation. Chapters 3, 4, and 6 of this book provide a deep investigation of these issues.

Memory, identity, the state

Soviet institutions and policies had a marked impact on the personal choices, opportunities, and interpretations of wartime events of Jews who had been born in eastern Belorussia in the late 1920s and early 1930s.[45] Though the Soviet state promoted ideas of equality among all nationalities, suggesting that a universal Soviet identity stood above national differences, it also discriminated against particular nationalities. Jews, for instance, were restricted from access to specific universities, positions of power, and resources in the postwar period.[46] This unequal treatment of Soviet Jews, many of whom were survivors of the Nazi genocide, reflects an inherent contradiction of Soviet policy. For many Soviet citizens, it was thus easier and more useful to foreground their Soviet identity rather than their national—Jewish—identity. The collapse of the Soviet Union in 1991 brought an end to these policies. In many cases, this end was marked by interethnic strife, which was an important motive for many former Soviet republics to secede and form sovereign states. For individuals, however, the breakdown of this oscillation between national particularism and Soviet universalism, with the latter now absent, often meant deep soul-searching about their own beliefs, their identities, and their worldviews.[47]

In that moment, late in life, many elderly Soviet Jews developed a renewed interest in their Jewish origins and began to develop a strong sense of self as "Jewish."[48] Memories of the war are filtered through this dual and shifting sense of self and point to the unstable nature of identity. Narrators reach toward a time and space in the past in which they acquired a specific position in society, based on personal choices as well as social restrictions and opportunities. The narratives thus question the use of categories such as Jewish identity to such an extent that it is perhaps more appropriate to simply describe the ways in which individuals position themselves within a larger social and political framework and in relation to other people.[49] This approach avoids the pitfalls of assigning categories of identification to people that may have more to do with the scholar's understanding of what it means to be Jewish, Soviet, or both than with what the narrator considers important. For Soviet Jews, this positioning ranged from assimilation into a secular, Soviet framework to being excluded from it to developing a distinct ethnic identity rooted in cultural and religious practice.

The narratives suggest that in the prewar decades, interethnic solidarity had been promoted by the state and, to a considerable degree, was a lived reality. Following the breakdown of Soviet state institutions at the beginning of the war in June 1941, which left Soviet civilians to fend for themselves, the apparatus of the Communist Party, trade unions, and the Party's youth organizations reemerged in the process of developing underground organizations and partisan formations that were essential for young Soviet Jews' survival. Underground and partisan networks, including the so-called *semeinye otriady* (family units) within the Soviet partisan movement, drew upon the themes of interethnic solidarity and Soviet patriotism. They recreated a sense of belonging to a larger group that was central for the youths' socialization before the war. Postwar Soviet portrayals of the war further described it as a shared Soviet experience, focusing on the role of state and Party for the successful military defeat of Nazi Germany, achieved by the Soviet people.

At the same time, narrators highlight where the state-sanctioned portrayal of the war did not give justice to the specific wartime experiences of particular groups. Monuments and annual celebrations largely focused on victory and liberation, on the successful military struggle against German troops, and on heroic fighters who sacrificed their lives. Civilians who died on the home front, veterans who had been injured and returned home as invalids, but also prisoners of war and forced laborers rarely figured in the public memory of the war.[50] Among the memories that were overlooked were the mass murder of Jews, the collaboration of Soviet citizens in the violence against Jews, and discrimination against both Jewish ghetto refugees and women within the Soviet partisan movement. Interviewees address the failures of Soviet modes of remembering the war to include a memory of the dead, pointing specifically to the lack of memorials to identify mass graves for Jews shot by the Germans and the postwar use of such killing sites as airports or dachas.[51]

A coherent and unifying framework of interpretation, focusing on the victorious end of the war, was essential for individuals and for Soviet society as a whole during and after the war.[52] Nevertheless, such a framework silenced different experiences that either did not fit into the narrative of victory and unified struggle or could have stained the memory of the victorious army and partisan movement. This silencing also resulted in social and economic discrimination against Jewish survivors or veterans. These women and men often were denied recognition and material resources such as additional pension payments, subsidized housing, access to high-quality health care, or vouchers for visits to sanatoria that were available to other esteemed participants of the war. Despite these discriminations, Jewish survivors of the Nazi genocide in the former Soviet Union joined the celebrations on May 9, the anniversary of the German surrender in 1945. For them, enthusiasm for the liberation from the Nazi regime, achieved in large measure and with great losses by Soviet soldiers and partisans, and disappointment about unequal forms of recognition go hand in hand.

Soviet state institutions played a pervasive role in shaping pre- and postwar Soviet society, individual reintegration, and war commemoration practices. This is the scaffolding for survivors' descriptions and assessments of their own life experiences. When citizens of the former Soviet Union remember their past, they recall a life within a collective, a life in relationship to others and to state institutions.[53] And while the Soviet collective of the 1930s and later does not exist anymore, it is nonetheless the group in which elderly Jewish women and men spent their youth and their adult lives and with which they communicate in history and memory.

Recognizing the complex and often contradictory attempts of Soviet Jews to integrate into Soviet society is crucial to understanding the Jewish condition in the Soviet Union, before, during, and after World War II. Such a framework recognizes the possibility for people to "occupy the space of devastation by making it one's own, not through a gesture of escape but by occupying it in its present-ness," a strategy by oppressed subjects to survive that is at times wrongly dismissed.[54] In this spirit, I trace the experiences and perceptions of those who stayed. For the most part, I spoke to women and men whose grandparents did not join the masses of Jews who emigrated from Eastern Europe between 1880 and 1920 and whose parents did not leave for Palestine to participate in the Zionist project of the 1920s and 1930s. I worked with individuals who stayed in the Soviet Union, even returned there at the end of World War II, and remained despite a wave of emigration in the late 1960s. Only a few of the narrators cited here left the post-Soviet space in the early 1990s. While many Soviet Jews saw a way out of a life determined or threatened by discrimination in leaving for pre-Nazi or post-reunification Germany, the United States, or Israel, a large number of what was once the world's largest Jewish population stayed to live in tsarist Russia, the Soviet Union, or the post-Soviet Russian Federation and other successor states of the USSR.[55]

However, the fact that many chose emigration points to difficulties in living in these entities as a person of Jewish origin. This life involved negotiating between being a Russian or Soviet citizen who wanted to become equal to others, and the fact that others identified Jews as different or even inimical to the Soviet population. The notion of a "double-consciousness," diagnosed by W. E. B. Du Bois as an essential instrument of African-American survival, is useful in considering this perilous balancing act. Without aiming to equalize experiences of Jewish persecution, genocide, slavery, or other forms of racist discrimination, one can say that the necessity to "look at one's self through the eyes of others" is deeply connected to the hope of escaping death and isolation, in history and in memory, an experience shared by many victims of repression and discrimination.[56] Attempts to balance belonging and outsider status leave a distinct mark on narratives of elderly Jewish women and men in the former Soviet Union. They inform the stories throughout the book, but are most specifically articulated in chapters 2 and 5.

Trauma, community, reproductive labor

The racist German occupation and extermination policies challenged the Soviet project at its core by destroying the moral fiber and social cohesion of a multinational society. Soviet citizens were taken by surprise when German troops invaded the Soviet Union in 1941 and began a war of annihilation and exploitation. Jewish Soviet citizens in Belorussia were shocked to discover that some of their neighbors and classmates, as well as strangers they had never met before, actively participated in the German efforts to identify, humiliate, and torture their Jewish compatriots. Violence, deprivation, and ideological indoctrination targeted a population abandoned by both the political leadership and a Soviet army that had been defeated within days. The civilian Jewish population quickly learned that it would be treated differently than most non-Jewish citizens, however. Public humiliation, internment in ghettos, and finally killing actions signaled that Jews would suffer disproportionally from Nazi racism. In this context of war-related violence that shook the whole Soviet population and discrimination and violence that singled out Jews, access to food and other supplies and protection from terror was in large part contingent on quickly organized self-help. For Jews across Nazi-occupied Europe, stripped of rights and political and legal status, friends and allies were the only resources for survival. For Belorussian Jews penned up in ghettos, connections with non-Jews proved essential for survival; the emerging support relationships with former neighbors, colleagues, teachers, classmates, or nannies are the only reason some survived. The case of Jewish Soviet citizens and their survival thus also exemplifies the resilience of personal relationships across national (ethnic) divisions in the moment of a shared trauma.

The extent of such relationships varied across different regions of the German-occupied Soviet Union. The divergent attitudes among the non-Jewish population toward their Jewish compatriots' plight are yet to be fully understood. For instance, it is an open question whether eastern Belorussia is distinct from other areas in this regard and whether there were more such networks here than, for example, in Ukraine. In both Belorussia and Ukraine, local residents actively collaborated with the Nazi occupation regime.[57] They looted Jewish property and formed divisions of the so-called *Schutzmannschaften* or *Hilfspolizei*, collaborationist auxiliary police battalions, which actively participated in execution drives, supplying much needed support for the enormous murder campaign.[58] (Survivors regularly refer to members of these divisions summarily as *"politseiskie,"* or "police.") The central question here is whether the proportionally higher number of Ukrainian policemen increased the likelihood that Jews or those who were willing to harbor them were discovered in Ukrainian territory. The intensity of anti-Jewish violence before World War II, the widespread participation of locals in denunciation and looting, as well as the lack of non-Jewish leaders to help organize the rescue of Jews are, however, well documented, and suggest a different, more difficult environment for Jews in search of help in Ukraine than we can discern for Belorussia.[59]

In addition to interethnic self-help and support networks, and in some instances facilitated by them, young Soviet Jews also forged close bonds with peers who shared experiences of orphanhood, hunger, and displacement. Ties with other teenagers roaming the streets of the ghetto or Russian districts, bunkmates in orphanages, or fellow workers in forced labor settings delivered a semblance of emotional stability, but also provided crucial access to information about impending killing actions or available food supplies.

An outstanding example of such peer-to-peer support and communality based on a shared traumatic experience are the so-called family units, detachments within the Soviet partisan movement comprised of civilians. One of the largest family units in Belorussia was the so-called "Zorin" unit, a detachment—named after its commander, Shalom Zorin—that housed up to 800 civilians, among them 150 orphaned children and 280 women. The detachment was an anomaly within the Soviet partisan movement because of its gender ratio and the large number of noncombatants. Simultaneously, the detachment was an essential part of the Soviet partisan movement, as the work of the "family partisans," the production of shoes and clothing, medical care, and organization and processing of food supplies, was beneficial for several other partisan units.

Chapters 5 and 6 provide insights into the internal structures of the Soviet partisan units that became safe havens for several thousand refugees from the Nazi ghettos. Survivors speak about the difficult inclusion of ghetto refugees—largely untrained, impoverished, and traumatized civilians—into the militarized environment of the Soviet partisan movement. Their stories reveal the significance of reproductive labor, that is, labor directed at the maintenance of individual and communal lives, in the context of ongoing warfare and genocide.

State-sponsored detachments such as the "Zorin family unit" also helped to reintegrate children and adolescents who fled the ghetto into Soviet society. Schooling, Party lessons portraying the war as an attack on all Soviet citizens, as well as military discipline reinstituted a sense of stability and acceptance into youths' lives. Portrayals of war and occupation as a shared experience of the whole Soviet population came at the cost of denying the role of Soviet citizens' antisemitism and collaboration in the Jews' suffering. Yet the concrete bonds with other members of partisan detachments, as well as the partly real, partly imagined ties with other Soviet citizens, recreated a sense of belonging and purpose that was essential for both physical and emotional survival and remained operative long after the war. Whereas collective experiences of mass starvation, war, and other forms of systematic violence often lead to the dispersal of existing communities, in the case of young Belorussian Jews and their peers the collective trauma of war and genocide resulted in new or revived communal bonds that suggest an understanding of trauma as a productive social force.

Scholars have analyzed how the collective experience of deportation to, and internment in, the concentration camp intensified bonds among preexisting friends or groups. For instance, a group of ten women, the so-called "Plaszow Zehnerschaft," formed a close network of support that aided them and others in the Płaszów concentration camp.[60] All but one of the women shared the same educational and religious background; the women between the ages of sixteen and twenty-six had studied at the Beis Yaakov shool for girls in Krakow before the war and drew on their shared values to form a support group.[61] Other scholars highlight the role of testimony, of remembering, to create community, arguing that "recounting the extreme . . . sometimes has the power to form a community entangled together through the act of listening."⁶²

The family units, Jewish networks, or networks that included Jews and non-Jews show elements of both processes; they are forged based on experiences of violence and the knowledge of other people's suffering. Few members of the family unit had known each other before the war, but they came together because they shared the experience of living through and witnessing the violence of Nazi warfare, mass executions, and hunger resulting from the robbery of resources. The family units coalesced because Jews were persecuted as Jews, which one may consider a preexisting bond. Yet before the war young Soviet Jews had hardly formed a distinct community, and only the Nazi persecution forced this group identity upon them. In that sense, the experience of the Nazi genocide was instrumental for the revival of Soviet Jewish collective identity.⁶³ More concretely, for some Jewish survivors this revival had a social location, namely, in the family units.

It is no accident that the emerging community within the unit is identified as a family. Whereas bonds between individual members were not determined by kinship, the function and purpose of the unit resembled those of traditional families. Joining this group in the forest, the ghetto refugees received the bare necessities for physical survival, but they were also integrated into, or socialized into, a social system with distinct social and cultural values and power structures. Soviet and partisan leaders portrayed the work of the partisans as part of the collective struggle against the enemy and suggested that defeating the German occupants would be beneficial for the whole Soviet population. This deeper sense of meaning found in belonging to a partisan detachment strongly motivated the participants to give everything they could to protect the Soviet people. Helping them to survive and to secure a specifically Soviet way of life inspired many ghetto refugees who had grown up in the Soviet Union.

Like family systems that rely on patriarchal authority and teach family members to accept it, partisan units expected members to follow the orders of unit commanders. These leaders, however, were also seen as representatives of the Communist Party and the Soviet state. Respect for the father figure, as it were, was here replicated in the partisans' allegiance to the state government and its leader, Stalin. Organizational structures and activities within the detachment reflect this submission to authority, for instance in the form of school lessons in which the unit's youth were encouraged to prove their loyalty to partisan and state leadership by writing a letter to Stalin. Likewise, instances of sexual domination and violence within the family unit and other partisan units show that particular ideas about gender roles were deeply ingrained in state and military institutions. These ideas shaped how partisans related to each other and how the larger Soviet public viewed the partisans. The participation of Jews and women in partisan units was largely omitted from public view, both during and after the war. It was widely assumed that women did not fulfill any important tasks within the partisan movement, but merely provided sexual services for male combatants.[64] For fear of humiliation, many women, Jews and non-Jews, kept silent about their time in the partisan movement. As a result, a history of internal discrimination and violence remained largely off the record.

The silencing of women and noncombatants also sidelined what is often described as women's work, the daily labor to provide food and care, a crucial element of the struggle for survival against the Nazi regime. The Soviet portrayal of World War II favored the experiences of almost exclusively male military fighters and the heroic and victorious struggle against the Nazi occupants.[65] In focusing on military struggle and achievements, the value of strategies aimed at survival, of building networks of mutual support and the fulfillment of day-to-day chores in a dangerous environment, was deemed negligible. But the narratives of the participants demonstrate that hiding places, partisan units, and family units were the spaces of survival. These spaces were often established and maintained by women's labor, the work necessary to reproduce human life and its productive capabilities.

Survivor's descriptions of life-saving strategies that are traditionally tied to the private, or domestic, sphere and understood as women's work ask us to reflect on what we understand as valuable work and, in times of war and conflicts, as "resistance."[66] Scholars of the Nazi genocide generally agree that the provision of food, care, and mental well-being and the transfer of a cultural heritage were central forms of resistance against the genocide, yet especially with regard to the Soviet context there is still a higher emphasis on Jewish armed resistance and the participation of Jews in the Soviet armed forces.[67] Without denying the importance of military engagement, the silencing of life-saving activities suggests that military agency—men's work—is more valuable than other activities. This not only pushes aside women's lives but also marginalizes actions that are not geared toward seizing power, but rather strive to make life livable.

Remembering the daily realities of survival in the context of war, genocide, scarcity, and emotional damage, the stories told by eastern Belorussian Holocaust survivors like Frida Ped'ko offer a new perspective on survival during the Nazi genocide.[68] While individual and collective strategies to survive in a situation of extreme violence are the subject of many volumes, there continues to be a lack of studies of these issues with regard to the Nazi-occupied Soviet Union.[69] Alongside the symbolic recognition of specific people's experiences that comes with including them in the record, this study diversifies knowledge of the Nazi genocide and of survival in an area where about a third of all Jewish victims of the Nazi regime perished.

This book does not offer a comprehensive account of the destruction of Soviet Jews in eastern Belorussia, even less so of the economic, administrative, or military infrastructure of the Nazi genocide. Rather, it strives to highlight how and where the experience of growing up as a Jew in the Soviet Union in the 1930s, and generally of living within the purview of institutions of the Soviet state, shaped the struggle for survival during the war, and how and why some of these experiences were excluded from postwar portrayals of the war.

The oral histories of elderly Jews from the former Soviet Union bring into conversation scholarship on Soviet and European history, the Holocaust, and feminist analyses and approaches. Placing the experience of individuals at the center of attention provides insight into how subjects marked by nationality, age, and gender experienced their everyday lives under conditions of violence. More specifically, orphaned children and their everyday struggle for survival offer an important lens through which to understand the scope and force of Nazi terror. These adolescents, without any family member to relate to, personify the detached Jewish individual removed from the political community that the Nazi regime strove to produce so that it could annihilate them physically. A process in which European Jews were stripped of their political status and legal personhood had been set in motion for the first time during the interwar period. Stateless Jews who had no place to go and no one to ask for protection were forced into a narrow private sphere, outside the purview of law, where they had to find resources and allies who were willing to assist them.[70] For Soviet Jewish youth, survival against war and Nazi genocide was enabled by interpersonal bonds that drew on the shared experience of war and on a community that had, in part, been built before the German occupation. Survival thus relied on building communality in private, removed from the occupants' view. It is no accident that this community is revealed in the semiprivate/ semipublic space of oral history. Oral history once more emphasizes its significance by bringing hidden, personal histories to the surface, all the while pointing to the limitations we face in trying to uncover such personal experience.

Conducting oral history interviews and combining them with other sources provides a unique opportunity to create an archive that otherwise would not exist. It is also a delicate endeavor, asking individuals to share very personal and often traumatic experiences for a public purpose. Associated problems are discussed in the following chapter; readers who are interested in the story rather than how it is produced may advance immediately to chapter 2.

1

On Methodology

Oral History and the Nazi Genocide

After our first interview, Alevtina Kuprikhina commented, "Next time, when you speak better Russian, we can have a better conversation."[1] Questioning my ability to communicate with her in a foreign language, she clearly considered our conversation to be filled with misunderstandings and obscurity. Listening to the interview tape, I recognize that, though my Russian was intelligible, it was at times clumsy. My inability to formulate precise questions, and indeed my insecurity about this, resulted from my own confusion about a narration that was hard to track. Alevtina Kuprikhina transitioned between themes, time periods, and names quickly, making it difficult to follow her train of thought. Such seemingly disconnected narrations are common in interviews with survivors of genocide and other traumatic experiences. They raise questions about whether the content of the narration reflects contradictory and disruptive experiences, or is a product of broken and fragmentary memory that cannot be restored.[2] Reading Kuprikhina's narration alongside a testimony she gave to the Shoah Visual History Foundation in November 1998—one that is far less entangled and follows a linear chronology—it appears that details about times, places, events, and decisions are consistent.[3] The question therefore is: what are the reasons for confusion among narrators and listeners? Which factors play a role in determining how narratives are constructed and interpreted?

Interviewing Alevtina Kuprikhina was one of the most challenging parts of my research in St. Petersburg. We met only once in person, in September 2002, and our conversation about her survival of genocide proved to be very difficult. This is not unusual; oral history interviews are often confusing and even unsatisfactory. Studying issues of history and memory through personal narratives is complicated, the emerging portrayal sometimes contradictory, provocative, and often fragmentary. And there are a number of reasons why participants may feel uncomfortable or even insecure during the encounter. First, oral history interviews are deeply personal, and sharing intimate and personal details does not come easy to anyone. In addition, the narratives are geared toward a public audience; encounters between interviewees and researchers are encounters between two historical subjects and take place with the public purpose of the researcher bearing witness in mind.[4] Thus, the act of remembering in the oral history interview is itself a historical event that deserves scrutiny, for instance, of the different positions participants occupy in the world in terms of access to resources, power, or audiences.[5] The context of the interview, the participants' social and historical positions, but also historical relations between two societies, mirrored here in the encounter between two people, shape what is said and what is not.

The narrative of this book is, in large part, rooted in interactions between elderly Jews and a young, German-born, female researcher in post-Soviet Russia and Belarus. I met these women and men on multiple occasions, beginning in the year 2000, after contacting associations of survivors of Nazi persecution. I wanted to find out about the application and payment process for financial compensations recently allocated by the German government and to see whether I could help file claims for such compensation. Working as a volunteer, I heard stories about the Nazi genocide that were unfamiliar, despite my being raised and educated in Germany, and I began to ask questions.

Over the course of eight years, I conducted many interviews with twenty-one members of one particular association, the Association of Former Prisoners of Ghettos and Concentration Camps, with branches in St. Petersburg (Russia) and Minsk (Belarus). In addition, I was able to access fifty-three video interviews recorded by the Survivors of the Shoah Visual History Foundation in post-Soviet countries.[6] My research also includes eighteen interview narratives produced by the United States Holocaust Memorial Museum's Oral History Branch, several accounts held at the Archives of the Yad Vashem, and archival materials of both German and Soviet provenance. A number of written autobiographical accounts, published and unpublished, complement my source basis. Using a method of inference to make connections between these different sources, which are, each in their own way, fragmentary, I pursue strategies employed by historians of largely undocumented historical experience.[7] Such a methodological approach acquires special urgency when we try to confront a scarcity of historical documentation produced by the systematic exclusion and violation of specific historical subjects. Working with interviews and testimonies, however, raises thorny questions about efforts to account for destruction, including the roles politics, resentment, and trauma play in individual attempts to narrate historical experience.

Oral history as memory work

"Should we have lunch first, or will we work before eating?"[8] Minutes after I arrived at her apartment, Rita Kazhdan asked me this simple question.[9] I was taken aback. I remember wondering, how can she think about eating shortly before we are going to talk about her experiences in the Minsk ghetto, about life under terror, about her being constantly surrounded and threatened by death? I quickly realized that one should not be driven by an image of survivors as people identified only by their traumatic experiences; such an image is blind to the energetic, busy lives that people like Rita Kazhdan have lived for many decades.

Her simple question destroyed my preconception. It also drew attention to the notion of collaboration in uncovering history, in making memory work through our interaction, through the "shared labor" between the narrator and the researcher.[10] It was a reminder that her narration would not merely be a spoken flow of memories activated by pressing the button on a recorder. Recalling the past is an activity, it is work: memory work. Memory work also involves listening to those who remember and talk about their lives, about violence and its effects on their lives and relationships, and then arranging these recollections. Memory work with people like Rita Kazhdan questions the unspeakability of the Nazi regime's violence against Jewish Soviet citizens and other Soviet civilian victims. It criticizes the politics of memory employed both in Germany and the Soviet Union that have largely excluded these victims' experiences from portrayals of the war. Kazhdan's question also shows that the memory of war and genocide is a constant part of her daily life. In some ways, her attitude reflects the interest that this book takes in the dailiness of survival, highlighting how memories that to others appear exceptional continuously shape the lives of genocide survivors.

When, in 2001, I began to interview Jewish women and men who had survived the Nazi genocide in occupied Soviet territories about their lives, I was able to do so as a result of two major political processes leading up to the breakdown of the Soviet Union in 1991 and the lifting of the so-called Iron Curtain between western and eastern, or capitalist and socialist, countries: *perestroika* (restructuring) and *glasnost* (openness). Without the latter, I would not have been able to freely travel to St. Petersburg or Minsk. Likewise, ongoing efforts to enable free speech in the former Soviet Union enabled me to visit survivors of the German occupation of Soviet territories and talk about their experiences before, during, and after the war. Thus, I used the opportunities for conversation and disclosure that these processes created, both within the former Soviet Union and across long-term political and geographical divisions, to learn about the forms and repercussions of the violence that the German occupation had posed to Jewish citizens of the USSR.

Beginning in the early 1980s, activists of perestroika and glasnost sought to reevaluate Soviet history by attending to voices that had been overlooked by the official historiography.[11] Former POWs, people who had been deported and forced into labor for the Nazi regime, Jews who had been subjected to the Nazi genocide, and Soviet citizens who had been victims of repression by the Soviet state began to speak out and question the official portrayal of the Great Patriotic War. The state portrayal had largely omitted these experiences, foregrounding the heroic defeat of the Nazi regime based on the unified struggle of the Soviet population and the government's ability to direct all resources toward victory.

For different reasons, yet with similar results, Eastern European victims of World War II had been largely neglected by politicians and scholars in the Western hemisphere. An image of the USSR or its population as a victim (of World War II) was irreconcilable with the perception of the Soviet Union as the Cold War enemy and a threat to world capitalism. One of the results was that no individual compensation for physical, mental, or material damage was allocated to East Europeans until 1991: West Germany limited such benefits to citizens of countries with which it had diplomatic relations.[12] Furthermore, West Germany was released from reparations related to World War II to socialist countries until a formal peace agreement was concluded.[13] At the same time, as a form of reparation, factories, production facilities, and railway lines located in East Germany were taken apart, transported to the USSR and reassembled there. Individuals, however, could not hope for support from the East German government either.[14] This closure, in conjunction with the Iron Curtain, effectively shut off communication with victims of the Nazi regime in this area of the world, limiting a portrayal of the war past largely to that given by the former perpetrators and their progeny (West Germany) or to the portrayal of communists and anti-Fascists who were persecuted by the Nazis (East Germany).[15]

When in the mid-1980s these restrictions—on free communication and travel—were lifted, alternative portrayals of the past could emerge. There were opportunities to talk about a shared history of violence and its repercussions, a history that continues to affect the relationship between Russia and Germany and between the citizens of these states.

However, while it became possible then to discuss a shared history of violence, that same history necessarily affected the dynamic between survivors of Nazi violence and me, a German-born researcher in the former Soviet Union. Our interactions were bound to a history of systematic violence and attempts at erasure that its perpetrators—German occupants—strove to achieve. Our conversations had a strong ethical dimension, because the act of remembering, of making destruction and its effects visible, is an attempt to ensure that destruction is not complete.[16] Nonetheless, the interviews testify to long-lasting ruptures in individual lives and societies: the interviewees and I are entangled with past violence and with the moral burden this violence poses in the present. These entanglements became strikingly obvious, for instance, when interviewees questioned public forms of commemoration. My interviews indicate that recent, especially German, attempts to both publicly memorialize the Nazi past and curtail the memory of suffering by way of financial compensation do not adequately respond to the violence experienced in the past. Rather, the conversations reveal wounds that are impossible to heal and the feeling that "there is no former time or space of wholeness to which we might return."[17] These wounds were frequently manifested in remarks about my German origin. My presence was an obvious reminder of the historical rupture resulting from Nazi violence, and this played a role in conversations I had in St. Petersburg and Minsk.

The interpersonal dynamics that emerged in the interviews clearly reflect a historical relationship. Both the interviewees and I are members of societies that might be denoted as "the victims" and "the perpetrators": in 1941, German troops attacked the Soviet Union.[18] At times, the women and men interviewed addressed this relationship explicitly and in different ways that are instructive for understanding the process of remembering. Interviewees would express their feelings about this relationship in a rather informal setting, before or after the official, taped interview, during lunch or when we had tea, and often in indirect ways.

At times, these moments made me gulp, literally. Mr. and Mrs. Pudovik invited me to lunch after we had finished a difficult interview.[19] As always, it was challenging for me to explain that I do not eat meat, not even chicken. "Hitler was a vegetarian too, you know?" was Roman Pudovik's response to this, pronounced as he handed me a basket full of bread. Minutes later, he offered me more food, still trying to understand why I choose to abstain from meat, saying, "This leads to Hitler," as if to convince me of the danger entailed in my eating habits. I am still unsure what exactly he meant, but his statements definitely had an effect: I was reminded of who I am, and what that meant for my interviewees.

Many women and men addressed the question of compensation, a question that is directly rooted in the past experiences of violence, dispossession, and genocide. Presumably, this question was salient because I met most of the interviewees for the first time in the winter of 2000, a few months after the German government had approved a law that allocated financial payments to former forced laborers.[20] At the time we met, people were submitting applications and documentation of their personal suffering to the various institutions, often struggling to bring evidence of ghetto internment and forced labor. Almost sixty years after the occupation and war had ended, and because there were few documents issued to ghetto prisoners, this was a demanding task. The majority of my interviewees, however, welcomed the attempt at reconciliation, though for different reasons: one would take the payment out of principle, acknowledging the need for the German government to pay for past mistakes; another one was happy because the funds would help to buy medicine or to support children and their families. An acknowledgement of the collective responsibility of German society for the lives of former ghetto inmates and forced laborers underlay most of these positions.

Soviet historiography and politics also shaped how interviewees evaluated the Russian-German, or Jewish-German, encounter. Sometimes people showed resentment toward Germans, but they also used specific terms that indicated how Soviet policies had formed their view of the past and of people like me. The Soviet state had actively pursued the building of an anti-Fascist bloc that consisted of Eastern European countries. To achieve this, it focused its efforts on conciliation between the Soviet and the East

German populations, including war veterans and criminals who had participated in the attack on the USSR. These efforts affected people's understanding of history; some interviewees frequently apologized, implicitly or explicitly, for speaking to me of "Germans (*nemtsy*)," that is, for generalizing about Germans.[21] Generally, narrators worked hard to carefully distinguish between soldiers (members of the Wehrmacht) and members of the SS, the Nazi regime's paramilitary Defense Corps that was actively involved in the mass shootings in the Soviet territories, who were equated with either Germans or Nazis/Fascists. In the Soviet portrayal, a criminal and terrorist elite, the true Nazis, had exploited regular German soldiers, who were thus exempted from guilt. However, this differentiation sometimes collapsed, especially in instances when narrators described the extreme physical violence that they witnessed.[22]

Although some interviewees directly implicated me in speaking about the Germans when addressing the question of compensation, I understand the differentiation between Germans and Nazis as an attempt to differentiate between the perpetrators of that violence and me.[23] The labor put into this distinction enabled our conversations, but at the same time it turned into a request for labor on my side: assisting in the search for answers as to why and how the extermination of European Jewry was possible, why it took so long for German society to admit and take responsibility for the crimes committed against the Soviet population.

To take responsibility for past violence means to ensure it is not forgotten. The oral histories at the center of this book are essential for the study of Nazi violence in German-occupied Soviet territories. There are hardly any other sources available that show how people survived. Moreover, narrators bear witness for the dead when they describe those with whom they grew up, with whom they worked, and who they lost in a killing action or to starvation. Hence, oral histories with genocide survivors enable us to learn how people lived with death, and how they live with the dead. Knowing about those who lived; the violence that took away family, childhood friends, and possible fiancées; and remembering them are at the center of an ethical approach to the present. Documenting survivors' accounts thus has taken on special urgency, and it has recently turned into an international endeavor. At times problematic, large-scale efforts such as the Shoah Visual Foundation to collect survivor narratives have enabled, among others, this study, but also new perspectives on genocide, trauma, and memory more generally.

Oral history, testimony, and Holocaust scholarship

Oral histories have proven useful in reconstructing knowledge about aspects of life that are not typically captured by archival records, among them daily or domestic life and affective dimensions.[24] The windows they provide onto, for instance, experiences of the Holocaust are invaluable. Early historical accounts of the genocide often ignored forms of violence that targeted diverse populations in distinct ways, and notably ignored the role of gender in shaping individuals' experiences and memories of the Nazi regime. The move to include this perspective coincided with a refocusing of Holocaust scholarship more generally, when in the early 1980s scholars began to shift their gaze from perpetrators to victims and from mass murder to everyday life under Nazi rule.[25] There are still gaps in the historiography, however; we still know rather little about the experiences and perceptions of Roma, homosexuals, or physically and mentally disabled persons, especially those in occupied Eastern Europe. Issues of daily life in this region are similarly understudied; apart from a comparatively small number of memoirs, case studies of a partisan unit and the Minsk ghetto, and a recent attempt to illuminate life in the *shtetls* (small towns) of the *Kresy* (the Borderlands, a former territory of eastern Polish provinces) before their destruction, there is little material available on how Jews survived in Eastern Europe, and next to nothing on Soviet areas.[26]

In an effort to remedy this situation, several scholars and institutions have collected and conducted oral history interviews, utilizing advanced technologies, including video, since the early 1980s. The largest such collection has been produced by the Survivors of the Shoah Visual History Archive (VHA), an initiative of film director Steven Spielberg in 1994. The ambitious goal of the VHA was to "give thousands of Holocaust survivors ... the chance to testify to their experiences," and to preserve the stories on videotape.[27] The goal of collecting the testimonies of 50,000 survivors in the United States, Israel, states of the former Soviet Union, Germany, and other countries was reached in 2000.[28] The project has been criticized for various reasons, most prominently for favoring quantity over quality and facilitating an "Americanization" of the Holocaust that prioritizes the individual story over history.[29] The interviews follow a format that enables certain insights while inhibiting others, and which produces a particular type of narrative, identified as "testimony." Despite these limitations and the distinct manner of production, I have used a number of these testimonies alongside the interviews that I conducted myself.[30]

The foundation's interviewing guidelines highlight the interviewer's role in ensuring that certain topics are addressed and clarified, that an overall length is followed, and that the technological infrastructure fits the needs of the project. These requirements are in tension with the aim to let narrators "speak in their own terms," to follow the narrators in defining the content and pace of producing the oral source. Especially problematic are instances where the interview team failed to bring enough videotapes, so that the interview had to be cut short.[31]

The VHA testimonies have a strong performative function; it often seems as if the interviewee delivers a speech rather than developing a narrative in the moment and in collaboration with the interviewer.[32] This becomes especially palpable in the way interviews are structured. VHA interviews usually consist of three parts; they begin with narrators' portrayal of their childhood, family members, and schooling, they continue with an account of experiences during the German occupation and war, and end with an often very brief account of postwar lives. By including these three periods, the testimonies aim to show the survivors' lives in their entirety. At the same time, the proportions allocated to these periods, as well as the projected end of the interview, reflect the VHA's desire to impart a distinct framework for interpreting the lives of survivors. This framework marks the Holocaust as the end to an idealized prewar Jewish community, and the end of the war as the beginning of a new life in societies free from anti-Jewish hatred or other forms of inequality and violence. A scholar criticized the VHA interviews as contributing to "Jewish post-memories focused on romanticized notions of Jewish prewar life, followed by Jewish persecution and death, and then redemption."[33] The testimony collection, in other words, and its emphasis on Jewish regeneration may indeed reflect the need to construct a coherent Jewish group identity more than people's actual lives.

The interviews accessible through the VHA that I used have important characteristics in common with the interviews that I conducted myself. Specifically I was interested in interviews with people who had grown up in the Soviet Union and lived their adult life there. Furthermore, since I had conducted interviews in the territories of the former Soviet Union—Russia and Belarus—I also selected VHA interviews that were produced in the post-Soviet context. Postwar accounts included descriptions of return to former hometowns, the difficulty of rebuilding a life without family, and experiences of antisemitic policies and attitudes in Soviet state institutions or by individuals. Such descriptions mark the most important difference between interviews in Eastern Europe and the former USSR and those that were conducted in the United States, Israel, or Germany. Accordingly, volunteer interviewers were alerted to adjust their interview strategy.[34] In line with the procedure adopted across the project, however, are the efforts in all interviews to show survivors' current and carefree life by introducing family members at the end of the conversation.

However, the romanticized version of Jewish prewar life is less prominent in the testimonies by survivors who grew up in Soviet territories; interviewees describe the decreasing role of traditional Jewish lifestyles, and some interviewers ask for information about Soviet repression instead. Nonetheless, many testimonies that I used introduce family members or end with requests for a message for the future. Most narrators respond with generic phrases of hope that future generations will never experience war and genocide. These abstract addresses inject a moment of distancing into the testimony that removes the narrator both from the interviewer and from the larger audience represented through the interviewer. Rather, they establish a connection between the past experiences of the survivor and anonymous future generations; the present, however, is notably absent (or made absent) from the narrative and the testimonial moment.[35] Secondly, the testimony created in this way asserts a moment of closure. Oral history as memory work, in contrast, tries to acknowledge that the narrated events are not self-contained, that they are rooted in a history, and that they have an aftermath. The contrast, Alessandro Portelli pointedly puts it, is between a self-enclosed story where the ending of a narrative restores an order that may have existed at the beginning, and recognizing "the burdens and tensions that pervade the lives and feelings of those who were left behind," hence, unrestorable order.[36] Kuprikhina's story is perhaps the strongest iteration of such continuing disruption, but most other interviews do not follow a chronology of major life periods either. Childhood experiences, for instance, were often shared only upon request, because narrators immediately proceeded from their day of birth to the beginning of World War II.

Mobilizing Hannah Arendt's insight that telling stories "reveals meaning without committing the error of defining it" helps to sharpen this analysis.[37] The oral histories of elderly Jews in the former Soviet Union unlock the meaning of the Nazi genocide for Jewish life in the Soviet Union. Disorder and fragmentation are first of all located in the inability to place these lives in a neatly defined framework, whether Jewish or Soviet. They question certainties of scholarship on, and public memory of, the Holocaust by showing that the extreme experience of genocide and sustained systematic violence in the German-occupied Soviet territories is deeply intertwined with the non-Jewish population's experience, both at the moment of the genocide and in the period before the war which prepared the ground for responses to the violence during the war. Drawing on these experiences, these stories make unmistakably clear that a specific war and a specific genocide targeted a specific population and must be recognized in their specificity.

The systematic destruction of human life, often in an industrialized manner, during the Nazi regime exceeded traditional frameworks of perception and interpretation and put to the test attempts to describe, analyze, and understand the events.[38] Many inquiries of survivor accounts employ a concept of trauma that is borrowed from psychoanalytical practice to address the complex relationship between experience and expression, or between experience and representation.[39]

The focus on trauma is manifest in the attention to silences, repetition, or the use of symbols to detect unconscious processes that bar the traumatizing event from fully entering into consciousness, and which result in the inability to fully represent the experience.[40] The basic assumption here is that our cultural frameworks, and specifically our language, are inadequate to make sense of the experience.[41] Successfully narrating it is then considered to be the cure for trauma.[42]

It is indisputable that the moment of being interviewed, of being heard, for many survivors is of utmost importance, as it validates their personal experience. But cultural historian Catherine Merridale powerfully reminds us that not all people respond to grief and loss equally all over the world, not "all silences are pathological and need to be cured." Considering "silence . . . as a sign of damage, talking . . . as therapy, and testimony, though painful, as rebirth" may be a violent illusion of scholars.[43] Indeed, oral history interviews cannot, and are not designed to, fulfill therapeutic purposes.[44]

The literary scholar Thomas Trezise provided an insightful analysis of the slippage that is at the root of confusing testimonial interviews with psychoanalytical practices that address traumatic disorders. Among others, he highlights aspects of privacy necessary in the therapeutic setting that are in stark contrast to the public purpose of interviewing. He also emphasizes the competing notions of narration as cognition (as in psychoanalytical practice) and cognition as precondition of narration (as in historical study). Finally, the position of the listener (as witness to the witness and for a community of listeners) requires attention to the information that the narrator gives and its clarification, rather than an analysis of the narration's performative dimensions: "to fulfill the responsibility of listening for others might well be considered a way of welcoming the witness herself to the community of listeners."[45] Assuming the powerful position of the therapist who alone enables trauma to be represented and is able to make sense of the narration puts the narrator, who is scrutinized but presumably freed from difficult unconscious memories, in a new position of dependence and must be avoided.

Pursuing oral history as memory work that aims to undo relationships of dominance is difficult. It requires serious attention to what narrators have to say, rather than treating their accounts as "raw material" for a discussion of remembering or for the "psychologization" of "survivors."[46] Ruth Klüger, a scholar of German literature who published an important account of her imprisonment in several Nazi concentration camps as a child and her life after the war, finds that this is often the focus of analyses of oral histories with survivors of the Nazi genocide.[47] It is my aim to take her critique seriously and to be attentive to the thinking being who is coping with her or his life, and who "has perhaps spent more time thinking about the difficulties of remembering than the listener" and, consequently, chooses her words carefully and consciously.[48] This approach, I believe, demonstrates that Soviet Jews' experience of the Nazi genocide, and how they remember it, differ in significant ways from those of other Jewish populations.

It is here, in the task of listening to what is said, that the VHA interviews are appropriate and important sources, although they contain problematic elements. In the absence of other ways to trace the life and survival of Soviet Jews who survived the Nazi genocide in eastern Belorussia, the work of the foundation is commendable. Of course I would have liked to have been able to work with material that corresponds with my approach and reflects the ethical dimensions of oral history work in different ways. At the same time, the resources available for gathering more oral accounts of this life and this survival work were not in my hands. They were available to the VHA, enabling a regionally and experientially diverse portrayal that was impossible not long before and after volunteers visited 244 survivors in Belorussia and 673 in Russia, among them a number of women and men whose narratives are included in this book.[49]

Mindful of the methodological challenges, I cite a number of stories about growing up in Soviet Belorussia, surviving in the Minsk ghetto, and living on in a partisan detachment that were recorded by the VHA. At times fragmentary and short of enabling memory work, these stories provide insights into the dailiness and complexity of life under the German occupation and beyond. Together with the interviews I conducted, these stories are unique, and sometimes the only way of accessing this reality.[50]

Stories can be unsettling because of their content or their unfamiliar structure. They can also alert listeners, or readers, to their own entanglement with ways of thinking and interpreting the world that do not align with that of the narrator. For instance, this book is about Jewish children and adolescents living through and with the Nazi genocide in eastern Belorussia. What may be considered a statement of the obvious in fact marks a moment of realization that came to me late in the research process. When I began my interviews, the women and men were in their late seventies and early eighties, and many of them have passed away over the past fifteen years. It took me a long time to acknowledge and hone in on the fact that those whom I met as old people had been children or teenagers at the time that they experienced what we talked about in the interviews: occupation, life in the ghetto, and survival in partisan units or in hiding.

In hindsight, two factors facilitated my slowness to realize the disconnection. The stereotypical image of survivors at the end of the war shows adults, or people who look old, in many cases as a result of years of starvation and suffering. My failure to see or hear thus reflects my own involvement in, to borrow Marianne Hirsch's term, the "post-memory" of the Holocaust, a knowledge of the events transmitted through images and the memory of others.[51] My ignorance possibly indicates an inability to see, or resistance to seeing, the violence that is at the root of these images, violence which makes it impossible to identify the proper age of the person. Similarly, the narratives that I collected over the past decade often entailed descriptions of situations and actions that one tries to separate from ideas of childhood and youth. The witnessing of violence or murder, the constant need to strategize and develop "illegal" actions to procure food and shelter, and involvement in violence, for instance in partisan units, are all events one resists associating with ideas of growing up. This book addresses this failure, taking note of the age of those I and others were able to interview, who, in the absence of other sources, are key figures for understanding the struggle for survival in German-occupied Belorussia. The worldview and perceptions of children and youth as remembered six decades later, their needs, endangerments, and problems, but also their attachments to individuals or institutions, form the scaffolding for the following account.

The history and memory of adolescents surviving the Nazi genocide in the occupied Soviet territories has been buried under layers of ignorance, forgetting, and marginalization. The experiences of a crucial generation of Soviet Jews, those who lived through the prewar promise of a new society, the Nazi genocide, postwar Stalinism, and finally the dissolution of the USSR, provide deep lessons about dramatic social changes and how individuals deal with them.

2

Between Tradition and Transformation

Soviet Jews in the 1930s

Rita Abramovna Kazhdan, born in Minsk in 1927, experienced the effects of Soviet nationality policies, the secularization and assimilation of Jews and other national groups into a Soviet collective, through language: "We never spoke Yiddish at home, because the family was a Russian family. I learned Russian in school so that I would not have an accent . . . These were Soviet times."[1] Kazhdan recalls her parents' aspirations to remake their Jewish family into a Russian one, to erase any linguistic trace of their stigmatized cultural heritage. But Kazhdan also suggests a layer of resignation and a lack of choice behind this aspiration by situating it in the larger Soviet context: this is what one was supposed to do at the time. Furthermore, Rita Kazhdan acknowledges the role of hindsight in her interpretation, of looking back to the past from the post-Soviet present. Her account thus brings into focus questions of social and cultural transformation in prewar Soviet society that shaped and continue to shape Jewish lives and self-perceptions. Especially for young Soviet Jews, born after 1924, this perspective determined how they perceived the German attack on the Soviet Union in June 1941, and how they remembered and represented it several decades later.

The story of prewar Soviet Jewish youth that emerges from the oral histories is one of positive social change: Soviet policies of secularization and the propaganda of internationalism and patriotism had effectively transformed Soviet society to such an extent that young Jews saw themselves as equal to their peers.[2] They enthusiastically supported the building of a society that would overcome traditional limitations for women and the poor and include previously marginalized national groups. This perspective primarily emerged in the interviews when narrators described their female relatives joining the labor force or when they compared their wartime experience, especially interactions with non-Jewish peers, to prewar classrooms and leisure activities that created interethnic friendship and solidarity.

To some extent this account contradicts the familiar story of the 1930s Soviet Union, which emphasizes party purges and terror, the violence of collectivization and industrialization, antireligious campaigning, and antisemitic assaults in factories, farms, and schools.[3] Recent scholarship has challenged this portrayal and gives a more complex account of how, for instance, Soviet nationality policies reshaped Jewish life in the USSR. Religious practices such as kosher slaughtering and circumcision continued well into the 1930s, and a new secular Soviet Jewish culture developed out of the very attempts of the Soviet state to Sovietize Jewish traditions and language.[4] Both of these trends complicate the destructive potential normally ascribed to Soviet policies. Similarly, the women and men introduced in this book do not appear to see this change as grounds for frustration or disappointment. Rather, they remember their adolescence largely in positive ways and emphasize their integration with peers of different nationalities and their affirmative engagement in Soviet schools and youth organizations.[5]

A simple explanation for this rather positive portrayal may be that narrators strongly identified with the ideologies of communism and internationalism.[6] The limitation may also result from the fact that those who did survive the Nazi genocide in occupied Belorussia did so because of underground or partisan networks sponsored by the state. Because of this support, survivors are thankful for, and loyal to, Soviet policies. Both of these explanations are of potential value, yet the situation is more complex.

For one, as children, the narrators were dealing with situations not of their own making. Their parents had made decisions about which languages to speak in private or in public, and had enrolled them in Jewish (Yiddish), Russian, or Belorussian schools; the youths accepted their conditions as given. More importantly, their reconstructions of 1930s socialization are shaped by what came afterwards, especially such turning points as World War II and the collapse of the Soviet Union in 1991. In both instances, periods of relative calm and sufficiency, at least in the urban centers and European parts of the USSR, ended abruptly and were replaced by conditions of insecurity and instability. And while the material deprivation and ideological disorientation that elderly Soviet Jews experienced in the 1990s is, of course, not the same as starvation, war, and genocide, it is significant that when compared to both moments the prewar decade appears a remarkably stable and promising period. In this sense, the story of the 1930s is a nostalgic one, one in which, in the words of cultural historian Svetlana Boym, nostalgia is more than regret for what is lost, but also for the "unrealized dreams of the past and visions of the future that became obsolete."[7] The affirmative account of life in the 1930s has roots in lived experience, but it is also a counterimage to what came after: Nazi occupation, postwar Stalinism, and the collapse of the Soviet Union. This relationship between the past and the present attests to the dynamic nature of experience and memory and structures how elderly Jews in the former Soviet Union talk about the Nazi genocide.

Jewish Pioneers and Soviet nationality policies

It was very hot when I met Boris Gal'perin, a retired engineer, for the first time. Many Petersburgers tried to escape the city on that day in May 2001, going to their *dachas*, seasonal second homes in the nearby countryside. For some, the better off, this meant driving to a comfortable cottage house outside of town; others would make a longish trek by public transportation to a simple cabin on a plot of land, which they often also used to grow fruit and vegetables to supplement meager diets. Gal'perin, seventy-two years old, would have liked to join his wife as she went to check on the couple's plot. Confined to a wheelchair for the past three years, though, he was visibly upset that he was unable to leave his apartment on the fourth floor of a residential building. The thresholds were too high for his wife to lift him across; unless his son came to help, Boris Gal'perin was bound to their home. For a man who had always felt "a special connection to living soil," this difficulty was but one of many.[8]

The unaffordability of health care and medicine, a result of the Soviet collapse that left many pensioners struggling to make ends meet and deal with illness and disability on their own, was even more frustrating. Gal'perin was also upset that his former colleagues at a company developing high-voltage networks had forgotten to congratulate him on his birthday, an omission that had occurred for the first time that year. In light of all of these worries and troubles, the man was clearly delighted at my interest in his life long before the botched operation that restricted him to the wheelchair. During this first visit, Boris Gal'perin provided me with a written account of his wartime experience so I could learn about him before we talked.[9] Clearly, he was excited to speak about this life, but he also expected me to be prepared for our conversation.[10] As I was about to leave, Gal'perin handed me a picture of himself at age twelve, dressed in the uniform of a Pioneer, a member of the Young Pioneer Organization of the USSR (the Soviet organization for children age ten to fifteen), and wrote a personal dedication to me on the back of the photograph, which appears in this book.

When I met Boris Gal'perin the second time a few weeks later, he was eager to talk, and I was able to learn about his growing up in Ryzhkovichi, one of three mostly Jewish *kolkhozes* (collective farms), near the town of Shklov, and about his life after the war. Neither of these themes was included in his brief written account, which focused on the war.[11] This was the last time I was able to meet Boris Gal'perin. He died nine months later, in February 2002.

The ties to living soil that Boris Gal'perin frequently pointed out are rooted in his childhood in the former Pale of Settlement, in a rural setting where farm work was the daily norm. While for him his childhood was untroubled and full, it was also a time of hard labor and of historical changes that affected both his life and the community he grew up in—a life he remembered with sparkling eyes.

Young Gal'perin's childhood reflected the impact of Soviet policies since the Russian Revolution. As soon as the tsarist regime was deposed in 1917, the provisional government lifted the restrictions on Jewish settlement in the Russian Empire that had been mandated by Tsarina Ekaterina II in 1792.[12] Boris and his peers, born in the second half of the 1920s and early 1930s, grew up in the first twenty years of the Soviet Union, a period that was shaped by the overthrow of discriminatory bureaucratic and economic structures and power relations. Several interviewees grew up in former shtetls, the emblematic space of Jewish existence in the Pale of Settlement.[13] Varying in size, these shtetls had been shaped by Jewish religious law and customs, as well as by traditions that determined family life, educational careers, and the government of local communities. Following the October Revolution in 1917 and the subsequent founding of the Soviet Union in 1922, life in the shtetl underwent reformations that redefined the framework for growing up Jewish. Thousands of Soviet Jews' lives were profoundly reshaped by rural-to-urban migration and relocation to the two cultural centers of the European parts of the Soviet Union, Leningrad and Moscow, as well as entry into previously closed educational institutions and professional employment.[14]

The communist regime, having seized power, aimed to create a new society that was formally based on principles of class, national (ethnic), and gender equality.[15] To achieve ethnic equality, the Soviet policy on nationalities encouraged the strengthening of ethnic cultures, referred to as *korenizatsiia* (indigenization or nativization), as well as their secularization.[16] Eventually, the government strove to create Soviet peoples that were "national in form, socialist in content."[17] While these policies targeted Belorussian as much as Jewish culture, the interviewees largely focus on the latter. Although they grew up in a context that was shaped by both, their narratives rarely speak to the role of Belorussianization in their adolescent lives.

The destruction of religious institutions and the prohibition of religious congregations began in earnest in 1921 as part of the groundwork for creating socialist Soviet peoples.[18] These antireligious campaigns were a point of contention for Jewish political parties and individuals that were generally supportive of overthrowing the tsarist regime and worked to gain individual and collective rights for Jews.[19] For them, the protection of Jewish religious and cultural customs did not contradict the notion of social and political equality among all Soviet citizens. Groups that promoted national autonomy, either within the Soviet Union or outside (in the form of a Jewish state), whether socialist parties, such as the Bund or Poale Zion, or more centrist and religious parties, sooner or later were prohibited.[20] In their stead, a Jewish committee within the Communist Party, the so-called *Evsektsiia*,[21] was to represent Jewish citizens and their interests. First of all, and in line with the project to create a secular Soviet state, the Evsektsiia took over directing the socialist revolution "on the Jewish street," facilitating the secularization and modernization of everyday Jewish life that had been the goal of Eastern European Jewish activists since the 1880s.[22]

In addition to the decreasing role of religion in the molding of everyday lives, schooling and language use surface in interview narratives as significant for young Soviet Jews' development. Both were regulated in accordance with the Soviet regime's aims to construct secular Soviet peoples, to overcome illiteracy, and to increase the level of education more generally. For Jews, the Evsektsiia determined, secularization meant first of all communicating not in Hebrew but in Yiddish, which the committee considered to be the true "language of the Jewish proletariat."[23] As in other instances of nation-building, Soviet theorists located the "form," or expression, of nationality precisely in a nation's language.[24] By promoting the native languages and cultures of Soviet nationalities, the Soviet leadership hoped to overcome national distrust and reach out to different national groups. In other words, supporting national cultures would help remedy the historic inequality of cultural development in the Russian empire, facilitate enlightenment, and eventually spread revolutionary consciousness and communism.[25] For Soviet Jewish citizens, maintaining their language was also important, because they could not claim territorial concentration or residence in a particular republic, unlike other nationalities.[26] The establishment of the Jewish Autonomous Region Birobidzhan in the Soviet Far East in 1928 was an attempt to remedy this lack, but very few Jews actually settled there, which marks the creation as an artificial outcome of Soviet nationality policy in the 1920s.[27]

Activists modernized local native languages by using live popular speech to codify literary standards; they saw this as an attempt to link up linguistic self-determination to cultural development.[28] For the Jewish national community, this resulted in the suppression of Hebrew, the language used in religious services; Yiddish was considered to be the only legitimate national Jewish language. Consequently, Hebrew schools and publishing houses were closed, and cultural activities in Hebrew, such as theater performances, were discouraged.[29] At the same time, the Yiddish language experienced widespread support; for instance, pupils in newly established "Jewish schools" throughout the country were instructed in the Yiddish language. Over four years, between 1922 and 1926, the number of students in Jewish schools doubled, so that eventually more than 22,000 children and youth were instructed in Yiddish, but not in Jewish history or culture.[30] Focusing on providing education for as many children as possible and the transmission of traditional disciplines, these Jewish schools were part of the project to train workers, cadres, and Soviet citizens—a new type of human who supported socialist ideas and was devoted to the cause of the Communist Party.[31] This training is reminiscent of political education, yet it did enable some sections of the Soviet population, especially young people, to overcome illiteracy and poverty.[32]

In the early 1930s, the Soviet leadership, proclaiming that such problems as poverty and inequality between different national groups had been resolved, downplayed policies designed to improve the situation of women as well as Jews and other ethnic groups. They redirected nationality policies toward a select few national groups—Ukrainians, Belorussians, or

Armenians—whose loyalty was crucial to achieving industrialization and centralization. These groups were strong in numbers and resided in areas that were strategically important for either agriculture or oil production.[33] One last and momentous element of the nativization campaign, however, was the introduction of internal passports for Soviet citizens in the early 1930s. Part of an effort to curtail the free movement of laborers and to purge cities of undesired social groups, the passports included a section on the bearer's national origin, or nationality.[34] These concurrent trends culminated in the closure of "national institutions" such as Jewish schools and publishing houses and the dissolution of the Evsektsiia.[35] The repression of national cultures coincided with a broader trend to persecute supposedly anti-Soviet sentiments and activities; thousands of party functionaries and ordinary citizens were deported to special settlements, interned in prison camps, or killed.[36]

At the same time that collectivization and industrialization, famine, and political repression drained people and society, hopes for a better future prevailed, especially among the youth.[37] After decades of life in poverty and restrictions on Jewish life in the Russian Empire, the Soviet project promised better days for individuals and the society as a whole. Yakov Negnevitzki, who was born in 1925 and grew up in a workers' family, is convinced that his father was excited about the new society, despite both long bread lines in the early 1930s and the Russo-Finnish War's undoing of the improvements the family had experienced before: "He compared it to the conditions of his childhood and they were of course much worse."[38] Like Boris Gal'perin, Yakov Negnevitzki is suggesting that Soviet policies were successful in reshaping private lives and were welcome as such.

Young Soviet Jews actively participated in building a new, better, Soviet society, alongside their parents. They thereby realized the concept of childhood promoted in the young Soviet Union, where children were seen as agents of the revolution and allies of the state in educating older generations.[39] Gal'perin's gift to me, the photograph, is thus both a representation of his 1930s self-conception and a reminder of a still self-valued social function he once occupied as a Pioneer. The memory of this role sharply contradicts his current life. The perhaps nostalgic picture of a happy Soviet childhood acquires double meaning in reminding us of the ideological position of being a Pioneer as well as of the socially highly valued physical prowess of adolescents: Gal'perin describes his own adolescence with great excitement while displaying discontent about being sidelined in old age.

"He wanted to teach me Hebrew, but . . . I always ran away"

Once restrictions on Jewish life in tsarist Russia were lifted, many Jews, especially younger ones, left their hometowns in what is now considered Belorussia and moved to larger cities outside of the former Pale. They went to Leningrad, Moscow, or Kiev, often to continue their education or to find work outside of the agricultural settings of their childhood.[40] Liubov Belen'kaia recalls how one sibling after another left her home in Slavnoe, a settlement in the county of Tolochin with about 600 residents in the 1930s:[41]

> I wanted to become a doctor when I was a child, but I did not make it. My oldest sister Margolia (Fridliand) moved to Leningrad, found herself an apartment and then invited the next sister, Liuba. And then my older brother Paia followed too. When it was my turn, my little brothers had grown up and my mother decided that if I leave too, they would be by themselves and fool around. So they all went, one after the other, but I stayed. Mother needed help, she was ill and weak . . . My sister worked in a factory and took evening classes at the Engineering School [in Leningrad].[42]

Belen'kaia attests to a trend that rocked many families in former shtetls and furthered the separation of family members across large distances. It also opened up new possibilities of professional development, especially for women.[43] Indeed, between 1932 and 1937, 82 percent of the 4,047,000 workers who entered the Soviet labor force were women.[44]

These opportunities for women, and their employment, contrast strikingly with the limited educational opportunities previously available to them in the shtetl. Synagogues and cheders, schools where children were taught how to read the Torah, had largely been inaccessible for women. Leaving the shtetl, as Liubov Belen'kaia indicates, often meant a farewell to the limits of religious schooling, learning Hebrew, or receiving no education at all.

In the former shtetls, however, previous patterns of everyday life persisted, albeit paralleled or disrupted by the ascent of new ways of thinking about religion, education, and the division of labor. Boris Gal'perin explains:

My grandfather lived with us. He loved my mother very much and used to say that there was no better daughter for him than she. He was very religious, and she prepared everything separately for him, we had an extra set of dishes for him. He prayed every morning; he had his own bench in the synagogue. . . . He wanted to teach me Hebrew, but at the time that was not welcomed in the schools, and so I always ran away, I did not want to. Now I really regret that I don't know it. Grandfather had many books in Hebrew, he owned a lot of Jewish literature, and he read it to me. I loved listening to him . . . .[45]

Boris Gal'perin, born in 1927, fondly remembers his grandfather as the center of family attention in their home. Exercising religious obligations and customs such as the daily prayer and observing kashruth, the grandfather personifies the continuing influence of Jewish religion and cultural traditions in Ryzhkovichi. There, Boris's parents worked and lived in the Jewish cooperative Der Emes (The Truth), which was transformed into the Jewish kolkhoz Iskra (Spark) in the early 1930s, a development that shaped many Jewish agricultural settlements in the 1920s.[46]

Gal'perin recalls the enjoyment of listening to stories in what was for him an inaccessible language, a pleasure that presumably resulted from the sound of Hebrew speech rather than the content of the stories. At the same time, he describes the diminishing influence of his grandfather on his personal development and his resistance to the transmission of traditional cultural knowledge, a resistance that was supported by Soviet authorities. The failure of his grandfather to motivate him to study Hebrew and the Torah indicates a shift in how important belief and traditions were for young Jews in 1930s Belorussia, but also the role of Soviet nationality policies in shaping these perceptions.[47]

Gal'perin's mother, Esfir Zakharovna Gal'perina, cared for her father in-law, Boris's grandfather. The young Boris enjoyed his mother's culinary skills as well as her efforts to care for both her family and her community:

Mother had geese; she had 150 geese every year. She always chased them to the riverbanks; we lived near the Dnepr. She then left them there for the whole day, and when she came for them in the evening, they all came flying up to her and gathered around her. She was a real housewife, she worked very hard, and managed to provide treats as well . . . We had an icebox, there was a pit with ice in it, it did not melt, all peasants brought their milk there so it would not go bad. And mother even knew how to make ice cream, for the whole kolkhoz, on holidays. She was such a good person . . . When in 1939 a Jewish family from Poland came to live in Ryzhkovichi, they had fled the German occupation, they were really poor. They had nothing, and worst of all, they had never done any farm work. So mother helped them . . . She gave them milk every day, and some geese, when it was time to slaughter them . . . I liked it when mother helped others, that was a great joy for me. I was very proud of her.[48]

Thus, while Liubov Belen'kaia's sister Margolia Fridliand left her family in Slavnoe and received a higher education, Boris Gal'perin's mother continued to run a rural home. She took care of a multigenerational household infused by tradition and contributed to the sustenance of the cooperative-turned-kolkhoz. Gal'perin's emphasis on his mother's engagement in domestic labor is repeated in his account of her later involvement in the partisan movement, where she worked as a cook while Boris participated in combat missions. The emphasis on these activities and the absence of other details about his mother's interests or activities reflect traditional gender roles, in which women were expected to care for the family and community above all else.

Margolia Fridliand's decision to leave and invite her siblings to follow her, along with her sister Liubov Belen'kaia's need to stay behind to help her mother, also attests to a situation that was typical for many, especially in families with many children: not all adolescents had the same opportunities. Some had access to education and independence; others did not. Limited resources as well as traditional expectations of women restricted opportunities that were otherwise available to Soviet citizens.

In introducing his family, Boris Gal'perin reminds us of these limitations, though without questioning them. His paternal uncle received professional training as a furrier and went on to found the fur company Rot Front in Leningrad, laying the groundwork for a successful and renowned enterprise. Another uncle worked as an accountant, his father as a farmer. His aunts, in contrast, "were all seamstresses. This, as people used to say, 'gave bread and food.'"[49] And Gal'perin's cousin Galina Slutskaia explains that their grandfather "did not want them to study further," and so Sarra Klebanova, her mother and one of the two seamstresses, quit her education after graduating from gymnasium and learned a trade.⁵⁰ Whereas Boris Gal'perin describes his mother's trajectory as matter-of-fact, Galina Slutskaia delivers an explanation of the grandfather's influence and allows for a critical perspective on the reasons for women's confinement to the home.

Had Sarra Klebanova continued to study, she might have been among those who took on important positions within the Soviet administration of kolkhozes or specialized in new agricultural technologies. Liubov Belen'kaia, for instance, worked as a laboratory assistant in the grain department of the local collective farm in Slavnoe and helped monitor the quality of grain seeds.⁵¹ Employment in such departments provided access to material resources, and also promised social prestige.

Frida Ped'ko, born in 1934, also grew up in Slavnoe. She recalls that her mother, Maria Iosifovna Sirotkina "had a very good salary ... She was head of a department for grain distribution. We had our own house; we lived together with my grandfather, my mother, and my sister. And mother also had a brother and one sister, we all lived in one house."⁵² Frida's mother was also the local secretary of the Communist Party, and as such could provide for the family even after her husband died unexpectedly of typhus when Frida was one year old.

I met Frida Ped'ko in 2001, when I volunteered in the association of Jewish ghetto and concentration camp survivors. Ped'ko had married a Russian man after the war, and in our conversations she was very reflective about the ways in which people of different nationalities lived together in the Soviet Union and were treated by the state. Often she argued that there should be no differences, identifying herself as a "true internationalist," that is, she emphasized that she did not harbor prejudices toward other nationalities and that all are equal. Her life reflects the transformations in the lives of young Soviet Jews and their families similarly to, if not more clearly than, Boris Gal'perin's biography. Gal'perin emphasizes that his grandfather and his parents continued to observe Jewish holidays, yet "did not force me to participate."⁵³ Frida Ped'ko, in contrast, remembers how she and her parents' generation actively undermined such customs:

> Grandfather observed [traditions], but we did not. On Passover, when grandfather did not eat bread, only matzo, we snuck into the other room and ate bread. He had kosher dishes and everything and went to the

synagogue, but we were all atheists. We were Pioneers, members of the Komsomol ... .[54]

Descriptions such as these suggest that at times there was a stark generational difference with regard to the observance or abandonment of religious traditions.

As Frida Ped'ko, Liubov Belen'kaia, Galina Slutskaia, and Boris Gal'perin convey, the importance of religious and cultural traditions in Slavnoe and Ryzhkovichi was changing. Their narratives indicate that the project to create a union of Soviet peoples in the 1920s first of all affected the role and significance of a religious heritage in structuring the everyday lives of especially the younger generation. In addition to these changes, women's access to education and career opportunities outside the home was increasing. Both of these processes were, of course, contradictory and uneven, but indicated larger social and cultural shifts.

"I did not have Jewish literacy"

Alevtina Kuprikhina and Grigorii Erenburg's narratives focus on the interaction of young Jewish women and men with their peers and their integration with other nationalities, especially in schools, in Rogachev and Bobruisk respectively. Both towns had been centers of Belorussian Jewish cultural and religious life, and both grew considerably during the first three decades of the twentieth century. Kuprikhina and Erenburg's recollections address the schooling, language, and political engagement of those whose grandparents had been trained in cheders and synagogues, whose parents negotiated between these and Soviet schools and universities, and who themselves often did not have a choice with regard to the language of instruction in school, their religious education, or membership in political associations. The adolescents and their parents were agents of integration into Soviet society.

I met Alevtina Kuprikhina only once, in September 2002, and our conversation about her survival of genocide challenged us both. Hampered by poor health and nervousness, Kuprikhina gave an account that was hard to follow as she switched themes, time periods and names quickly. But her story provided important insights into how youths experienced the war, and the testimony that she gave to the Shoah Visual History Archive (VHA) in November 1998 is even more revealing. This testimony was far less entangled and follows a chronology, yet the details about times, places, events, and decisions that she provided there confirm those that she gave during our interview.⁵⁵ Overall, her adolescence, much like our conversation, was filled with movement and rapid transitions symptomatic of the time.

Born in 1931 in Bobruisk, Alevtina Kuprikhina grew up in two worlds. Solomon Igol'nikov and Riva Rivkina, her parents, separated shortly after she was born. Her unhappy father "kidnapped" little Alla, as she was called, from her maternal grandparents' house in Rogachev and placed her in the care of his parents in Zhlobin, about 25 km (15 miles) from Rogachev. Both Alevtina's father and mother moved separately to Leningrad to continue their educations, and Riva Rivkina was later deployed as a military surgeon in the Russo-Finnish war. Thus, Alevtina was mostly raised by her grandparents, moving back and forth between Rogachev and Zhlobin: "Whenever I was upset with one pair of grandparents, I got onto the train and went to the others."⁵⁶ These trips translate into a commute between a generation's different choices to adapt to changes in traditionally Jewish towns.

In 1923, Rogachev housed 6,320 Jews; this number shrank by 1939 to 4,601 Jews, a third of the town's total population. The town had once had a strong Zionist presence and was the home of influential religious Jewish thinkers.⁵⁷ Following the closing of Jewish religious and cultural institutions under the Soviet regime, young Alla's maternal grandparents struggled to make a living.⁵⁸ The head of the household, Mr. Rivkin, was a rabbi with limited income, requiring the family to mobilize other resources: "We had our own vegetable garden . . . and we rented out two rooms to another family."⁵⁹ And yet, Alevtina Kuprikhina has bright memories of Rogachev. In her memory, the town was

> very green, it was a very neat and cozy place, very lively . . . I remember all these gardens, flowers, there were almost no brick houses. We lived on Tsimmermannovskaia Street, No. 74, right next to a park that was also named after Tsimmermann, a Jewish hero from the Civil War . . . in the evening, people liked to walk along the streets, there was music, all over town, [and] girls wore such nice dresses.⁶⁰

Aleksandr Gol'din, a man who was interviewed by the VHA in 1997, was well into his twenties when little Alla enjoyed this peaceful life. He shares her impressions and describes Rogachev as a surprisingly "lively town" where people of various nationalities treated each other respectfully. At the same time, he invokes the dynamic and well-developed Jewish community, his own education in cheders and synagogues, and recites "Passover, Hanukkah, Rosh Hashanah, Yom Kippur, Succoth, and Purim" as important days of celebration.[61] Remnants of such a life are reflected in Kuprikhina's description of her grandmother's observance of religious customs and Jewish culture: "She sent me to the attic all the time to get the special dishes ... for Passover. They made their own matzo, but not at home. My grandparents spoke Yiddish, grandmother did not even know Russian that well."[62] The Rivkins, it seems, found their place largely within the limits of the Jewish community. But granddaughter Alla, who did not speak Yiddish, was positioned somewhat outside of this community, as her use of the third-person pronoun in discussing Jewish customs indicates: "they" made matzo, not we, whereas "we" rent out rooms and have a vegetable garden.

Whenever she stayed in Zhlobin, a town of about 19,000, Alevtina Kuprikhina joined a household that was deeply influenced by the drive to secularization and Sovietization. Her grandfather Lev Igol'nikov directed a large wood factory and "as a party member—at that time one had to be one—did not observe Jewish traditions."[63] It is hard to tell how many of the 3,709 Jews who lived in Zhlobin in 1939 followed a similar path.[64] What is clear is that Alevtina's trajectory followed in analogous footsteps; her narrative shows that the absence of specifically Jewish institutions, such as schools, facilitated her integration into a community that was indifferent toward national or religious heritages, including linguistic skills. "I spoke Belorussian very well,"[65] she said. That is why she "enrolled in Rogachev in a school that used to be a Jewish school, but then it was a Belorussian school ... [my] father had graduated from that school as well, he spoke and wrote Yiddish fluently. I don't know if there were many Jewish students in the class. We were all equal, Russians, Jews—it did not matter."[66] Alevtina Kuprikhina might not have had any other choice than to enroll in a Belorussian school at the time; the Department of Education decreed in 1938 that Jewish schools in Belorussia were to be closed.[67]

In memory, Kuprikhina's childhood experiences are filled with positive experiences, despite her growing up in a complicated family environment. She does not speak about what it meant to deal with the different degrees in which religion and cultural traditions shaped daily life, or what it meant to her to grow up with her grandparents rather than be raised by her own parents. A sole hint at a sense of confusion appears in Alevtina Kuprikhina's statement that "until I turned six, I did not know that I had a father; I called them [the grandparents] father and mother."⁶⁸ However, her adaptation to increasingly secular and Soviet environments, including the renunciation of the Yiddish language, appears smooth. Young Alla was not alone in this, as students of the time did not assign a great deal of meaning to whether they learned in Belorussian, Russian, or Jewish schools—perhaps because adolescents are generally flexible and open to new developments.⁶⁹ One may also see this as an expression of indifference.⁷⁰ Individual recollections, however, suggest that in some cases this reaction was rather a manifestation of enthusiastic support for the Soviet project, pragmatism, or a mix of both, and these sentiments were shared by adolescents and their parents, as interviewee Grigorii Erenburg reveals.

Grigorii Erenburg welcomed me several times to his home, always alert and eager to share all he knew about his own life and about Soviet history in general. He was concerned that I, and thus the public beyond the interview, would be able to make sense of his memories, and therefore often explained overall historical trends rather than speaking about himself. It turned out to be difficult to encourage Erenburg to share personal impressions and perceptions of events he described; he repeated his account in almost identical fashion in the four interviews I was able to conduct with him. Reading across our four interview transcripts as well as listening to the VHA interview, Erenburg's narratives allow us to trace the emergence of a consciousness that, while rooted in both curiosity about Jewish history and culture and communist and Soviet patriotic convictions, is oriented more pointedly toward becoming a Soviet—later, Russian—patriot.

Boris Davidovich Erenburg and Rakhil' Gertsevna grew up in Shchedrin, married there, and had two children before they turned twenty-four. Grigorii was born in 1927, his brother Iakov in 1931. Boris and Rakhil', a shoemaker and housewife, were engaged in the sort of gendered labor that many of their ancestors had performed in the Jewish shtetls in the Pale of Settlement; men were usually artisans and craftsmen, and while a few women worked as seamstresses, the majority were housewives who took care of large families. Yiddish was the common language: "even the few Russians and Belorussians in Shchedrin spoke Yiddish," recalls Erenburg.⁷¹ Religion was at the center of Jewish communal life; the small town, inhabited by 1,759 people in 1926, had three synagogues (earlier in the century, Shchedrin had had eight), and members of Grigorii Erenburg's grandparents' generation continued to observe traditional religious practices well into the 1930s.[72] Furthermore, while remembering a lively community, the elder Erenburg highlights the high value placed on education among the Jews of Shchedrin:

> They were very cheerful people, and there were many talented people among the residents. That is because Jewish culture, or better, religion, requires that every Jew be able to read the Torah, i.e. everybody has to be literate. So children were supposed to get a good education, and many young people went to other places to go to school ... In the summer, they all came back and there were many festivities; that was a lot of fun.[73]

In the late 1920s, however, this form of social organization began to fall apart, many people never returned to the shtetl, and the economic situation was increasingly difficult. It became impossible for people like Grigorii's father to make a living. As Erenburg says, "this was not an easy time for our economy in the Soviet Union, father did not have enough clients, and so we decided to move to Bobruisk."[74]

In the past, Bobruisk had been considered the capital of Belorussian Jewish culture; numerous yeshivas and synagogues had been frequented by believers and rabbis, Bundists and Zionists had worked there, and in the 1920s more than 2,400 students went to twelve Jewish (Yiddish-speaking) schools.[75] But by the time the Erenburg family went there, in 1934, most of these institutions and organizations had been shut down. Strong Jewish artisan cooperatives were converted into state factories.[76] Erenburg's father began to work at a wood factory, putting in extra hours to support a growing family; in 1935 and 1939, Grigorii's two sisters, Ol'ga and Zhenia, were born.[77] The family was among a continuing stream of immigrants to Bobruisk and other larger towns such as Rogachev and Minsk. Between 1926 and 1939, the Jewish population of Bobruisk grew from 21,558 to 26,703, forming a third of the city's total population.[78] The city was a prime example of urbanization, modernization, and associated migration patterns within Soviet society.[79]

Grigorii Erenburg's narration further indicates the success of attempts to Sovietize and secularize the population, to remove them from traditional, religious ways of life. Especially the turn toward Soviet patriotism in the 1930s destroyed the institutions that supported the specific cultural heritage of national groups: Jewish theaters, publishing houses, and schools were closed, depriving the population of a public infrastructure to maintain and promote even the Soviet, secular version of Jewish culture and tradition.[80]

Grigorii Erenburg's parents decided to enroll the boy in a Belorussian school but did not completely give up on Jewish traditions. After describing the area as an "interesting and international district," comprising Russian, Polish, and Latvian villages, Erenburg continues, "so when it was time for me to start school, we decided that I should go to a Belorussian school, because I did not have Jewish (*sic!*) literacy. As hard as I tried, I could not learn the Hebrew alphabet. Also, my friends were Russians, and the neighbors' son went there too."[81] What comes across as a rather pragmatic decision upon closer examination reveals Grigorii's increasing distance from his Jewish origins—if not in reality, then in memory. In his own words, Jewish culture requires every Jew's ability to read the Torah in the Hebrew original. Similarly, speaking Yiddish, but being unable to read or write it, places him outside the Jewish community in the strict sense.[82] Erenburg reinforces this with the caution that he "also did not look like a Jew. Now I may look like a Jew. But our family, we all looked like Russians, we were blue-eyed and had blond hair."[83] However, the family kept some Jewish traditions alive, celebrating Passover and inviting many guests to share the delicacies Rakhil' Gertsovna prepared, including matzo that had been made by a group of women.[84] Guests at these meals were both Jews and non-Jews; "father's colleagues came often."[85]

In the Soviet Union, such interethnic friendships and the theme of culinary differences were common, but they were seen more as grounds for curiosity than for conflict or to mark distinction. Liudmila Kriuchkova, for instance, says: "I had a Russian girlfriend in school. She always asked me, 'Why does your grandmother make these delicious rolls on Saturday, but mine—on Sunday?' I told her I didn't know."[86] The Erenburg family's preservation of the custom of celebrating Jewish holidays reflects a tendency to confine religious practice to the space of the family.[87] Yet opening up the celebrations for Gentiles questioned their role in facilitating Jewish community cohesion. In Judaism, different food items often have a specific meaning and remind eaters of particular moments in Jewish history that are invoked by storytelling during the meal. It is unlikely that these interpretations were delivered during interethnic meals, which voided them of their role in building connections between ancestors and present-day participants.

Young Grigorii Borisovich was an avid reader; he remembers that "on weekends I did not leave the public library" and that "mother gave me money for breakfast, but I saved it up and bought books with it."[88] His favorite book was Nikolai Ostrovskii's *How the Steel Was Tempered*. Grigorii Erenburg repeatedly encouraged me to read this book, stressing that even now he considers it a very important publication:

> This is a very patriotic and heroic book. As a young man, the writer participated in the Civil War and was seriously wounded. He wrote two very good books, they were the most popular books in our country, in the Soviet Union. He [the main figure] was my role model. I was so impressed by him. I was very romantic.[89]

How the Steel was Tempered is a fictionalized autobiography of the author, who fought in the ranks of the Bolsheviks during the Civil War of 1917–1922. Despite physical injury, the hero Pavel Korchagin uses all his energies to advance the communist cause. Ostrovskii describes his principles this way:

> Man's dearest possession is life, and it is given to him to live but once. He must live so as to feel no torturing regrets for years without purpose, never know the burning shame of a mean and petty past; so live that, dying, he can say: All my life, all my strength were given to the finest cause in all the world—the fight for the Liberation of Mankind. And one must make use of every moment of life, lest some sudden illness or tragic accident cut it short.[90]

The book was not only widely distributed in the Soviet Union, but was compulsory reading for students in East Germany and many other Eastern European countries as well. Full of the adventures of a rebellious student, it was even more useful to promote the young generation's potential and obligation to help further the socialist revolution.

Erenburg invoked Korchagin's morality multiple times to explain his involvement in the partisan fight against the German occupation. But his enthusiasm for participation in the exciting endeavor of building a new society began during his tenure at the seven-year school: "From my early years on I was an activist, I was a cork to every bottle, so to speak. I edited the wall newspaper in our school. I became a Pioneer, to this day I remember how they put the neck scarf around our neck... I was a very active Pioneer."[91] According to these descriptions, Erenburg embodies the desired outcome of Soviet schooling in the 1930s: he spoke Russian, read patriotic literature, saw himself as a potential hero, and actively worked for the communist project.

Speaking Belorussian and Russian rather than Yiddish, engaged in the communist youth organizations and liberated from religious influences, Grigorii Borisovich was on his way to becoming a committed and productive Soviet citizen; he planned to enroll at the local *tekhnikum* (technical or engineering school) after graduation in June 1941. Encouraged by his parents, who sent him to a Belorussian school and largely abstained from passing on cultural knowledge, Grigorii was Jewish by passport, but did not live as a Jew.

He was not the only youth in such a position, but he also does not personify the only available choice: there were a considerable number of Jewish women and men who were not yet ready to give up their Jewish religion and culture. Their efforts went so far as to resist antireligious campaigns and introduce students in Jewish schools to the skills of the local synagogue's cantor, or even prepare matzo with their students.[92] And yet, a combination of pragmatism and hopes for the future is evident on the part of Grigorii Erenburg's parents. They sent him to school together with his friends, assuming he could continue to study outside Belorussia if he acquired the necessary language skills. Grigorii Erenburg was excited about building a society based on ideas of internationalism and patriotism. His efforts to bring this project to fruition made his life differ markedly from the lives of his grandparents and even his parents, but it coexisted with other people's ways of adapting to, or even rejecting, Soviet society.

"Perhaps we did not understand the larger implications"

Minsk, like Bobruisk, was a center of Belorussian Jewish culture and religion. The city had been the home of a lively Jewish community and its institutions, which had evolved over several centuries.[93] Elena Drapkina, Rita Kazhdan, and many other young residents of the city followed paths that resemble Grigorii Erenburg's portrayal of growing up in a place previously shaped by Jewish customs and practices. Because it was the capital of the Belorussian Socialist Republic, the influence of Soviet politics and propaganda on personal lives was more pronounced in Minsk than in the eastern parts of the Republic. The newly established Soviet administration and cultural and educational institutions changed the large Jewish community and, eventually, facilitated its demise. Jews born after the founding of the USSR perceived these changes with varying degrees of awareness. Growing up in an urban environment made the impact of worldwide trends toward militarization, the rise of fascist regimes in Europe, and modernization very palpable. This experience emerges as more powerful in shaping the memories of elderly women and men than the disappearance of Jewish schools or synagogues.

At the time I conducted my research, many of the Soviet institutions that had guided interviewees' lives had stopped functioning a second time, and for good. The effects of political and social transformation in what once had been the Soviet Union was tangible in St. Petersburg, yet appeared not to exist in Minsk, the capital of the newly independent Republic of Belarus. I remember my first visit to Minsk, in September 2002, like a journey through time. Having spent several months conducting many interviews in the heavily modernized and Westernized city of St. Petersburg in the northwest of Russia, I had been eager to go to the place that I seemed to know so well already, based on the narrations by Elena Drapkina, Rita Kazhdan, and Pavel Rubinchik. Of course, the prewar city, its architecture, and its people were long gone, many of them destroyed during the German occupation.

At the same time, walking along the streets of modern-day Minsk felt strangely familiar. The cleanliness, the massive concrete buildings complemented by socialist-classicist housing complexes, the introverted passersby who hardly deigned to look at each other, police officers scolding drunken people, all of them surrounded by the bustling traffic of outdated cars, stinking buses, and the occasional bicyclist—I recognized them as having been a part of my own youth. Growing up in East Germany, I had encountered the remnants of Soviet socialist creations in the 1980s, and their impact was all too visible in the Minsk of 2002. They had nothing to do with the life that emerged in Elena Drapkina and Rita Kazhdan's portrayals of the wartime city and ghetto. Minsk had been in ruins at the end of World War II and was rebuilt over several decades, so there were almost no physical traces of what they had described. At the same time, with its buildings reaching for a new type of grandeur, a river enclosed in concrete, nature tamed by man, and people following strict discipline, the society I encountered was a reminder (or remainder?) of the project to build a new society, a project that shaped Drapkina and Kazhdan's childhood and youth.

Elena Drapkina was born in 1924 as Elena Askarevna Levina, Rita Kazhdan in 1929 as Rita Abramovna Fridman. They both had parents who worked in administrative or managerial capacities and could thus provide very well for their families.[94] Abram Fridman, young Rita's father, directed the Belorussian State Film Studios (BelGosKino). His wife Rozaliia Fridman worked as a dispatcher at the train station, but had begun to do so only after both Rita and her younger brother Grigorii (Grisha) had started school.[95] Elena Levina's parents were both well educated and had given up teaching positions to work in the city *Ispolkom* (Executive Committee).[95] As the women remember, the families lived a comfortable life. They had sufficient access to food and other resources and were able to integrate fully into Soviet society. The children especially made full use of Soviet schooling, afternoon programs, and sport groups, all activities that reflected the socialist project of emancipation and progress and replaced traditional Jewish culture.

Like Boris Gal'perin, Grigorii Erenburg, and others, Elena Drapkina recounted that her grandparents used to live according to Jewish religious and cultural traditions, while she and her two brothers were "raised in an atheist family" that did not celebrate Jewish holidays or follow any traditions.[97] The generations lived such different lives that "grandfather often came to visit, but since we did not keep kosher, he did not eat in our house."[98] Rita Kazhdan was not introduced to Jewish culture as a child, which created a sense of confusion when she visited her grandfather in Leningrad:

> I remember he was always praying when we visited. He wore a tallith [Jewish prayer shawl] and those little cubes [tefillin], I don't know what they are called.[99] I always asked him a lot of questions, but he never answered as long as he was praying and wore the tallith and those cubes. I thought they were strange. I don't remember what I asked him, but I knew that we were not supposed to interrupt him, but I always wanted to see what he would do when I disturbed him. I was being silly.[100]

While the grandparents' generation continued to celebrate Jewish customs, their children and grandchildren increasingly distanced themselves from this cultural framework, up to the point that they are unable to identify basic religious practices such as wearing tefillin during prayer.[101]

Encounters with grandparents or parents practicing religious belief were the only reminder of the family's (and thus the youths') Jewish heritage, but at times religious rituals acquired very pragmatic meaning. Samuil Volk, born in 1930 or 1931, when asked "Did you consider yourself a Jew?" responds in the affirmative, explaining that his father

> observed traditions, he prayed, he had a Talmud, and he wore these black things [tefillin], I don't know what they are called, a yarmulke, and we celebrated holidays, but I wasn't terribly involved, neither were my siblings, and father didn't make us do anything. I think he used to be a believer and tried to make the family at least observe a few traditions.[102]

Samuil Volk recalls that his mother struggled to gather enough food for her five children, the husband, and herself. Folia Volk worked as a carpenter; his wife Revekka was a seamstress but spent considerable time on maternity leave during Samuil's childhood. The family's income was thus limited, and often there was not enough food on the table. He therefore remembered Jewish holidays primarily as days when there was something good to eat, not for their religious significance.

By educating her in the state language, Russian, Rita Kazhdan's family actively supported her full integration into Soviet society, she recalls: "We never spoke Yiddish at home, because the family was a Russian family. I learned in a Russian school so that I would not have an accent,"[103] an accent Rita's parents apparently deemed detrimental to their aspirations. They largely succeeded, judging from Kazhdan's narrative. She recalls her shock, then, at the anti-Jewish verbal abuse she received in the first days of the war. Before the war nationality was a concept disconnected from her personal life:

> I remember, in third grade, the teacher asked which nationality we were; she had to fill out some lists. And when she called out my name, Fridman, Rita, my maiden name, I said, I don't know, I'll ask my mother. There were no divisions between us. After all, these were Soviet times, I grew up in the Soviet state.[104]

Enrolled in a Russian school, young Rita did not develop a strong sense of Jewish identity or, in the Soviet framework, nationality.

Sending children to Russian schools was a privilege, as Elena Drapkina argues: "Russian schools were only for the upper crust, people in important positions."[105] Kazhdan's father surely belonged to this elite—the family even had a housekeeper, Marusia Gubinskaia, throughout the 1930s.[106] Young Elena and "everybody else went to Belorussian schools."[107] Until their closure, however, some Jewish children also went to schools where instruction took place in Yiddish.[108]

The increasing renunciation of Yiddish as the language of choice for children's education anticipated the closing of all Jewish schools and the complete erasure of Jewish institutions by 1940.[109] This closure and the Kazhdan family's efforts to excel in Russian are responses to a shift in Soviet nationality policies in the mid-1930s that foregrounded a Soviet identity, which translated into favoring Russian language and culture above all else.[110] None of the people I was able to interview noted this as problematic. In contrast, many interviewees remember fondly the indifference toward national origin and difference when they describe friendships with Russians, Belorussians, Ukrainians, and others. Vera Smirnova, for instance, smiles at the thought of Russian neighbors asking her mother for recipes of Jewish dishes such as gefilte fish.[111] According to these accounts, the idea of Soviet internationalism, in which difference merged into equality, had become a reality in the everyday lives of Jewish children and youths.

Teenagers also experienced this sense of unity beyond the classroom, in *kruzhki* ("circles," here meaning regular afternoon workshops), sports clubs, Pioneer camps, and elsewhere. Many of these programs catered to youths' personal interests, but they were also places for political instruction and recruiting labor for utopian projects. Elena Drapkina, for instance, ironically mentions her attempts to grow cotton in the *Detskaia Tekhnicheskaia Stantsiia* (Children's Technical Station), saying, "of course that had to fail, it was too cold in Minsk for it to grow."[112] Though this project failed, young Elena perceived herself as a valuable contributor to Soviet society and put her energy to work.

The Pioneers Palaces—youth centers where Young Pioneers engaged in such extracurricular activities as sports and arts and crafts, and which were often housed in former residences of the tsar or the nobility or newly built structures of similar size—emerge in several accounts as centers of after-school activity. Vera Smirnova attended dance classes, Elena Drapkina followed her love of literature and participated in theater workshops, Vladimir Mordkhilevich trained to become a singer, and Mikhail Treister practiced gymnastics three times a week.[113] Both Mordkhilevich and Drapkina recount their participation in performances and plays based on novels such as *How the Steel Was Tempered*, *Timur and His Team* (by Arkadii Gaidar), or *The Snow Queen* and *The Emperor's New Clothes* (both by Hans Christian Andersen), all of which convey strong moral messages about the struggle between good and evil. The element of heroism on behalf of the socialist cause, especially in *Timur and His Team* and *How the Steel Was Tempered*, further strengthened their consciousness as Soviet citizens. Whether they adopted these ideals is an open question. However, the excitement with which they recall these activities suggests that young Elena Drapkina, Rita Kazhdan, Vera Smirnova, and Vladimir Mordkhilevich welcomed the opportunity to participate in activities guided and approved by the new Soviet regime.

Roza Zelenko suggests, in hindsight, that this attitude may be questionable: "Perhaps we did not really understand the larger implications, but especially the summer camps were really nice. And everybody had access to free education, not like today."[114] Elena Drapkina argues that she was "basically raised in the Pioneer camps. Both parents worked and so I often spent three months in the summer camps. One camp was organized through father's employment, one through my mother's, and the third was offered by my school."[115] Her statement points to the important role that teachers in Soviet institutions played in child and youth development, increasing the degree to which communist and socialist values and ideology were able to guide the mindset of young Soviet citizens. Memories of summer camps, workshops, and other state-sponsored youth activities and the largely affirmative portrayal indicate that the state's effort to replace the family as the main influence on youth were successful.

Soviet schools and summer camps provided often crucial food supplies to families who were not part of the upper professional or Party strata. Samuil Volk, for instance, recalls that he was often upset when his mother put only black bread with butter in his lunch bag. This stood in stark contrast to his classmates' delicious *piroshki* (buns filled with potatoes, mushrooms, or other ingredients) or *bulochki* (yeast rolls). To alleviate the pain, his teacher "noticed this and sometimes put sandwiches or rolls in my desk drawer."[116] Support such as this for individual students occurred in a context where teachers were trained and officially encouraged to look out for the well-being of children beyond their intellectual development. Promoted and implemented since the early 1920s, this approach marked a substantial shift from tsarist practices.[117] The change here lies not only in the attempt of the teacher to remedy the hunger, but also in the fact that the teacher is a comrade supporting a member of the collective rather than an authoritarian representative of power.

Despite food shortages and even famine, resulting from the redirection of resources away from agriculture and toward export industries, the 1930s was a time of widespread support for the Soviet project.[118] But the decade also brought war into the consciousness of young Soviet citizens. This danger bolstered an emerging sense of belonging and collectivity. It also reminded young people of what they might have to sacrifice to preserve this community: individuality, the ideal of the friendship among all peoples, or their physical well-being.

Yakov Negnevitzki recalls a discussion among fellow Pioneers in which they assumed that Hitler's rise to power would lead to war, sooner or later.[119] Anticipating war, the Soviet government mobilized considerable resources to prepare the population for war and the state's defense.[120] Half laughing, half embarrassed, Amaliia Moiseevna Iakhontova hints at the rising fear of international conflict in summer camps in the mid-1930s, when she recalls she and other pioneers attempting to "catch spies" roaming the countryside. Her tone of voice suggests an ambivalence that Amaliia experienced either at the time or when she looks back at her youth. Her doubts may be rooted in insecurity about the success and purpose of her actions or in astonishment about the state's unpreparedness for the war as it unfolded despite these maneuvers. She may also be embarrassed about her participation in military operations that she generally does not condone.[121]

The process of militarization shaped all sectors of society, involving all generations, and women and men alike. Elena Drapkina, for instance, participated in the training program of *BGTO* (acronym for *Bud' Gotov k Trudu i Oborone SSSR*, Be Ready for Labor and Defense of the USSR, a paramilitary organization educating Soviet civilians), which included both athletic exercises and practice in handling weapons and shooting.[122] For young Elena, the program provided entry into professional sports: discovered by a swimming coach during tests for BGTO, she began to train regularly and competed for several years on the republic level, setting several records in butterfly and breaststroke.[123] Slightly older, Elena might have participated in exercises offered by the *OSOAVIAKhIM* (acronym for *Obshchestvo sodeistviia oborone i aviatsionno-khimicheskomu stroitel'stvu*, Society for Promotion of Defense, Aviation, and Chemical Development). Rita Kazhdan's mother, "a very progressive and dedicated person [who] went to all sorts of kruzhki, OSOAVIAKhIM, BGTO," was one of tens of thousands of young women and men who strove to be able to fly planes, parachute, and shoot in case of emergency in order to help defend the Soviet Union.[124] The inclusion of women in training programs which taught skills previously deemed appropriate only for men indicates a revision of gender roles promoted by the Soviet regime. The explicit inclusion of women in the industrial labor force and military formations suggests the striving for progress and for emancipation from bourgeois ideals of family and gender.[125] Yakov Negnevitzki illustrates how his mother managed to negotiate these objectives:

> My mother, Berta Gottlibovna, worked as a controller in the Krupskaia factory... She got up at 4:00 AM to heat and prepare food for the day. Then she went to work at 6:00 AM, trying to get to work on time so that she would not be penalized for tardiness, and after work she went to buy groceries.[126]

The "radical undoing of traditional gender differences" in 1930s Soviet society offered new opportunities for women and men.[127] However, this undoing was incomplete, since it asked women to shoulder a double burden: working for the state in public while also keeping house and raising future generations in private.[128] This overload of expectations clearly emerged from Negnevitzki's recounting of his mother's arduous daily schedule.

Despite this imbalance in the distribution of labor, images of women working, taking leadership positions, and participating in military operations supported social change and overall progress. They enabled Elena Drapkina, Rita Kazhdan, and others to envision themselves as actors in areas that their grandmothers were unable to enter as a result of religious, social, or cultural restrictions. The inclusion of women in the labor force, necessary to make up for lack of resources and to avoid deepening the housing crisis, enabled economic growth in the 1930s.[129]

Women's presence in the two central areas of constructing a Soviet society heightened the sense of strength and invincibility among the population. The assumption was that if everyone helped, failure was impossible. Elena Drapkina speaks for many when she recalls a popular sentiment regarding the German invasion: "We were absolutely convinced that war would never reach us. There was this song, 'If war comes tomorrow,' it said that we 'will defeat the enemy on his own land,' but not on our territory.[130] Perhaps because we were Pioneers and *komsomol'tsy* [members of the Communist Party's children and youth organizations] we were so sure."[131] This belief was quickly shattered, and along with it the ideal of equality among nationalities and between genders, when German troops invaded Soviet territories in 1941. And yet the possibility for valuable relationships across national lines, confidence in personal abilities, and belief in the ideology they acquired in their youth remain as deeply entrenched values in the consciousness of Jews who grew up in Soviet Minsk in the 1930s.

Lenin on his face
In our third conversation in 2005, Elena Drapkina mentioned that she did not know Yiddish: "It is a pity that I don't even know my own language; nobody taught us."[132] When I probed further, Drapkina expressed an increased interest in her family heritage and Jewish religious customs, mentioning that she had begun catching up on some of the knowledge she missed. Initially startled by this description, which seemed inconsistent with her own sense of her "atheist" upbringing, I came to understand this as part of an ongoing process of negotiating her relationship to the memory of her family, who had been killed by the Nazis; to the Jewish community in the postwar USSR; and to the society that had succeeded the Soviet Union. In this active process of reorienting herself in the 2000s, Elena Drapkina is not alone. Neither were she and her family in the 1930s, when thousands of Jewish families in Belorussia (and elsewhere in the Soviet Union) came to develop new ways of life, including a farewell to the religious frameworks that had shaped their family's past, a liberation from restrictions on certain nationalities, but also a redefinition of gender roles. They spoke Russian or Belorussian, developed friendships with children of various nationalities, eagerly participated in Pioneer campaigns, and were ready to help defend the country against enemies of communism and the Soviet project more generally. Only their grandparents continued to visit synagogues or observe Jewish dietary laws in private, alerting the adolescents to a bygone past that was now, figuratively speaking, banned from public view.

One may call the parallel existence of public loyalty to the Soviet state and private religious practice a life of double standards.[133] But one may also think this a site- and time-specific iteration of reconciling difference with universalism, an approach at the heart of the Jewish emancipation and assimilation movements. Specifically, left-leaning Eastern European Jewish social movements of the early twentieth century, such as the Bund, advanced and fought hard for similar ideas. While the interviewees' parents' generation was very familiar with this struggle, for 1930s Jewish adolescents this way of life was normal. They showed no interest in ensuring the longevity of Judaism; it did not play an important role for them. Similarly, politics to promote gender equality enabled the participation of girls and women in previously inaccessible spheres and institutions, such as in nonagricultural labor and the military. The double burden emerging from women's inclusion in the labor force and their continued responsibility for private households is noted in passing, likely because the interviewees themselves were not old enough to have been in that position.

While this Soviet project was under way, Nazi Germany introduced the Nuremberg Laws of 1935, which excluded German Jews from society, prepared an assault on European Jewry more generally, and readied itself for an imperialist and racist war. Soviet Jewish youth, in contrast, experienced a society that had the potential to do away with discrimination based on essentialist categories. In reality, Soviet authorities often neglected personal interests and pursued exaggerated expectations of reshaping the whole society that cost many people's lives and health.

The failure to implement equality and justice, and indeed phenomena that contradicted this goal, hardly arise at all in the accounts. It bears considering why the effects of collectivization, famine, state intervention in private lives, repression, and incidents of antisemitism, themes that are regularly addressed in scholarship on the 1930s in the Soviet Union, do not figure prominently. Young Frida Ped'ko, Elena Drapkina, and others may not have recognized or experienced them as meaningful for their personal lives at the time. Or they may not be willing to address those themes, as they continue to be marginalized and unwelcome in public discourse in Russia seventy years after the fact.

In a more complicated way, this omission expresses narrators' desire to maintain a powerful image of a promising period and social vision that was shattered several times, first by Nazi occupation and war, then by postwar Stalinism, and, finally, by the 1991 dissolution of the Soviet Union. Compared to these, the friendship of peoples, gender equality, and state protection against war, supported by schools, Pioneer activities, and sports activities, seem blissful.

The significance of this repeated experience of breakdown is perhaps nowhere else as powerfully described as in Samuil Volk's reminiscences of an encounter in Minsk at the beginning of World War II. His description encapsulates his disappointment in the destruction of the Soviet state, despite his family's poor living conditions. Ten-year-old Samuil returned to the city of Minsk from his first summer camp adventure shortly after German troops had bombed the city on June 22, 1941. He reacted strongly to the destruction around him: "When I was close to our house, I passed the House of Government. There used to be a Lenin statue, but now he was lying on his face, the Germans had knocked him over. I got really upset somehow, and I couldn't go any further. I started to cry."[134] The ten-year-old could not know that the German troops' attack was not only aiming to overthrow Soviet rule, but also paved the way for the murder of more than 800,000 Soviet Jews. His portrayal, however, indicates that the experience of physical destruction was accompanied by shock about the destruction of the Soviet project, of communist and internationalist ideals. The fact that he recalled this moment in detail and shared it with an interviewer in 1998 indicates the significance of the destruction and challenge to Soviet state power for him, if only in hindsight—here represented in a shattered monument to one of the founders of the Soviet state. Volk's postwar life and work, which revolved around service in the Soviet military, suggests that his recent experience of the collapse of the Soviet state, in many places accompanied by the destruction of monuments to Lenin and other Soviet leaders, mirrors his shock about the state's defeat in 1941. The project to build a communist society was thus invalidated for a second time. The collapse brought back and enhanced memories of the first time it happened, in the form of Nazi violence.

Of course, salvaging the ideal of prewar Soviet society has, first of all, personal value. During that period, families were intact, relatives were alive, and a powerful ideological framework, in which people were seen as builders of a new society, assigned meaning to people's lives. Nonetheless, knowing about interviewees' self-image and their position in Soviet society before World War II is essential to understanding the ways in which they experienced, survived, and responded to the German invasion of Soviet territory in June 1941. Drawing on insights about the prewar environment and the relationality of memory, the following questions are useful in approaching post-Soviet oral histories of the Nazi genocide: Did interviewees' perceptions of nationality and gender, or internationalist solidarity and equality, prove sustainable under conditions of occupation and genocide? How did they influence the youths' general perception of war and occupation? How did they affect the choices interviewees made with regard to their personal survival, relationships to others, and resistance against the occupation regime?

3

The End of Childhood

Young Soviet Jews in the Minsk Ghetto

When Sonia Zalesskaia returned from summer camp to her family's home in Minsk, the capital of the Belorussian Socialist Soviet Republic, in June 1941, she found her mother incapable of caring for either herself or Sonia and her three siblings, Tsilia, Abram, and Roza.

> She had a nervous breakdown when the Germans came, she was completely indifferent, paralyzed. When we had to move to the ghetto, I had to organize everything. I was the oldest sister. When they moved us to the ghetto, mother did not know what was going on . . . I found a peasant who drove our belongings to the ghetto on his cart. I figured I had to give him something, so I gave him our sewing machine and some fabric. That meant we had nothing left to trade with.[1]

Sonia Zalesskaia gives a sense of the multiple dimensions of breakdown that Soviet Jews experienced when Nazi troops occupied Minsk and, within a few weeks, established a segregated residential district for Jews, enclosed by barbed wire. Her story also highlights how age and gender affected people's reactions to violence, displacement, and starvation. Many adults, much like the Soviet authorities, were paralyzed by the swift invasion and ensuing terror regime; others were arrested or immediately killed. In either case, remaining relatives, often children, found themselves responsible for supplying whole families with food and other necessities. This critical labor, most often performed by women and girls, was crucial to surviving the extreme deprivation of the ghetto. This was often an impossible task, however; the prewar emphasis on social equalization had left people with little personal property to use or exchange, thus complicating access to necessary supplies and exacerbating the effects of Jewish segregation. With the establishment of the Minsk ghetto, young people faced both the breakdown of Soviet society and a profound scarcity of basic materials for survival.

Vera Smirnova's assessment—"my childhood didn't last very long. Childhood was when people were burned and killed"—was shared by thousands of people who were trapped in the Minsk ghetto.[2] Many of them did not survive, and cannot tell us about it.[3] Those who did survive, however, speak about individual and collective survival in the face of terror and oppression. Their narratives explicate the distinct features of Belorussian ghettos in the Nazi-occupied Soviet Union; these were killing sites rather than transitional places of internment. Their stories also make a case for paying special attention to the diversity of experience—according to age, gender, and geography—of the Nazi genocide.

Rita Kazhdan, Elena Drapkina, Mikhail Treister, Sonia Zalesskaia, Samuil Volk, and others experienced internment in the Minsk ghetto as children or teenagers. Children and youth were at once the most vulnerable and the most resourceful group within the ghetto.[4] Though roundups, murder, and starvation claimed thousands of children's lives, adolescents could move about within and outside the ghetto more freely than adults. And because they were smaller, they were able to cross the ghetto fence, sometimes merging with groups of homeless children in the Russian district. They also made use of those friendships and relationships with non-Jewish teachers or other adults that had been established before the war and remained immune to racist ideology. Further, ghetto youth developed bonds with each other, which provided emotional stability and enabled such forms of mutual assistance as sharing information, food, or other essential resources. Lastly, adults both within and outside the ghetto made great efforts to save children from the ghetto, organizing food and smuggling children out of the ghetto and into hiding.

Soviet Jews' experience of Nazi occupation and genocide was shaped by gender in several ways. Broadly speaking, the ghetto population was predominantly female; many men had been drafted by the Soviet military in the first days of the war, and many of the remaining men, targeted as potential resisters, fell victim to the first killing actions in July and August 1941.[5] Within the ghetto, however, the gendered division of labor meant that men were more likely to evade execution than women: whereas men and boys were often engaged in skilled and valued work in war-related production facilities, women and girls cooked and cleaned for the occupation administration, and were easily replaced by other Jewish or non-Jewish workers. Circumstances in the ghetto, however, often also produced a reversal of traditional gender roles; young women, for instance, engaged in underground political work, and boys and young men performed domestic and care roles. And finally, as survivors' stories bear out, young women in the ghetto faced threats of sexual violence from both Nazi and collaborating Ukrainian, Latvian, and Belorussian militia forces.

Jews' experiences in Minsk were similar to the experiences of Jews elsewhere in Nazi-occupied Europe and the Soviet Union but also distinct, due to both the Soviet framework that had determined city residents' lives before the war and the comparatively long existence of the ghetto, from July 1941 until October 1943, a time when most other ghettos in German-occupied Soviet territories had long been destroyed. For the thousands of young Soviet Jews in the Minsk ghetto, who had been raised to believe in the equality of all people and who were unfamiliar with a history of antisemitism, pogroms, war, and sexual violence, the emotional and physical traumas of the war and the ghetto would have been especially shocking.

Life in the Minsk ghetto was, more than anything else, a life immersed in death. Unlike elsewhere in Europe, Jews were not deported to concentration or extermination camps; they were shot right in the ghetto or at nearby execution sites, trenches or ravines on the outskirts of Minsk: Drozdy, Blagovshchina, Koidanovo, Trostenets, or Tuchinka. Others were herded into gas vans, the so-called *dushegubki* (soul killers), and asphyxiated on the drive from Minsk to prepared mass graves. Survivors of the Minsk ghetto liken life there to that in an extermination camp, with very little, if any, time and space to adapt to the circumstances.[6]

The Minsk ghetto offers a disturbing chronology of death. In September 1941, more than 2,200 Jews were killed, allegedly as punishment for resistance or acts of sabotage. During the pogrom on November 7, 1941, approximately 18,000 people were killed. On November 20, 15,000 people were shot; on March 2, 1942, another 8,000 inmates of the ghetto were killed, including many children who had been rounded up in the ghetto orphanage as well as the unemployed. In the summer of 1942, the Nazi leadership again ordered the killing of so-called "nonproductive" Jews, that is, people who were not employed in producing essential goods for the war effort. Between July 28 and August 1, 1942, as many as 25,000 Jews from the Minsk ghetto were murdered.[7] And in 1942 and 1943, Gestapo, SS, and police forces frequently rounded up groups of between 20 and 150 Jews from the ghetto, hospital, or work sites and executed them. These killings, raids during which gas vans were used, were sometimes planned long in advance; at other times they were acts of retaliation for attacks on German officers.[8] One of them targeted the whole city of Minsk; the Germans purportedly attempted to identify "Bolsheviks, spies," and people unwilling to work, but primarily rounded up Jews.[9]

In June 1943, in the shadow of the Warsaw ghetto uprising, Heinrich Himmler, Reichsführer of the SS, ordered the destruction of all existing ghettos in the Reichskommissariat Ostland.[10] Simultaneously, Himmler and Hitler alleged that Soviet Jews collaborated extensively with partisans and thus posed an additional danger for the German war effort.[11] After a series of arrests and executions of worker columns, by October only 1,500 people were left in the Minsk ghetto. Most of them were murdered during the last raid on October 21, 1943.

These waves of murder were closely tied to economic considerations as well as the genocidal plans of the Nazi regime. For instance, the killing of Jews in Ukrainian ghettos slowed somewhat in early 1942 when German leadership realized the need for Jewish labor, but intensified again after food shortages in the Greater Germany (the so-called *Reichsgebiet*) were avoided when Ukrainian wheat, produce, and livestock were taken away from residents of the occupied territories and given to Germans. Jews, already concentrated in ghettos and therefore easy targets, were killed to limit the number of eaters and thus prevent hunger revolts in Ukraine.[12] There was a similar dynamic in Belorussia, where ghettos, sites of preemptive concentration in preparation for murder, served to solve local housing shortages and organize forced labor.[13]

Surviving this genocide took a huge toll, especially on children and young people under the age of eighteen, who often had not completed professional training, who had lived in sheltered households, and who grew up in a context largely unperturbed by nationalist or antisemitic conflicts. How did these young Soviet Jews live with this destruction in a holding area in preparation for genocide, and in the wake of a war of annihilation that destroyed the moral and social fiber of the surrounding society? How did Jewish people survive in a context where they could not rely on communal Jewish or state institutions to address scarcity, violence, and ongoing humiliation? Did people organize and strategize to rescue themselves and others?

The dangers that, according to Nazi propaganda, Soviet Jewish collaboration with partisans posed to the German war effort and the genocide were real, even if only to a limited extent. The underground movement in the Minsk ghetto organized a number of diversionary activities, supplied partisan units outside of Minsk with arms and other equipment, and smuggled a number of Jews out of the ghetto and into the forest "so that they could fight and take revenge on the enemy."[14] This movement drew heavily on women and men who, before the war, had been members of the Communist Party, trade unions, and other organizations, hence people who were twenty or older and often knew each other.[15] And while a number of children and youth did participate—as couriers or scouts, or in other roles—most young survivors remained largely unaware of the underground's work and tried to secure resources and safety on their own. Interviewees suggest that they conceived of themselves as individual nomads facing deprivation and violence, a perception that was exacerbated by the fact that Jews were isolated in the ghetto and had little insight into broader developments.

"I really wanted to live to the moment when I saw at least one German soldier in captivity"

Throughout the 1930s, Soviet citizens constructed industrial factories and power plants, mostly geared toward the development of heavy industry producing coal, iron, and machinery. Industrializing the then largely peasant-based economy was a major objective of the Soviet government's effort to modernize the country. Improving living conditions was a subordinate goal, whose realization took several decades.[16] The hard, often manual labor of thousands of Soviet workers and activists thus remained largely unrewarded by personal access to consumer goods or housing. One modernizing project, however, designed to tame the frequent floods threatening settlements around Minsk, did produce an immediate collateral recreational benefit.

In the spring of 1940, the local authorities and public institutions of Minsk joined forces to create Komsomolskoe Ozero (Komsomol Lake) northwest of the city, between the settlements Veselovka and Storozhevka. The Svisloch River, which runs through Minsk, repeatedly flooded these and other settlements in the springtime. A manmade lake surrounded by a recreational park would provide both a retention basin and a spot for swimming. A lack of funds and friction among local and state leaders about resources for building the lake necessitated a large amount of volunteer work.[17] Since excavators and bulldozers were unavailable for the project, the government instructed all factories, universities, and hospitals to send workers to help dig, and many Komsomol members and even Pioneers volunteered. Others were forced to do so: Leonid Okon recalled, "Inmates were sent there too, and there were many accidents and people died."[18] The construction was characteristic of the time; masses of Soviet citizens were enlisted for government projects, which, if successful, would serve the common good, at great personal cost. Nevertheless, several interviewees recall their excitement about the lake's opening on June 22, 1941.

For many, that Sunday marked the beginning of their summer holidays, and they had planned to attend various festive activities. Some, like twelve-year-old Leonid Okon and sixteen-year-old Yakov Negnevitzki, went to celebrate the completion of the lake and took a swim; Ekaterina Tsirlina, eighteen, was looking forward to joining friends at the opening. She did not manage to leave her home: "At noon Molotov gave a radio address and announced that the war had begun. Our guys came and said that they couldn't come with us; they had been summoned to the *VoenKomat* [Military Registration and Enlistment Office] for the next day. So we all sat there, talked, and cried."[19] Similarly surprised was Elena Drapkina, who was attending a guest performance of the Moscow Art Theater in the Pioneers Palace. Amaliia Iakhontova, who had tickets for an upcoming performance, was sad it was canceled, and Pesia Aizenshtadt, who was preparing for her final exam at the Pedagogical Institute, turned off the radio when it blasted a siren, thinking it was just an air raid drill.[20] Hundreds of children had just arrived at summer camps outside the city, ready and eager to spend time away from home.[21]

The failure of the Soviet government, and Stalin in particular, to take seriously warnings of an impending German attack on the Soviet Union or to inform Soviet citizens about Nazi anti-Jewish policies put all these young people, as well as their parents, friends, and neighbors, in extreme danger.[22] None of them expected a rapid, aggressive invasion, and they were accordingly unprepared. Living in the capital of the Belorussian Socialist Soviet Republic, neither they nor their parents could have known much better. Throughout the first days, while German troops advanced deep into Soviet territories, the Soviet radio station falsely reported that Soviet troops were defending the border and played war songs, encouraging people's optimism and fulfilling the promise that had seeped into the population's consciousness over the past years: *If tomorrow there is war, we will defeat the enemy on its own territory.*[23] As a result, Anna Borisovna Pekhman-Khurgina, Amaliia Iakhontova's mother, was sure that "the Soviet troops would win the war the next day," and Mikhail Treister was upset that the war would end "without my participation . . . after all, our troops are already in Warsaw, or even Berlin."[24] People do recall that refugees from Poland, many of them Jewish, had reported Nazi brutality, and that they knew they would be in danger once German troops seized Soviet territory. But all of them assured me and other interviewers that they did not expect an invasion, much less that it would happen so fast and be such a crushing defeat.[25]

Young women and men believed in the state's, and their personal, ability to fight off the invaders and that it would only be a matter of enduring a short period of war. Trained as a member of the BGTO, a paramilitary organization for Soviet citizens, and thus considering herself ready to participate in military efforts to drive out the Germans, Elena Drapkina recalls her thoughts at the sight of marching German soldiers entering Minsk on June 28:

> When the war began, I saw the German troops marching, they were all very young, beautiful and healthy, and they had all this equipment. I stood there and thought: "My God, I really want to live to the moment when I see at least one German soldier in captivity. I wonder what they will look like then" . . . We were patriots.[26]

As German troops attacked the Soviet Union and the Soviet people, it roused the patriotic sentiments of Elena Drapkina, Pesia Aizenshtadt, Mikhail Treister, and many others. These sentiments, in turn, were the basis for people's hope for, and trust in, the Soviet army's successful response to the invasion.

The case of Minsk illustrates the consequences of the German offensive. After two days of heavy bombardment, the leadership of the city and party administration left Minsk on June 25. They ordered the evacuation of some factories, yet failed to ensure any safety measures for residents.[27] Thousands of Minsk civilians tried to leave on their own when German bombers attacked the city, setting it on fire and destroying major parts of it. Under conditions of danger, scarcity, and insecurity, relationships between neighbors and within families began to shift. Jews especially confronted the erosion of the interethnic communality that had been a central element of the first Soviet generation's upbringing.

Survivors report that local, non-Jewish residents around Minsk refused to provide assistance to refugees, even threatening to report them to the advancing German troops.[28] Rita Kazhdan's narration of her family's attempt to evacuate is emblematic of these experiences, and it also explains the role of emerging anti-Jewish sentiments among local residents in her entrapment in Minsk. Rita's father worked hard to evacuate the equipment of the state film studios and did not come home to fetch his family until late on June 24. He missed Rita, her brother Grigorii, her mother, and their maid Marusia Gubinskaia by minutes. They had left him a note, explaining that they had left for the village where they had spent many summers. Passing through multiple checkpoints and avoiding air raids, it took Abram Fridman three days until he found his wife and his children. Rita remembers,

> But in the evening people began to complain to us that "because of you Jews the Germans will burn the whole village." They knew we were Jewish, because we had come there for the past twelve years. It was impossible to listen to this, more so since we had no idea what antisemitism was. Well, but when these arguments came up, mother and father immediately decided to go back to the city. We had no place to stay, our house was destroyed, ... and so we moved into our neighbors' apartment. After the mass flight from the city many homes were empty.[29]

Like Rita Kazhdan, many Jews returned to Minsk, seeking shelter with relatives, in abandoned houses, or in public buildings that housed stranded refugees. Still others had not left, staying with relatives who were unable to move. Others remained in the city because family members remembered German soldiers who had occupied Minsk during World War I and were sure that the Germans who cam now would not do particular harm to Jews either.[30]

Ultimately, this assumption proved false, yet it bears noting that accounts such as Kazhdan's indicate that even before the German occupation regime had arrived, distributed antisemitic propaganda, or implemented anti-Jewish policies, some Soviet citizens felt compelled to distance themselves from their Jewish compatriots or even deny them assistance because they were Jews.[31] These mostly verbal acts of aggression were far from the pogroms against Jews that were committed by locals either before German troops even arrived, as in Lithuania, Latvia, or the Ukraine, or where they left the decision about the treatment of Jews to local gentiles, as in Jedwabne, Poland.[32] At the same time, these open hostilities show that the idea of social cohesion among the Soviet population on the basis of internationalism had failed to take hold comprehensively and that, instead, the Soviet collective was susceptible to antisemitism and racism, especially under the extreme circumstances of an unforeseen invasion.

Members of the first Soviet generation, born after 1920, were particularly shocked at the emerging discrimination. They had not experienced the pogroms of 1905 or the Civil War of 1919–1921. They had grown up sharing school benches, food, and plans for the future with contemporaries of all nationalities, and were excited about the educational, professional, and cultural opportunities that the Soviet project provided for them. In contrast to Rita Kazhdan, who noted rising local hostility, Mikhail Treister recalls the shock at how quickly German racial policies turned Minsk Jews from equal members of society to outcasts. The sarcasm of his memoir should not deceive the reader about this lasting irritation:

> *Zhid*. [Russian term used to insult Jews, close to "kike" in English.] I knew before the war that there was such a word. You could get one and a half years for it. One had to be a really enthusiastic antisemite to pay that much for the modest pleasure of calling someone a zhid. The liquidation of Orthodox and Catholic churches, mosques and synagogues, as well as mixed marriages had relegated the nationality question into the realm of some virtual platitudes. I was not a Jew. And I wasn't a Russian either. I was nobody. And all of a sudden ... there were posters at each gate and at every ruin with the decree of the field commander, dated July 19, 1941, "On the Creation of a Jewish Residential Area in the City of Minsk."[33]

Shortly after segments of the Heeresgruppe Mitte and Einsatzgruppe B had reached and occupied Minsk and its vicinity on June 28, the German military command established, in quick succession, a series of different administrations.[34] The interests of the army and the *Einsatzgruppen* (task forces, in this context, mobile killing units) aligned in many ways, but particularly with regard to treating the Soviet Jewish population as political opponents, possible resisters, and generally "inimical" individuals (to which Jews belonged by definition), as well as balancing the exploitation of valuable Jewish labor skills as long as necessary with killing Jews them as soon as possible.[35] The most direct outcome of this interaction was the killing of up to 10,000 male civilian prisoners, among them many Jewish men, and the establishment of a ghetto for the Jewish residents at the order of Field Commander Karl Schlegelhofer, signed on July 19, 1941.[36]

Jews, who prior to the war had lived in many different areas of the city, were forced into a single two-square kilometer area.[37] The movement of several thousand residents within a period of three days was chaotic; interviewees note the incredible noise from wooden carts rumbling along paved roads as well as the high material and emotional toll on the displaced.[38] Non-Jewish residents who were forced to abandon their dwellings in the ghetto-to-be often benefited from the population exchange within the city, moving from damaged small wooden houses or buildings into better-equipped houses. Amaliia Iakhontova recalls that several people were looking at apartments inhabited by Jews and chose which apartment would suit them better.[39] Jews, in contrast, did not have the luxury of such a choice and had to move to wherever there was some space. In addition, Jews were allowed to move what they could carry or pull in small carts. Thus, many of them left behind furniture, sewing machines, and the majority of clothes and other household items, things that were taken over by non-Jewish people who moved into their homes.

The confinement of between 30,000 and 50,000, possibly even 80,000, Jews behind barbed wire segregated them from the overall population and enabled exploitation and extermination.[40] Among the 50,000 inmates were local Jews as well as several thousand who hailed from surrounding towns and villages; later they were joined by around 35,000 Jews transported to Minsk from Germany, Austria, Czechoslovakia, and Hungary.[41] For Soviet Jews, including youths, their Jewish origin became the central category of identification. From now on, this identity would be the basis for how they would be treated, both by occupiers and by many locals. From July 15 onward, any Jew over the age of ten had to wear a yellow patch ten centimeters in diameter on their chest and back. The patch stigmatized anyone who would try to leave the ghetto and thus enabled immediate punishment.

Many Jews were thrown in jail or shot when they were discovered either on their own outside the ghetto or without their patch.[42] In one incident, sixty-four Jewish women were shot for refusing to wear the patch inside the ghetto.[43] Initially, the ghetto was to be surrounded by a brick wall, but this plan was soon abandoned and the streets of the ghetto were cordoned off by multiple layers of barbed wire.[44]

With 1.5 square meters (16.1 square feet) allotted to each adult, with no allowance for children, homes in the ghetto district were overcrowded. Elena Drapkina describes what happened when she, her parents, and her brother moved in with her uncle's family:

> My uncle's family consisted of three people, so we were seven, and then there was another uncle who had a daughter; his wife had died before the war. That means we were nine people, and we lived in a room of 14 square meters [150 sq. ft.]. We lived ... well, we slept on and underneath the table.[45]

Survivors felt this crowding—in private homes as well as schools, movie theaters, the opera house, and other public buildings—so intensely that most cite a much higher ghetto population, between 80,000 and 120,000, than documents of the German authorities suggest.[46]

Overcrowded living quarters were only one form of an aggressive assault on people's lives. The German occupation administration limited access to the small daily food rations to only those who worked.[47] Violence and terror posed immediate and deadly threats to the occupied city, targeting certain segments of the population more than others, deliberately and effectively. The social cohesion of the Soviet populace fell victim to both military attack and propagandistic fervor, singling out Jews as racially inferior and subject to humiliation, exploitation and, eventually, extermination.

"One could get everything for money in Minsk"

At the beginning of the war and occupation, Jews in Minsk could not rely on community institutions or a communal body to provide organized self-help. The dismantling of Jewish cultural and religious institutions during the Soviet antireligious campaigns and, later, drives to eliminate any cultural, political, or social institutions that promoted a particular nationality's culture had devastating, if unintended, consequences. People had to deal with hunger and humiliation largely on their own.

The absence of material and spiritual community bonds was, however, partly reversed when the city's Jews were interned behind barbed wire and thus physically separated from their compatriots. The forced cohabitation of various generations of Soviet Jews resulted in a revival of religious rituals and cultural traditions, including the use of Yiddish as an important means of communication, at least among large parts of the ghetto population.[48] Vladimir Mordkhilevich relates his unease about this return to religion and tradition: "Around Rosh Hashanah my grandmother took me to a Hebrew teacher; she was very religious and wanted to make sure I learned the language. I thought that was ridiculous, I always wanted to run away. I did not like it; the prayers appeared mystical and inaccessible to me, scary even."[49] The German politics of separation and isolation forcibly created a Jewish community, even though many Jews in the ghetto, especially younger ones, had not previously considered themselves as members of a religious community.

In contrast to their prewar life, youth were now in a situation where they had to seek out ways to survive within and beyond a restricted space that disrupted many ties established before the occupation. The lack of food, heating material, and supplies to treat illnesses, as well as the looming threat of violence all contributed to the physical and mental exhaustion of the interned population, and made many hope for some kind of organized institutional support, rescue attempt, or a powerful resistance movement. Members of the *Judenrat* (Jewish Council), a Jewish leadership body imposed by the German authorities, attempted to respond to this hope.[50] A creation of the Nazi regime, the Judenrat was designed to help execute plans for exploitation and extermination by registering all ghetto inhabitants, organizing work details, and fulfilling any order of the German command. The Minsk Judenrat, however, differs markedly from similar bodies whose leaders were told to mediate and organize deportations to killing sites, as in Łódź or Białystok. The absence of such demands freed the Minsk leaders from dangerous strategizing over whom to deport and whom to keep, resulting in rather favorable portrayals of the first and second Judenrat by survivors.[51] On the other hand, the noninvolvement of the council in the preparation of killing actions also meant that it did not have the opportunity to warn ghetto inmates.

Though corralled into this position, the first Judenrat in Minsk, under Ilya Mushkin, did its best to use its authority to assist those in need. A ghetto hospital, an orphanage, and a soup kitchen were set up to support inhabitants of the ghetto who were not able to find work, among them many elderly and children.[52] Mushkin and several other council members also supported the ghetto underground that began to operate in the fall of 1941 by helping to organize donation drives for clothes, medicine, and other supplies. Mushkin, the chair of the Judenrat, was later hanged for supporting the underground, but his successors, Moisei Ioffe and Zamenshtein (first name unknown), also did their best to assist those without homes or food and those who were ill, and staff members of the Judenrat continued to support the underground movement.[53]

However insufficient, the attempts of the Judenrat addressed emerging inequalities within the ghetto; there were those who had access to jobs and thus food, and there were those who did not and required the support of others.

The lack of food overwhelmed many other concerns, such as the desire for religious or spiritual activity. When asked whether she or her family were able to celebrate Jewish holidays in the ghetto, Tatiana Gildiner replied laconically, "we often had Yom Kippur, we had to fast very often."[54] This "fasting" was not a choice, but was forced upon the inhabitants of the ghetto. The resulting hunger, one of the major concerns for Jews in the ghetto, was part and parcel of the German war strategy. The so-called *Generalplan Ost* (Master Plan East), a document outlining, among others, the aims and purpose of the war against the Soviet Union, calculated that the death of up to 30 million people, mainly residents of urban centers and 50 percent of Belorussia's rural population, was necessary to secure enough resources—food and land to grow produce—for troops active in the region and for the German population more generally. Jews were a specific target of this plan, comprising about 30 percent of the prewar urban populace.[55] The plan forced many Jews to sneak out of the ghetto to the so-called Russian district in search of food. Rita Kazhdan left the ghetto repeatedly and visited the family's former maid Marusia and other acquaintances, and "when I came to visit, they already knew that they should feed me and give me something to take with me ... they knew what situation we were in."[56] In other cases, non-Jewish friends came to the ghetto and brought badly needed food supplies. They were conscious of the danger this entailed; David Taubkin remembers that his former nanny Lenia "literally shivered when she came to the ghetto."[57] Eventually, many Jews urged their friends to stay away from the ghetto to avoid punishment, forgoing displays of support for the sake of their friends' and acquaintances' well-being.[58]

The other side of the ghetto fence, where Jews were officially outcasts, was a dangerous but important part of ghetto life—at least for those who had either the courage and strength to cross over or non-Jewish friends who, violating the German policy of Jewish segregation, were willing to smuggle food in. Roza Zelenko and her sister, Lilia Tsukerman, gathered valuables and clothes from their household and from other Jews, brought them to her friend Ol'ga Glazebnaia and her sister, and received food supplies in return. Glazebnaia reasons that, as non-Jews, she and her sister were able to provide food to her friend because

> We were not in the ghetto, and my sister was very active and frequently went to the countryside to exchange clothes and other things for food. Back in Minsk, she would sell the produce; that was our income. One could get everything for money in Minsk ... It was easier for us; we had more freedom.[59]

Ol'ga Glazebnaia's sister frequently traveled with other women to the countryside, where they helped to harvest crops or potatoes or exchanged personal belongings for food with the peasants. For Jews, the possibility of acquiring food through barter in the Russian district was limited, as a number of Jews had lost their belongings when air raids destroyed their homes in the early days of the war or when they had had to abandon their homes to move to the ghetto.[60] Moreover, Soviet policy before the war had stripped the majority of Soviet citizens of valuable capital, and this form of "social equalization" now stood in the way of trading personal property for food, as many did not own valuables to begin with.[61] In addition, prices for goods skyrocketed: Mikhail Treister remembers exchanging a sewing machine for a handful of potatoes; David Taubkin exchanged a pocket knife for two potatoes and a sewing machine for a bag of rotten flour.[62]

Despite these challenges and difficulties, the trade of goods across the barbed wire was a crucial means for Jews in the ghetto to acquire food, not least for German, Austrian, and Hungarian Jews, who were interned in a special section within the main ghetto, the so-called *Sonderghetto*. They had no other way of supporting the nonworking population than to offer their valuables in exchange for food. Soviet Jews often served as intermediaries between them and people outside of the ghetto, keeping a small share of the yield while the bulk provided crucial sustenance for the doubly isolated foreign Jews.[63]

Mikhail Treister unmistakably and vividly insists on the difference between Jews and non-Jews, here identifiable in the difference between the watery soup given to Jewish workers and Russian workers' lunch packages:

> While we were eating our so-called soup, the Russians brought bread, lard, pickles, and on the side chewed on these unimaginable delicacies. We tried not to look at each other. They were also paid for their work. And we left work differently: they went to their families, we—in a column, under escort, toward our netherworld where most of us had already lost our families.[64]

Both this and Ol'ga Glazebnaia's account demonstrate that the gentile population was aware of the Jews' misery, but also that some of them thought it unacceptable. Their statements show that there was a difference in experience; while all inhabitants of Belorussia suffered from the war, Jews were especially targeted. Both interview transcripts and carefully worded memoirs debunk myths pervasive in both popular assumptions and Soviet historiography that life in the ghetto was not especially bad and that Jews, consequently, should not claim a distinct status among war victims.[65] Mikhail Treister's recollection makes a direct connection between hunger policies and Nazi murder policy and their distinct impact on Jews, emerging, for him, during daily lunch breaks or the memory of them.

Physical violence—such as raids or executions—specifically targeting Jews marks a fundamental difference. In the face of pogroms and mass murder, the Russian district served as a safe haven. Roza Zelenko and her sister could rely on a stable friendship with their friend Ol'ga and her sister Varvara. They hid at her house when SS troops and collaborating police formations of Ukrainian and Lithuanian volunteers conducted pogroms in the ghetto, often staying for days:

> During the night we slept in their house, but in the morning Varvara removed two planks from the floor, and underneath there was a hollow space, she threw some blankets and clothes in there, and we went there and sat there all day. In the evening they opened the planks and we came out, ate with them, and slept there.[66]

Vera Smirnova and Mikhail Treister could count on similar refuges during the many pogroms, highlighting the importance of sustainable relationships with non-Jewish people living outside the ghetto.[67]

Other ghetto inhabitants had to face newly expressed hatred by Belorussians whom they had known before the war, as Amaliia Iakhontova comments: "My uncle was a doctor, and before the war he had treated a seriously ill child. When he asked the child's family for shelter during a pogrom, the youngster yelled at them and said that 'zhidy' don't deserve protection, and my uncle had to leave."[68] Sonia Zalesskaia once hid when a workers' column that she had joined to leave the ghetto was rounded up by SS troops, only to hear a Belorussian woman yelling at the SS that they should look for a "zhid" hiding in her outhouse.[69]

The Russian district was an ambivalent space, perhaps more so than the ghetto, where encounters between Jews and non-Jews were predictably fraught with violence. Outside the ghetto, such encounters could go both ways. The different experiences of receiving help or assistance outside of the ghetto mark the rifts that divided Soviet citizenry to a substantial degree, with members of non-Jewish nationalities on one side and Jewish people on the other. Whereas all residents of Belorussia faced hunger during the occupation, ghetto inmates had even fewer opportunities to obtain food, as their access to markets and farms was strictly prohibited. Non-Jewish Soviet citizens were aware of this inequality. They were also aware of the killings inside the ghetto and outside of town, since they were visible, audible, and palpable to all residents of the city and its immediate surroundings, and Jews in search of hiding were living evidence of the fatal danger.[70] Whereas war and occupation targeted the whole population, mass killings and genocide marked a deadly difference between Jews and non-Jews.

Crowding large numbers of people into a restricted area of the city institutionalized the separation of people according to national categories. Beginning in mid-August 1941, systematic raids and executions of ghetto inhabitants disrupted efforts to survive in the ghetto. Arbitrary mass killings frightened the residents, as the Nazis treated human beings as mere objects to be destroyed. As Rita Kazhdan explains,

> Now people don't speak of "raids" anymore, but of "actions." We called them raids, and when there was such a raid, they [German and collaborating police formations] closed off a district within the ghetto and caught

everyone they could get hold of. Or they were assigned a quota, and then they rounded up a certain number of people and took them to the execution.[71]

The term used by Kazhdan, *oblava*, may also be translated as "drive hunt" and no doubt accurately describes how she and her neighbors perceived the attacks on the ghetto.[72] During these operations, people were driven out of their homes at gunpoint, and infants and small children were thrown against walls or speared by bayonets.[73] Frequent invasions of the ghetto added to the fear, as German SS and police as well as local police regularly broke into homes in the ghetto district to steal property and abuse residents.

Connections between the ghetto and beyond were under constant threat; the German occupation regime mercilessly persecuted both Jews who moved around outside the ghetto and non-Jews who helped Jews. Solidarity within the ghetto was even more fragile. Nightly raids and large-scale pogroms—killing several thousand Jews—ended with the German ghetto command shrinking the borders to reduce the area of the ghetto. Both family and newly established bonds were broken when survivors were forced to move to new homes in the remaining ghetto area.[74] Mariia Boiko emphasizes not only the fear, anger, and grief produced by these pogroms, but also their effects on efforts to survive in the periods between them: "After each pogrom we had to move, there were always new people to deal with, it was like a new beginning every time."[75] To orient oneself in new surroundings was a challenge. In many cases, the loss of parents, aunts and uncles, or other caretakers during the pogrom put children and youth in a precarious situation; access to food and housing was tied to employment inside or outside the ghetto. For children, however, employment was largely inaccessible, and they had to find other means of existence.

"There my independent life began, so to speak"

The situation of orphans in the Minsk ghetto and how they reacted to violence and segregation is particularly instructive. They personify the unattached, disassociated individuals that the German occupation regime strove to produce, and they were particularly vulnerable to violence against the nonworking ghetto population.

For orphans, war, terror, and pogroms had blown up familial bonds, turning youth and older siblings into guardians or breadwinners. Everyday life in the Minsk ghetto thus redefined roles that women and men, young and old took on within families. The ways in which these distinct groups were able to fulfill this task largely depended on their age; youth over fourteen (boys) and sixteen (girls) were considered employable and thus had access to daily food rations, meager as they were, but younger ones had to find other means of subsistence. The ten-year-olds Sonia Zalesskaia and Samuil Volk, as well as Rita Kazhdan, Elena Drapkina, and Mikhail Treister, all over thirteen, cared for themselves and others in a variety of ways, which required them to make a variety of difficult decisions and choices in their quest for survival.

Sonia Zalesskaia and Samuil Volk had each just arrived in one of the many summer camps around Minsk when German troops invaded the Soviet Union. Following complicated routes, they made it back to their hometown, each confronting a family in disarray. Sonia's father had left Minsk together with other employees of the bread factory, whose equipment had been evacuated further east to avoid capture by the Germans. Later, her father was drafted into the army, leaving behind Sonia's mother Nekhama Portnova and four children. Samuil's parents had quarreled over leaving Minsk and eventually split up. His mother, Revekka, had pleaded for his father to wait for Samuil's return, but he chose to abandon the family for fear of finding himself again in German captivity; he had been a POW in World War I and had suffered permanent damage to his hearing while in captivity.[76]

Sonia returned to the destroyed city and, confronted by her mother's mental paralysis, was required to take care of the family. Like many other youngsters, she regularly left the ghetto and roamed abandoned homes and factories in the Russian district in search of food, coal, and other essential goods. As a rule, adolescents did not wear the yellow patch when they were in the Russian district: Rita Kazhdan and Vera Smirnova removed it when they crossed the barbed wire, usually in the midst of a worker column; Sonia and Samuil took advantage of the fact that children did not have to wear the patch.[77] Leonid Okun was aware that removing the patch could pose a danger too, as there could be a mark on the coat where the patch had protected the fabric from the bleach of sun and repeated wear.[78] Young Sonia repeatedly visited her family's old apartment, which was now occupied by a former neighbor. The old man fed her whenever she showed up at his doorstep.[79] Her efforts yielded only small amounts of food and were not sufficient to support the whole family. A few months after the family had moved to the ghetto, her mother died of starvation.

Relatives sent Sonia and her three siblings to one of the ghetto orphanages that had been founded by Ester Chernis in agreement with the chairman of the Judenrat, Ilya Mushkin. Despite Mushkin and others' best efforts, food supplies were insufficient in the orphanage.[80] Older children were encouraged to seek food themselves and return only to spend the night.[81] So Sonia continued her trips to search for sustenance:

> There were many children, but these were not children, they were like living corpses. They were so emaciated . . . I brought food for my siblings, but my brother could not eat already. The next time I came, after a couple of days, all three of them had died and had been taken away already. That was three months after the invasion.[82]

At the age of ten, Sonia became an orphan and had to find ways to sustain herself, in a climate of violence, scarcity, and soon, a harsh winter.

Zalesskaia remembers that she roamed the Russian district for food, and she also saw it as a safer place than the ghetto, where raids and pogroms posed a constant threat: "I was in the ghetto only during the night, I left during the day."[83] She shared the fear of being trapped in the ghetto with other children. Many of them used their ability to crawl underneath the barbed wire or hide in the middle of worker columns to leave the ghetto and gathered at central places to beg for food. Regular raids, targeting especially Jewish children, however, could quickly turn the Russian district into a trap like the ghetto.[84] Hiding one's Jewish identity from both German police and local residents was thus an essential strategy for the young people's survival.

Samuil Volk's account illustrates the different forms of violence and deprivation that newly orphaned children experienced in the ghetto. In the early weeks of the occupation, Samuil's mother asked him and his siblings to stay home, fearing for their lives. She responded to the many questions the ten-year-old asked about what was going on with explanations that taught him one important thing: "She explained to me that Germans don't like Jews, and that Hitler wants to exterminate them."[85] Consequently, as soon as he found the courage to do so, he went in and out of the ghetto with great caution, knowing that he must not be seen crossing the barbed wire. Having observed the abuse and killings in the first months of living in the ghetto, Samuil knew how to interpret what was going on around him. When Samuil, his mother, and his three siblings were among a group of people that was led from Minsk to Tuchinka for execution in November 1941, he understood that he should leave as soon as possible. Once his mother had nodded to him in agreement, he waited for an opportunity to escape.

> So I waited until the guards didn't pay attention. All of a sudden I saw a woman with a child step out of the column and hide in a doorway. I followed her. I heard bullets flying over my head, and when I turned around I saw that Ziama was running after me. I waited for him and shoved him into the next barn I could find.[86]

Samuil and his six year-old brother found shelter with an aunt, but after a couple of days the woman registered them in the orphanage because she was unable to provide for them as well as her own children. "There my independent life began, so to speak," Volk concludes.[87]

Like Sonia, Samuil did not stay permanently in the orphanage. The lack of food and the sight of children dying of hunger impelled him to leave the ghetto and beg for food in the Russian district, preferably in areas farther away from the center. He fed his brother and gave the rest to other children. Soon he teamed up with another Jewish boy, Leva, who "had made contact with some Russian guys at the freight yard. They were cleaning toilets and shoes for the Germans, and sold newspapers to them. He took me there too and they taught me how to clean shoes." Laughing, he explains that he got his equipment "like everyone else. I had two brushes, a rag, polish, a little box that served as a stool." The laughter indicates that the supplies may have been stolen, though he never said so specifically.

Samuil and Leva slept in the basements or attics of abandoned buildings: "we tried not to go back to the ghetto because it was dangerous to stay there and to go in and out every day, but every once in a while we went to the orphanage to wash ourselves, every week or so."[88] In contrast to Sonia's assessment, for the boys the Russian district served as a safe haven from pogroms and mass killings, an observation shared by many other adolescents who relied on friendship or other acquaintances to hide them when SS troops and collaborating police formations of Ukrainian and Lithuanian volunteers conducted pogroms in the ghetto.[89]

An alternative to hiding outside the ghetto was to seek shelter in a hiding place that was prepared in advance, a so-called *malina* (Russian for raspberry, a slang term for a hiding place).[90] These *maliny* (plural for malina) were spaces, often collectively built, to escape discovery by the police, reviving a tradition of evasion that Jewish men had used to skirt the draft into the tsarist army in the nineteenth century.[91] Speaking for many, Elena Drapkina describes how she was able to survive a large pogrom on November 20, 1941, but she also calls attention to the ambiguity of the maliny, which rescued some and endangered others:

> Some men had covered the space underneath the stairs with plates of tin. In front of it, they mounted a laundry line and hung some rags and underwear to cover the plates, and they made a door. When we got there, there were already so many people that the narrowness itself was dangerous—if someone fell, people would step on them, and for lack of air one could have suffocated ... We stood like sardines in a can ... There was a woman with an infant, and in the moment that the Germans were walking up the stairs, the child began to cry. People almost jumped on her, but she began to nurse the baby and he stopped crying. ... We stood like this for a whole day and the following night.[92]

When Elena and Lenia emerged after the pogrom, Elena's uncle had been murdered in the living room. The man was one of many older ghetto inhabitants who volunteered to close and disguise entrances to the hideouts, hoping to meet mercy among the killers, or consciously giving their lives to ensure other Jews' survival.[93] Other accounts reveal that infants were deliberately suffocated when they started crying, and sometimes children died in the overcrowded hiding places.[94] Maliny were often the last resort, but they also pointed out who were the most vulnerable groups within the ghetto, the very old and the very young. For children, hiding in a malina was often precarious, and thus many of them chose to leave the ghetto and wait out the violence beyond the barbed wire.

Soon after Samuil started to spend most of his time in the Russian district, he took his brother Ziama with him. He was afraid that the little one might fall victim to a raid or one of the pogroms, which, as on March 2, 1942, often targeted children's homes and the hospital. Samuil Volk says that he had already "said goodbye" to his brother when he realized that the orphanage had been surrounded and the children inside were murdered. Days after the pogrom, he went to see for himself, and "there he was, running around with some other children. ... He had hidden in a pile of dirty laundry. . . . He said to me, 'I knew you would come at some point, so I stayed here.'" After that, the boys tried to evade the danger in the ghetto by sleeping in the Russian district, utilizing, like other homeless youth, ruins, basements, squats, or even cisterns.[95] Ziama would only return to the ghetto orphanage to wash or eat if he and his brother were unable to find sufficient supplies themselves. The constant danger fostered the bond between the two brothers, as Volk explains. They were separated once more during one of the large killing actions, presumably during the pogrom in late July 1942; afterwards the younger boy's attachment to his older brother grew, and he literally clung to him:

> He never let me go; after once we were outside the ghetto and one of the boys told him I would leave him, he never let me go again. Whenever I wanted to go somewhere, he started to scream and cry. Once he had a bellyache, he didn't let me get out of bed and I had to go the toilet with him. He was so afraid I would leave him.[96]

One of the central places for homeless children like Sonia and Samuil was the freight yard. There, begging for food from wounded German soldiers who arrived on hospital trains, cleaning their shoes, selling newspapers to them, or performing Russian and Yiddish (which sounded like German) songs and dances for them yielded crucial supplies in the form of food, money, and other salable goods.[97] A substantial group of youth, both non-Jewish and Jewish, gathered there every day, attempting to earn a living for themselves, their family, or other dependents. None of the interviewees and narrators address the absurdity of this encounter between Jews and Germans, an indicator perhaps of the normalcy of life under occupation, and likely more so of the lack of choice in the situation in which the youth found themselves.

Among the youths at the freight yard were several boys who had been smuggled out of the ghetto by women associates of the underground movement and placed in an orphanage in the Russian district.[98] There was a great deal of cooperation between Jewish women in the ghetto and non-Jewish women living in the Russian district. The women's rescue efforts were successful because most of them had known each other as colleagues or fellow union or Party activists before the war.[99] Even today it is impossible to determine how many Jewish children were saved by being placed in Russian orphanages in Minsk, partly as a result of the necessary disguise of their

Jewish identity, which some of the youth never reclaimed. One estimate suggests that there were as many as 500 Jewish children among the 2,000 children in all the orphanages in Minsk.[100]

The directors of children's homes encouraged some of their charges to roam the streets of Minsk to panhandle or to work for small payments to acquire food. However, probably as a precaution against the threat of rape or other forms of abuse, girls were forbidden to leave the orphanage where David Taubkin survived.[101] Vladimir Mordkhilevich also reports that his aunt banned his cousin Zhenya from leaving the ghetto with the boys, and Elena Gringauz's mother had her daughter stay home rather than go anywhere.[102] Sonia Zalesskaia also noted that she returned to the ghetto at night after roaming the Russian district in search for food. While none of the narrators specify the reasons for these restrictions on women's movement both within the ghetto and outside, special danger to girls and women in the form of sexual violence is reported in other accounts and may have been the motivation.[103]

But the boys were not safe either. German and collaborating troops were free to abuse and randomly punish children and youth, and it is likely that the abuse included sexual violence against boys as well as girls. Beatings, denial of payment for services, and even raids against crowds of children were daily occurrences. Many children, Belorussian and Jewish, were deported to Germany to be included in the so-called *Lebensborn* (Spring of life) program, designed to "Germanize" suitable parts of the population of occupied countries. Other children were used to provide blood "donations" for wounded German soldiers, draining them literally of their scarce bodily resources.[104]

Jewish boys were particularly eager to avoid arrest or too-close interactions with the police, since some of them were circumcised and would hardly have survived discovery. Accounts of this fear reveal that the religious practice of circumcision had persisted in prewar decades despite the attempts to secularize Soviet Jews before the war, yet there are no data available as to how many of the youth in question were or were not circumcised.[105] As a form of protection against discovery, many took on other names; Samuil Volk went by Misha, Vladimir Mordkhilevich chose "Buratino [a character in a Soviet children's novel based on Carlo Collodi's *The Adventures of Pinocchio*] because I was always funny and a little naughty," and others teamed up as Zhilin and Kostylin.[106] In addition, boys dirtied their faces with soil so as to look like homeless children.[107]

Yet neither the pseudonyms nor the change of appearance protected youth against denunciations by other boys who recognized Yiddish accents or faces from previous common school enrollment, and who thereby renounced the interethnic solidarity they had been taught in the very classroom they had shared with the Jews. The false names were also no protection against German officers' hatred for or retaliation against Soviet patriots stealing weapons: twelve-year-old Samuil was once apprehended and severely beaten because he was suspected of stealing weapons from German soldiers in the restroom of the train station. Later, his friend Liova confessed that sometimes his brother Lenia mingled with the boys at the freight yard to obtain weapons for underground members and partisans.[108] Samuil dragged himself back to the hideout because "that was the only place I could imagine to find someone to help me. And there was Ziama, all in tears. He then cried even more, he was so happy I was alive."[109]

The fear of discovery, violence, and death never disappeared; combined with living in the streets, it took a huge toll on the orphans' physical and emotional strength. Like the two brothers, Sonia Zalesskaia spent nearly two years in and out of the ghetto, sleeping here and there, hiding from pogroms, feeding herself by panhandling, sometimes supported by prewar acquaintances. The unsteady supply of food, unstable housing, and constant threat of death drained the orphaned youth, both physically and emotionally. Strong bonds with siblings or other people, like Sonia's former neighbor, were essential for surviving in a situation where there was no official guardian.

"Another German wanted to just kill me"

The Nazi occupation relied on various forms of violence, several of which were determined by the victims' and perpetrators' gender and perception of sexuality. Physical violence targeted women and men for different reasons and in different forms. Rape and harassment, injury and murder served distinct purposes in the system of humiliation and exploitation that German officials established within and beyond the ghetto.

Nazi policies in Minsk were directed at an urban population that included a disproportionally high number of women, youth, and elderly people, since many men over eighteen years of age had been drafted into the Red Army when the war began.[110] This imbalance was further, and deliberately, boosted when Germans arrested and executed men between the ages of eighteen and fifty shortly after the invasion. On July 1, all men of draft age were arrested and interned in a makeshift camp near the forest of Drozdy, where several thousand Soviet POWs were already jailed behind barbed wire under the open sky. The conditions in the camp were miserable; food was not supplied, and there was no shelter against the hot sun or, later, rain. Relatives tried to alleviate the pain by bringing food to the prisoners. Some people, wives of internees as well as Communist activists, were able to rescue a number of men by supplying them with women's clothes. The men wore these dresses and, disguised as civilian visitors, escaped the camp.[111] The horrid conditions upset even a German official, who observed that the small number of guards led to a ruthless use of arms against the interned to secure order.[112]

The German military's internment practices quickly turned into systematic murder. Frequent selections among the prisoners by national, professional, and political categories resulted in the shooting of communists, members of the intellectual and cultural elite, and Jews. In July alone, 10,000 Jews were shot for no other reason than their national identity.[113] The special targeting of Jewish men continued when, during the first raids within the ghettos, up to 1,500 men between the age of fifteen and fifty were arrested and executed in August 1941.[114] Rita Kazhdan, Elena Drapkina, Ekaterina Tsirlina, Vladimir Mordkhilevich, and many others lost fathers, brothers, and uncles that month.[115] Afterward, assuming that men, and especially male communists, were the prime targets of Nazi persecution, many men remained in hiding for several months, hiding in attics or other concealed spaces in residential buildings or the hospital.[116]

Securing access to food for families who had lost male relatives to the killing or could not rely on their contribution was thus often the task of young or female family members. Their only means of securing a stable supply of food was employment; in the Nazi ideology and war plans, Soviet Jews' right to live was tied to their economic utility, to providing labor that was essential to maintaining public infrastructure or producing and repairing equipment necessary to win the war. Survival in the Minsk ghetto was therefore tied to work at construction sites; in one of the shops where tanks, uniforms, or shoes were repaired; or in serving military and civilian administrations as cooks, cleaning personnel, or laundresses.

Rita Kazhdan describes how first her mother and then she herself took on the role of breadwinner. Both of her parents were killed in ways that targeted them, at different times, because of their gender. Abram Fridman,

Rita's father, was killed because the Nazi regime considered men potential resisters and saboteurs. Rozaliia Fridman, her mother, was murdered during a pogrom in the ghetto with a child in her arms that was not her own. Kazhdan vividly remembers the situation. Buildings in the ghetto had no access to hot water, and what remained of bathrooms was often converted into living space. Occasionally, workers had the opportunity to use public bathhouses. On March 1, 1942, a Sunday, Rozaliia Fridman took her daughter Rita and her son Grisha to the Russian district to visit a *bania* (public bathhouse). Unexpectedly, the hot water was turned off while the three were lathered in soap. Rita's mother was worried that her children would get sick and used a towel to remove the soap rather than showering them with freezing cold water. Covering the yellow patches on their coats, the family rushed home through the Russian district, independently of the column of ghetto Jews. Rita Kazhdan explains,

> And on the way, you know, as if she had a premonition, she told me: "Remember the address [of relatives] in Moscow." And as we walked home, she said, "Well, and if they kill me tomorrow, at least I will enter the grave a clean person." That was on March 1, and on March 2 she was killed.[117]

Rita Kazhdan's mother fell victim to the frantic hunt for 5,000 Jews during the pogrom on March 2, 1942. She was caught while trying to find some food for her children and some friends who were hiding in a malina; a militiaman put a child in her arms as she was pushed into the group of people who were designated to be killed. The image of Kazhdan's mother carrying an unknown child while she was murdered is a stark reminder of the overall goal of the Nazi genocide to deny Soviet Jews their future, both as individuals and as a community.

Rita and Grisha were now orphans; after the killing of their father, aunt, uncle, and a cousin, their mother was the last of their relatives to be taken away. At fourteen, Rita was in charge of her ten-year-old brother. Access to food was limited to the working population, and so far the two siblings had relied on their mother's income. Rita decided to send her brother to the orphanage to receive a bowl of watery soup every day around lunchtime, yet she also urged him to come home immediately after he had received his meal. "First, because he was the only one I had left, and secondly, the children's home was plagued with scabies and lice, dangerous germ carriers, and we had enough of them already."[118] Begging for food in the Russian district was not a sustainable option, for fear of discovery and because it had only minimal success. Furthermore, being unemployed jeopardized her very existence, because a work permit could provide some degree of security during raids and pogroms. Assisted by former classmate Ania Lianders, who also lived in the ghetto, Rita found employment in the *Panzerwerk* (tank workshop) run by the German company Daimler Benz. Kazhdan is sure that her non-Jewish appearance, "blond, and with thick pigtails," helped to persuade the shop foreman, Willi Scheimer, to admit her into the work detail.

Every day, after cleaning the repair shop and offices of the German administrators, Rita received a piece of bread and a bowl of soup. Her friend Lidiia Parfimchuk, who worked in the workshop kitchen, encouraged Rita to leave her soup container in a corner near the kitchen so that she could provide Rita with an extra portion. At the end of the workday, Rita picked up this container and shared the contents with her brother, who, afraid to leave the house, had waited patiently at home all day. Women's work in the kitchen here turned into an advantage, supplying some with precious extra food.

But there was never enough food, and Rita Kazhdan's description of her condition borders on the hallucinatory:

> Often, the shop foreman would request that I wash his laundry. In return, he brought me a sandwich with butter and jam. This was a great support . . . And I remember like it was yesterday, downstairs they ran the engines of tanks that were ready to be sent away, and there were these exhaust fumes. I took the bread and sat down near the tanks. It felt like I was eating sprats, bread with sprats.[119] That was the condition I was in.[120]

Rita Kazhdan shared her concern for food, her relatives, and her very existence with other youth. Mikhail Treister and Elena Drapkina found themselves looking for work early on. Fourteen-year-old Mikhail pretended to be older in order to join a shoemakers' workshop. Capitalizing on the loss of identification cards during the pogrom on November 7, 1941, he said he was sixteen years old and a shoemaker. The boy successfully hid his lack of professional training, and found understanding colleagues, mostly Jewish artisans who had arrived in Minsk from Poland at the beginning of the war, who taught him the craft within a few weeks. For the following nineteen months he worked for the German air force, leaving the ghetto every day. His mother and sister managed to find employment as seamstresses in the same building, and, like Mikhail, received a bowl of watery soup and 150 grams (5.2 oz.) of bread daily.[121]

Elena Drapkina joined the thousands of women and men searching for work and eventually registered with the Judenrat's labor office. She was assigned to the freight yard. As part of a group of sixteen women workers, she cleaned arriving trains, removed snow from the tracks, and received a daily food ration. Like Mikhail and Rita, she used her employment to acquire additional resources. Work sites served as places to exchange valuables, clothes, or household items for food: "Whatever people had left, we took it to work and exchanged it with Russian workers for flour, pearl barley, anything, really."[122] This barter was possible because access to food supplies was much greater outside the ghetto.

Work sites and the contact with residents of the Russian district were also spaces of connection with the underground movement, enabling both welcome and dangerous encounters. Rita Kazhdan regularly interacted with Russian POWs and Jewish men working in the boiler room of the tank shop, where she made use of the hot water supply to launder the German officer's garments. Soon enough, she was asked to collect bullets and other useful things when she was cleaning the upstairs offices.

> One of the guys made a container that had a double bottom, and I put the bullets, or carbide, in the lower part, covered it, and on top of it Lidiia ladled soup or whatever food was available. I hid the bullets at home until I was able to pass them on to a young man, Iuzik, who took them to partisans; in return he had promised that he would make sure my brother and I would be able to join them . . . But after a while he disappeared and didn't come back, so I was stuck with the bullets. One of my roommates found them when she was cleaning the house. They almost killed me, because if the Germans had found them, they would have killed all of us.[123]

Ekaterina Tsirlina and Mikhail Treister, who both worked for the air force, albeit in different workshops, were also engaged in supporting the underground. Ekaterina and her friend Tsilia Botvinnik smuggled a number of weapons out of the shop where they worked, and Mikhail retrieved leather or complete shoes to sell or pass on to underground members. One day, they had to witness the potential consequences of smuggling, when they were forced to watch the hanging of three men who were caught engaging in similar transactions.[124] Knowingly or not, Ekaterina Tsirlina and Rita Kazhdan utilized stereotypical assumptions about women to deceive the occupation regime. Notions of passivity and activity that are prominent in the stereotypical imagery of women as well as Jews, for instance, may have facilitated their success in smuggling weapons and bullets from their workplace, as these preconceptions denied the possibility that Jewish women would actively work against the regime.[125]

Contributing to the armed resistance was dangerous and promising at the same time. German guards, who checked workers returning to the ghetto, posed a daily threat to the young women, as did Jewish housemates who feared retaliation for real or alleged links to underground activity. At the same time, connections with partisan liaisons allowed the women to harbor hope that at some future time there would be an opportunity to leave the ghetto and join a partisan formation outside of town.

Securing employment outside the ghetto was advantageous; it provided opportunities to obtain food and make connections with potential helpers. Daily absences from the ghetto also provided a form of protection from the terror; because the pogroms in November 1941 and March and July 1942 targeted "disposable" individuals—children, the elderly, and other nonemployed people—they began only after the workers had left the ghetto. Rita Kazhdan's description of the mass killing action in the summer of 1942 underscores how work outside the ghetto offered a sort of protection to laborers as well as the anxiety they suffered not knowing the fate of friends and family who had stayed behind in the ghetto:

> They did not send us home from work, we stayed in the workshop, and in the ghetto there was a horrid pogrom. That time, they took everybody, they dragged people out of malinas and houses, everybody. I remember, when we left for work, the sun was shining. But then, as if nature would accompany this whole act, it started to rain. And for two or three days, I already don't remember how long this was, to us it seemed like an eternity, the rain didn't stop. When the pogrom was over, they sent us back to the ghetto. The ghetto was located around a hill, and as we walked up Respublikanskaia Street, blood was streaming down the road with the

water. And at the top we saw those who had survived, who had been able to save themselves. And Grisha was among them.[126]

Rita's brother had survived in a malina that a family friend, the pharmacist Abram Levin, had built in his house. Trying to avoid a repetition of such a situation, young Rita urged her supervisor to employ Grisha. She succeeded, and her brother now daily left the ghetto with her, working as a messenger boy within the workshop, receiving a daily food ration, and evading the trap that the ghetto became during mass raids. "This Willi Schott [the foreman] saved us," says Rita Kazhdan.[127] Employment equaled survival, but it was an option only granted by those in power.

The generosity of some was accompanied by the aggression and violence of others. Once mentioning that she was "almost raped," Kazhdan refused to elaborate in our conversations, which only increased my attention to things said, unsaid, or hinted at. In an interview with the VHA in 1995, however, she described how a German worker named Jupp assaulted her, indicating that such attacks were the norm:

> When this Jupp had already thrown me onto the bed and covered my mouth so that I could not scream—but I also was afraid to scream, because technically I wasn't allowed to clean the rooms of Germans, this Kruglenitsa [Jupp's roommate] came, and Jupp went into one corner, I into the other. But that was horrible. Another German wanted to just kill me because once I had not properly put away a broom in the workshop. Things like that, all the time. It was very difficult.[128]

Rita Kazhdan's hesitance to detail these forms of abuse and violence may be due to shame, embarrassment, or the desire to hide the events from family members.[129] These omissions or distortions are echoed in a similar fashion by others, pointing to difficulties of representing gendered and sexual violence. Mikhail Treister describes how Sarra Friedman, a housemate, approached three German soldiers for help when the house was on fire. Promising help, they took her away and she never returned. "Till today," Treister writes, "I try not to think about the end of this episode."[130] Albert Lapidus and others vividly remember how the ghetto commander Rübe chose thirteen young Jewish women who were first forced to walk around the city of Minsk. They were then taken to the Jewish cemetery in the ghetto, where they had to undress and dance in front of the commander and his entourage. Eventually he shot them at a prearranged pit.[131]

Such instances instilled a constant sense of fear among the ghetto population. Elena Drapkina's description of a warning system set up by her neighbor shows the limited options for self-defense:

> She drilled a hole through the wall next to her window, and on one side she had a string, on the other she hung up a bell. And when at night she noticed anything or heard people screaming somewhere, she pulled the string [and rang the bell]. That was such a noise, like in church. . . . Well, now this sounds funny, and sad at the same time. I am telling you this now, like that, but at the time, you heard this at night, and your stomach turned.[132]

While we cannot know whether Sarra Friedman was sexually abused, killed, or both, all of these options are both possible and likely, given the number of reports on the sexual abuse of women in Minsk and elsewhere in the occupied USSR.[133] The physical reflex produced by the sound of the bell thus had a very real basis: members of the German forces and collaborating militias frequently used the cover of night to invade homes, take whatever possessions remained after confiscations and barter, and abuse the residents. Many women and girls were brutally raped and, more often than not, killed.[134] It is likely that men were also the target of sexual violence, though there is little information available. In addition to the actual violence committed, the rapes established a sense of terror and fear; every woman could be the next to suffer from abuse and violence.[135] Sexual violence thus had symbolic value, highlighting the vulnerability of not just female Jews but any Jews who were unable to prevent the violence. Moreover, it demonstrated the vulnerability of the whole Jewish community, whose biological reproduction was contingent on women's bodies—a concept shared by both attackers and Jewish heritage law.

The assault on Jewish women continued in the context of labor assignments and selections. Working for a food ration entailed bureaucratic registration and an increased risk of pickup for summary execution. For instance, when the Judenrat refused to assemble 5,000 ghetto residents to be killed on March 2, 1942, German and Lithuanian police killed all the children in the orphanage and a number of patients in the ghetto hospital, and randomly selected passersby such as Rita Kazhdan's mother. They also used the return of workers in the evening to complete the cruel assignment.[136] Elena Drapkina gathered from a German foreman's discussions that something was going on in the ghetto. To assure herself, she asked me whether "Gefahr," the word the men used, indeed signified "danger." It does, and despite their concerns and after long hesitation, the supervisors made the women mount the truck that took them to the ghetto gate on the intersection of the streets Ulitsa Chornaia and Ulitsa Obutkovo. There, she says,

> They made us get off and line up along the ghetto fence. This was at night, it was already midnight, it was a moonlit night. I will never forget this scene... A German guard checked the documents at the gate, and I noticed that he sent those with a *Facharbeiterausweis* [skilled worker card]—mostly men—to the ghetto, the other ones, younger people and women, to a second column.[137]

Elena Drapkina explains that she took her worker card, which identified her as a worker but not as a "specialist," showed it to the guard, and thus passed the control. On her way to reach the German guard who was checking the documents, she was held up several times by Polish legionnaires assisting the German occupants, and was beaten up for trying to bypass the line of Jews to be checked.[138] The only other women from Elena's column who survived the selection at the ghetto gate was Elena's friend Oktia. "She ran away from the gate and hid in the Russian district. She could do that because she was blond and did not look like a Jew."[139] German and Russian workers alike were shocked when only Elena and Oktia showed up for work the next day; all the other women from their group had been killed.

A few days later, two Russian workers offered to get Elena a passport that identified her as a Polish woman and would enable her to leave the ghetto. Drapkina did not leave the ghetto immediately, as she did not want to endanger her housemates or coworkers. Frequent inspections and additional marks on people's coats, identifying the person's residence and the number of residents, helped the ghetto command to detect the absence of individual people. If such an absence was discovered, all residents of the building were taken into custody and killed.[140] For this reason, Elena waited until a suitable moment occurred. The chance came after the July 1942 pogrom. It was unclear who had survived and who had been killed, because all the data and registration records were in disarray. Drapkina left the ghetto immediately after the pogrom, passing as a gentile woman; she first found refuge in a farmer's household west of Minsk and later joined a partisan unit.

Drapkina embarked on an escape route that several thousand ghetto inmates used to save their lives, including Samuil Volk, Sonia Zalesskaia, Mikhail Treister, and many others. Efforts to leave increased in 1943, when inmates began to sense the impending destruction of the ghetto. Alerted by rumors that a special killing squad was making the rounds in Minsk in the summer of 1943, Rita Kazhdan, for instance, noticed the arrival of a suspicious German command at the Panzerwerk and decided to stay home the next day.[141] She warned some of her colleagues, but they accused her of panicking. "You understand, they couldn't imagine that they would kill everyone. People grabbed for the last straw, hoping that they would just be transferred to another place for work, they didn't believe it. Not even the Germans with whom we worked."[142] She and her brother were the sole survivors of their work detail and realized they had to leave if they wanted to survive. Two years after its creation, the Minsk ghetto had nearly disappeared. In the summer of 1943, between 3,000 and 6,000 of, over the course of two years, up to 100,000 inhabitants were alive, and the ghetto area had shrunk "like shagreen leather," as Rita Kazhdan says.[143] She and many other young people left the ghetto over spring and summer 1943.[144]

Even the putative degree of reliability and stability that the inmates' work for German military or civilian institutions provided could not ensure that their ultimate fate would not be extermination. Both individual assaults and repeated pogroms in the ghetto were a constant reminder that Soviet Jewry figured in German war plans as a category of people to be used and killed. The ghetto was destroyed in the fall of 1943, shortly after Rita, Grisha, Mikhail, Sonia, and Samuil had left Minsk. Between October 21 and 23, 1943, all remaining inhabitants of the ghetto were murdered.[145] By then most other ghettos in eastern Belorussia had been destroyed by Einsatzgruppen and collaborating militia.

The Minsk Ghetto in Oral History

If ever there had been a playful and unburdened childhood for young Soviet Jews in Minsk, it ended immediately after the arrival of German troops, who steadily increased and refined their system of violence, intimidation, and threat. As Tatiana Gildiner notes, "children in the ghetto did play, but they rarely smiled."¹⁴⁶ Jewish children in German-occupied Minsk had to fulfill roles that, before the war, were largely reserved for adults: working to supply their family and themselves with food, as well as to protect themselves and others against the intrusion of strangers and violence.¹⁴⁷ Interviewees did not volunteer any information about schooling during the war. This absence points to a stark difference between the lives of Jews and non-Jews during the war. Belorussian children were offered education and other cultural activities, even if these did instill Nazi ideology.¹⁴⁸ Starving, exposed to the elements, battling illness, and fearing for their lives, Jewish youth were physically and mentally exhausted, and thousands of them died. How many children, Jewish and non-Jewish, fell victim to the Nazi extermination policy, is hard to establish; children and women were often excluded from Soviet statistics of the dead, and we may thus never know.¹⁴⁹ We can, however, use the existing materials—oral histories and memoirs—to try and reinsert the experiences and perceptions of teenage and other young people into the historiography of the Holocaust in the USSR.

Understanding the perceptions of teenagers and children is especially significant in a context where not only did war destroy and change the material conditions of existence, but where the newly established political power structure abruptly challenged and invalidated previously acquired attitudes and perceptions. Recognizing oneself as and being treated as members of a racialized nationality at the bottom of society came as a reversal of what both family members and teachers had taught Rita Kazhdan, Elena Drapkina, Sonia Zalesskaia, and their contemporaries: that Soviet society was unified in patriotism and interethnic friendship. They had internalized the idea that a person's national identity had no impact on how they would be treated, and it played little, if any, role in their everyday lives. During the German occupation, Jewish communality was forced upon the youth, their families, and strangers in the form of ghetto internment, yellow patches, and anti-Jewish violence. In order to survive, Soviet Jews had to adapt to a regime that saw them as either a source of labor power or a disposable, superfluous people.¹⁵⁰

Rita Kazhdan and, until she was murdered, her mother stand for many young and adult women who provided for their families after male family members had either been drafted into the Soviet army or murdered by the Germans. In other societies, this could have come as a reversal of prewar gender roles, for instance in Polish ghettos.¹⁵¹ Yet, for Soviet families, especially in cities like Minsk, both parents' participation in the labor force and contribution to the household income had been considered normal in the 1930s.[152] Labor policies and practices implemented in the 1930s in the Soviet Union were reversed during the German occupation. Girls and women, many of whom had been employed in the education sector and in administrative positions—or looked forward to such employment—in the prewar period, were now confined to unskilled labor, often as janitors or cooks. This not only devalued the professional training they had acquired, it also made them vulnerable during selections, when skilled workers were favored and unskilled laborers led to execution sites.

In addition to the distinct forms of work assigned to women and men, violence and abuse targeted people differently, but these specificities are difficult to uncover. The silences around young women, especially given their absence in official statistics, are particularly noteworthy. Rita Kazhdan and Mikhail Treister's vague but disturbing remarks on sexual violence, for instance, highlight the need to explore the intersection of gender and historical memory. The difficulty they have elaborating on these stories—because of either shame or absent knowledge—underscores the challenge of reconstructing particular histories of violence. Narrators may downplay sexual violence because they consider it less important than the persecution and extermination of a whole national group.[153] Moreover, the difficulty with speaking about sexual violence, or violence that targeted women, is bound up in the discriminatory practices that emerged in the postwar Soviet Union, which erased the wartime histories of women, young people, and Jews.

In the postwar Soviet Union, silencing targeted women in compounded ways. It included the denial of recognition for female Soviet war veterans, a history that has been uncovered by Beate Fieseler.[154] The active writing out of history of a young, Jewish woman's contribution—Masha Bruskina—to resistance efforts is further evidence for deliberate omissions within the official Soviet war portrayal; Bruskina's name was reinstated and included in the memorial to her group's execution in Minsk only in 2008, after a decades-long struggle of scholars against Minsk authorities' claim that her identity was "unknown."[155] Furthermore, silence brought women into close association with Jewish child survivors of the Nazi genocide. First of all, the special targeting of Jews during the Nazi occupation was not typically acknowledged in memory as cultivated by the Soviet state. Secondly, people under eighteen years of age were not legally considered veterans of the war and thus were not entitled to veterans' benefits.[156] Adolescents occasionally were glorified as heroes, especially those who died, such as Zoia Kosmodemianskaia, but the experiences of Soviet youth were largely neglected in Soviet historiography and were not officially part of the history of World War II.[157] Compounded by the denial of distinct Jewish suffering during the war, Soviet Jewish youth thus had no voice in the canon of Soviet war commemoration and historiography. While the oral histories, testimonies, and memoirs introduced here are decidedly personal, they also have significant political importance, locating the experiences of Jewish youths, especially women perhaps, within the history and memory of Nazi occupation. They help overcome an exclusion produced by an extreme violence that nearly succeeded in destroying even the few voices we have available, the voices of those who barely escaped the genocide.

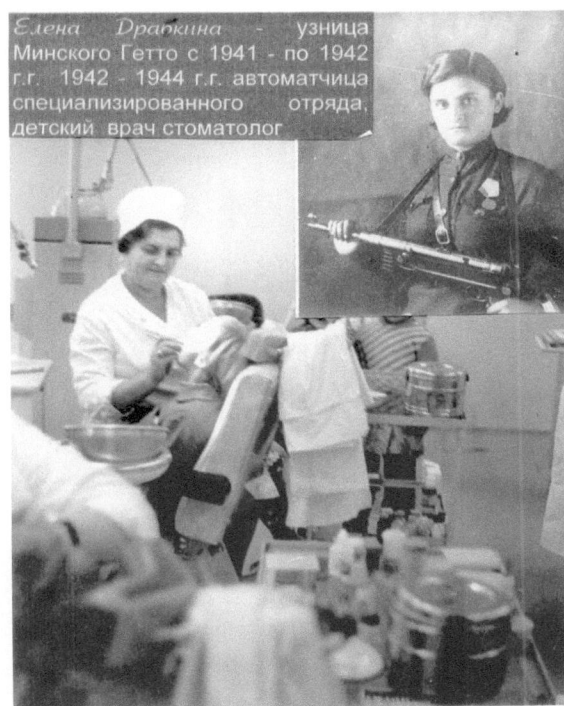

Elena Drapkina, at work as a dentist in the 1960s (left) and in partisan uniform in 1944 (right). *Collage courtesy of Elena Drapkina.*

Elena Drapkina, St. Petersburg, May 2005. *Photo by Anika Walke.*

Grigorii Erenburg, St. Petersburg, May 2005. *Photo by Anika Walke.*

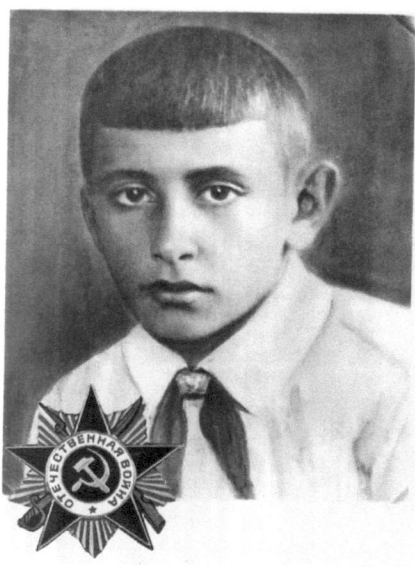

Boris Gal'perin as a pioneer in the 1930s. *Photo courtesy of Boris Gal'perin.*

Boris Gal'perin, Leningrad, early 1990s. *Photo courtesy of Association of Former Prisoners of Nazi Ghettos and Concentration Camps, St. Petersburg Branch.*

Leonid Gol'braikh, Beshenkovichi, 1930s. *Photo courtesy of USC Shoah Foundation, Visual History Archive.*

Leonid Gol'braikh, Pushkin/St. Petersburg, May 2005. *Photo by Anika Walke.*

Amaliia Iakhontova, Novosibirsk, April 1998. *Photo courtesy of USC Shoah Foundation, Visual History Archive.*

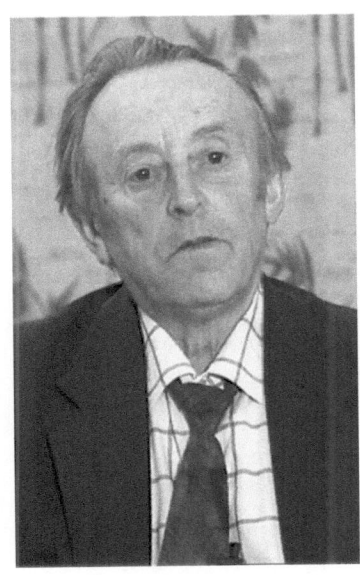

Sholom Kaplan, St. Petersburg, October 1995. *Photo courtesy of USC Shoah Foundation, Visual History Archive.*

Rita Kazhdan (née Fridman) with her parents, Rozaliia and Abram Fridman, and brother Grigorii, Minsk, late 1930s. *Photo courtesy of Rita Kazhdan.*

Rita Kazhdan (née Fridman), Leningrad, late 1940s. *Photo courtesy of Rita Kazhdan.*

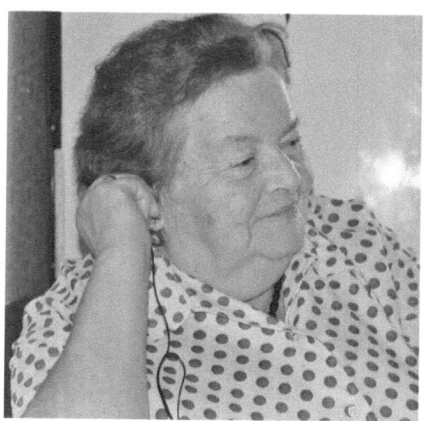

Rita Kazhdan, St. Petersburg, May 2005. *Photo by Anika Walke.*

Rita Kazhdan and Elena Drapkina, St. Petersburg, May 2005. *Photo by Anika Walke.*

Alevtina Kuprikhina, Leningrad, early 1990s. *Photo courtesy of Association of Former Prisoners of Nazi Ghettos and Concentration Camps, St. Petersburg Branch.*

Zoia Oboz, Minsk, January 1997. *Photo courtesy of USC Shoah Foundation, Visual History Archive.*

Frida Ped'ko, St. Petersburg, May 2005. *Photo by Anika Walke.*

Mikhail Treister, St. Petersburg, April 1995. *Photo courtesy of USC Shoah Foundation, Visual History Archive.*

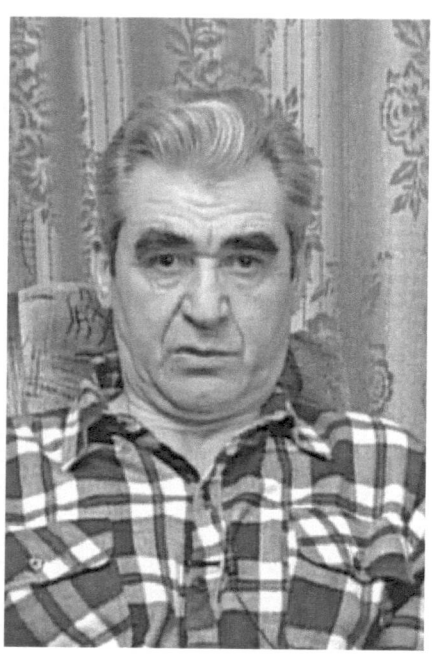

Samuil Volk, Novosibirsk, April 1998. *Photo courtesy of USC Shoah Foundation, Visual History Archive.*

Sonia Zalesskaia, Minsk, May 1997. *Photo courtesy of USC Shoah Foundation, Visual History Archive.*

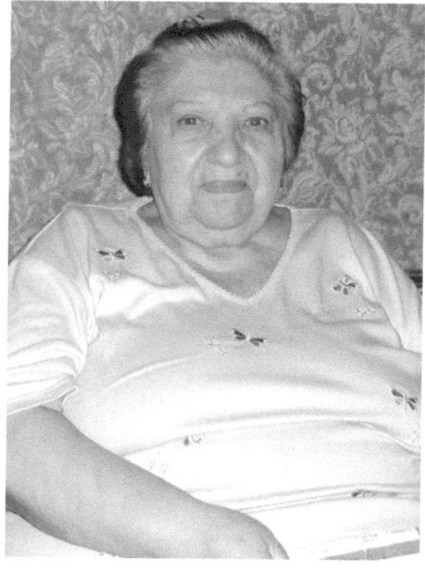

Roza Zelenko, Minsk, October 2002. *Photo by Anika Walke.*

4

Suffering and Survival

The Destruction of Jewish Communities in Eastern Belorussia

The inmates of Nazi ghettos in the German-occupied Soviet Union were constantly confronted with death, loss, and grief. There was, however, rarely time or space to mourn the dead. Amaliia Iakhontova recalls her reaction to the killing of her mother when she was sixteen years old. When two German officers raided her home in the Minsk ghetto, they forced her mother to let go of Amaliia and took her to a neighboring room.

> A second later I heard a shot, but I didn't understand what happened . . . I went to mother and said, "Mama, get up!" She was on her knees in front of the bed, and blood was trickling down her temple. I did not understand that mother could have been killed. I yelled at the neighbors, "Bring me some water for her!" They all stood around me and said that wouldn't help. I kept screaming, so they brought me water. I wanted to give it to my mother, but they made me drink it and put something in my mouth and then put me to bed so that I wouldn't cry so loud. They were afraid the Germans would come back. Only one woman said to me, "Amaliia, you have to remember the day this happened for the rest of your life." Then I began to understand what happened, but I kept calling for her.[1]

The German ghetto command in Minsk limited permissions to bury deceased Jews in the Jewish cemetery to persons who had died of illness or old age. Against this prohibition, friends and former colleagues of Amaliia's mother organized a funeral for her. An uncle put up a gravestone, but it was destroyed the same day, leaving Amaliia with only a vague place to go to mourn her mother.² Documenting memories such as Amaliia Iakhontova's poses thorny questions about how to write about destruction and violence. How can we represent death and the dead without perpetuating the violence of stigmatization and anonymization, where victims and the violence committed against them remain obscure and unnamed?

Oral histories of elderly Jews in the former Soviet Union play a special role in commemorating the Nazi genocide; they commit to memory and knowledge those dead whose killing has been obscured. German policies of destruction in occupied Soviet territory included, first, actual murders, and then attempts to erase any physical trace of those murders. Not only were the remains of victims of mass shootings dumped in largely unmarked mass graves, but beginning in 1942 Jews and Soviet prisoners of war had to dig up those graves and burn the remnants of corpses. *Aktion 1005*, the code name for this final obliteration, completed the cruel and destructive agenda of the German occupants and condemned the victims to yet another death.

Iakhontova's account emphasizes the attempts of the Nazi regime to produce deaths that had no meaning. When the dead are denied proper burial, and death has no place, it is removed from the realm of the living, and the life of the dead is obliterated. Mass killings in ghettos and the disposal of corpses in mass graves are an assault on death itself, specifically on death in the Jewish tradition. In this tradition, to die as a human being is "to affirm that life is very good," and rituals of prayer and burial recognize the life of the individual.³ Where murder ignores individuality, however, where the dead and death remain unmarked, extermination targets both the dead, who are deprived of life, and the living, who are deprived of memory. Iakhontova's neighbors and friends tried to withstand this assault. Similar to the *maliny*—collectively built and occupied hiding places—the emotional support they gave to young Amaliia offered a communal challenge to the Nazi regime's attempt to create a society of atomized and disposable individuals. Iakhontova's description, however, also insists on the limits of the ghetto inmates' efforts. These limits are marked by the unscrupulous and arbitrary, yet systematic, invasion and destruction of personal lives, as well as by the eradication of sites of death and burial. Hannah Arendt's diagnosis, that the Nazi murder of the Jews presupposed their legal, political, and social death, comes into focus here in a disturbing way.⁴ The destruction of the moral person, here obvious in the prohibition of grieving and remembering, coincides with the physical destruction of persons stripped of their juridical personality and individuality.

The description of a teenager's struggle to acknowledge and commemorate the loss of her mother is an account of complete destruction. The Nazi murder of Soviet Jewry left few traces. And the near complete absence of physical reminders of Jewish deaths—true of both individuals, such as Amaliia's mother, as well as incidents of mass murder—erases the destruction several times over. For many localities in the occupied Soviet territories, there are no lists comparable to inmate lists of concentration camps: Jewish residents were often rounded up and shot without leaving a trace on paper. The efforts of the Extraordinary State Commission for the Investigation of Atrocities Committed on Soviet Territory (hereafter, Extraordinary State Commission) after the war to draw up lists of the dead presupposed that someone remained who was able and willing to serve as a witnesses of their former lives and their deaths.[5] This logic of the necessity of others' willingness to testify and to witness the suffering and death is inscribed in Vera Pogorelaia's decision to postpone her escape from her hometown Slavnoe after the mass execution: "We thought we shouldn't go too far at first, so that if we died, at least someone will know, otherwise nobody would recognize us."[6] Her fear evokes the problems we face by studying destruction and how people responded to it: What if there were no witnesses? What if there was no one who would bear witness to the Soviet transformation of Jewish communities and to their destruction during the Nazi occupation?

The violence of the Nazi genocide in Belorussia continues on in haunting images and in the simultaneous absence of images, which challenges people's desire and ability to know; many women and men, while aware that their relatives were killed, never learned, how, where, and why they died. They try to compensate for this lack of certainty by developing stories and images that cover up the destruction of familial networks, borrow from state portrayals that capitulate before senseless violence, and share narratives that are fragmentary and incoherent.

Our attempts to uncover omissions and distortions can only succeed partially insofar as oral histories can emphasize only those who are available in memory and imagination; they thus mark exclusions in both history and memory. What is true for most Holocaust and genocide testimony generally acquires special urgency in the case of narratives about the ghettos in Minsk and eastern Belorussia: the dead exist only in memory; there are no paper records; and, as a rule, there are no individual gravestones. Mention of parents, classmates, or acquaintances who did not survive populate the narratives and are a reminder of the destruction. They forcefully point out that any account of the systematic extermination of Soviet Jewry will remain partial and incomplete because those who were killed cannot report their experiences. I do not say this to echo scholars who argue that the absence of the complete witness to "Auschwitz" means we can never fully know the Holocaust.[7] I do believe that we can understand Nazi atrocities without the knowledge of those killed. Acts of violence, the survivor and writer Ruth Klüger says, can be "described just fine and in all detail," and survivors do exactly that; to claim that the "Holocaust" is indescribable is a form of "sentimental self-adulation that claims to be a sign of empathy; in fact, though, it is a way to evade facing the reality of (and the responsibility for) atrocities committed by human beings."[8] There may be no immediate witnesses to the killing, they are dead, but we often have sufficient information to discern who was murdered and how the murder was committed, and in most cases we can identify the perpetrators.

Yet, at times, survivors do not have concrete information, or find themselves unable to speak the violence they know occurred, or are troubled by it to such an extent that a coherent narrative is impossible. In these cases, we can glean from other sources what likely happened to those who are evoked in their narratives. Through such an approach we may infer the events, but we also understand the difficulty in accounting for them. In addition to oral histories, we must therefore resort to other memoirs, scholarship, wartime journalism, fiction, and archival documentation—for instance, in the form of reports and witness testimony collected by the Extraordinary State Commission or by the Soviet Army.[9] These latter materials, often written in specialized terms, reflect the state's attempt to document unprecedented atrocities committed against people and country. In disturbing ways, these reports and other materials provide a language for individuals who try to understand, right down to specific phrases and images used by survivors.

Frida Ped'ko, Alevtina Kuprikhina, Grigorii Erenburg, and Boris Gal'perin, who were introduced in chapter 2, were confined to ghettos in eastern Belorussia that have not been subject to substantial historical inquiry. In multiple interviews, these women and men revisited their pasts in Slavnoe, Rogachev and Zhlobin, Bobruisk and Shchedrin, and Ryzhkovichi, respectively, speaking about their childhoods in peace and war and about how difficult it is to remember. Their narratives address a problem that applies to an overall concern of this book: how do we learn about the past if there are no—even insufficient or distorted—records? How do we learn about a past of destruction that was, at least in part, successful? Or, in other words, "how does one write a story about an encounter with nothing?"[10]

The Nazi genocide in eastern Belorussia

Boris Gal'perin arrived in Ryzhkovichi in mid-June 1941, looking forward to spending the summer school break at his parents' house. The fall before, he had moved to his uncle and aunt's household in Leningrad and enrolled in School No. 19 of the former capital's Vasileostrovskii district.[11] On July 11, Ryzhkovichi and the nearby town Shklov were captured by Wehrmacht troops, trapping Boris, his parents, and approximately 8,000 local residents behind the front line. At the end of the month, all Jews residing in the towns were forced into two ghettos.[12]

Gal'perin's experiences reflect those of thousands of other Jews of his age. He had enrolled in a school in Leningrad, following in the footsteps of his aunt and uncle, who had left the former Pale of Settlement in the 1920s and later offered to let Boris stay at their house while he studied. Schooling in Leningrad promised Boris better prospects for the future than he would have found in the agricultural setting of the kolkhoz in Ryzhkovichi. His movement between Belorussia and Leningrad thus points to Soviet Jews' personal, familial, and communal roots in the former Pale of Settlement, but also to the changes that shaped Jewish life in the first two decades of the USSR. When he returned to Ryzhkovichi during the school break in the summer of 1941, he was unexpectedly caught in a war zone. Soon he confronted anti-Jewish policies and harassment from German troops as well as a few neighbors, an experience he shared with thousands of Jewish residents of the area.

The process of military occupation, destruction, ghettoization, and extermination affected the Jewish population all over Belorussia in similar ways. But one important difference is in the timeline of these processes in distinct areas. The Minsk ghetto was created in July 1941 and existed until October 1943, and the grip there of constant threats and murder actions consistently reduced the ghetto population. Jews residing in eastern Belorussia, the territories that had been part of the Soviet Union since its foundation in 1922, faced an even quicker and more thorough destruction. Survival in these areas thus relied even more on swift and ad hoc decision making than in Minsk. Sustainable networks of support or underground movements, which proved essential to organizing collective and mutual support as they emerged in the ghettos of Warsaw, Łódź, Vilna, and Białystok, for the most part did not exist in eastern Belorussia.

Grigorii Erenburg, Frida Ped'ko, Boris Gal'perin, and Alla Kuprikhina were trapped in areas that remained under German military control until 1944. In this region, under military occupation they thus faced not only ongoing battles between Soviet and German troops in some areas, but also the continued presence of individuals prepared and willing to use their weapons against anyone who posed an imagined or potential threat. Ghettos in these areas were often not designed to house "useful labor." Rather, they were zones of concentration in preparation for extermination. Structurally, these ghettos compare to many ghettos in Ukrainian territories where "the Nazis had redefined the term *ghetto* altogether, from Jewish quarters with some form of self-administration and life-sustaining conditions to makeshift death traps and staging areas for genocide."[13] In Belorussia, ghettos with this purpose were often established in large buildings guarded by local police or SS troops, housing local Jews for only days, weeks, or a few months before they were shot in nearby trenches, natural ravines, or on the spot.[14]

The Nazi genocide in these areas was not only committed more quickly than in western parts of Belorussia, it was also emblematic of the coupling of economic planning and a racist agenda in the war against the Soviet Union: Jews in the so-called Old Soviet territories were considered deeply committed Bolsheviks. From an ideological standpoint, they therefore posed a particular danger to the German people and had to be exterminated as soon as possible. Consequently, the destruction of Jewish communities between Borisov and Minsk began in late August 1941.[15] From a strategic standpoint, fighting troops required local resources to sustain themselves; eliminating a portion of the civilian population reduced competing claims on those resources.[16] The ghettos in eastern Belorussia exemplify the dynamics and goals of Nazi policies in the occupied Soviet territories by showing the coincidence of rational pragmatism and ideological concerns that were resolved through the killing of a racially defined group of people. The effects of such policies on individuals and communities, in particular the repercussions of the destruction for a long time to come, are yet to be fully understood.

"We decided to go to the local commander and ask him to kill us"

Accounting for death is a difficult task. It does not only involve the images of those who died. It also includes thinking about the threat of murder, of death, that consistently lingered over those who survived. Frida Ped'ko, a former resident of Slavnoe, a small village twelve miles to the southwest of Tolochin, described how she contemplated the end of her life during the occupation. She thus touches upon an issue—the possibility of her own death—that few narrators articulate and which interviewers (myself included) are reluctant to address. And yet this is an important dimension when considering the implications of genocide. Notably, the figure of the mother surfaces as central to efforts to come to terms with terror and the dread of death. Simultaneously, in remembering her mother Maria Iosifovna Sirotkina, Ped'ko's oral history is contradictory. Her attempts to remember her mother display that desire and longing for stability thread through her efforts to represent a major rupture in her life.

Seven years old when the war began, Frida Ped'ko found herself trapped in the occupied village in early July 1941. Her mother, Maria Iosifovna Sirotkina, was a member of the *sel'sovet* (short for *sel'skii soviet*, village council), and heavily involved in organizing the evacuation of local residents. She managed to get her two children, Frida and Elena, and herself onto the last train out of Slavnoe. The train was bombed, however, and the family had to return to Slavnoe. Within days, the approximately 150 local Jewish residents were ordered to move into a few houses in a heavily damaged part of the settlement.[17] Everyone over the age of ten was forced to work: adolescents collected pine and fir cones in the nearby forest that were then sent to Germany, and older women and men worked on repairing roads and cleaning military facilities.[18] Germans regularly burst into ghetto homes, stole property, and abused the inhabitants.[19]

It is unclear whether Frida's mother was present during the occupation. Ped'ko gave two differing accounts of the occupation, each conjuring a competing image of her mother. Within the stories themselves, there are important clues as to why the versions differ and even how they relate to one another. One version emerged when I interviewed Frida Ped'ko for the first time in the spring of 2001, and it is also included in an autobiographical statement that she supplied for an application to receive benefits and compensation as a former underage prisoner. She described how after enduring eight months of hard forced labor, lacking both food and heating material, all Jewish residents of Slavnoe were killed. On the evening of March 15, 1942, Frida Ped'ko's uncle got word that a German *Einsatzkommando* (task force) was preparing to round up all Jews the next day and kill them. "Mother made me and my sister run away from the ghetto at night, she told us to go to nearby Pogrebishche and hide in the house of some friends. On the way a police patrol caught us and took us to the local command post."[20] The police decided that the two children would not pose any harm and sent them to a local peasant, ordering him to take care of them and make sure they would be raised as proper Belorussians.

When I interviewed Ped'ko for the second time she revealed that her mother, since she was Party secretary, had been "among the first to be shot" in Slavnoe; "they made them dig their own grave, near the river, and there they shot her."[21] In keeping with German war plans to destroy the Bolshevik leadership, Party activists and functionaries were regularly singled out and, in many cases, murdered in the first days of the German occupation. For instance, Liubov Belen'kaia, a member of the Komsomol, was arrested and threatened with murder; Belen'kaia assumes that she was singled out because of her activism.[22] Even more to the point, Menukha Boroda, a woman who escaped the destruction of Slavnoe's Jewish community, reports an incident in the summer of 1941 when she and seventeen other Jews, "mostly from the sel'sovet, Russians and Jews, Communists, were lined up" to be shot. Boroda was released after a neighbor lied and told the Germans in charge that she was not a Jew; the others were killed. This arrest and execution presumably involved Frida Ped'ko's mother; she was a member of the Communist Party, she was Jewish, and she occupied a high post in the sel'sovet.[23] The combination of these three attributes made her a likely victim of the Germans' first murders in Slavnoe. From this we can discern that Ped'ko's mother was probably killed early on during Slavnoe's occupation and was not present in March 1942.

According to this second version, Frida and her sister lived with relatives from the summer of 1941 until they were lined up with the other Jews on March 16, 1942, and led to the execution site. Young Frida's thoughts, familiar to the reader from the Introduction of this book, were:

> I didn't really understand, when they took us and told me, "We're going to mama." I had understood that she was shot and that that was terrible, but

I didn't understand that that was forever. I thought she is somewhere . . . But when my sister said, "They'll shoot us," I was terrified, asked, "What do you mean, they will shoot at me? That will hurt and will make me bleed!"

Rescue from these thoughts, or from their becoming reality, appeared in the form of a policeman who pulled the two sisters out of the column. He pushed them into the arms of an old man, P. I. Stasevich, and told him to take the children farther away, saying, "there is no need to shoot these kids."[24] Stasevich took the children to a chapel, had them baptized, and took them to a nearby hamlet in the woods. He thus rescued the two children from sure death: up to 150 Jews residing in Slavnoe were shot on March 16, 1942, at a ditch near the village of Gliniki.[25] Among the 123 names listed in a Soviet document are at least 26 children under the age of twelve who were killed that day.[26]

The rescue by P. I. Stasevich unites both stories; the only difference is how the siblings ended up in his care. Were they indeed singled out by a compassionate German soldier, or were they released into his care after they had been arrested? Did their mother send them out of the ghetto to try and save their lives, or had she been dead for months? Why, we must ask further, did the sixty-seven-year-old Frida Ped'ko share first one, then, four years later, another version? To ask this question is not an attempt to deconstruct her story as unreliable, a trap one may easily fall into. Rather, one needs to understand the function of both stories to grasp the perceptions of violence by a young child and how the survivor remembered and narrated those perceptions several decades later.

It is likely that Frida Ped'ko's reflections on her own thoughts facing execution resulted from the rapport between her and me, built over several years. Her willingness to explore her memory of emotions may have triggered a remembering of a much earlier loss that, until the interview, she had suppressed. This suppression might reflect the way in which the young child reacted to the loss of the mother in the summer of 1941. By this logic, Ped'ko's memory of considering her own future death includes the realization that her mother was dead; Maria Iosifovna had been shot, but only when Frida contemplated being shot herself did she realize that that meant physical pain and death. Living in the ghetto for several months and watching numerous killings, she then understood that her mother was, indeed, gone forever and that there was no hope she would ever return. In other words, this is the moment when Frida Ped'ko realized she was an orphan, putting her in a situation that, in hindsight, made it difficult not only to survive war and genocide, but also to rebuild a life in the postwar Soviet Union.

The contradictory stories also speak about agency and belonging, and the struggle to understand how both were shattered. Each mother figure, the one that was present during internment in the ghetto and the one that was killed in the summer of 1941, personifies differing degrees of agency in protecting her children. Whereas the party member, shot for being a communist, has no chance to care for her children and leaves them behind in uncertainty, the mother who sent them away on the eve of destruction was able to make a decision, albeit one that sent them into an unknown future.

The aftereffects of parental loss are crucial for deciphering the construction of Frida Ped'ko's and others' oral histories. How children experience and perceive the destruction of child-parent relationships in contexts of extreme violence is yet to be fully understood.[27] An ongoing fear of separation, abandonment, and further violence, as well as lack of self-worth and feelings of anger, guilt, or emptiness as a result of losing parental safety and security, have all been diagnosed among many child survivors of Nazi persecution.[28] In addition, literary explorations of slavery in the United States, which dwell on the forced separation of mothers from their children, are suggestive of how a mother's inability to protect her offspring produces in those children compounded moments of humiliation, self-hatred, mistrust, and feelings of abandonment and rejection and shed light on oral histories such as Frida Ped'ko's.[29]

Did Frida Ped'ko understand, or accept, the death of her mother? Or did young Frida need the illusion that her mother would return, support, and protect her to survive? Did she have to hold on to the idea that her mother still "is somewhere"?[30] Did elderly Frida Ped'ko try to preserve the mother's image as capable and independent, exemplified by raising two children on her own after the father's untimely death and, as both a worker and a mother, by being a role model of Soviet modernization? The latter was the reason for her quick death, and for her inability to care for the sisters and to rescue them. At the same time, the successful fulfillment of the double role as mother and worker was deeply inscribed in Soviet discourses about womanhood and femininity that shaped Ped'ko's life over multiple decades.[31] She fulfilled these social expectations after the war; she gained a professional degree, raised a family, and worked until she was too sick to continue.

Placing her mother in the midst of the family although she was already dead is, therefore, an attempt to come to terms with the violence, rooted in the child's needs as much as in prewar and postwar Soviet realities.

Frida and her sister Elena survived, one way or the other, in the middle of the forest around their hometown. The peasant P. I. Stasevich brought food and constructed a hut from logs and branches. After more than two years, however, in the summer of 1944, the two children discussed giving up come winter. "We decided to go to the local commander and ask him to kill us. We were so wasted, there was no real food."[32] They saw no prospect for surviving any longer; with the war going on around them, they were starving and without shelter. Seeing no other option, the girls considered their own deaths as a relief. When Soviet troops liberated the Vitebsk region in June 1944, these plans became moot: Frida and Elena survived. They then rejoined a society that was deeply affected by the occupation. Over a period of three years, 6,596 people had been killed in the Tolochin region, and 375 deported to forced labor—all in all, about one-third of the prewar population was either dead or had been forcibly removed.[33]

Frida Ped'ko's narrative is haunted by the emotional and physical pain of surviving, of knowing that survival depends on the actions of others, and that death would be a relief from a hellish life. The narrative is a powerful reminder that the ghettos in Eastern Europe challenged notions of life and death by "transforming life into an antilife before it is lived," in other words, devaluing life by defining it by death.[34] Ped'ko's oral history also points to a quality of oral histories—their potential to be fragmentary, even contradictory—that can be discouraging. But I see this as a productive challenge. Learning about personal interpretations and attempts to make sense of what happened, but also about the inherent contradictions and fragmentary character of oral histories, highlights the breakdown of reliable frameworks of interpretation during the Nazi genocide and the dramatic destruction of people's sense of self and agency under occupation, terror, and violence.

"In fact, we don't know what happened"

Grigorii Erenburg, an avid reader of patriotic literature who had dreamed of becoming an engineer, found himself and his family among thousands of residents of Bobruisk who fled their city when German troops forced their way into town in late June 1941. After a failed attempt to move in with relatives in Rogachev, the six family members trekked back to Shchedrin, the village where both parents had grown up. Within a few days, a Belorussian acquaintance who had often visited the family before the war informed them that their house in Bobruisk was intact and encouraged the family to return to their home. Upon arrival there, the Erenburgs discovered that the information had been false, their house was in ruins, and they had to find shelter in some other abandoned building. By mid-August, together with approximately 30,000 other Jews of Bobruisk and up to 4,500 Polish Jews who had sought refuge in Bobruisk since 1939, the family had been robbed of valuables, money, and fur and resettled in a ghetto.[35] Grigorii Erenburg recalls the regular incursions of German military or SS into the ghetto, hunting for men to be taken away during daytime and women to be humiliated—and, as other accounts suggest, raped—at night:

> Big trucks stopped in our street, and the Germans went from house to house and dragged out Jewish men. I saw how they were beating up our neighbor, and then I ran home and told my father to hide. Father went into the outhouse in the backyard. The Germans came into our house ... it was still early in the morning and grandfather was praying in one of the rooms in the back. All of a sudden I hear this terrible scream of my grandfather, they dragged him out of the room. In the evening we heard from a young man who managed to run away, a distant relative of ours; he told us that they had taken all the Jews who had been caught to a fortress outside of town, beat them, and finally shot them all ... And the Germans destroyed everything. At night they went from house to house, searching for young women, and they beat them. Once they came to our house and pushed several women into our house. My aunt was pretty young. They brought a gramophone, played music and made all the women undress and forced them to dance in front of them. Then they left. So the nights weren't quiet either.[36]

In October 1941, a family acquaintance from Shchedrin came to the ghetto; he and other farmers were planning to trade food with the inmates and to pick up horses that could be used in the fields. They had been given twelve travel permits, but since they needed only eleven, the friend offered to take Grigorii's father. Some days later, Grigorii's mother arranged for the fourteen-year-old to be taken away too; she was worried that he might be caught during one of the raids. Dressed in farmer's clothes and posing as a peasant's nephew, Grigorii and the family friend left the town. Together with his father, Grigorii stayed in a village not far from Shchedrin, where they worked in the workshop of a prewar friend and made plans to get the rest of the family out of the ghetto.

In November, just four months after the Nazis had arrived, Grigorii and his father heard of the destruction of Bobruisk's Jewish community. Already in July 1941, several hundred Jews had been killed under the accusation of organizing sabotage and spreading anti-German rumors. In September and October, 2,200 Jews were shot near the Jewish cemetery of Bobruisk and close to the nearby villages of Eloviki and Kamenka. Another 7,000 Jews were killed near Bobruisk's airfield. Following a selection of professionals and skilled workers and their placement in a work camp within the ghetto, 5,300 unemployed Jews were taken to Kamenka and shot on November 7, 1941. People who had managed to hide within the ghetto during earlier killing actions were murdered by December 30, and the specialists singled out in October were killed in February 1942. Bobruisk continued to be a site of execution in 1942 and 1943, when Jews from Poland and other areas in Belorussia were taken to Bobruisk and shot there.[37]

Until November 1941, Grigorii's father was unaware of the extent of the murder of Jews in Bobruisk and agonized over the fate of his wife and children. Eventually, he sent an acquaintance to determine whether they were still alive. In the end, Grigorii and his father were told that their loved ones were alive and hiding in a village near Bobruisk. When father and son investigated after the war, they were told that no woman with three children had ever been there. "In fact, we don't know what happened to our family," Erenburg said.[38]

The unsuccessful search for mother and siblings, and for hints of what had happened to them, never came to an end. The absence of clear information has crystallized in a painful image, indicating Erenburg's concern for the dead and for the effects of the murder: "Now, when I am thinking of my mother, how it was for her to go to the execution with the little ones, it just doesn't make sense. . . . I am trying to imagine how she went, with three children . . . she probably held the youngest in her arms, the others were already . . ."[39]

This image, often drowned in tears and with slight variations, was one of the few things Grigorii Erenburg repeated in all the interviews I conducted with him, and it also emerges in the video testimony produced by the VHA in 1995. Erenburg is one of only a few narrators who share their imagination of an unwitnessed loss; while all interviewed survivors report the loss of parents, friends, and others, few ever describe the dead. This is understandable, given that very few witnessed the concrete circumstances of their close ones' deaths. In most cases, they did not see them, having managed to hide during pogroms or escape from executions.

Grigorii Erenburg's narration thus stands in for the images and imaginations that haunt, and in many instances are avoided by, survivors. Moreover, in accounting for his own and his father's rescue in response to raids for men, and the humiliations and systematic killings of women and children, Erenburg points to how gender factored into the course of the genocide, the chances for survival, and the destruction and losses that shape both history and memory. Others do so as well. Rita Kazhdan was told her mother was handed a child when she was caught during the March 2, 1942, raid on the Minsk ghetto and subsequently shot.[40] Elena Drapkina hid in a malina while her mother and younger brother were taken away.[41] And Yakov Negnevitzki recalled that he was inconsolable when he learned about the death of his mother and sister; he had agreed to leave the ghetto and go to the partisans without them, hoping to pick them up at a later moment, which never came. He does not know when and where his loved ones died.[42]

Memories of the dead, images of the genocide, appear to be populated by women, children, and the elderly. These groups likely comprised the majority of the victims of the Nazi genocide. Many men were serving in the Soviet army when the war began or were drafted immediately; Einsatzgruppen often killed those men who had remained in the area early on during the occupation, presumably with the aim of preventing possible resistance. Later, according to a different logic, women and men, young and old alike were caught during raids and pogroms devised to eliminate nonworkers. The genocide was thus simultaneously all-encompassing, targeting all Jews, and particular, killing more women, children, and elderly people than men. Yet, it bears asking, why did Erenburg remember, or imagine, his mother's death in such detail, especially in contrast to the deaths of other men he is aware of as well? While Grigorii Erenburg mentioned the death of fellow partisans only in passing, he continued to evoke this very concrete image of his mother's and siblings' deaths.

In popular thinking, men go to war, ready to kill and be killed. Women and children, traditionally, do not, and the fact that they, as noncombatants, were targeted by the Germans has resulted in long-lasting puzzlement. Erenburg was shocked about just that, and his search to make sense of his mother's murder in this particular way reflects a prominent trope in talking about war: the killing of women and children, the innocent, as a signal of unprecedented and unbearable violence. Witnesses and writers worked within this framework already during and immediately after the war, affecting the way in which mass murder was to be represented for decades to come. In 1942, the journalist Ilya Ehrenburg, for instance, explained and encouraged hatred toward Germans as follows: "And death came with them to our country. I don't mean the death of soldiers, for no war is without its victims. I refer to the gallows from which the bodies of Russian girls are dangling, and the terrible pit near Kerch' in which the children of Russians, Tatars, and Jews are buried."[43] In one of the first photographic documentations of mass murder, showing pictures of the dead bodies of civilians shot by Germans in Kerch', a similar emphasis is repeated twice: "Wherever the Germans found themselves, they murdered thousands of women and children ... (see above photograph). Among the murdered were many women and children (see lower photograph)."[44] Lastly, the phrases "peaceful Soviet citizens" and "innocent civilians," often specified as "elderly, women, and children," were included in hundreds of reports and testimonies collected after liberation by both the Soviet Army and the Extraordinary State Commission. Used throughout the war in official communication and Soviet media outlets, these phrases then found entry into many publications on World War II in the Soviet Union. Grigorii Erenburg's emphasis on the death of his mother and sibling, on the image of the mother holding her child, reflects the ways in which both individuals and state-censored media described the genocide.

Emphasizing the killing of vulnerable, defenseless women and children fulfills a crucial public function, increasing the urge to fight back against the enemy's senseless slaughter. At the same time, these images carry symbolic meaning—mothers and children symbolize the future of the state and the population as a whole.[45] The damage, in this sense, is doubled: it is done to both individuals and the group.[46] The strength of these images is enhanced by their juxtaposition to images of male fighters, such as in writings by Ehrenburg or in other media portrayals of German atrocities that call on the reader to defend the victims on display. The male fighters called upon include both (young) male civilians, who are not typically included in either the photographs or the textual accounts and thus are not part of the dead, and the male soldiers who died, but do so understandably, "for no war is without victims" (Ehrenburg, see above). Grigorii Erenburg joined the partisans and did what was expected of young males: fighting and avenging the death of loved ones, who simultaneously symbolized the absolute horror inflicted by the Germans and the threatened society in which he believed.[47] The murdered mother and sibling, a quintessential personification of the vulnerable and innocent, thus (likely) served as justification for Erenburg's and many other Soviet men's actions. While the military fight was necessary and deserves respect, the logic of writing about it according to this scheme also reinforces problematic notions of female passivity and male activity. These identifications are used to create exclusions in historical writing by marginalizing women's contributions.[48]

In a different reading, the visualization of his mother holding her two-year-old daughter and dying instantly from a gunshot may be the only way that Grigorii Erenburg can bear the knowledge of their death. There are other images available, some of which the survivor himself evoked late in our last interview: "I saw so many horrific things, the piles of corpses . . . or there was this young mother who was hanged, a little child next to her, . . . or when they cut open the womb of a pregnant woman . . . the Germans committed such atrocities . . ."[49] Other images are included in the forensic reports by the Soviet Army, describing star-shaped cuts, bruises on inner thighs, and bullet wounds inflicted on a woman who, the medics conclude, was raped, shot, and finally dumped in a river.[50] Babies and young children were reportedly often torn from their mother's arms, ripped apart, thrown against trees or walls, thrown into the air and gored with bayonets, or dumped into the mass graves alive.[51]

Grigorii Erenburg from Bobruisk, Mikhail Treister from Minsk, and many others remember the women who were humiliated in the ghetto, raped, and taken away, never to be seen again. The memory of nightly raids and humiliations witnessed by fourteen-year-old Grigorii before his departure from the Bobruisk ghetto, and the specter of the violence witnessed elsewhere, suggest that Erenburg's imagination of the execution is a protective shield against knowing other pain may have been inflicted on his family. One may even consider the work of shame in Erenburg's repeated reference to his search for knowledge; he and his father left the family behind and thus physically denied themselves the ability to protect them from the terror of humiliation, rape, and murder. "Protector" was a role that men were expected to fulfill, as communicated for instance through Soviet war propaganda.⁵² In the context of German violence, they had to fail to do so in order to survive, yet Erenburg and many others may perceive this as a personal insult and breakdown.⁵³

We do not know how Grigorii Erenburg's mother and siblings died, and probably never will. Their names are not included in the lists of victims compiled by the Extraordinary State Commission, though the lists are by necessity incomplete. Erenburg's search for information, and the image that has to stand in for the details, mark the painful coexistence of knowing and not-knowing, of the presence and absence resulting from destruction. Like him, thousands of others lived on with double death. In German-occupied Belorussia, we may even have to speak of triple death: during Aktion 1005, *Sonderkommando* 1005 (Special Task Force 1005) of the SS was in charge of concentration camp prisoners, ghetto inmates, and others who were to exhume the mass graves left behind by the Einsatzgruppen killings in occupied Eastern Europe and to burn the corpses so as to cover up the mass murders.⁵⁴ These efforts to disguise the killings failed, yet the intent is clear: to obliterate destruction once more. In Bobruisk, Kamenka, and Eloviki, these burnings began in the fall of 1943.⁵⁵

"My second mother"

At the heart of the German occupation regime in Soviet territories was the destruction of Soviet Jewry, accomplished through ghetto incarceration and destruction, mass killings, and antipartisan warfare. In addition, the German genocide regime produced massive population displacement in the occupied territories. The Nazi genocide was embedded in a brutal war against residents of the occupied territories irrespective of their national identity. Especially in the eastern parts of Belorussia, displacement often went along with, or was strategically employed to achieve, a high number of casualties among the civilian population. The Rogachev region, home to Alevtina Kuprikhina, exemplifies this. Kuprikhina's narrative, in many ways fragmentary and incoherent, reproduces in its structure the massive and repeated dislocation experienced by Jews and non-Jews during the occupation.

Survivors' oral histories bring to light, and reflect, the struggle of Soviet society at large to come to terms with the brutality of the German occupation.

The experiences of both Jews and non-Jews in the eastern, less urbanized parts of Belorussia disclose the indiscriminate and unbearable violence Soviet citizens suffered. Attention to attempts by the Soviet state and Soviet society more generally to account for that violence reveals both the close interaction between public and private discourses and the way in which many survivors maintained a positive image of the Soviet state.

Over the course of three years, between the summers of 1941 and 1944, the Rogachev region, located in the Gomel'skaia oblast, lost 51 percent of its prewar population.[56] This loss was felt with particular strength in some areas more than others. For instance, in the village of Zhlobin, home to Alevtina's maternal grandparents, only 20 percent of the prewar population was alive and present when Soviet troops liberated the area in the spring of 1944.[57] Hundreds were rounded up and deported for forced labor in Germany. Jews, Roma, Belorussians, and other non-Jewish locals were shot for real or suspected cooperation with the Soviet partisan movement or for hiding Jews or functionaries of the Soviet administration and Communist Party. Numerous civilians were used as "human shields" for the retreating German army in the last months of the war.[58]

As the war went on, the brutality of German troops was increasingly driven by attempts to curtail the activity of partisans in this area. Gomel' was one of the centers of the movement; up to 16,000 partisans were active in the region's forests and swamps.[59] Locals who were in touch with partisans and supported them by providing food, equipment, or information often also chose to extend their anti-German activity to helping victims of the Nazi extermination policy. Hiding or supporting Jews was thus often an "offense" committed in conjunction with assisting partisans, increasing the risk of detection and punishment. Such people saved Alevtina Kuprikhina, ten years old when German troops occupied Rogachev. Her story reflects regional trends and dynamics of genocide and rescue, and it shows the brutality exerted by the German regime. This violence produced a sense of uncertainty that ended only with the advance of the Soviet army, which, consequently, assumes a stellar role as savior in survivors' accounts.

When the war began, Kuprikhina stayed with her grandparents in Rogachev. Soviet troops and locals were able to hold back German troops until early August 1941, but the confrontation produced many thousands of deaths that summer, and large parts of the city were on fire. Relatively few of the approximately 15,000 residents of the town were able to evacuate.

In part, escape was hindered because, upon final surrender, Soviet troops destroyed the bridges across the river Dnepr, the only route that would have allowed flight away from the German advance. Within a few weeks, the Germans had taken the city, and the approximately 3,000 remaining Jewish residents were confined to their own homes. By September, the nonworkers among them were resettled into the former heating and power plant of the city; others considered employable who were over ten years old were interned in a labor camp in the basement of the former military warehouses. The inmates of this camp were forced to perform often degrading tasks that lacked clear purpose, such as moving piles of sand at the banks of the river from one place to another, and they received no food. The only sources of food were the sparse supplies that the resettled Jews were able to bring with them and some produce and grain that locals outside of the ghetto fence tried to provide. After a short period, all Jews were gathered in the power plant buildings, apparently in preparation for executions. In October, Jews from the surrounding villages were also transferred to this ghetto. The systematic mass killings began in late fall 1941; on November 6, together with Jews from nearby Gomel' and Korma, 2,365 Jews were murdered.[60]

Alevtina's grandmother was among those who died in these early months of the occupation: "Later they told me that my grandmother almost lost her mind, she looked for me everywhere, our house was set on fire, she dug through the ruins with her bare hands, then she was killed. That's what people told me later."[61] The young girl lived through the day she lost her grandmother in a state of panic. She frantically tried to find the woman, searching for her caretaker in a town that had been bombed by the Soviet army to hold back German troops:

> The town was on fire. I went, I was not afraid, nothing, I looked for our house—and I couldn't find it. Across from the house was a bunker, and so I figured out where our house was. The corners were still hot, I cried and looked for my grandmother. Rogachev was bombed by Soviet troops, because Germans entered the town, and so I went to the Stalin school, I was really hungry and was exhausted. I sat down on the stairs of the school and fell asleep.[62]

Like young Frida Ped'ko, Alevtina was unable to fathom that she had lost the one person who had cared for her, and searched in vain for her all over town. A German soldier picked her up and took her in, sheltering her for an unspecified period of time. However, he offered his support only after he had established that Alla was not a Jewish child:

> We got there, and I saw that they were taking everything apart, some were in the library, screamed "Moskau kaputt! Stalingrad kaputt!" and such things. That was all very interesting, I was a very curious child, and all of a sudden a door opens and I noticed that the German got nervous. He pushed me into that door, closed it and left. There were two older officers, with a radio, and they started asking me, 'Jude? Rus?' But I remembered that movie and said, 'Rus'. He slapped me on my shoulder and said, 'Gut gut', and motioned me to exit through the door.[63]

The elderly Kuprikhina explained that she knew to lie because she had watched *Professor Mamlock*, a 1938 Soviet film based on the German writer Konrad Wolf's play about the Nazi regime's increasingly aggressive antisemitic policies in 1930s Germany.[64] Once Alla had passed the interrogation by other German officials, the officer took her to the trenches where other Germans were, supplied her with food, and built a shelter. "He watched me at all times and made sure I wasn't going anywhere, that I wasn't talking to anyone, that no one saw me. They dug a little pit and built something like a tent, and there I slept."[65] Eventually, the soldier's division moved on, and he asked a local woman in the nearby village of Kolosy, Anastasia Ustinovna Tristsenetskaia, to take in young Alla. Alla had a hard time letting go of this man who replaced her absent family: "I ran after them, I clung to his leg, screamed, 'Uncle, don't leave me behind.'"[66] The elderly Alevtina Kuprikhina suspected that the German was a Communist and interested in supporting Soviet resistance against the occupation. This may explain why the soldier chose to drop off the girl at a Belorussian woman's house. Tristsenetskaia had already been under scrutiny by German authorities; she had been arrested and jailed by the Gestapo. This persecution is likely related to her son Kolia's involvement with a partisan group. Kolia frequently left the house for the woods, and, among other acts, helped shelter a number of youth from the town in a dugout outside of the village. "There was a whole trench full of youngsters, I was the only girl, but Kolia took care of me."[67] Finally, Kolia had to leave the village and remain with the partisans because a search warrant had been issued. When the German antipartisan warfare intensified, it was too dangerous for the woman to keep Alla, and she asked a partisan unit stationed nearby to take her in as well.

Tristsenetskaia and her son took an immense risk, both by being involved with the partisans and by hiding Jews and others. A report from nearby Staraia Dubrova, 150 km to the west of Rogachev, shows the brutality with which German troops searched for and punished families involved with the partisans. In 1944, the resident Nadezhda Alekseevna Zhulega reported to the Soviet Army a number of German atrocities, including the killing of a woman whose husband had been with the partisans:

> Someone denounced the family of the partisan Semen Odinets, i.e. his wife Matriona and her four children who were all sick with typhus. to a so-called punitive squad in April 1944. The troops stormed her *zemlianka* [dugout] and started beating up the ill woman, then they cut off her nose, her ears, trying to force her to say where her husband is. She did not say anything and so they stabbed her to death and killed the children.[68]

Were the Germans to have discovered the Jewish girl Alevtina and the other youth in hiding, Anastasia Tristsenetskaia would likely have suffered in similar ways. Many Soviet children were rounded up by the Germans and abused as blood donors for wounded German military, or included in the deportations for forced labor.[69] Hiding them thus constituted a crime as well, and those who tried to protect them were subjected to severe punishment if discovered.

Despite these threats and examples, there were many hundreds of Belorussians who did what they could to rescue adolescents, Jewish or not. Parichi, a town about thirty miles from Rogachev and eight miles from Grigorii Erenburg parents' hometown Shchedrin, exemplifies these efforts in a unique way. Like Rogachev, the town withstood German occupation until August 1941, but many homes were destroyed or damaged by then. Out of 1,881 Jews, more than half were unable to evacuate and stayed. Once Parichi was in German hands, the Jewish residents were brutally abused and received no food rations at all, and even those who were forced to work suffered from intense starvation. In October, 1,013 Jewish men and women of all ages were summarily shot because, as the report of the Einsatzgruppe B states, "they displayed a hostile attitude toward the Germans and had close links to the partisans."[70] This was a typical phrase used to justify the mass murder of Jewish civilians. The number of victims might be even higher; the Soviet Extraordinary Commission reports that "up to 1,500" people were shot in the fall of 1941.[71]

In late fall 1943, however, a new Jewish presence developed in Parichi. At that time, a small stream of refugees from the Minsk and other ghettos reached the settlement. In several groups, forty children arrived. The local residents adopted them and put them up, individually or in groups of two or three, in their own homes. Partisans in the surrounding swamp helped to supply food. They also helped to evacuate the whole population into the nearby forest when German troops attacked the settlement or when the fighting intensified during the Soviet army's operation to liberate the area in 1944.[72] All forty children survived until summer 1944.

Staraia Dubrova, Parichi, Zhlobin, and Rogachev exemplify the sharply contrasting elements of living through the German occupation. On the one hand, there was unprecedented brutality against civilians, because they were Jews or Roma, because they (allegedly) supported partisans, because they were Soviet citizens. On the other hand, there were the numerous people, civilians, partisans, or soldiers, who readily exposed themselves to retaliation by rescuing threatened children, Jews, and others.

The German regime's unscrupulous use of violence and military force against the Soviet population peaked in early winter and spring 1944. At that time, the German army and Einsatzgruppen drove the residents of Zhlobin out of their homes in the direction of Bobruisk. They were loaded onto freight trains that took them to open spaces in the middle of the frosty swamp. Barbed wire surrounded hundreds of people who formed a human buffer between German and Soviet troops.[73] In addition, persons suffering from typhus were placed in the middle of the overcrowded camps. A confession by a collaborator confirms what survivors suspected: the Germans intended to spread typhus among the civilians and the Soviet troops who would liberate the region and thereby weaken their force.[74] These camps and horrific forms of biological warfare resulted in thousands of casualties. People died of illness, but also starvation, or because they were shot for attempting to retrieve food or water. Inmates of these camps were largely women, children, and the elderly, a pattern familiar from the ghetto: most men of working age were serving in the army, had left to join the partisan movement, or had been arrested, sent away, or killed by the occupation authorities or the German army. In some way, these operations resembled other attempts to erase witnesses to the German genocide regime by covering up the traces of the mass murder. Whereas in Zhlobin, Ozarichi, and elsewhere the living witnesses—the local residents—were murdered or left to die, in Parichi or Shchedrin local residents and prisoners of war were ordered to exhume the mass graves from the mass killings since 1941 and burn the corpses.

The dead of the last months of the war included people, many of them women, who took care of children, both their own and orphans. Soviet authorities thus faced yet another wave of displaced and violated adolescents who required attention and support. Many in the generation of Alevtina Kuprikhina thus shared the experience of living in orphanages: between 1943 and 1945, reception centers in the USSR processed more than 840,000 children who had lost their families to war and genocide or whose families were unable to provide for them, among them 17,200 children of military personnel and partisans alone.[75]

Kuprikhina's experience resembles those of many Soviet youths, Jewish or not, and thus requires attention: she was rescued by non-Jews in the occupied territories, and further survived war and genocide in the care of state institutions. Her and Frida Ped'ko's narratives, witness statements collected at the end of the war, and many other sources thus not surprisingly align in one aspect: emphatic gratitude to the Soviet army. Whereas the statements of 1944 include direct thanks to the soldiers interviewing the survivors, Alevtina and others mention in interviews long after the war their sparkling memories of Victory Day, May 9, 1945, when Jewish and non-Jewish citizens alike celebrated, cried, and began to hope for the return of loved ones. Alevtina Kuprikhina, who had been relocated to an orphanage for teenagers in the Ukraine, remembers the day vividly: "I can't tell you how exciting it was. I had very good friends there, we lived together in a dorm room. We shared everything. . . . And at the day of victory, all these trucks and vans, people threw flowers, so many flowers, people were so happy!"[76]

What is more, this moment marks the point in the interview after which her narrative became much more coherent and ordered. The end of the war thus signals a turn away from the highly mobile and problematic sequence of displacement and violation during the occupation. The testimony produced by VHA and my own interview with Kuprikhina both include strong references to the only wartime fixtures of her life, the two individuals who provided, albeit temporary, shelter and protection. Both the German soldier and

Anastasia Tristsenetskaia are identified as surrogate relatives: the German, Kuprikhina remembers, was like an uncle, the Belorussian woman a "second mother."[77] These entangled relationships, perhaps at least partially a result of imagination, result in part from the destruction of familial cohesion.

At the end of the war, Kuprikhina managed to find her paternal grandparents in Sverdlovsk. They had survived because they had been evacuated as workers of the factory that her grandfather directed. However, in 1945, they, like many other Soviet citizens affected by the postwar famine, were struggling to find enough food for themselves. Fourteen-year-old Alevtina therefore decided that she and they would be better off if she returned to an orphanage:

> When grandmother came home from work and found me in her living room—did we cry! It was a nightmare! It was horrible. Many others who had been evacuated from Leningrad came over, they were so happy to see a child from Leningrad that had survived. ... But then I realized that the grandparents had nothing to eat. A loaf of bread sold for 500 rubles. What should I do? So I went to the city administration and asked them to place me in an orphanage.[78]

Several years after the war, Alevtina Kuprikhina found her father; he had entered a new relationship and lived in Leningrad. She remembers the encounter as rather distant: "He was of course very surprised, 'You are alive? I thought the Germans had killed you!' He had never inquired about me, did not concern himself with this, but I loved him very much. So we met."[79] In the interview with me, she did not mention this encounter at all—the connection with Solomon Igol'nikov was effectively destroyed. Alevtina Kuprikhina was also unable to reunite with her mother: Kuprikhina's mother served in the Soviet army and did not return after the war. Like thousands of others, she is listed as "missing in action." Up until late in life, Alevtina regularly went to the gatherings on May 9 near the front line in Krasnoe Selo, where she was informed that her mother's regiment was destroyed by the German adversary. Like many other Soviet citizens, she would display a picture of her mother, asking passersby and other attendees and veterans for information. She never learned her mother's fate.[80]

Alevtina Kuprikhina's story of survival is complex and characterized by movement, shifting alliances, and risks. As an adolescent she may not have registered these changes, but in hindsight they make her trajectory difficult to organize. Structure and orientation are provided by individuals, and finally by Soviet institutions such as the partisan movement and orphanages. The former are thus integrated into a concept of an extended family, the latter never lost their shine. Both challenge common understandings of the Nazi genocide, highlighting, firstly, images of Germans by noting how individuals, even if all too few, chose to act against ideological indoctrination and military order, and secondly, why for survivors of World War II in the Soviet Union the Soviet regime deserves to be recognized and defended.

The Nazi genocide as triple death

Frida Ped'ko, who had imagined how it feels to be shot; Amaliia Iakhontova, who had tried to revive her bleeding mother when she was shot in their home in Minsk; Grigorii Erenburg, who does not know where his family was killed; and Samuil Volk, who had seen his mother and siblings walking to the execution site—they all carried, and carry, disturbing images of death. Survival in the absence of relatives or caretakers depended on various factors, including the help of others and, eventually, escaping spaces controlled by the occupation regime. Close relationships to others, siblings or other peers, proved essential to emotional and physical survival, as we shall see in following chapters, in partisan units as much as in hiding. Sometimes locals were willing to support ghetto refugees, even if that meant endangering their own lives. The history and perception of these relationships remains an open field for exploration, as does the struggle for survival in ghettos like Slavnoe. In the former shtetl, only ten Jewish residents survived the extermination of both the Jewish population and local Jewish history and culture. It may thus be impossible to comprehend how Jewish and non-Jewish residents lived there together under conditions of extreme violence, and how Jews managed to survive genocide. The near complete absence of records that describe life in the ghetto, the destruction of the local synagogue as well as witnesses to Jewish life in the area—only exacerbated by the passing of survivors and eyewitnesses in the time since the end of the war—are powerful forces that make writing this history very difficult.

The oral histories of survivors are invaluable sources for attempting to understand what happened. They identify those who died, how they lived before war and genocide, and how they attempted to survive against it. At the same time, they are limited in their capacity to give an exact and comprehensive account of events. In conjunction with other sources, however, the narratives of Frida Ped'ko, Alevtina Kuprikhina, Grigorii Erenburg, and Boris Gal'perin show the effects of systematic humiliation and violence on individuals and communities. They do so on two levels. First, they entail important markers to reconstruct events, providing a scaffold for explaining how individuals of a specific age, gender, and nationality experienced the German occupation of eastern Belorussia. And second, a close look at their narratives, at fragments and insecurities reveals the effects of destruction on individuals' abilities to make sense of mass murder and to live in its aftermath. Images are used to frame experiences in a familiar way, even if they may not have a basis in reality, and thus play a crucial role in enabling the survivor to live on after destruction and talk about them. Notions of motherhood, women's and children's vulnerability, and substitute families are at the center of their descriptions.

The survivors' difficulty in representing the Nazi genocide in Soviet territories reflects ongoing struggles among scholars and artists. Several Soviet Jewish writers tried to develop adequate literary forms to account for Nazi destruction and genocide. And again, mothers are central figures for authors' ruminations about the intricacies of witnessing. For instance Vasily Grossman's works *For a Just Cause* and *Life and Fate* strongly relate to his own family's destruction and are works of history and commemoration simultaneously.[81] We cannot miss the similar prominence of mothers and family connections in the oral histories introduced here. The older family members remembered by Ped'ko and others signify the speakers' past as well as their future. Their destruction unmistakably took away parts of the speakers' own past and future, and their narratives highlight the gaps and shards that were indefinite elements of their lives. Understanding these helps us to understand the violence and how individuals responded to it. While we cannot see or hear the violence, we can and must pay attention to its effects and consequences, as they provide a window into the workings of cruelty.[82]

On a different, yet related note, the memories reflect the impact of postwar and recent experiences on survivors' narratives. Frida Ped'ko's reluctance, both as child and adult, to pinpoint the absence of the mother and main caretaker of a family is, in part, related to her own postwar biography. After the war, Frida Ped'ko completed a professional degree and occupied leading positions in a production facility while also raising a family.[83] That her mother, who had joined the Communist Party and participated in modernizing the village cooperative, should have been unable to develop a similarly successful career as worker and mother was perhaps too much to bear. Ped'ko's history and narrative thus reflect the crushed hopes of an eager parental generation and her own disappointment about, and shock at, the violent end to their aspirations.

During one of many interviews, Grigorii Erenburg mentioned that, for a short time, he joined the Jewish survivor association's efforts to commemorate and educate people about the Nazi genocide by creating a small museum. He quit shortly thereafter, because "I always left there in pain; I thought, what if at some point I see my mother in a picture." The images of women and children at the shooting pits drove him out.[84] Whereas he and his father never exactly found out what happened to their relatives, these photos showed what might have been, in a stark and irrefutable visual form. In the absence of concrete information, they now stand in and occupy the man's imagination about how his mother and siblings died. The notion of post-memory among second-generation survivors (the offspring of survivors), whereby photographs substitute for personal memories and transmit traumatic experience, thus applies to members of the survivor generation themselves; Grigorii Erenburg is, by all measures, a survivor of the Nazi genocide.[85] Nonetheless, his memories and narrative reflect the impact of images that are prominent in museums, films, and other visual forms of representing or commemorating the genocide, but do not necessarily reproduce his own experience. Thus, other people's representations and the culturally available material visualizing the past affect the relationship between historical experience and memory.

The impact of postwar experiences and discourses, especially those related to a collectively shared experience, is further obvious in Alevtina Kuprikhina's account. Her narrative reflects the impact of extreme violence, producing fragmented lives that are difficult to comprehend. It further centers on the substitute families or individuals who take on the role of personal caretakers. In emphasizing the roles of strangers and the state in the upbringing of children, Kuprikhina is one of 2.5 million Soviet children who lost their families during World War II and between 1945 and 1953 were placed in Soviet orphanages or, later, were adopted by other citizens.[86] Her insecurity about her mother's fate, and her inability to find out what happened to her, mirrors that of about a million Soviet families who never learned where, how, or even if their relatives who were in the military died.[87]

What unites Ped'ko's, Erenburg's, and Kuprikhina's lives is that they were never able to find conclusive information about their loved ones' fate. Mourning and remembering were thus doubly problematic. They included not only the loss of a person but also a void created by the absence of knowledge. The impact of German policies to disguise murder, from locals as well as from the victims themselves, thus reaches far beyond the actual moment of committing violence. The perpetrators of genocide intended to produce double death by targeting "not only a type of human being, but also [depriving] a people ... of their generations," that is of those who mourn each other's deaths.[88] This "murder of death" was radicalized by the practices used by Nazi administrators to devalue death and to deny the ability to mark death. In an escalation of the double death of denying the possibility of mourning, as in Amaliia Iakhontova's case, the unearthing and burning of mass graves constitutes a triple death. The Nazi genocide in eastern Belorussia is thus not only a catastrophe in history, but also a catastrophe for memory.

5

Fighting for Life and Victory

Refugees from the Ghettos and the Soviet Partisan Movement

"Nobody knew about my existence. And I didn't know about them either, only then [in 1948] did I learn that they were alive."[1] Leonid Gol'braikh describes here his struggles to find his relatives and rebuild his life following the German occupation of Soviet Belorussia. Gol'braikh was an orphan; his mother and two sisters had been killed, his father was missing in action, and a distant uncle had no idea that he was among the few survivors of Beshenkovichi, a small town in the eastern part of Soviet Belorussia. With few exceptions, German Einsatzgruppen had killed the 1,100 or so Jews of the town.[2] Gone was the prewar community of Beshenkovichi, where Belorussians and Jews lived rather peacefully together, as Gol'braikh says: there "had been no hatred toward the Jews . . . Belorussians understood or even spoke Yiddish."[3] But in early February 1942, a German Einsatzkommando surrounded the makeshift ghetto of Beshenkovichi, assembled its inmates, and drove them, on foot, to an execution site on the outskirts of town. Eleven-year-old Leonid Gol'braikh managed to slip out of the column of people and run away: "I went to this family, ten kilometers away, and I made it there only at night, because I tried to avoid the villages and settlements. I arrived there in the middle of the night, I was in such a state, I was shivering violently. The woman held me in her arms for the whole night."[4] Foma and Elena Kuiko, family friends who lived in the village of Svecha, took care of Leonid for several days. Eventually the boy had to move on, since other residents who also knew him from before the war may have reported him to the Germans. By the fall of 1942, after almost ten months, Gol'braikh made contact with partisans. Initially, the partisans asked him only to scout out the village—he does not remember its name—and its surroundings while he was working as a herdsman, but eventually they admitted him into the detachment, where he remained until the summer of 1944.

Leonid Gol'braikh, like thousands of other young Jewish Belorussians—many of them orphans—had limited options for survival during the German occupation. The systematic and summary killings of Jews, as well as the ongoing war, left little opportunity for rescue operations within or outside of the ghettos. Gol'braikh ultimately survived because he was able to join a Soviet partisan detachment, a group of guerilla fighters who had gathered in the woods. Significantly though, it was not the Jew "Leonid Gol'braikh" who shared the experiences of about 100 men and a very few women, but the Belorussian "Leonid Vasilevich Andrichenko."[5] The unit commander, Mikhail Sol'nikov, had recommended that Leonid change his name and disguise his national Jewish identity from his comrades.[6] The use of this pseudonym, ironically, erased the main reason for Leonid's partisan involvement—escaping and surviving the German anti-Jewish genocide.

Gol'braikh's statement that "nobody knew about his existence" could have described the situation of young Soviet Jews within Soviet society both during and after the war more generally, where to exist as a Jew meant negotiating being simultaneously present and absent. On the one hand, Gol'braikh's experiences speak to the Soviet state's ability to provide stability and orientation in a context of destruction and displacement. On the other hand, the Soviet government promoted a form of Soviet patriotism that pushed rights to national particularity and distinction to the margins. One of the dramatic effects of this policy was the refusal of the partisan leadership to combat anti-Jewish behavior among Soviet citizens or to acknowledge the Nazis' particular targeting of Soviet Jews. Gol'braikh's pseudonym served not only to protect but to obscure, effectively writing the experience of the young Jew out of the history and memory of the Great Patriotic War and the Soviet partisan movement: the facts that Jews were both singled out for murder and, in some cases, survived the Nazi genocide by joining and making significant contributions to the Soviet partisan movement disappeared.

The deliberate indifference of the Soviet government to the plight of Jews under the Nazi occupation found a dramatic continuation in the outright denial of a Jewish woman's participation in the Minsk underground movement. Elena Drapkina had barely finished telling me about her own wartime experiences during our first encounter when she began to tell me about her friend Masha Bruskina. The story of sixteen-year-old Bruskina is a tragic and well-publicized example of a Soviet postwar politics that attempted to erase the Jewish experience from official portrayals of the war.

As a member of a small group of Soviet citizens who helped captured Red Army soldiers to flee Minsk, Masha was denounced and arrested in the fall of 1941. On October 26, 1941, twelve members of the group were killed in the first public execution of anti-German activists. Pictures of Masha's execution, by hanging—together with sixteen-year-old Volodia Shcherbatsevich and forty-plus-year-old Kirill Trus'—are a staple of accounts which depict both German brutality and Soviet postwar antisemitism. In contrast to the two men, Masha's name was not listed at a memorial erected in the 1960s in Minsk; she was only identified as "young woman/name unknown." Belorussian authorities agreed to correct the plaque only after several decades of protest by survivors and friends of Masha's, among them Elena Drapkina, and numerous scholars' interventions. This late recognition, in 2008, brought to an end the denial on the part of the Soviet and post-Soviet states that a Jewish woman played a crucial role in underground and resistance efforts.[7]

Masha Bruskina's actions challenged preconceived notions of both female and Jewish passivity, especially the idea that Jews "went like sheep to the slaughter." Evidence of their resistance needed to be silenced in order to maintain the illusion. Masha Bruskina's denial of recognition and honor as a member of the Minsk underground is certainly a result of the antisemitic campaigns that gripped Soviet society beginning in the late 1940s. In the early postwar decades, governmental authorities restricted Jews' ability to mourn their dead as victims of a genocide specifically targeting Jews. They also denied the existence of antisemitism within, and complicity in the genocide on the part of, the Soviet population during the war.[8] Moreover, the denial of Bruskina's achievements reflects a general tendency in the postwar USSR to deny or marginalize female participation in the anti-German effort. A few female snipers and pilots, most of whom died during the war, were included in official Soviet accounts of the war, but in general, women were portrayed as grieving mothers or persons in need of protection.[9] Bruskina's upright posture while walking to her execution contradicted images of both cowardly Jews and helpless women, which was perhaps another reason for Soviet authorities to obscure the real person involved in sabotage and resistance.[10]

Furthermore, the case of Masha Bruskina demonstrates a particular aggression against Jews. The pictures and stories about her were always there, but publicly her identity was covered up. The case thus mirrors Leonid Gol'braikh's experience of being hidden in plain sight: here the woman who is there but not named, there the Jew who is there but not named. The initial denial of Leonid Golbraikh's existence of course took place during the war, but it was extended in the postwar period when Jewish contributions to the Soviet partisan movement were silenced among the Soviet public. The two cases of marginalization are thus conjoined in the moment of memory, but draw both on, and refer us to, specific historical experiences of gendered Soviet Jewish subjects during the war.

How did people like Leonid Gol'braikh and Elena Drapkina—people who, or whose close ones, were denied proper identification and thus recognition in the historical record—deal with the fact that they were both part of the unified Soviet struggle against the Nazi genocide and regularly reminded of their precarious status as not quite Soviet enough? Jews and women found that the officially promoted brotherhood of Soviet people did not quite apply to them. Jews often had to disguise their national identity and assume non-Jewish names. Women and girls were often relegated to kitchen labor or medical service for partisan units, without the opportunity to choose otherwise. And many women were pushed into sexual relationships they did not want. Postwar accounts of the partisan movement regularly omitted women's participation, or alleged that any women associated with the partisans were prostitutes. Partisan detachments integrated ghetto refugees into the Soviet war effort, but they also showed that promises of gender equality and interethnic solidarity, so important for many citizens in the prewar period, were hollow, even within the realm of a movement that, by 1942, was officially led by the Communist Party.

This simultaneous assimilation and exclusion raises a question: how are experiences of marginalization written out of history? Rather than rehearse arguments about discrimination against Jews in the Soviet military and partisan movement and their exclusion from official histories—which has been rectified to some extent by non-Soviet scholars—I shift the focus and ask, how did people experience the tension of their simultaneous inclusion and exclusion?[11] How do they construct a narrative of their past, a past that has been the subject of ideological and cultural interpretation for more than six decades? The survivors whom I interviewed were constructing personal narratives of wartime experience against the backdrop of Soviet war portrayals that favored Soviet masculine heroism and downplayed the experiences of nonhegemonic nationalities and female activity.[12] The memories of former partisans demonstrate the significance of deliberate silence for producing fragmented histories and further the exploration of incomplete historical reconstruction.

Several youths managed to escape death and the ghetto in eastern parts of Belorussia in the winter and spring of 1942. Boris Gal'perin (Ryzhkovichi), Alla Kuprikhina (Rogachev), Grigorii Erenburg (Bobruisk), and Elena Drapkina (Minsk) were admitted to one of the several hundred partisan units emerging in the forests and swamps of Nazi-occupied Belorussia, each to a different one. Often considered too young to participate in partisan combat, ghetto refugees nonetheless participated in dangerous military operations as messengers or scouts, by planting bombs, or assisting in supply and maintenance detachments as cooks and nurses.

In particular, Gal'perin's and Drapkina's accounts are examples of how narration itself can produce (and reproduce) lacunae in the histories we are able to write by deliberately not naming specific people—women—or experiences determined by the subjects' gender identity. While Ped'ko, Erenburg, and Kuprikhina have no certainty about their mothers' fates, Gal'perin chooses not to mention his mother except in an addendum to an otherwise detailed description of his activities in a partisan detachment that he and his mother joined together. Drapkina's oral history, in turn, proposes a closer look at gender and sexual relationships, especially among partisans, pointing to how the Soviet concept of morality limits the possibility of speaking about them publicly.

These stories help develop a framework to understand the mindset of Soviet Jews who participated in the Soviet partisan movements and dealt with varying forms of discrimination. For them, the passionate desire to defeat the Nazi regime overrode conflicts within the partisan movement. Loyalty to this movement which, together with the Soviet army, helped end war and genocide produced forms of self-censorship about negative elements of their experience, including the anti-Jewish and sexist behavior of other partisans. The image of heroic Soviet partisans could therefore persist untainted. We confront here a dynamic of historical representation specific to Soviet war memory, but also a more general social pattern in the Soviet Union, where citizens operated with different biographical self-representations carefully constructed for different occasions.

Jewish resistance and the Soviet partisan movement

When Elena Drapkina left the Minsk ghetto in late July 1942, she did so with only scant information and hope. A fellow worker had told the seventeen-year-old that she might find shelter and work in one of the many farm households to the west of Minsk. Drapkina is convinced that the farmer recognized her as a Jew when she arrived at the farmstead, despite the passport that identified her as the Pole Iadviga Aleksandrovna Skrotskaia: "the farmer knew who I was, I had thick black hair."[13] Nevertheless, the farmer took her in as a housemaid. A few days later, Elena ran into a small group of Soviet parachutists who had been deployed to the area to set up a partisan unit in the rear of the German front line, efforts that the NKVD had undertaken since late summer 1941.[14] Convincing them of her intention and desire to take revenge against the Germans, Elena, now eighteen, became a partisan and joined her comrades in combat operations for the following two years.

Young Elena was one of a few refugees from the Minsk ghetto who succeeded in joining a partisan unit. Of the 6,000 to 10,000 people who were able to escape the Minsk ghetto, most left much later than the summer of 1942, and many young Jews fled between spring and October 1943, when the ghetto was finally destroyed.[15] The majority of them found refuge and purpose in the newly established partisan detachment No. 106, a so-called family unit under the leadership of Shalom Zorin. The unit provided a safe haven for several hundred civilians—men, women, children, and the elderly—and, through their work, acquired a crucial role within the Soviet partisan movement. (Life in a family unit will be described in detail in the following chapter.) Others, like Elena, joined so-called combat units, formations that focused on sabotage operations against German infrastructure and personnel.

The uneven development of opportunities to escape the ghettos in Minsk and elsewhere was rooted in the state of war and occupation, the ability and will of the Soviet partisan movement to admit ghetto refugees, and changing opportunities for, and preparedness of, Jews to leave the ghetto and traverse large distances across the countryside. Escape from the ghetto and survival in a partisan unit were thus circumscribed by the effects of nationality policy (both German and Soviet), military conflict, and Soviet political and military agendas. They also indicate that Jews in German-occupied Soviet territories tried to undermine the German murder campaign in various ways—a story that is all too often discussed solely under the rubric of "resistance," a term that comes with preconceived notions of military and armed rebellion and often overshadows more mundane acts of self-preservation and rescue.

The history of Jewish resistance against the Nazi genocide in Belorussia, in fact, is yet to be written.[16] In the early postwar decades, the portrayal of Jewish resistance to systematic annihilation primarily aimed to show that accusations that Jews had willingly given themselves to their murderers were invalid and unfounded. Thus, many authors highlighted Jewish groups that acquired arms to engage German troops and their collaborators in military form.[17] Over subsequent decades, this celebration of heroic fighters willing to die in battle to preserve "Jewish honor" gave way to more comprehensive approaches to Jewish responses to the genocide. Consequently, referencing the notion of *amidah* (literally 'standing up, stand'), life-saving strategies or attempts to preserve Jewish culture, must be included in studies of Jewish resistance. Incorporating, for instance, "smuggling food into ghettos; ... cultural, educational, religious, and political activities taken to strengthen morale; the work of doctors, nurses, and educators to consciously maintain health and moral fiber ... and ... armed rebellion or the use of force (with bare hands or with 'cold' weapons) against the Germans and their collaborators" allows us to go beyond a one-sided view that focuses on Jewish armed resistance and the participation of Jews in the Soviet armed forces.[18] The latter is important in order to deconstruct stereotypes that portray Jewish survivors of the German occupation as passive and cowardly.[19]

However, it is equally important to consider the particular challenges experienced by individuals who differed in age, gender, social background, or physical stature from regular combatants in order to blur the distinction between "survivors" and "resisters," i.e., fighters. Such differentiation conjures up notions of heroism that juxtapose self-sacrifice and efforts to save lives with armed combat and that place excessive ethical and ideological demands on the shoulders of people who had very little choice and opportunity. If we try to define "resistance" based on what people were working against, the destruction of Soviet Jews, one ought to focus on the interplay between efforts to save lives and the eventual destruction of the occupation regime. Jewish responses in the occupied Soviet Belorussian territories included collectively planned assaults on German military, SS, and collaborating police forces that also coincided with rescue attempts.

Inmates of the ghettos in Slonim, Nesvizh, Kopyl', Mir, Kamenets, Białystok, Glubokoe, Novogrudok, Kobrin, Liakhovichi, and Derechin built and procured weapons; and people in the ghettos of Disna, Druia, Sharkovshchina, and Nesvizh set houses on fire to prevent or obstruct killing actions.[20] These efforts were always "planned for the eve of the certain, complete destruction of the ghetto, when an uprising was the only alternative to going to the pits to be shot."[21] Where an uprising seemed unlikely to organize, flight was the only other option. Other than in Minsk, mass escapes took place especially in western Belorussia, such as in Gantsevichi, Novogrudok, Kletsk, Nesvizh, and Slonim, and were at times supported by partisan detachments.[22] Overall, between 30,000 and 50,000 Jews fled from the ghettos in Belorussia and tried to hide in the forests.[23]

In the beginning, partisan units were primarily comprised of Soviet soldiers trapped behind the front line. Later they included civilians who escaped German rule. The movement played an important role in the Soviet military campaign against Germany. In addition to groups consisting of Soviet citizens of different national identities, there were groups formed exclusively by Jews, for instance those founded by Lev Gil'chik, Kirill Orlovskii, Boris Gindin, Israel Lapidus, Pavel Proniagin, and Hirsh Kaplinsky, who assembled primarily male Jews who wanted to take up arms against the German occupants.[24] Overall, a recent estimate suggests that up to 345,000 Jews—14,000 in Belorussia alone—participated in the Soviet partisan movement.[25] For Jews, the partisan movement provided a space of safety outside of the ghetto. Moreover, Jewish participation in the movement highlights the fact that the murder of the Jews was embedded in a war that targeted a whole population. While Soviet Jews responded to a campaign targeting them as Jews, they also responded to an assault on them as Soviet citizens and thereby joined thousands of other people. They did so based on their personal ability and outlook, and within the framework of developing conflicts within Soviet society, especially conflicts involving anti-Jewish hostility. In order to study Jewish responses and resistance in this area, it is thus imperative to account for this complexity, and the following pages on Jews in combat formations of the Soviet partisan movement should be read in combination with the following chapter on a so-called family unit almost exclusively harboring Jews.

German troops invaded the Soviet Union in June 1941. They quickly occupied large portions of the Belorussian republic, surrounding thousands of Soviet soldiers along with the majority of the civilian population. Between June and September 1941, up to 2,050,000 Soviet soldiers were either killed or taken prisoner, most often in makeshift camps surrounded by barbed wire. There, inmates slept on bare soil, starved, and were often shot indiscriminately.[26] Only a comparatively small number of Soviet soldiers managed to evade capture. Some dumped their uniforms and began working on local farms; several hundred retreated into swamps and forests. Some of these scattered individuals created new groups, acquired food and clothing, and were the first to call themselves "partisans." They also responded to the Soviet government's call to local party officials in June and July of 1941 to organize partisan struggle against the occupation in locales where topography and support from the local population allowed them to do so.[27] For Jews like Leonid Gol'braikh, Boris Gal'perin, or Grigorii Erenburg, however, joining the partisans was very difficult.

First, it was problematic for Jews to move about freely within and outside of towns. Even if Germans did not use yellow patches or stars to easily identify and track Jews, local residents might identify their former neighbors, colleagues, and even friends to the Germans. Further, large parts of Belorussia remained war territory; while civilian administrations governed the western parts of Belorussia, the east continued to be administered by the military. This area was populated by German soldiers, police, and Einsatzgruppen—all permanently prepared to arrest, punish, and kill whomever they perceived as inimical to the German "war for living space." The constant presence of combat-ready troops made leaving the ghetto particularly dangerous. Moreover, many chose to remain in the ghettos rather than plan for an insecure future in the forests and countryside. Some hoped "that people would just be sent to other places to work."[28] Others refused to abandon family members.

Moreover, Soviet authorities instructed partisans to collaborate only with trustworthy individuals—specifically, individuals for whom the unit could establish party or Komsomol membership, or other evidence of loyalty to the regime.[29] Obviously, this policy was rooted in a fear of engaging with spies and traitors who would undermine partisan efforts. In practice, however, the policies excluded any civilian searching for refuge from the occupation who could not draw upon previous connections with military or party members. Essentially, this cast suspicion on anyone other than young male soldiers or loyal party members, including women, youths, suspected *kulaks* (affluent peasants), and people previously convicted of anti-Soviet behavior.[30] The anticivilian attitude of Soviet partisans disproportionally affected Jewish civilians, since Jews were more likely to leave their hometowns and to look for shelter elsewhere.

More civilians—Jewish and non-Jewish alike—were integrated into the partisan movement after it was reorganized under central commands and a Central Staff. The Communist Party appointed Panteleimon Ponomarenko the movement's leader in May 1942.[31] In addition to Ponomarenko's Central Staff, there were separate central command staffs in each of the German-occupied Soviet republics and, subordinate to these, regional command structures. In Belorussia, the Party ran ten provincial, seventeen interregional, eight city, two city-regional, and 166 regional committees to help steer partisan activity.[32] In the forests near Mogilev and elsewhere, the Party established training centers, where future partisans were introduced to such techniques and rationales of guerilla warfare as how to build and place mines or pursue intelligence missions.[33] Dispersed soldiers of the Soviet Army and volunteers from occupied territories enlisted in these centers to join guerilla groups located in swamp and forest areas. Meanwhile, thousands of untrained locals saw the partisans as their only hope of evading German brutality and asked for admission.

In September 1942, Stalin declared a "People's War" and ordered the partisan movement to incorporate any female or male Soviet citizen willing to fight. Another order from May 1, 1943, requested partisans to protect Soviet citizens, an order that may well have resulted from the recognition that partisans and the Soviet army were unable to protect local village populations from the terror of the occupation.[34] And yet, despite the partisan movement's increasingly powerful Central Staff pressing for the admission of women, Jews, other minorities, and people of various physical capabilities, partisans persisted in scrutinizing Jewish refugees' attempts to find protection. This attitude marked a problematic coalescence of security considerations, antisemitic prejudice, and, in many cases, sexist attitudes that created dangerous and challenging spaces for people like Leonid Gol'braikh, Boris Gal'perin, and Elena Drapkina, who had nowhere else to go and possessed little to no military training that would have equipped them with immediately recognizable skills. Nonetheless, once they were admitted, they learned how to handle weapons, live outdoors, and stand their ground against not only German enemies but also Soviet citizens who tried to abuse their precarious status. Their stories have much to tell about the individual challenges experienced by youths and women who were part of a movement that, in Belorussia, counted more than 240,000.³⁵

"Childhood, scorched by war"

Boris Gal'perin's father was drafted by the Soviet military when the German invasion began. Following his departure, Boris and his mother, along with other farmers, attempted to evacuate the kolkhoz's cattle, but they were forced to return to their hometown on July 11, 1941. For young Boris the occupation began as a test of his patriotism:

> My personal hero was Ded Talash (Grandfather Talash), a Belorussian partisan during the Civil War, and like I had been taught before, for about five days I did not remove the portraits of V. I. Lenin and K. E. Voroshilov in my corner.³⁶ Only when some Germans came into the house and one of them kicked me with his boots and yelled "Bolshevik!" I took them and threw them onto the floor. When the Germans had left, I took the portraits and hid them carefully in the attic.³⁷

Within a few days, the Jewish families of the kolkhoz were forced into a ghetto. When men between the ages of fifteen and sixty-five were singled out by SS men during the resettlement, purportedly for work detail, thirteen-year-old Boris was also pushed into the column of men. "Luckily, the Germans entertained themselves by robbing houses along the way, and I was able to use one of those moments and left the column, I ran toward the [River] Dnieper. I heard shots, but I was already in the water and swam to the other side." Gal'perin mentioned several instances in which he escaped arrest by crossing the nearby river, or by hiding in a sack of flour that his grandparents sat on while police searched the house. Hiding from the raids was crucial; men supposedly taken to work never came back, and most likely they were killed immediately in a nearby meadow.³⁸

Living in the ghetto included experiences of humiliation, physical violence, and hunger, as described by Gal'perin:

> There were frequent beatings of elderly people, women, and children during robberies, when they took the few modest things, such as watches or earrings, which the ghetto inmates used in order to trade valuables

for bread. Only our neighbors sometimes brought some boiled potatoes, milk, or some buckwheat porridge. We were thankful for a glass of water, because the ghetto was a little outside of Ryzhkovichi, near the ruins of the church above the Dnieper.[39]

Life in the ghetto was short. In the fall of 1941, a number of Ryzhkovichi's Jewish residents were moved to the buildings of the flax factory in Shklov, where they and several Jews from Shklov were held under curfew and not given any food. Boris Gal'perin vividly remembers how, as some were fasting for Yom Kippur, an Einsatzkommando surrounded the ghetto the morning of October 3 or 4, 1941, and how his mother woke him, warning him "Quick, the Germans!" She left the house with Boris's grandmother and told him to run away too. Barefoot, young Boris made his way to the river, where he found the two women. Jews who were rounded up in the flax factory were taken to the village of Putniki, about two miles from Ryzhkovichi, and shot at a ravine. Ninety-six Jews from Ryzhkovichi, Shklov, and possibly other places were killed that day.[40] Between October and December 1941, the nearly 3,000 Jews of Shklov, Ryzhkovichi, Maloe Zarechie, and Bolshoe Zarechie were killed at various sites.[41]

For several months, Boris, his mother, and his grandmother found shelter with a number of peasants. Many had known the family before the war and were ready to take the risk to hide the Jewish refugees, though not all together and only for short periods.[42] When the three relatives reunited in Polykovichi in July 1942, joining a partisan unit appeared to be the only viable option for them and for two other survivors of the massacre in Ryzhkovichi, Lev Makhover and his mother.[43] In partisan detachment No. 10 of the brigade "Chekist," Boris had the opportunity to replicate his role model Ded Talash's partisan career. He became a scout and also participated in a number of attacks on German garrisons and mining operations that destroyed German war equipment. Several decades after the war, he detailed his partisan exploits in an autobiography, which he shared with me as part of his interview. His account is peculiar in its silence about his mother; this contrasts sharply with his prewar narrative, in which Esfir Zakharovna Gal'perina is a central figure. A close reading of the silence reveals the problematic structure of portrayals of the partisan movement.

Generally, Gal'perin's experiences with the partisans are representative of those of many civilians, especially Jews. Boris's grandmother, together with a number of other women and children who had sought shelter in a unit, died during a German antipartisan operation in the summer of 1942.[44] By then, partisan groups posed a growing challenge to the German war effort, blowing up bridges or freight trains, cutting telephone lines, and attacking police garrisons. Initially, partisan units consisted of between twenty and 200 people. These *otriady* (units), the core element of the partisan movement, were pooled into brigades that brought between 4,000 and 10,000 partisans together under one central command in 1942; at a later stage these brigades were organized into *soedineniia*, partisan formations that united two or three brigades and whose coordinated actions increased their impact on the occupation regime.[45] Responding to the increasing impact of the partisans, the German army, cooperating with SS and police battalions, mobilized resources and personnel to capture and kill partisans and destroy their bases, including the premises of local peasants who supported partisans.[46]

In September of that year, the regional partisan command ordered all women and children in Soviet partisan detachments to be sent across the front line. Six partisans were assigned to guide the group that included Gal'perin's mother and, because she refused to leave him behind, Boris as well. En route, at night when everybody was asleep, the guides abandoned the evacuating civilians. Unable to find the correct route, Boris and his companions hoped that they would come across other partisan detachments. One partisan commander, identified by Gal'perin as Gurskii, rejected the group because, Gal'perin recalls him arguing sardonically, "he didn't need such a 'treasure.'" He even confiscated the only weapon the group had in its possession. In the fall of 1942, detachment No. 345 of the brigade under the command of S. A. Iarotskii admitted Boris and his mother, but only after a detailed interrogation.[47]

However, the unit commander suggested that he disguise his Jewish nationality in order to avoid humiliation—or worse—from fellow partisans.[48] Like Leonid Gol'braikh, who joined the "Stalin" Brigade in the eastern regions of Belorussia, Boris Gal'perin thus participated in state-sponsored resistance at the expense of his Jewish identity. Being a Soviet partisan allowed young ghetto refugees to partake in the fight against the occupation regime. Simultaneously, though, they were both reminded that their precarious position as Jews had brought them to the woods in the first place and forced to conceal that fact. Even fellow fighters displayed resentment toward Jews, a clear contrast to how they had perceived Soviet society before the war, and an attitude with no basis in anything Jewish partisans may have done wrong.

Gal'perin's written account describes a number of military operations in which he participated and which endangered him as both a partisan and a Jew. The summary on page one states, "Gal'perin actively participated in the Belorussian partisan movement. With his help, six trains were blown up, two armored cars and two tankettes destroyed, five locomotives derailed, and twenty-eight Germans killed in open battle."[49] Together with a group of partisans, he guided several members of an NKVD task force across the front line after they had completed an assignment in Minsk.[50] In the account, Gal'perin also describes the partisans' dangerous task of acquiring food and hay for their horses.[51] During these "economic" or "household" missions, as the partisans called them, they often had to engage with German troops or, in the cases described here, local residents or members of the Vlasov Army who collaborated with the Germans to capture Soviet partisans when they emerged from their hideouts in the forests and entered villages. In many cases, these missions were military operations that included the exchange of fire and, often enough, ended in partisans being killed or wounded.[52] Gal'perin gives a detailed description of how he moved from house to house with a fellow partisan, how they arrested several *"vlasovtsy"* (a term used for members of the Vlasov Army or other collaborators), and managed to evade a group who pursued them.

The partisans also used the skills Gal'perin had acquired by growing up on a kolkhoz. During an attack on a garrison in Skripnitsa, the partisans were to retrieve a bull that would inseminate the cows that were with the partisans. Despite another battle, the mission was accomplished, but only because young Boris knew how to properly tie a rope around the bull. Even when the animal, scared by the gunfire, tried to escape, the boy did not let go and was dragged along until the bull fell to its knees, choked by the rope. To celebrate the success, the partisans put Boris on the bull, and he rode home to the base while everybody else had to walk.[53]

In late 1942, the Communist Party, in an effort to regain power in the occupied territories, began sending activists to the German rear to reestablish party committees. This endeavor to reestablish Soviet power relied significantly on the ability of partisans to secure the activists' passage. Boris Gal'perin and his fellow partisans were among the otriady that participated in the move to the western parts of Belorussia.[54] As Gal'perin recalled, in the spring of 1943 the commander of the Mogilev soedinenie

Soldatenko-Sergienko announced to the partisans that they should feel honored to be among the first to complete such a raid deep into western Belorussia.[55] The 700-km hike surely did not at all times feel like an honor. Gal'perin especially highlights the insecurity he experienced; he had a hard time reading and understanding military maps and was unfamiliar with the area that the partisans traversed.[56]

Eventually, Gal'perin and his otriad participated in the so-called *rel'sovaia voina* (railroad war), during which partisans helped Soviet troops by cutting German supply lines and destroying hundreds of miles of railroad. The railroad war, conducted in waves during the decisive battle in the Kursk-Oriol salient in 1943 and during the Red Army advance through Belorussia in summer 1944, helped decide the result of the war, as Soviet officials emphasize.[57] Gal'perin devotes a separate section to this campaign, describing several explosives missions in detail.

Boris Gal'perin is undoubtedly proud of his contribution to these achievements; a list of orders and medals for the partisan struggle and for his postwar achievements as an engineer illustrates the importance of institutional recognition for him.[58] Yet, he also points out, "not everything went smoothly in our partisan group. Once we stepped on a mine, and one partisan lost part of his leg. I had a concussion, I lost my voice, and my legs were wounded." Despite these setbacks, including a month-long stay in the field hospital, his account highlights both the participation and value of several strata of Soviet society in the partisan movement. He also implicitly places himself within this collective: "Hitlerite Germany forgot that throughout history, nobody could ever defeat Russia, which always was and will always be, because adults, women, the elderly, and weak children's hands took to arms to protect their homeland."[59]

At the same time, this statement and its purpose—to identify a transhistorical unity of people—contradicts his own experiences during a war in which a number of partisan commanders rejected him and his fellow Jewish ghetto refugees. He explained this with a reference to antisemitism, "which was always there, even in the partisan movement."[60] He overheard anti-Jewish statements by a fellow partisan, and knew that fellow partisans had shot other Jews.[61] And yet, despite the failure of the Soviet project to capture everyone's attention and produce empathetic attitudes toward each other irrespective of national identity, he remembered that his and other Soviets' participation in the movement was motivated by loyalty to the Party and, by extension, the state: "Our youth, we went consciously into battle. We had no other goal, there was a mobilizing force to it that directed people's actions. And that was the Party."[62] People, Gal'perin proclaims, shared in the "unconditional hatred for the enemy and everyone who had betrayed the Homeland or was loyal to the occupants."[63] In my interview with him, he mentioned that he even declined to be sent to the rear and chose to stay with the partisans and continue the fight against the German occupation.[64] Gal'perin joined the Komsomol in 1943, while he was a partisan—a further expression of his devotion to defending the state and standing up for its ideological tenets.

Local police were aware of his activity as a scout, and a monetary reward was offered for his capture.[65] Asked whether he ever experienced any fear or difficulty adjusting to military discipline, Gal'perin said:

> We did what we were told to do ... Fear, that is such a relative concept: a strong person suppresses fear; a weak person surrenders to fear. That's how I think about it. And also, I was at an age where I was convinced that a small bullet could not kill a person. That wasn't as much a philosophical reflection as it was just a simple thought in my mind. Therefore I cannot claim that what I did was an expression of heroism. Whatever assignment was given, one had to fulfill it without question.[66]

At the same time, he points out, qualifying his response, that, "Finally, many say that war is not that horrible—this is a lie. War in itself is horrible, but for the participants it is even more terrible."[67]

Boris Gal'perin experienced a "childhood scorched by war," first in the ghetto, and later in the woods as a young partisan who participated in combat and endured German antipartisan operations.[68] His experiences thus resemble the paths of many other Soviet citizens and military personnel who joined the partisans. At the same time, his and his mother's presence in a partisan detachment marked an exception. Only a few Jews survived the killing actions in eastern Belorussia; there, in the *oblasts* (provinces) of Mogilev, Gomel', and Vitebsk, organizing Jewish partisan formations (family units) similar to those which emerged from the Minsk ghetto—from which several thousand Jews escaped—was largely out of the question.

Leonid Gol'braikh, Boris Gal'perin, Grigorii Erenburg, and other men who did reach a partisan unit willing to admit them were often the only

Jews in the detachment, and often also the youngest members. These detachments were not interested in providing a space for the survival of noncombatants; rather, they focused on attacking and sabotaging collaborating and occupying forces. The only way for Boris, Grigorii, and their parents to earn respect and the right to stay with the partisans was to subscribe to the military purpose of the unit, obedience to established patterns of discipline—including the silent acceptance of antisemitic attitudes—and the successful fulfillment of assignments. There was no respite from the horrors of war and genocide, and there was hardly a communal space to communicate and work through experiences of humiliation, disappointment with friends turned antisemites, or the loss of both home and family.

We observe here a regional inversion of Jewish prewar and wartime experiences of communality and Soviet belonging. In Minsk, where prewar secularization and Sovietization had made being Jewish largely socially irrelevant to children and youths, wartime terror and occupation produced a sense of Jewish communality in ghetto and partisan detachments that these youths had not experienced before. In eastern Belorussia, especially in former shtetlach (small, primarily Jewish towns) like Ryzhkovichi, Slavnoe, or Shchedrin, remnants of Jewish communality had continued throughout the 1930s, if only in the form of a Jewish demographic majority. Mass executions, however, thoroughly destroyed these remnants, leaving behind a number of dispersed Jews who often concealed their national identity and scrambled individually for survival in hiding or in partisan combat units.[69]

Gal'perin's account is very detailed with regard to the military assignments he fulfilled together with fellow partisans. What is largely absent from his account, and which also emerged only marginally in the interview, are details about the conditions of daily life; we learn little about how his unit ate, lived, or clothed themselves. This is a common omission in the portrayals of the Soviet partisan movement. A recent account notes that information about daily life—about the struggle to survive hunger, cold, rain, sleepless nights, and the constant sense of danger—is all too rare, in official documentation and reports as much as in accounts by individual partisans.[70] In focusing on the military purpose and achievements of partisan detachments, available accounts written in official language often marginalize the significant labor and experiences of nurses and cooks, those who produced footwear and clothes, and those who collected and processed food supplies for the partisans. Since women performed much of this labor, it is they who have largely been written out of the history of the partisan movement: "female labor is only rarely depicted in the heroic cast with which male labor is endowed."[71] Boris Gal'perin's account also fails to account for the experiences and contributions of women.

Esfir Zakharovna Gal'perina escaped the ghetto with Boris, accompanied him on a difficult journey to find partisans willing to admit refugees, and eventually joined the same detachments as her son. Boris Gal'perin includes just three short paragraphs on his mother's role in the partisan detachment, in a final section he added later, as an afterthought to his autobiographical account.[72] Esfir Zakharovna worked as a cook, preparing food for the thirty members of a platoon within the unit. Among other things, she baked bread for the partisans, including "one small extra loaf" for her son—who, technically, was in a different squadron than the one to which she was assigned. At night, she scraped out the fat from freshly slaughtered animals' intestines to use for frying food. Work and war seemed to have worn her out, Gal'perin notes:

> She looked much older than her thirty-five years. Time does that, but in this case, the horrors of the ghetto that she lived through, the loss of close ones, the worry about father, who had been in the army since the first day of the war, the worry about me until I came back from my assignments—all of this had to leave a trace in her appearance.[73]

Within the official Soviet portrayal of the war, the experiences of civilians, of surviving war and genocide in the rear, or of those who did not blow up trains or shoot Germans, were rarely included or considered worthy of recognition.[74] Women like Esfir Gal'perina were rarely compelled, or asked, to write down their memories. Without Boris Gal'perin's short account, we might not have any, but we are left without any knowledge about the impressions and perceptions of the woman herself. Only in recent years have former female partisans been asked to talk about their lives.[75] Elena Drapkina's remembrances demonstrate that these former partisans—their stories and their voices—do not necessarily suffer from memory loss due to the passage of time; they suffer social taboos and political restrictions bound to the celebration of masculine heroism and military struggle.

"It was perfectly clear that I had to ... do everything I could to avenge these murders"

Elena Drapkina had trained as a member of the BGTO (a paramilitary training organization for Soviet civilians), so she considered herself ready to participate in military efforts to drive out the Germans.[76] From the very beginning of the war, as German soldiers marched into Minsk on June 28, 1941, she imagined—as many at the time must have—how defeating the Germans would feel in the words already familiar to the reader:

> When the war began, I saw the German troops marching, they were all very young, beautiful and healthy, and they had all this equipment. I stood there and thought: "My God, I really want to live to the moment when I see at least one German soldier in captivity. I wonder what they will look like then" ... We were patriots.[77]

Elena Drapkina's story offers insight not only into the situation of Jews among the partisans, but more specifically that of Jewish women. Her account demonstrates how gender, even more than nationality, could mark difference within the partisan movement. Her Jewish identity appeared to have little meaning for her fellow partisans, and she herself shrugs off issues of anti-Jewish behavior. For instance, when she encountered a group of parachutists who had arrived in the German rear as part of an NKVD operation to strengthen the partisan movement, they immediately admitted her because she was a Jew: "I told them I was a Jew, and they understood everything, they obviously knew what was going on."[78] Even later, once the unit had grown and "there were antisemites who humiliated Jewish members of the unit ... I was fine."[79]

Asked about her motive for joining the partisans, she responded, "because I needed to take revenge, for my mother's death, my father's, for my brothers. There was no question. It was perfectly clear that I had to go to the partisans and do everything I could to avenge these murders." In addition, to explain how she was able to make it through the ensuing difficulties in the partisan unit, she says,

> Of course it was difficult. But you see, when you are eighteen or twenty years old, you don't think about the fact that it is hard. But when I saw all the abuse, when I worked at the freight station [in the Minsk ghetto], we

worked there with Jews and Russians, and Germans, well, the Germans supervised for the most part. And once, one of the Russian guys mixed up the rail switch, and two wagons crashed into each other. And one of the Germans, a younger one, he beat him up so badly ... I don't know if the guy stayed alive or not. I saw this with my own eyes. Do you understand? There was not a drop of compassion, he obviously enjoyed doing it ...[80]

Witnessing German brutality and terror proved to be a strong motive for her to join the partisans, which provided an opportunity to avenge the violence visited upon those close to her and other Soviet citizens.

Elena Drapkina joined a group of eight partisans under the leadership of I. M. Timchuk. The group grew quickly, and by February 1943 it counted forty members.[81] Every member was assigned a specific task, and so was Elena. Because of her desire to participate in combat and take revenge, she was displeased with the commander's initial order sending her to the kitchen. When she refused, the commander sent her to work as a nurse in the medical tent. She says she told the commander that she could not stand the sight of blood: "I had fainted multiple times before when I saw lots of blood." In the end, she was enlisted in the combat group. A certificate about her membership in the partisan unit, however, states that she worked as a nurse's aide and later on as a nurse, a contradiction I was unable to resolve.[82] The information Drapkina gave in the interview suggests, however, that she did indeed participate in combat missions.

Drapkina's explanation of her treatment in the partisan unit shows that there were strong opinions among commanders (and presumably other partisans) about suitable tasks for young women—even women like Elena Drapkina, who had had BGTO paramilitary training before the war. Elena's struggle to find a suitable task in the partisan unit reflects a general trend, especially in the first years of the war. Stalin, P. P. Ponomarenko, the chief of staff of the Soviet Partisan Movement, and other leaders' attempts to include everyone in the partisan movement were met with resistance on the ground; many local residents complained to the Central Staff that they were not admitted into partisan units.[83] Gal'perin's mother, as well as a number of other women, were confined to household tasks whether they wanted it or not, though many apparently expressed their discontent. In May and June 1943, for instance, the general secretary of the Komsomol, Nikolai Mikhailov, filed a complaint based on information submitted from Komsomol members in German-occupied territories to Ponomarenko. He wrote that

> in a number of cases there is an incorrect attitude toward young women, and there is a widespread degeneration among combatants and commanders. For instance, in the units under the command of comrade Fiodorov (Chernigov province), many young women ask to be enlisted for combat, but they are confined to the kitchen or other ancillary work. In other cases, women are not considered fit for combat and they don't receive proper military training. This limits the women's military effectiveness and undermines their authority as combatants.[84]

Other women complained that they were not included in demolition details.[85]

There are parallels here between the partisan movement and the Soviet Army, which officially called on everyone to fight against the German occupation and yet for a long time struggled to admit female volunteers. Rank-and-file partisans and partisan leaders, too, were reluctant to recruit women, resulting from an ambivalent attitude on the part of the Soviet leadership that can best be described as "discouragement without prohibition."[86] A strategy marked, on the one hand, by calls for volunteer service that were directed at everyone and, on the other hand, by the absence of provisions for women to participate seems to have applied to the partisan movement as well. Whereas the Komsomol called on everyone, specifying "women and men," to defeat the enemy, the Central Staff and local commanders seemed unclear about the incorporation of women into partisan units on an equal footing.[87]

On the ground, this could lead to dangerous situations for women. Elena Drapkina, for instance, mentioned her lack of access to a weapon. Especially during the first months of its existence, her otriad had trouble acquiring weapons and ammunition. She received a small pistol, but there was only one cartridge. A short time after she had survived a German shelling, the otriad heard from locals where a Soviet soldier, killed during the first months of the war in 1941, was buried. The partisans dug up the corpse and retrieved his weapon and ammunition. The comrade who took this rifle passed on his sawn-off shotgun to Elena. "This gun had a terrible shot, it was horribly loud, and there was a horrific recoil.

But still, I was armed."[88] Eventually, Elena received a machine gun in the spring of 1944, when supplies were dropped in the partisan zone by airplanes from the Russian rear.[89] During the interview, Drapkina showed a picture, included in this book, that displayed her with the gun, visibly proud. "Unfortunately," she said, that picture was taken [in summer, 1944] just to show off once more, right after that I had to surrender the gun." At the same time, I sensed some hesitation in her narration about the role of weapons. When I asked whether she used the gun, she answered, "I can't say that I did very often, but I did shoot, I had to . . ."[90] Where Boris Gal'perin proudly lists the number of Germans he killed, Elena Drapkina neither declares her count nor details her use of the weapon.

Elena Drapkina emphasizes that she knew to avoid, at all costs, capture by the Germans. "We all had a hand grenade, an Efka [F-1 model], that's what it was called. It was better to kill yourself than to fall into their hands." Partisans knew that capture would result in horrible torture before the inevitable execution. The depth of Drapkina's fear emerges in her narration of the capture of a fellow partisan: "A woman from the Luninskii otriad was captured. They took one of her legs and tied it to one tree, and the other leg to a second tree, and so they tore her into pieces . . . Do you understand? That's what they did. It is hard to believe."[91]

Indeed, scholarship on the German war against the USSR shows that hatred for Soviet women combatants was extraordinary, and expressed in extreme brutality. The "Flintenweiber" (shotgun dames), as the female fighters were called derogatorily, stirred the aggression of German soldiers. They saw not only an enemy combatant but also the absolute negation of a Nazi ideology that, in addition to racism, rested on a conservative patriarchal gender order in which women were to comply with their "natural" roles as mothers and wives. The Soviet project to include women in all socially valuable tasks, including industrial work and military activity, stood in sharp contrast to this ideology. By this logic, combat encounters with Soviet women fulfilled the anti-Bolshevik propaganda that had been driving the war and warfare against the Soviet population; it was evidence of the racial inferiority of the Soviets.[92] The immense brutality with which Zoia Kosmodemianskaia and other women were killed—faces disfigured, breasts cut off, sexual organs mutilated—testify to the merger of racist and sexist hatred. In this light, Drapkina's elaborations on procuring a functional weapon reflect her strong desire to protect herself by carrying her own weapon.

In passing, Drapkina mentioned that she and four other women in her unit always went together to the "bath," a place assigned for washing a short distance away from the unit's base. On the one hand, these collective outings enabled the women to watch out for outsiders—Germans, police, spying locals—who were trying to determine the location of the partisans' camp while they were away from the fortified base. On the other hand, there is reason to believe that fellow partisans might also have posed a danger to women by trying to persuade or coerce them into relationships they may not have wanted or would not have engaged in in other contexts.

Elena Drapkina reluctantly spoke about gender and sexual relationships, though the first time she talked about it in the interview she asked me to turn off the recording device. What followed did not incriminate her in any way, even by measures of taboos on extramarital relationships. Yet even her proximity to such behavior, by choice or force, appeared problematic for her. It took many years of discussion until she agreed to include this information. It is worth both narrating the story and trying to understand her hesitation, a hesitation that reinforces silences in the historical record and pushes women's experiences, especially of violence, to the margins of the historical record.

The otriad "Bol'shevik" included a number of women, many of whom, according to Drapkina, had joined because they were relatives of male partisans and were threatened by German retaliation. When I asked her about relationships among partisans—being deliberately vague about their nature (friendship, intimate, marital)—she asked me to turn off the microphone. Most of the women in the partisan unit were very young, between fifteen and eighteen years old. Except for Tania, the wife of one of the commanders, none of them had experienced intimate relationships with men before the war. Furthermore, Elena and most of the other women had lost relatives who could have given advice on emotional or physical aspects of intimacy. Tania perceived it as her task to warn the young women to be careful in their choices, to think twice before they engaged in a relationship with one of the partisans. In her experience, the women would have to deal with possible consequences by themselves. To underscore this danger, Drapkina related the case of a woman who became pregnant, was expelled from the unit, and whose lover, the father of the child, did not care about her or the baby. Moreover, Drapkina explained how she tried to avoid engaging in any sort of relationships and remembered how she had to fight off the advances of a young man:

> I told him, "I came to the partisans a virgin, and I will also leave a virgin." So he said that we would die anyway. I replied, "OK, then I will die as a virgin." He, again, said "Then there won't be any birds flying over your grave."— "I don't care, so be it." That was it, after that, he left me in peace.[93]

At the same time that Drapkina helps in writing the history of the Soviet partisan movement by describing the involvement of Jews, specifically Jewish women, she initially contributes to the silencing of history—in this case, to the silencing of women's exclusion from partisan units because of pregnancy, and advances by male partisans toward young women.

The cases Drapkina described were hardly unique; other women were kicked out of partisan units for being pregnant, and she was not the only object of desire for a fellow partisan. The commander of the "Voroshilov" otriad in the Briansk area, for instance, was reported to the Political Department of the partisan movement's Central Staff because he expelled from his unit a pregnant partisan woman who refused to abort the fetus.[94] Other unit commanders "cohabitated" with several women each under their command, often against the women's will.[95] One of them sent a woman whom he had impregnated to Smolensk for an abortion. On her way to the doctor she was accosted by a German patrol and executed.[96] Partisans also committed sexual violence against local Soviet citizens; a number of complaints by women of the village Klitskii in Vitebsk province provide clear evidence.[97] And yet, there are few concrete descriptions of such instances; the subject is still buried under shame and official cover-ups that try to preserve the image of the proper, heroic partisan.

Elena Drapkina's narration and reluctance to include details about the precarious status that women like her occupied are glimpses into a history of the Soviet partisan movement that is yet to be written. On the surface, partisans are known for surviving in the woods and amid fierce military battles, and for participating in the defeat of the German army by fulfilling dangerous sabotage missions against railway lines or garrisons. Had Drapkina not agreed to include her memories of the women's experiences in her unit, we would be left with a similar story from her, a story of military, patriotic, and heroic struggle determined largely by men.

Elena Drapkina spoke about the new commander of her unit, Frants Ivanovich Garak, a man of Czech origin who had joined the partisans after defecting from the German army, with mixed feelings. (In spring 1944, her otriad "Bol'shevik" was regrouped once more and some members joined partisans from the "Budionny" otriad to create the otriad "Spartak."[98]) "He took such risks! Of course it was necessary to take risks, but he actively risked people's lives. He was even reprimanded by the brigade commander." But Garak also led the group out of an ambush that could have easily cost the partisans' lives. After a local resident had told a German troop that partisans were in his village, the Nazis surrounded the house and threw grenades at it.

> Our commander told us to leave through the river—that was the only exit they had left us. It was November, there was a layer of ice on the water … We lost one of our group, another one was injured. How they were shooting at us! But we made it. I was probably lucky because I used to be a swimmer before the war, and that's why I made it across the river.[99]

The group then had to wait until nightfall until they could warm up, since the smoke from lighting a fire would have directed the Germans to their hiding place.[100] Drapkina indicates an ambivalent relationship to her commander here, one in which he jeopardized other people's lives, but also one in which she can acknowledge his skills in leading the unit to safety from dangerous situations.

In addition to preparing sabotage missions and protecting their own lives, partisans in Belorussia and elsewhere in the German-occupied territories of the Soviet Union often helped protect the local population from German terror and attacks. Once, in early 1944, when Elena was appointed commander of the village Morozovka in the area that her brigade oversaw, she had to organize the evacuation of the whole population because a troop of unknown combatants was passing through the area. "There were these impenetrable swamps, and we didn't think that the troops would get in there. So we took all the residents there and waited until the troops had passed."

Drapkina hints here at the reciprocal effect of the increasing presence of the partisan movement. The growth of the partisan movement increased the ability to target German supply routes and infrastructure; while there were 50,357 partisans in December 1942, there were 68,498 in April 1943 and 121, 903 in January 1944.[101] The actual success of the partisan movement in undermining the German war effort continues to be contested, but there is no doubt about the German response to these efforts. Aggressive operations by German police, SS, Wehrmacht, and other forces targeted partisans, Jews, and their (potential) supporters alike, with increasing brutality.[102]

Especially in the years 1943 and 1944, the partisans essentially ruled whole areas in the German rear.[103] By April 1942, there were eleven so-called *partizanskie raiony* (partisan zones) in the German-occupied Soviet territories, covering a space of 50 km² in total.[104] These zones were often areas that were difficult to access because of thick forests or extensive marshes and swamps and that only locals knew well enough not to get lost in them. As a result, German authorities complained about their lack of influence and the partisans' success in driving out local administrations established by the occupation regime, resulting in up to 50 percent of arable land under partisan control.[105] To undermine the partisan presence, German authorities organized coordinated attacks that included army divisions, SS battalions, and police troops. The frequency and intensity of the attacks increased after the defeat of German forces at Stalingrad in February 1943.[106] Amassing personnel and mobilizing airplanes, tanks, and other heavy armor, the Germans then systematically combed the assigned area, trying to capture and destroy anyone or anything that might assist the partisans and to seize foodstuffs and other resources that would be useful to support the German war effort.[107] Rather than trying to find the partisans, the German strategy consisted primarily in destroying the livelihood of partisans and civilian residents who were suspected of supplying the partisans with food and other necessities. It is estimated that up to 345,000 combatants and civilians died from German antipartisan operations.[108] In Belorussia, 186 villages were wiped out; another 441 settlements and villages were nearly destroyed but could be rebuilt after the war.[109]

In all our meetings and interviews, Elena Drapkina described how she barely escaped these attacks, blockades of areas with a high concentration of partisans. During Operation Cottbus, army divisions, SS, and police forces numbering 80,000 swarmed an area between Molodechno, Vileika, Parafionovo, Polotsk, and Borisov. The campaign included a task force of Gebietskommissar Vileika, dispatched to register grain, crops, potatoes, fur, animal skins, cattle, and horses.[110] From a military standpoint, Operation Cottbus was an attempt to push a number of partisan units based in the area toward the swamps around Lakes Palik and Domzheritskoe.[111] Drapkina remembers,

> The Germans came from all sides, they drove us partisans toward Palik Lake. Only a third made it out alive. It was horrible ... If the merger with the Soviet Army had taken place just a little bit earlier, many could have been saved. I didn't go toward the lake, I came out through the lines ... I simply couldn't run anymore. The Germans just set the whole forest on fire; there was no way to go. Better not to remember this ... I ran into two girls from the Luninskii otriad, we met in a little pit and waited it out there.[112]

The three young women hid for several days in the forest before they reunited with their units, surviving on Elena's iron ration—a piece of dried bacon and a piece of bread.

Double consciousness and the Soviet partisan movement

Elena Drapkina's request to erase her portrayal of complex personal relationships that were deemed illicit reveals the difficulty of studying practices of marginalization in the past. "Cultural memory is always about the distribution of and contested claims to power,"[113] and it is useful to probe the location of gendered lives in the memory of the Soviet partisan movement to see which relationships of power are at stake. The major challenge to a nuanced reconstruction of the partisan movement is rooted in its heterogeneity and the nature of the Nazi genocide, which disrupted previous conceptions of war and showed the potential weakness of social cohesion among the Soviet population. Conflicts about the inclusion of Jews in the Soviet partisan movement are indicators of this weakness. The partisan units themselves consisted of men freshly trained for military careers and local residents who could draw on previous combat experience during World War I or the Russian Civil War. Moreover, the detachments also included a number of adolescents, women, and other civilians who unexpectedly found themselves in a militarized space. For them, for Boris Gal'perin and Elena Drapkina, antisemitism and sexism were often additional challenges to the dangers posed by war and hunger.

In the Soviet Union, where the victory over Nazi Germany served to further establish and support the Party's legitimate rule, the partisan movement and its achievements were a prominent and celebrated element in Soviet portrayals of what was called the Great Patriotic War. This portrayal is inflected by attempts to display the success of internationalist solidarity, the Soviet people's unified struggle for liberation, and the strength of the Soviet military. Problematic elements of the wartime experience—such as conflicts between various nationalities, antisemitism, or failures of military strategy—were largely covered up.[114]

Within the larger public, the participation of women in partisan units and the army was considered a myth. As a result, many women—including Drapkina—kept silent about their participation in the partisan movement for decades, thereby denying themselves benefits available to war veterans.[115] In the postwar period, women's roles were reduced to the domestic sphere, as mothers and wives.[116] In the same way that women are vulnerable to, and targeted by, sexual violence because of their symbolic role for the reproduction of imagined national collectives, they were now denied a place in the public memory of the war, and, with that, rightful claims to access the role of the (publicly visible) combatant, a role typically reserved for men. In Soviet war portrayals, women primarily figure as representatives of the nation that require protection—for instance the figure of *Rodina-mat'* (Mother Homeland), featured in wartime posters and in such postwar monuments as that at Mamaev Kurgan (Mamaev Hill), the memorial to the Battle of Stalingrad (today Volgograd) in 1943. There, Rodina-mat' beckons the invisible masses to enter battle and fight for "her" protection. At the memorial site in Volgograd, a second statue complements the female figure—a bare-chested male fighter, erected in front of the large female figure, is protecting Rodina-mat', putting his life at risk.[117]

Imagining the homeland as a motherly figure works both ways. When the nation is understood as a reproducing body and reliant on genealogical connection, actual women are bestowed both concrete and symbolic value: they are capable of and necessary for the biological reproduction of the nation or ethnic community.[118] The demobilization of women service members and partisans in postwar Soviet society, which explicitly called on them to build families and raise children, reflected this logic. Excluding female veterans from benefits and other forms of public recognition after the war, an experience that Elena Drapkina, Boris' Gal'perin's mother Esfir Gal'perina, and many others shared, is thus the logical consequence of a traditionally binary system of gender, in which both women and men assume distinct roles as reproducers and protectors, respectively, of the national collective.[119] Male activity is in contrast to female "passivity," a nexus that can function only by denying female activity and participation in the defense of the nation, should it occur. The Soviet effort to rebuild society after the devastating war included the material reconstruction of public infrastructure, but also of the social and moral fiber, including a gender order in which women raise children and are to be protected, while men protect them, make decisions, and have political power. It is important to understand Gal'perin's emphasis on his military achievements and his silence about his mother, as well as Drapkina's hesitation in this context.

Related to the silence about women's participation in the Soviet military, speaking about sexual harassment was even more complicated; it would have made speakers vulnerable to renewed accusations of dishonorable prostitution and self-interest. Women's feeling of shame led them to avoid the subject, and to this day it has produced omissions in, and distortions of, the historical record, a dynamic reflected in Elena Drapkina's reluctance to include her memories of sexual harassment in the public record.[120] The resulting silence (or silencing) of women not only disallowed an appreciation of their involvement, either in combat or noncombat functions, it also made it impossible to learn about instances of sexual violence, abuse, and the difficult position that women occupied in the male-dominated space of the partisan detachments.[121]

Studying Jewish women's participation in the Soviet partisan movement, hearing and writing about portrayals like that of Elena Drapkina, shows the intersection of different forms of marginalization and abuse that disguise these forms of violence. This intersection is a strong argument for an integrated approach to studying oral history, one that recognizes the impact of the ideologies and culture of the seventy years and describes social patterns of oppression alongside an investigation of the forces that make them disappear. To understand how narrators represent gendered experiences, it is thus important to trace the socialization of narrators as women or men within a specific cultural framework.[122] We need to take note of cultural modes of accounting for gender and sexuality that determine, for instance, how Drapkina and others are able to describe their experience in the semipublic space of an oral history interview.

How people in formerly Soviet societies speak about their lives is, in many ways, shaped by patterns learned during Soviet times. "Every Soviet citizen had two totally different biographies at hand ... They differed from each other in terms of the facts selected, of interpretation and the character of presentation, as well as the sphere of public the person ought to speak in."[123] The norms of everyday speech were determined by (party) ideology; following syntactic rules was understood as following overall order, in which the personal does not matter and is subordinated to collective and depersonalized principles: "The Party offered the code to decipher personal experience and the means to make sense of this experience."[124] Soviet citizens were regularly asked to write short autobiographies when they enrolled for school or higher education, employment, or social security purposes, and these autobiographies typically included a wealth of data on relatives, origin, career, etc. Wartime accounts such as Boris Gal'perin's were to include detailed descriptions of participation in the publicly celebrated and valued combat operations but marginalize instances of antisemitism within the movement. The latter tendency was reinforced by Soviet authorities, which destroyed the whole print run of a book documenting Jewish partisan life.[125] While the personal presentations were distorted to comply with official expectations, this "formal biographical work was part of a social control and self-censorship system" that remained valid even in private settings.[126]

In these publicly legitimate self-representations, matters of everyday life, and thus information about personal lives, were relegated to a realm outside state control and barred from consideration in public.[127] As the public presentation of individual life provided no space for interpretation or deviant information, autobiographical narration appears to produce a facade that covers up individual life experience rather than exposing it, and focuses on socially valued actions. Successful partisan combat experience overrides women's work in the kitchen and frictions along the lines of national identity. The demand to create such a facade is deeply engrained in people's consciousness and continues to shape their behavior in the post-Soviet period. Despite a general opening of public discourse, effectively enabling a challenge to, for instance, the official portrayal of the war, representations of personal experience are still subject to limitations (and will perhaps be even more so in the near future). The site of the oral history interview is an especially complicated one, given its orientation toward making private experience publicly available. Aware of this inclusion of personal history into public discourse, but also in response to the social interpellations governing their public presence, interviewees make choices about the content of their narration. They provide "situational knowledge," knowledge produced both in and for a specific context, and, we observe, in accordance with rules they have come to adopt.[128]

Drapkina's difficulty and discomfort in speaking about sexual relationships during the war and how they were imagined after the war shows both her awareness of her contribution to the memory of the war and her continuing loyalty to its production. Finally, her narrative is shaped by the ways in which she was taught and expected to speak about issues of sexuality and gender relations, topics that were largely taboo during Soviet times. From the 1930s on, communist morality denounced personal desires that were not directed at reproduction. Intimate relationships were conceivable only as spaces of reproduction, as contributions to the growth and sustainability of the Soviet people. Beginning in the late 1930s, the Soviet state actively intervened to circumvent opposing behavior and individual choice.[129] With the prohibition of abortion, the crucial site of intervention was women's bodies. Following the idea of the working mother, women were to bear children and raise them "in the spirit of loyalty to communist morality."[130] Functioning as role models for Soviet citizens, partisans and Soviet soldiers were required to conform to this morality. Potentially illicit desires such as those by male partisans, existing extramarital relationships, but also homosexual relationships within units counter such proclamations and must remain off the record. At the same time, childbearing was considered the real fulfillment of the woman's role, while partisan activity was not. In this logic, excluding pregnant women from partisan units was a legitimate course of action. Elena Drapkina's request for erasure therefore reflects her entanglement in the discourse on sexuality, decency, and the gendered division of labor, as well as with the official portrayal of the war. Her memories and her refusal to speak about them mirror how these issues were addressed within the partisan movement and the limitations to speaking about oneself in relation to them.[131]

Drapkina's discounting of gender discrimination, and both Gol'braikh and Gal'perin's reference to, but minimal critique of, anti-Jewish marginalization in the partisan movement, resemble the "peculiar sensation, this double-consciousness, this sense of always looking at one's self through the eyes of others, of measuring one's soul by the tape of a world that looks on in amused contempt and pity" that enabled survival for African-Americans in Du Bois's day.[132] In pointing to this parallel, I am not attempting to equalize experiences of Jewish persecution, Nazi genocide, and slavery and racism. Rather, this is to take up Du Bois's recognition during a visit to the remnants of the Warsaw ghetto that racial violence is not only a problem of color but of "cultural patterns, perverted teaching and human hate and prejudice, which reached all sorts of people and caused endless evil to all men."[133] The strategic acknowledgement of both victimization and resistance as an "expression of particular relationships between minority and majority culture," which Du Bois saw depicted in Nathan Rapoport's monument to the Warsaw Ghetto uprising, thus becomes thinkable as a general form for resisting exclusion.[134] The monument, showing a group of Jewish civilians driven toward execution on the back side and a group of fighters on the front, displays the split Jewish experience during the Nazi regime: "a resistance which involved death and destruction for hundreds and hundreds of human beings."[135] The monument also marks the ways in which Jewish existence found entrance into public recognition through participation in resistance against the Nazi regime. Claiming recognition, claiming a place among those who resisted, to "look at one's self" one must then adopt the gaze of others, seeing what they would see when they look at resistance: the eyes of the Soviet others see male fighters, but not women and how they are treated by male fighters; and they see Soviet citizens, but not Jews—two markers of identity and experiences connected to them that are, in variation, obliterated so as to maintain belonging.

Elena Drapkina's initial effort to keep silent marks a conflict between her and my analyses of history, a conflict in which notions of discrimination, privacy, and what needs to be critiqued are rooted in different concepts of how individual lives are connected to larger cultural and political formations.[136] For her, offensive behavior toward women appears to lose significance in light of the genocidal war the Soviet partisans resisted, while I am interested in lifting multiple buried forms of violation to the surface so as not to weigh one against the other. Her limitations to narration would, in the final instance, constitute limitations to the construction of the memory of the war. As historians, how do we respect this desire, yet also reconstruct practices of marginalization, in history and memory, which include abuse or discriminatory treatment based on gender or other socially constructed categories? The memories presented by Elena Drapkina, Leonid Gol'braikh,

Boris Gal'perin and many others show that forms of self-control learned during Soviet times remained operational even after the demise of the USSR. For all of them, experiences of discrimination as Jews and/or women within the partisan unit remain side notes compared to the violence they experienced from the Germans, and the valuable role of the Soviet partisan movement in ending it. To fully understand the tension between experiences of marginalization and willingness to accept them, we ought to recognize the complex interaction of limitations to public speech in the Soviet and formerly Soviet context, but perhaps first and foremost the strong identification of survivors with the Soviet struggle against Nazi Germany and its postwar portrayal.

6

Of Refuge and Resistance

Labor for Survival in the "Zorin Family Unit"

Amaliia Iakhontova remembers her arrival in the partisan unit as a moment of returning to life: "The fear was gone. We had a chance to make it. We were breathing. We had taken off the patches and numbers, and nobody would just come and kill us."[1] Like her, thousands of Jews trapped in the Minsk ghetto tried to leave the city, aware that evading German military and civilian authorities was potentially the only way to survive. Alongside hundreds of others, Amaliia sought to reach partisan unit No. 106. This unit, under the leadership of Shalom Zorin, was known to accommodate ghetto refugees from Minsk and elsewhere.[2] Zorin's unit, a successful collaboration of Jews and non-Jews, provided a space for survival in the Nalibokskaia pushcha (Forest of Naliboki) to the northwest of Minsk. The significance of the unit cannot be overestimated; nearly every account by a survivor of the Minsk ghetto includes a description of an escape route from the Minsk ghetto to this unit. The detachment was established by the leadership of the Belorussian Partisan Movement precisely to provide shelter for ghetto refugees, who had often been denied entry to other units on the basis of their perceived inability or unwillingness to participate in military action. In addition to participating in combat missions, the unit was charged with sustaining itself and other partisan units by providing for essential needs.

To my surprise, Rita Kazhdan ended a several-hours-long conversation about the ghetto, partisan unit No. 106, and the postwar decades by remarking, as an aside, that she "had not told anyone about her time with the partisans after the war."[3] When I asked why, Kazhdan replied with an ironic undertone: "Only fools like myself kept it a secret . . . because partisan women were considered to be fallen women. And for God's sake, nobody should think that about me!"⁴ Her statement explicitly addresses Soviet postwar discourses that denounced women partisans as prostitutes rather than "real" partisans. The accusation was that they were neither trained nor fit for combat, and that they had engaged partisan leaders in sexual relationships to secure their place in the unit and save their own lives. These women, according to this logic, violated ideas of the modesty and morality expected of Soviet women.⁵ Framing her silence as an attempt to avoid stigmatization, Rita Kazhdan hints at widespread attitudes during and after the war that assigned civilians, women, and Jews a particular place in contexts of war, military, and the partisan movement.

The name of the partisan detachment that accommodated Rita Kazhdan, her brother, and many other refugees provides a clue to understanding the problematic position that this unit occupies in history and memory. For the first ten months of its existence, the detachment was referred to in the partisan movement's internal correspondence as "Zorin's family unit"; as of March 25, 1944, the Central Staff of the Partisan Movement in the Baranovichi Region ordered it to be named "Partisan detachment No. 106."⁶ Available correspondence within the partisan movement, however, shows that the unit continued to be identified as a "Jewish family unit."⁷ And documentation of the partisan movement, compiled in 1944, lists the unit as "operating separately," i.e., not included in any brigade and thus seemingly outside of coordinated partisan operations.⁸ This incongruence between uneven official attempts to numerically name and integrate the detachment into the larger movement and the persistence of its common family unity identity—in light of the important role the unit played in the survival of hundreds of refugees from the Minsk ghetto— deserves some attention.

The term "family unit," or interchangeably "family camp," was used to describe "special Jewish partisan units where there were refugees from the ghettos or from executions, including elderly, minors, and women."⁹ In other words, these units were sites where mostly Jewish civilians found refuge from the threat of annihilation and fulfilled specific tasks to ensure their own and other units' existence. Compared to the scope of the Nazi genocide and the density of the Jewish population in Belorussia, the number of family units was small. But considering the circumstances of war and terror, the numbers are impressive—and higher than anywhere else in Nazi-occupied Europe. Between 6,500 and 9,000 people lived in such units throughout the occupied Soviet Union; in Belorussia alone there were between 3,700 and 5,200 members.[10]

Despite these large numbers and the family units' contribution to the partisan movement, many members were deprived of recognition as veterans of the resistance movement after the war. Ekaterina Tsirlina, for instance, was repeatedly denied "war veteran" status, which would have granted her both public recognition of her wartime deeds and access to such special benefits as preferential medical treatment and other social services. Her applications to the local Party Committee in 1962 and 1963 were turned down.[11] In 1963, the resolution of the *Minskii promyshlennyi oblastnoi komitet KP(b)B* (Regional Industrial Committee of the CPB, Minsk) observed that, while several witnesses confirmed that Tsirlina smuggled weapons for the Minsk underground and indeed was a member of the Zorin family unit, she also "according to her own words did not participate in combat operations." The document concludes by refusing her application to be recognized as a veteran of the Minsk underground due to insufficient evidence.[12] This refusal to acknowledge the contributions of certain individuals is complemented by the omission of detachment No. 106 (and likely several other family units) from a 1983 publication claiming to provide a comprehensive account of the organization and personnel of the Belorussian partisan movement during the Great Patriotic War.[13] The refusal to validate Ekaterina Tsirlina's activities in the unit, as well as the unit's exclusion from scholarly accounts, raises questions about institutional recognition of the struggle for survival.

At the root of this refusal is a distinction between family units and combat units pursuing armed resistance. It is true that the majority of refugees who populated family units neither participated in combat nor identified this as a reasonable goal. At the same time, family and combat units were closely connected and acted in a shared context of war, occupation, and hunger. Together, they all faced a situation in which parts of the multinational Soviet population turned to antisemitism or anti-Soviet attitudes. This shared history of survival and resistance disappears when the actions of those who "fought" are honored and memorialized, while those who procured or produced weapons and enabled the day-to-day survival of civilians and combatants are forgotten, refused, or maligned, as happened in the postwar Soviet Union.

Rita Kazhdan, Samuil Volk, Sonia Zalesskaia, Mikhail Treister, Maria Boiko, and Amaliia Iakhontova were among the roughly six hundred

Jews—280 of them female, 240 younger than twenty—who escaped Nazi ghettos in Belorussia to spend between twelve and fourteen months in partisan detachment No. 106.[14] Their accounts indicate that the unit offered a safe haven to ghetto refugees, despite ongoing attacks by German and collaborating forces as well as Polish nationalists, who formed their own partisan units to combat both Soviet partisans and Nazi occupiers to regain sovereignty over territories that had been annexed by the USSR in 1939. They describe the unit's organization "from the inside" and highlight the value of mutual assistance for survival and the social dimensions of creating a community in the woods. Sharing experiences of loss, damage, and mourning and participating in the communality created by Soviet institutions—including a Pioneer brigade and a makeshift school in the detachment—were important dimensions of survival. Survivor accounts and archival material, including a collection of commands issued in the detachment, show that the unit reintegrated refugees into a Soviet value system but also increased the degree to which juveniles were included in militarized forms of sociality. The first orders issued by commander Zorin in June and July 1943 testify to his compliance with instructions from party functionaries, the chief of staff, and military commanders. They also reveal his attempts to establish discipline in the unit through setting up a daily regimen or penalizing individual partisans for noncompliance or rule violations.[15]

The exclusion of family units from history thus not only neglects their role within the larger partisan movement, it also prominently covers up the significance of reproductive labor and social relationships in surviving genocide, thus continuing an established pattern of disregard for women's work. The daily labor of obtaining or providing food, shelter, and emotional care—activities geared toward the maintenance of the individual and the community and traditionally assigned to women and performed within the family—does "not measure up" to modern understandings of labor, as it does not produce enumerable material or exchange value; it remains, consequently, invisible and unrewarded.[16] This invisibility also elides complex intracommunal, or intrafamilial, relationships that are shaped by affection as much as by discipline, (sexual) violence, or shame, making the lives of women and others who secure survival doubly precarious, a pattern repeated in the treatment of members of the family units.[17]

Overall, the problematic position of family units in the cultural memory of the Nazi genocide is not surprising. The term itself is a reminder of the role that these units played, which denied them equal attention. These units, after all, were not exclusively sites where families gathered. Rather, they were refuges for those who had lost all familial bonds and social networks, who were trying to make a living in a situation of extreme uprooting and instability, and who had seen the breakdown of moral norms and ideological frameworks. The family units were thus simultaneously sites of securing physical survival and social integration, both necessary, yet preferably invisible elements of maintaining loyal Soviet citizens.

In overlooking the emergence of these units we lose sight of the heterogeneity of the Soviet partisan movement and the ensuing challenges. The family units were not only necessitated by the Nazi regime's ruthless campaigns to kill Soviet Jews; their creation was also a reaction to antisemitic tendencies within the partisan movement. In turn, the presence of groups of civilians unaccustomed to living outdoors, in the midst of a military battlefield, required partisans to devise unprecedented strategies to coordinate military functionality and the presence and survival of civilians, an endeavor that failed in many respects and tainted the memory of the Soviet partisan movement.

The labor required for surviving within Jewish family units and that needed for the survival of the units themselves were interdependent elements of resisting the Nazi genocide in Belorussia. These two elements are also central to the whole of Soviet society's struggle for survival, a struggle that relied on the cooperation of Soviet army, partisans, workers, and civilians of varying ages. Rather than highlighting the number of German trains or vehicles that were blown up or how many Germans and policemen were killed in partisan missions, looking at the daily life of partisans, including adolescents and women who did not directly participate in combat, enables us to learn about the mechanisms that created social cohesion and enabled survival—in other words, the reproduction of the material and social conditions for human life. Eventually, these activities secured the reproduction of individuals and the community and created the preconditions for the more dramatic and visible elements of resistance. Zooming in on the daily efforts to survive thus challenges mechanical distinctions between "resistance" and "struggle for survival" that permeate scholarly debates. In order to do so, it is necessary to pay attention to the diversity of experiences, noting the roles of gender, age, ability, but also personal decision-making based on specific worldviews to account for individual and collective strategies of survival outside of Nazi ghettos.[18]

The family units, at once spaces of protection, military resistance, and reintegration into Jewish or Soviet communities (or both), have great potential for exploring notions of resistance against genocide and social injustice generally, and against the Nazi genocide in the occupied Soviet territories in particular. Ongoing military operations and systematic killings in occupied Belorussia, the loss of personal attachments and networks, and the lack of food, heating material, and medical aid each posed different challenges and required distinct responses, yet they were inextricably linked. Family units responded to these problems, and they show the possibilities and limitations of civilians trying to survive against the destruction of people and a cultural heritage.

Rescuing civilians in the "Zorin family unit"

Fifty-three years after the event, Polia Shostak is still indignant about how Soviet partisans treated her and her friend Ania as they made their way from Minsk to Staroe Selo, an important contact site for partisans. The four men inquired whether the young women were Jewish and whether they were spies sent by the German Gestapo. Shostak describes how the partisans explained that they already

> had killed a whole group of twenty female Jews who were sent by the Germans to poison the partisans and that, if we would not confess, they would do the same to us ... I was so upset and felt humiliated, now that I had made it to ours [our partisans] and then I would be killed by them.

Eventually the partisans staged a mock execution. "He shot right alongside my head. I was surprised I was still upright," Polia Shostak recalls. Since neither eighteen-year-old Polia nor her friend confessed even under these circumstances, the man "apologized and explained that they have to check on people."[19] Ania was not a Jew. She had volunteered to show Polia the route to Staroe Selo. Both women narrowly escaped execution, and the fact that both raised suspicion demonstrates the shared danger for Soviet civilians of various nationalities.[20] At the same time, the partisans' initial question points to the coupling of suspected Jewish origin and treason, providing justification for the killing of a group of Jews who claimed to have fled the ghetto.[21]

The largely anticivilian attitude among individual partisans and the partisan leadership can easily be interpreted as anti-Jewish and correlated with the Nazi project of systematically killing Soviet Jews. Many survivors believe this, pointing especially to a November 1942 order by the chief of the Central Staff of the Soviet Partisan Movement, Panteleimon Ponomarenko, that warned Soviet partisans against spies trained by the German Gestapo.[22] The order named anyone arriving from Minsk or other towns and did not point to Jews specifically. However, since the majority of escapees looking for partisan units willing to take them in were Jews, many, including partisan leaders, but also Jews themselves, interpreted it as an attempt to keep Jews out of partisan units, since the majority of escapees looking for partisan units willing to take them in were Jews.[23] In addition, in April 1943 the partisan leadership identified eight- to fifteen-year-olds as potentially dangerous spies and warned against their inclusion in partisan units. These warnings produced a dangerous threat for Amaliia Iakhontova, Mikhail Treister, and their young Jewish peers—some of whom indeed report being scrutinized by those they perceived as their saviors. [24]

It is hard to say whether Ponomarenko or other functionaries were antisemitic, or even whether these orders were designed to systematically exclude Jews from the partisan movement.[25] At best, though, their exclusion resulted from a combination of several factors, including these orders; local and, in some cases, antisemitic interpretations of them; and partisan commanders' concerns about limited resources.[26] None of this justifies or exculpates the deliberate killing of Jews suspected of being spies, or the robbery of any food and clothes they had. Rather, this discussion helps assess efforts such as those by Shalom Zorin, Tuvia Bielski, Gennadii Safonov, Hirsh Atlas, and others to set up specifically Jewish family units that would provide safe havens for ghetto refugees, or the efforts of Lev Gil'chik, Kirill Orlovskii, Boris Gindin, Israel Lapidus, Pavel Proniagin, and Hirsch Kaplinsky, who gathered Jewish combatants.[27] These decisions were responses to both the German occupation regime's systematic killing of Jews and to Soviet partisans who hampered Jews' attempts to find either protection outside of the ghettos or opportunities to engage in military resistance. For ghetto Jews, family units like Zorin's detachment were the only option.

Accounts of the unit's formation vary, though it is clear that the unit was established in spring 1943. By then, a considerable number of ghetto underground members had left Minsk to join various partisan units, and they were instrumental for setting up a safe haven for refugees from the Minsk ghetto.[28] Along with Shalom Zorin, who was leading the "Budionny" detachment's reconnaissance platoon, the underground activists proposed to Semion Ganzenko that they should rescue as many Jews remaining in the Minsk ghetto as possible and gather them in a partisan camp. The request acquired some urgency that spring when up to 500 refugees from the Minsk ghetto had gathered at Skirmontovo, a village near Koidanovo. The proposal was accepted, and by May 1—with the approval and support of Ganzenko and the regional partisan commander, General Vasilii Chernyshov (code-name "General Platon")—a base camp was established in the forest between the villages of Viertniki and Novosady in the Koidanov region. Fifteen (or eighteen) partisans of the "Budionny" brigade, equipped with rifles, were assigned to help Shalom Zorin, a carpenter who had fled the Minsk ghetto himself, to organize the rescue and shelter of Minsk's surviving Jews. The many children, youths, women, and elderly fleeing the ghetto were gathered in Zorin's family unit, while the majority of males that were considered combat ready were united in the "Parkhomenko" unit.[29]

The orderly creation of the detachment subjected it to the partisan movement's command structure from the very beginning. In this respect, the detachment was decidedly different than the group formed by Tuvia Bielski, which is the subject of a recent film based on an earlier monograph.[30] Together with his brothers, Bielski had gathered the core of his unit in the spring of 1942. Much later he opted to collaborate with Soviet authorities, and eventually the unit was forcibly subsumed under Soviet partisan leadership. But that happened only after the Bielski partisans had established both reliable relationships with locals who helped provide necessary supplies and their own value as combatants or providers of essential services for other partisan units.[31] Leonid Okon wonders whether the size of the "Bielski" unit, which eventually reached 1,400 members, as well as their more developed equipment and bigger fighting platoon, made them "a unit that they took seriously," as opposed to Zorin's unit, which was often considered a burden to the movement as a whole.[32]

The integration of detachment No. 106 into the Central Staff's command structure affected not only the internal organization of the unit and the definition of its tasks, but also its leaders' accountability. Zorin was bound by Central Staff orders, which had a broader party and military strategy in mind. He had to prove that his decisions conformed to the instructions, and to do so he kept a record of directives issued within the unit. This record includes orders concerning the detachment's internal organization, post assignments, disciplinary actions against individual offenses, and other issues pertaining to life within the unit. While this collection, first of all, gives insights into the official version of its activity, it also helps to fill gaps in the first-person accounts. In particular, the directives serve to place individuals' descriptions in a larger context of war and institutional structure, which were not accessible for the narrators at the time but were decisive for the unit as a whole. Additionally, articles submitted to the Soviet Yiddish newspaper *Einikayt*, in which authors celebrate the achievements of Shalom Zorin and other partisans, also yield information. In my account of the struggle for survival in a family unit, however, first-person accounts take center stage. Only these help us to understand how ghetto refugees perceived both the challenges of living in a militarized space and the significance of their contribution to creating a site of rescue.

The detachment faced constant danger: war, the elements, hunger, wild animals, and conflicts with residents who disapproved of partisans' living off local resources. Efforts to survive and resist were interdependent and demanded a lot from a diverse population that was largely untrained and unprepared for life outdoors and at war. In hindsight, the unit not only secured the physical survival of a number of refugees from the ghettos, but also provided a powerful framework for their reintegration into Soviet society, undoing the racist and deadly devaluation of human life guiding the Nazi occupation.

"It dawned on me that I was all by myself"

Rumors about both successful and failed attempts to leave Minsk circulated quickly within the ever-shrinking ghetto. These rumors were disturbing; some alleged that partisans were unwilling to accept Jewish refugees, others that partisans killed them as suspected spies, and still others that refugees were ambushed and killed just outside the city by German or Belorussian police. In 1943, the stories changed, promoting hope rather than fear. Word of both Shalom Zorin's unit and a general shift in partisan attitudes toward Jewish refugees made the rounds in the ghetto. At the same time, an increase in random daily killings of Jews, both in and outside the ghetto, in spring 1943 encouraged people to leave the ghetto.[33] The hope for a safe haven in Zorin's unit coupled with intensified mortal danger in the ghetto resulted in a wave of escapes in May 1943. The steady, if irregular, stream of ghetto inhabitants continued until the end of October, when the ghetto was destroyed. The number of refugees must not obscure the fact that leaving the ghetto was difficult. Many refugees failed to evade patrols or hostile farmers; others were unable to produce evidence of their good intentions—either rhetorically or as gifts to support partisan activity— toward partisans. One of the greatest challenges was knowing where exactly partisan units were and how to get there.

Many people went without precise information, hoping to either come across partisans or obtain information about their location along the way. Therefore, one of the first tasks that Zorin and the "Budionny" partisans set themselves was to send guides to Minsk who would direct refugees from the ghetto to the detachment's base.[34] Leonid Melamed and Mikhail Treister were two of many teenagers who became guides after they left the ghetto in May and July 1943. Fourteen-year-old Leonid and his mother were part of a group of people who left the ghetto one day as part of a workers' column. They separated from the column as soon as they had reached a previously arranged meeting point in the Russian district. As Melamed explains,

> One of the women knew somebody who lived on Grushevskaia Street and would show us the route, so we did not leave the column by chance. The women then put on other clothes so they would look like Russian peasant women. In the village Ptich' we ran into partisans who told us that we would find the unit No. 106 near Skirmontovo. Some guide from the unit came and took us to the unit. I then left the unit regularly to get other people from the ghetto.[35]

Mikhail Treister describes the dilemmas he faced as such a guide:

> They sent me for doctors, pharmacists, radio equipment, medicine, soap. People of course realized that I came and that I knew where partisans were. Some promised me weapons or gold if I would take them. I was of course hesitant to take them all; that would have been against my orders. But I had told my mother, my sister and the few others I was assigned to take to the partisans that we would meet in the infectious disease unit of the ghetto hospital. But many who had lost their homes had settled there, and realized what we planned to do. I felt horrible to say no to them, but I couldn't take them all. I also found Sasha Kaplan there, the son of a coworker, he sat there like an orphan, his brother was gone, and

his parents were dead. In the end we were thirty people, among them several elderly. I told them they should at least cover their shoes with rags to be quiet. We did make it out of the ghetto, but when we reached the railway line, something exploded and we had to hide. When the sun rose, we had to move on. We broke up in three groups and left at intervals of twenty minutes. Once I heard gunshots, the first and second groups were ambushed and many of them were killed. My third group later made it to Staroe Selo, and from there we reached the partisan unit.[36]

Thus, while access to a guide promised at least some direction, traveling in groups also exposed the refugees to great risks. And to join one of these groups an individual had to be attractive to the partisans in some way, having either training in a profession that was in demand, access to valuable equipment, or some personal connection to the partisans.

Rita Kazhdan was someone who had to make herself attractive to the partisans. She recalls that, as soon as she and her brother, Gera, recognized that escaping the ghetto was the only way they would survive the war, they knew they needed to accomplish two things: prepare gifts for the partisans and find a route to the partisan area. The siblings began to save parts of their daily rations and calcium carbide, and tried to trade them for tobacco. An old family friend, the pharmacist Abram Abramovich, supplied them with a bottle of iodine, some potash and aspirin, and several bandages. Prewar neighbors of the Fridman family, Zima, her son Ianka, and her two sisters, planned to leave the ghetto with Gera and Rita. Gera and Ianka once left the ghetto to scout out the area but were unable to identify a suitable escape route. Eventually the group decided, at the suggestion of a woman who had traded food across the barbed wire with Zima, to simply head in a westerly direction. There, they were told, they would find partisans or people who could direct them toward a partisan base.

In late September, when the group had everything prepared, no more workers' columns left the ghetto. On September 22, 1943, an underground cell had assassinated Wilhelm Kube, Generalkommissar Weißruthenien and head of the civilian German occupation administration in Minsk.[37] In retaliation, several hundred Jews were killed, and increased patrols made it nearly impossible to cross the ghetto fence secretly. "That is, we had to choose a moment when one patrol was far enough away, and the other was turning their back toward us. Then we crawled underneath the barbed wire and ran to the Russian side."³⁸ In that moment, Ziama's two sisters were too scared to continue and stepped away from the fence, chosing to remain in the ghetto. Gera had to return and retrieve the provisions that they were supposed to have carried for the group. Only then could he, Rita, Zima, and Ianka continue on their journey. Supplied with food and directions provided by a Belorussian woman along the way, the four eventually arrived in Staroe Selo. The last kilometers of their march were especially hard, as Rita Kazhdan recalls:

> We had to cross one stream after the other. It was cold, and it was raining the whole time. I was still wearing the shoes I had before the war; they practically did not have soles, only laces. I no longer took them off. In the beginning I always took them off, put them back on, and took them off again after two kilometers, and again and again. But then I ran out of strength, and I went through the water with my shoes on.³⁹

Physical exhaustion, cold, and inadequate footwear made the trip into the forest hard, especially for young people who had endured nearly two years of hunger and often hard labor. Ziama and Samuil Volk even had to abandon one group of partisans because they were too weak to keep up with them. A disgruntled partisan had told Samuil and his brother that they should go "find your people," Volk said. "I understood that he meant Jews, he didn't say it, but who else should 'we' mean." The boys eventually found a group of Jewish partisans who promised to take them to the "Zorin" detachment.

> They said we would have to walk around 100 km.... Halfway through, they didn't exactly chase us, but we had to walk very quickly, and for some reason it was really cold. So I said to Ziama, "Let's stay behind, we'll somehow find our way." We ended up in a house where there was another group of refugees. It turned out, it was a gathering point for people who had left the ghetto.⁴⁰

In Staroe Selo, groups like the one guided by Mikhail Treister, Rita Kazhdan's self-organized group, and many other individuals gathered, waiting for guides who would take them deep into the swamps to their final destination, the "Zorin" unit. Sooner or later, this village, 25 km to the west of Minsk, was the place where Samuil Volk and his little brother, Shalom Kaplan, Leonid

Melamed, Zoia Oboz, Amaliia Iakhontova, Sonia Zalesskaia, Arkadii Teif, Vladimir Mordkhilevich, and many others were greeted by Maria Kulish or other generous local farmers who were auxiliaries of the partisans. Kulish was a close ally of the partisan detachment and provided hot beverages and some food for the exhausted refugees.[41] While not everyone knew everybody in the unit, Rita Kazhdan and Mikhail Treister's encounter in this village, like those of Amaliia Iakhontova and Samuil Volk's, led to ongoing friendships during and after the war.[42]

From Staroe Selo, the ghetto refugees had to walk for another 50 km. Arriving in the unit was often painful, for several reasons. A bullet had struck Amaliia Iakhontova when her group left the ghetto and was ambushed by local police. "Mosquitoes had crawled into the wound. I couldn't walk anymore. They had to cut off the boots, and with them some skin came off too. But then they found some potash, and slowly it got better."[43] Rita Kazhdan suffered from frostbite, Shalom Kaplan's feet hurt badly, and Mikhail Treister also remembers "we had to cut off the shoes from some people after this long walk."[44] Alongside such physical ailments, the teenagers slowly absorbed the loss of relatives and friends and recognized that their farewell from the ghetto constituted an irrevocable parting from close ones. Zoia Oboz was at first surprised and then devastated to hear that she was among the last to leave the ghetto:

> My acquaintance Sasha asked me where my sister was. I told him that I had planned to find out where I could go and then go back to take her with me. He told me, "but we are going to the Nalibokskaia Pushcha today, and today they are destroying the ghetto in Minsk." I cried so much. I did not know what to do, where to go. We then walked during the night and slept during the day, after several days we arrived in the pushcha. I had no idea what was going on around me, I felt like I had lost my mind. It dawned on me that I was all by myself.[45]

Alongside this bitter reality, the detachment was a space of relief, providing shelter and companionship. The detachment was thus an ambiguous space. While it promised protection from genocide, it was also a constant reminder of the genocide that produced the need to provide for a large number of orphans. More generally, the detachment accommodated people who were outlawed by the occupation regime and, subsequently, for various reasons and on various levels, were rejected by influential forces within the Soviet partisan movement.

"Everybody had their task"

When Rita Kazhdan and her group arrived in the partisans' operating area in September 1943, the approximately 300 members of the unit had just gone through an extremely dangerous and exhausting period. Following the German defeat at Stalingrad in February 1943, the Soviet Army had gained the upper hand. In response, German troops increased the pressure on civilians and supporters of the Soviet regime. Refugees from the ghettos and Jewish partisans were doubly in danger, as both potential resisters and the enemy of Nazi racist ideology. The existence of a Jewish family unit was a provocation for those who consistently mobilized manpower and equipment to annihilate Jewish people.[46] Even before the war, the Germans had targeted "Judeo-Bolsheviks" for "indiscriminate and energetic" measures.[47] Any Jew outside the ghetto, for any reason, was free to be killed in the name of counterinsurgency.[48]

Shortly after the family unit had been established in May 1943, occupation forces intensified their attempts to destroy the partisans and their bases. The first three months of the unit's existence were fraught with fear. Vladimir Mordkhilevich recalls the terror that ran through the group on July 13, 1943, at the beginning of Operation Hermann, a large-scale antipartisan operation.[49] "There was an alarm once, I was woken up by some people, pushed around. We managed to flee into the swamps along some logs, Zorin hurried people to go faster. People panicked."[50] Operation Hermann aimed to destroy the five partisan brigades and approximately seven independent units located in the area between Lida, Stolbtsy, Minsk, and Molodechno. SS Infantry, SS Police battalions, Security Police, Security Service, forces of the Wehrmacht and Schutzmannschaften, and a few other organs gathered to crush the increasingly successful partisans.[51] Antipartisan troops typically deported large numbers of local residents to forced labor in the Reichsgebiet and burned down villages, remaining residents and all.[52] The Central Staff of the Belorussian Partisan Movement, aware that partisan forces stood no chance against the mass of war machinery and manpower concentrated in the area, ordered partisans to retreat rather than engage their attackers.[53]

Partisan intelligence units located in the Nalibokskaia Pushcha received information about the impending attack in the summer of 1943, allowing partisans to prepare their defenses and escapes. In the case of detachment No. 106, this meant finding a safe place to hide. Samuil Volk emphasized that

> Our commander knew that we shouldn't leave without a battle, but he also knew that there were many women, children and elderly with us. Not far from us there was an island in the swamp, about 4 km from us. We began to build a bridge out of logs. We would use it and destroy it behind us. Other partisans passed by and laughed at us. But he knew what he was doing. And when the Germans started their operation, there was an order to all partisans to not answer the fire, but to retreat. And so we were not the only people to use that bridge, but many other units did too.[54]

While it is unlikely that the partisans really built a four-kilometer-long bridge, they certainly did lay a log path to aid their escape across the swampy terrain. Amaliia Iakhontova and others remember the physical challenges posed by the uneven path: "I fell in between the logs, but one guy pulled me out. Otherwise I would have drowned there. We had to hide in the swamps, because the Germans chased us with dogs, but they couldn't pick up our tracks in the swamp."[55] Most of the approximately three hundred *zorintsy*, as the members of the units were called, managed to remain undetected, hiding in the swamp for four days.[56] Some sat in the swamp up to their chin or even plunged in completely, using straws to breathe while patrols searched the area; others used their belts to tie themselves to trees so they could rest, afloat, during the night.[57]

"War," Yakov Negnevitzki explains when recalling this situation, "for me is first of all hard work. I was used to the idea of being killed, but in that moment that was less significant. There was no food, we were constantly moving around, there were lice, we couldn't wash ourselves—war is hard physical labor."[58] For Negnevitzki, war is not just battle or warfare, but the everyday, physically strenuous, struggle to survive; he uses the term "labor" to describe this struggle. A closer look at the efforts of Zorin's family unit to secure the survival of its members, and other partisans as well, reveals the significance of the labor, the productive human activity, that Negnevitzki may have in mind.

After the blockade, which had effectively cut off communications between the encircled units and the regional staff, 270 villages had been burned and up to 20,000 residents had been either killed or deported to the Reichsgebiet for forced labor.⁵⁹ According to different sources, fifty (or fifty-two) partisans were wounded and 130 (or 129) killed, among them a group of six *zorintsy* who had been discovered and murdered.⁶⁰ During the operation, all residents of the village Skirmontovo, who were important supporters of the detachment, were wiped out, and a number of refugees from the Minsk ghetto who had just arrived were also killed.⁶¹ To develop a new base and find protection through mutual support, the units' leadership and members of the Minsk underground urged General Platon to allow relocation toward the village of Staroe Selo.⁶² Staroe Selo, for several months the entry gate into a life safe from daily pogroms, was destroyed during a similar operation in November 1943 when a number of partisans from several units gathered there and were attacked by German SS.⁶³ The Kulish family, who had welcomed many refugees from the Minsk ghetto, were also murdered for supporting the partisans.⁶⁴

In response to the destruction, particularly of their former base, and the loss of supplies, the "Zorin" unit relocated and restructured. Of the former base, Leonid Melamed explains,

> everything had been taken apart. The Germans had taken away all residents of the area, the villages were burned down, the cattle was gone. But it was September, the harvest was in the fields, and some chickens were running around. So all partisans started gathering the harvest.⁶⁵

The *zorintsy* split into several groups; one of the groups set up camp near the village Terebeinoe, another one near Rudnia.⁶⁶ Rita and Gera were formally admitted to the detachment in Terebeinoe, but then transferred to Rudnia to participate in the fieldwork there. Rebuilding the partisan base and collecting food from abandoned villages demanded hard labor. Both institutional records and personal accounts point to the effort that was necessary to accomplish the tasks.

Instructions to partisans in this period give a clear sense of the military organization necessary to establish a safe haven for ghetto refugees, as well as the new limitations and dangers it entailed. Reconstructing the campsite, the *zemlianki* (dugouts functioning as living quarters) and kitchen facilities, was "considered a military assignment" that was to be fulfilled between 5 a.m. and 9 p.m. on August 17. The military nature of the task was reinforced by the announcement that any partisans "responsible for the non-fulfillment of the task will be executed."[67] Later that month, the Interregional Headquarters of the Belorussian Partisan Movement instructed the detachment under Zorin's command to gather 600 poods (21,600 lbs.) of grain from fields associated with now-empty villages.[68] This task was also subject to military regimentation: four work brigades, comprised mainly of women, worked from 7 a.m. to 9 p.m., with one- and two-hour breaks for breakfast and lunch.[69]

Leonid Okon describes the morning roll call as an often funny event, with participants making fun of each other for counting incorrectly, or jokingly chastising women for having their chest stick out of the line. "People laughed, but at the same time we tried to keep some discipline, and everybody had their task."[70] Rita Kazhdan, who was assigned fieldwork immediately after arriving in the partisan camp, highlights the difficulties she and others experienced while fulfilling their tasks:

> We built up stocks of potatoes, carrots, beets, whatever was in the fields. We took all of that to the base camp and placed them in pits in the earth. Up until the first frost, we gathered the supplies. The norm for every day was one pood; everyone had to deliver that much per day. And it was so cold![71]

In addition to the fieldwork, a special platoon of the detachment visited nearby villages to collect or confiscate supplies. Survivors remember using force against local residents; this often targeted those who refused to support Jews. Though antisemitic behavior was seen as a form of Nazi collaboration and justified confiscations, a number of narrators regret the use of force and their involvement in the harsh competition for food.[72] They say that even the official endorsement of these requisitions through the Central Staff failed to make up for the burden that local farmers shouldered, facing both German and Soviet attempts to live off of local resources.[73]

Despite this hard labor, feeding more than five hundred people continued to be a challenge. Between June and October the unit had grown considerably, but supplies were limited to what people could find in the forest and the surrounding area. Mikhail Treister was so hungry that during the night he persistently ate small portions of his emergency ration until it was gone.[74] At some point he must have been so desperate that, together with three others, he broke into the unit's central emergency storage, a crime that sent him to detention for fifteen days, "with which [he] set a record."[75] Rita and her brother, who worked as a stoker in the camp kitchen, also resorted to unsanctioned ways to obtain food: "Gera suffered greatly, especially from the lack of salt; he couldn't eat the bland food. From the constant hunger he had sores on his legs. Sometimes we stole some potatoes from the storage and baked them in the fire."[76] Hunger thus continued to be a problem, though less so than in the ghetto.

Narrators also convey a palpable sense of pride when they speak about their hard work to find or produce food and other essential things for survival. Zoia Oboz specified: "We small ones collected branches and wood, farther away from the unit so it wasn't too obvious where our base was."[77] Others worked in the kitchen, peeled potatoes, dried grain, helped in the butcher shop, or worked as shoemakers, carpenters, tailors, and seamstresses.

Nearby detachments and the Central Staff of the Belorussian Partisan Movement also benefited from the labor of the *zorintsy* in different ways. The grain dryer and mill—built from millstones that partisans had found in the ruins of a nearby village and which they powered first with their own physical strength and later with horses—was an important device to process the grain that the *zorintsy* harvested.[78] Other units made use of the mill as well, leaving in return parts of the yield to the detachment.[79] The unit's correspondence and other interviews further testify to similar arrangements regarding the processing of meat to sausage, but also to sharing vegetables, salt, or cattle.[80]

The "Zorin" unit thus occupied an important position within the local and regional branch of the Soviet partisan movement. While in many orders it was referred to as a family unit, the unit acquired the status of a supply unit, receiving precise instructions as to how much food or goods were to be delivered. In preparation for winter 1943, for instance, orders issued by both the Central Staff and Zorin determined the amount of food to be stored and shoes and clothes to be produced.[81] At the same time, surrounding units were asked to help out with their supplies when the *zorintsy* were short of food in January 1944, and some delivered or agreed to support the partisans in their requisition activities.[82] One partisan commander, however, disapproved of the "Zorin" partisans' request to allow requisition in an area outside their usual base of supplies. He argued that the local farmers were currently very agitated because of German raids and propaganda efforts, suggesting they might react violently toward Jewish partisans rather than be supportive.[83]

Unit No. 106, its members, and many other family units occupied a crucial, yet difficult, place within the Soviet partisan movement and occupation society. On the one hand, people untrained and unprepared for military discipline and direct warfare, who had to be evacuated and protected, were met with suspicion, ridicule, and often rejection by other partisans. They slowed down mobility and flexibility, endangering not only themselves but also other detachments in their proximity. On the other hand, these family units supplied essential labor and services to other units and thus were an important element of the partisan movement. The work of specialists such as doctors, shoemakers, and locksmiths was indispensable for the collective and individual survival of partisans in the Belorussian woods.

"First they did not want her in Russian units, but then she was in high demand"

When the "Zorin" unit and other detachments had recovered and rebuilt their bases in the fall of 1943, more and more refugees from the Minsk ghetto arrived in Staroe Selo. This was partly because more Jews were escaping the ghetto, and partly because commanders of other units continued to refuse women, youth, and others supposedly unable to fight.[84] And yet, ghetto refugees' work was indispensable for the fighting partisans. Leonid Okon notes,

> There were shoemakers, tailors, carpenters—typical Jewish professions, and there were about 600 of them! Partisans from other units ordered what they needed and paid with arms or food. We were quite busy every day. . . . And there was a Dr. Livshits, first they did not want her in Russian units, but then she was in high demand.[85]

Professionals or craftspeople were of great use to the partisan movement, thus diminishing the initially hostile attitude of other partisan units. Several requests indicate that tailors, barbers, shoemakers, locksmiths, and typists were sought-after specialists; they were sent out to various units, and sometimes even kept there.[86] At times, Zorin had to decline requests from other units for a specialist visit because, for instance, the shoemaker's workload was already too high.[87]

In addition to the crafts people's qualifications, partisans were often in need of medical aid. Skirmishes or battles with occupation or collaboration forces, or with residents who resisted confiscations of food and other supplies, claimed a number of victims. A substantial number of physicians' assignments addressed injuries of partisan combatants, both members of the "Zorin" and of other detachments. Thus, medical specialists among the unit, including surgeons, dentists, and others, were sent to other units, or partisans were transferred to the hospital.[88]

Living in the forest with insufficient opportunity to maintain personal hygiene also posed a danger. Nurses and doctors worked hard to prevent the spread of lice and filth, transmitters of dangerous epidemics.[89] Vladimir Mordkhilevich recalls: "We children suffered greatly from lice. It was like a piece of fur walking away from us. We had scabs everywhere. They treated us with juice from birch trees; that made our skin very smooth but it also made all our hair fall out."[90] Samuil Volk remembers another treatment: "They smothered us with cart grease, for some days we looked like Negroes, then we washed it off and the scabs were gone. That was an impressive remedy."[91] Unlike in the ghetto, lice, scabs, and common diseases usually did not cause death in the partisan unit, as the medical unit tried to contain them as best as they could.[92]

Refugees from the ghettos brought in supplies for the medics' work, just as Rita Kazhdan described; other times such resources were requisitioned from locals and subsequently distributed among the various detachments.[93] At times, there were deliveries with essential goods by air from the Soviet rear. Demand for medical aid was high, and in the spring of 1944 courses to train partisans in basic medical skills were organized.[94]

Dr. Rozaliia Livshits, known to be an excellent surgeon and gynecologist, was in especial demand, particularly for women's health issues.[95] Sometimes she was requested to "perform an abortion," or "bring equipment" for this purpose.[96] Other times, "a gynecologist" or the "loan of tools for an abortion" were requested.[97] From the written records it is unclear whether all requests for Dr. Livshit's visits were aimed at gynecological operations or abortions, but several interviewees indicate—off the record—that she was in high demand precisely because of her qualifications as a gynecologist, and that there were many abortions.[98] That abortions occurred is often articulated in a hushed voice, in an allusive, ironic tone, as in Leonid Okon's comment above that Dr. Livshits was initially dismissed by Russian partisans but later "in high demand," or the descriptions are accompanied by insinuating looks that demand the subject not be pursued any further. My attempts to solicit more information about sexual relationships and their consequences commonly failed.[99]

Female members of partisan units were often assigned tasks typically understood to be women's labor, including preparing food, working as nurses, or keeping order in the detachment's base. Often they performed this labor in addition to other tasks, such as guarding the unit.[100] In addition, women partisans were often forced to engage in intimate relationships with male partisans, usually of higher rank, commanders of brigades or units, chiefs of staff, respected combatants. At the same time, romantic relationships rooted in true affection occurred as well. In several instances, however, the outcomes of such relationships were identified as problematic and, more often than not, the women were left to deal with them.[101]

Childbirth and child rearing in a partisan unit was a difficult proposition. However, coercive relationships potentially resulting in pregnancy or other adverse health conditions for women, coupled with the fact that the burden of addressing these results fell on women, indicate an ongoing disregard for women. They also suggest the unwillingness of partisan leadership to address the social consequences of promoting an all-inclusive partisan movement. This may itself be an extension of 1930s Soviet gender policies, which formally advocated equality but failed to implement it in factories and other institutions.[102] It is also indicative of the Soviet partisan movement's embeddedness in traditions of male-defined military spaces, the gendered division of labor, sexualized forms of violence, and the dismissal of shared responsibility for both. Either way, women and questions of gender have been placed at the margins of the partisan movement and its memory. This marginalization is intertwined with others, such as the division of labor in the unit and notions of militarized masculinity, authority, and the state.

Of partisan sisters and brothers

Relationships among partisans, sexual or otherwise, often emerge as one of the few fond memories of being in "Zorin's family unit." Interviewees speak about them in terms of mutual support and stability in a context defined by displacement and uncertainty. For adolescents, such relationships promised emotional bonds that were not continuously threatened by violence like other interactions they had had since the beginning of the occupation.

Furthermore, they were not exclusively defined by utilitarian considerations of procuring food or heating material or finding a way out of the ghetto.

Samuil Volk and his brother Ziama forged such personal connections when an older partisan, Isaak, "adopted" the two boys:

> He was a local, very combative and very strong. While he led us to the partisan detachment, he asked me about everything, and when we arrived at the camp, he said that we should stay with him. We couldn't turn that down and shared a zemlianka with him.[103]

Zoia Oboz, who had realized that she had lost everyone, found a similar substitute family:

> Slowly I started to engage with other children. My friend Ida's mother Rakhil then began to take care of me. She made sure I ate and washed myself. Then we moved to the winter camp, and there I ended up in a big zemlianka with many other children. We often gathered around the oven.[104]

Amaliia Iakhontova describes the moments around the campfire where she and her "partisan brother," Samuil Volk, shared stories and memories.[105] Similarly, Rita Kazhdan fondly remembers her "partisan sisters" Polia and Sonia Shostak, with whom she and Gera built a common hut. "Without a single nail," the four youth created a home in the midst of the woods, laying the groundwork for a long-lasting friendship.[106] Sharing the experience of surviving scarcity and danger required mutual support and resulted in strong emotional bonds.

The use of sisterhood and brotherhood to describe these bonds is interesting. The vocabulary is reminiscent of prewar Soviet propaganda and Stalin's speech of July 3, 1941, in which he addressed Soviet listeners as "Comrades, citizens, brothers and sisters!"[107] At the same time, these terms invoke the identification of the detachment as a "family unit." In both cases, the familial relationship is symbolic. Using the framework of the family is thus the result of a deliberate choice to characterize human relationships and allocate meaning to them. Sisterhood and brotherhood replace pervasive inequality and violence, reviving ideas of the equality of people across class, gender, and national boundaries popular in the visionary prewar period in order to build a community in which to survive war and genocide. The partisan detachment was a space built upon solidarity rather than difference, a sharp contrast to Nazi ideas about racial communities such as the Aryan race. Granted, the relationships described by Samuil Volk and others emerged within a largely Jewish unit, and yet they were the outcome of force and necessity. The unit, and ideas of family and solidarity therein, united people who had suffered displacement and violence because they were Jewish. These shared experiences brought adolescents together in the confined space of the partisan unit. Zemlianki were the literal roofs under which these teenagers gathered and developed sisterly and brotherly relationships.

Zemlianki in the summer camp were small, housing between five and twenty people. Toward the winter of 1943/1944, when the detachment's camp was more stable and secure, bigger ones were built, housing up to fifty people. They not only provided shelter, but were also sites of communality. Although Mikhail Treister's mother and sister were also present in the detachment, he chose to live separately from them:

> We young boys built our separate zemlianka, we called it 'Gop so smykom.' We talked a lot among ourselves, told each other stories, about what we had read before the war and such. We had a good time, considering what we had gone through and that we had just made it out from there.[108]

"Gop so smykom" (referring to a pickpocket) is the title of a folk song popularized by singer and artist Leonid Utiosov in the late 1920s and early 1930s. The song describes the life of a trickster who chooses to make a life on the streets as a petty criminal. While this song displays the optimism of a young male, the term *gopnik* is also used to describe young men under the age of thirty with problematic behavior, such as aggression against the weak or alcohol abuse. Treister's explanation of the dugout's name in his written account, "just like me, they were all romantics," juxtaposes the surrounding danger and grief with the teenage boys' drive to be wild and silly. This was also where Treister "realized that humanity consists of men and women"; here, he learned to dance and experienced his first kiss.[109] The boys' desire to be "real men" also entailed the desire to become "real partisan[s]."[110] Treister repeatedly highlights his unhappiness with his assigned task as a cobbler and how his stubbornness eventually enabled him to build a weapon for himself and convince Shalom Zorin that he should be a member of the military platoon.

Younger children, especially orphans like Vladimir Mordkhilevich, who was ten at the time, may have found the situation rather dull and limited their attention to finding food:

> Sometimes we children would talk to each other and concluded it was better in the ghetto. There were more adventures; we could find our own food and such. But here—there was hunger, rain, nothing to do. Parents who had come with their children took care of their children, brought them special treats. We didn't get any of this. There were thirty to forty orphans, we weren't friends, but we stuck together. We often tried to grab things from the kettle.[111]

Samuil Volk's remark that he and his brother were "probably in a better situation" because they had an *opekun* (guardian, foster father) indicates that adults' care for their own or "adopted" children was crucial for both the emotional and material survival in the unit. Isaak taught him how to ride a horse and explained how a gun functioned: "He regularly entrusted me with his revolver. I cleaned it; I knew how it worked. But I didn't have my own weapon, none of the children had."[112] The unit's leadership, it appears, actively tried to bar children from access to weapons, whereas rank-and-file partisans were much more lenient and had no problem introducing teenagers to them.

The "Zorin" unit was organized according to military principles, assigning individuals specific tasks and requiring them to follow established discipline. Underneath, or alongside, this regime, however, developed informal spaces in which these rules were partly irrelevant, and sociality among youth or within substitute family systems developed. These bonds, based on trust and shared experience, provided a strong foundation for mutual assistance and surviving genocidal threats and losses.

"And so I became a real partisan"

Living in the detachment was a social experience that enabled adolescents and adults to form new personal relationships and communality. At the same time, life in the unit was also deeply embedded in, and shaped by, the features of a partisan unit as a militarized space. Ongoing antipartisan operations by the occupation regime and, in the spring of 1944, the Soviet army's drive to liberate Soviet territory as well as German counterattacks, posed continuous threats to the partisans' bases and livelihood.

The challenges of surviving in the forest, of exhausting physical labor, of trying to hold on to newly established relationships, and of worrying about any remaining siblings increased in periods when the unit was under attack. In these moments, the safe haven became a site of renewed danger, in a double sense: German antipartisan operations targeted partisans for what they did, and Jews for what they were imagined to be. Moreover, many Jews among the partisan units were unarmed and relegated to maintenance units, and were thus the least able to defend themselves. The hundred Jews who lived in a family camp under the leadership of Hirsh Atlas, and who were killed as a form of retaliation for a previous partisan operation, are a clear example of both hierarchies within the partisan movement and the exceptional Nazi brutality directed against Jews.[113] Simultaneously, the vulnerability of noncombatants highlights the harsh realities and consequences of military discipline and order, which assigned specific tasks to individual people and often overrode their own will or needs.

Living with the "Zorin" detachment provoked a variety of emotions, ranging from relief to fear. The urge to survive existed alongside the desire for revenge. Narrators attest to their fear of wolves and raids, and describe their efforts to participate in evacuations and military assignments. For some, all of this was part of being with the partisans; for others, it was the combat assignments that turned them into "real partisans"; and for still others, they would always be denied the opportunity to become "real" partisans. The militarized character of the refuge in the forest is established by some common events that figure prominently in nearly all accounts. These moments include attacks by Polish partisans against Jewish partisans, the hard realities of establishing discipline in the unit, and the execution of traitors and German soldiers.

August and September 1943 were months of rebuilding and consolidating the unit after Operation Herrmann. An important aspect of this was increasing and intensifying the detachment's capacity to protect itself. As a result, Rita Kazhdan explains,

> all members of the detachment who were physically able and could handle a weapon participated in the protection of the unit. We had two posts, one was close to the unit, approximately 2 km away, and then there was an

outpost, about 6 km from the unit. So I was a part of the guard company. We were armed, and we always went in groups of four ... In the beginning I was scared, but now, after having been in the partisans, I am not afraid of anything anymore.[114]

Such statements suggest that partisans were aware that, whatever they did, they might fall victim to a variety of unexpected dangers. This vulnerability was made palpable in such moments as the killing of several members of the "Zorin" unit's combat platoon by Polish partisans in November 1943.

Leonid Melamed explains the tenuous relationship between Polish and Soviet partisans in unequivocal terms: "they were a greater nuisance than the Germans, it was unclear whether they were with us or with the Germans, whether we could work with them or should hide from them."[115] Arkadii Teif, fifteen years old, had been trained as a member of the demolition squad and frequently went on missions with small groups of the approximately 120 combatants to blow up rails or attack German or police garrisons. He describes one deadly assault:

In September 1943 we went on a mission and were ambushed by Polish partisans near Dubovnik. They beat us up all night, me less so than others. And then one by one they were shot. I was hit in the shoulder. I came to lie under corpses, covered in blood and brains.[116]

Arkadii was able to crawl out and escape; partisans later found him and he recovered after a long time in the detachment's hospital. Teif and Liova Cherniak, who had both managed to run away, were the only survivors of this attack.[117] Rita Kazhdan's remark that "this is our history, as people say, you don't need to read books for that. We saw it and lived it," points to her and others' knowledge of how vulnerable Jewish partisans were. The conflict between Polish and Soviet partisans was a long-standing one, connected with Polish attempts to regain Belorussian territories that had been annexed by the Soviet state in 1939. Decisive in the killing in September 1943, however, was a strong antisemitic attitude among Polish nationalists who were able and willing to kill those Jews who had barely evaded the Nazi genocide.[118]

Arkadii Teif's portrayal is a stark reminder of the dangers associated with being a "real" partisan, with participating in combat missions or requisitioning food in villages. Similarly, the defense of the family unit put guards at risk, and Germans or Polish partisans regularly ambushed guard posts.

Literally every interviewee recalls the last attack on the unit on July 6, 1944, with shock. Retreating from Soviet troops advancing across Belorussian territory, a German regiment passed through the area where the detachment was based. It is unclear whether German troops attacked, as a report by the Chief of Staff claims, or whether, as survivors argue, Zorin attacked, overestimating partisan capacities and hoping in vain for combat support from other units.[119] Six partisan combatants were killed in the ensuing skirmish, and two members of the family unit and two partisans were seriously wounded, including commander Zorin.[120] Those who were members of the combat platoon argue that they did not have enough weapons for a serious attack. Leonid Okon says, "we couldn't even scare them. They destroyed the camp completely."[121] It is unclear whether everyone in the unit was aware of the danger they were in. In interviews, nobody provided details about their whereabouts during the battle.

A partisan's life—whether in combat, utility, or maintenance units—was governed by discipline. Harsh punishments served to enforce both rules and fulfillment of assignments. Leonid Okon, for instance, was castigated for falling asleep while he was on guard: "I had to perform kitchen duty for two days and was not assigned to the post anymore."[122] Similar violations and punishment are documented in the detachment's report. Others are not, among them one that occurred during the blockade in summer 1943. There is a gap of documentation between July 10 and July 29, 1943, presumably the time when partisans where hiding in the swamp, but even if documents had been available, one wonders whether they would account for Mordkhilevich's reluctant description of how violations of discipline were prosecuted.

Hunger was a major problem, especially during the blockades when partisans were required to abandon their base and leave all supplies behind. One teenager was unable to bear the hunger when the detachment hid in the swamps. He left the group to pick some berries, thus violating the commander's order to stay put. Upon his return, Vladimir Mordkhilevich narrates, "Zorin shot him because Germans might have followed him and he wanted to demonstrate to others that what he had done was impermissible."[123] The elderly Mordkhilevich hesitated for a long time to report this incident and responded only to the interviewer's explicit push to do so. This hesitation, again, shows the reluctance to portray less favorable aspects of the partisan movement—here, the strong punishments meted out against rule violations among partisans themselves. Mordkhilevich is aware of the fine line that everyone in the partisan unit walked. Following his reluctant statement regarding Zorin's rigor he says, "I could have been shot too. They just didn't know what I did. I went to pick berries some time later, and when I saw a German plane, I yelled at them."[124] The anger of a child who has no other way of articulating his aggression against those who killed his family could have easily cost him his own life, this time at the hands of those whom he joined for protection. The commander's shooting of the young boy who did not follow orders ceased to have meaning for Mordkhilevich in this instant; emotions overtook his struggle to integrate himself into the unit, the space of survival. Mordkhilevich's portrayal thus highlights how ideas of military discipline conflicted with the personal experiences and perceptions of survivors of genocide.

Policies to secure discipline and order stood in stark contrast to the immediate needs and wishes of civilians who by force had ended up in a military formation, the partisan unit. In addition to the difficulty of making people follow orders, what the refugees had gone through in the ghetto at times resulted in uncontrollable anger and violence. For some of the *zorintsy*, the wish to avenge the loss of parents turned into a strong desire to fight. Both Mikhail Treister and Leonid Okon describe their mindset at the time in similar words: "I could not sit still. I wanted to fight the whole time. I wanted revenge. That was very boyish of me."[125] Leonid Okon also indicates that even those who had neither the opportunity nor ability to fight still wanted to act on their desire for payback:

> Once a German was caught and brought to the base. They didn't even manage to interrogate him. People basically tore him to pieces. That was a horrible picture; they ripped his hair out, women, elderly people. And everybody shouted "for my son, for my husband," etc. Somebody then shot in the air to stop this, and Zorin tried to give this an official coating, proclaimed that "in the name of the Belorussian Partisan Movement I sentence . . ."[126]

Okon did not finish the sentence, counting on us listeners to fill in the end. Zoia Oboz recalls a similar situation, describing how, when two German soldiers were captured in June 1944, "all children wanted to at least hit them once with a stick for all the suffering they had brought to them."[127] Vladimir Mordkhilevich gives an idea of what it was like to watch, or participate in, such forms of revenge:

> Once a group of seven Germans was caught. They made them undress and lined them up near a barn, then they shot them. I watched this, but then I ran away until I fell into the grass. There I cried for a long time. I couldn't comprehend that those naked people were Germans, Fascists. I understood that we were in a situation where there was no other choice, there was no place to keep them, but . . . If they would have worn uniforms it would have been different. I cried for a long time. I don't even know why, I never cried when I quarreled with other kids. I think I remembered all my relatives who were also naked when they were shot.[128]

Whether ten-year-old Vladimir indeed imagined his relatives being shot or whether the older Mordkhilevich's description is an attempt to rationalize his discomfort at the sight of an execution is only marginally important. Rather, his attempt to explain to the interviewer and future listeners the ambivalence, or even unease, with which adolescents looked upon death points to their problematic situation after experiencing murder and violence for twenty-four months, from July 1941 till the summer of 1943, when they were able to leave the ghetto.

It is striking that only a few of the narrators were able or willing to describe their feelings regarding revenge, pain, or emotional distress as a result of facing death and violence. These are difficult themes, yet it is possible that the interviewees' socialization in the Soviet Union, before, during, and after the war, plays a significant role in how they present these experiences. Some scholars argue that the repressions and purges of the 1930s normalized the use of violence against enemies, presumed or otherwise.[129] In addition, the portrayal and conceptualization of war and genocide in Soviet society as an affront to the Soviet project may have played a significant role in enabling a rationalized, objective narrative that rarely addresses individual experiences. The role of Soviet institutions, however, in shaping such accounts cannot be overestimated.

"To our beloved friend and father, our dear Iosif Vissarionovich Stalin"

The hope for survival that partisans found in the family unit was fragile and always under threat. But—what if? What if the war ended? What if there was a future without bullets and mines and hunger? Rita Kazhdan's descriptions of her thoughts at the time are a reminder of the rupture that the occupation meant for her:

> Although we barely hoped that we would survive, I kept thinking: "If I stay alive, I won't remember anything, I don't know anything... what am I going to do?" So I constantly repeated the multiplication table to myself. When I was lying on my bunk bed, there were these four logs above me, and I looked at them and practiced mathematics.[130]

She did not say whether she shared her thoughts with her friends, or whether others in the detachment entertained similar ideas about their future. The will to survive is what most narrators evoke when asked about their thoughts or wishes at the time. Plans for the future, it appears, were either difficult to devise or not sufficiently developed to be memorable.

The Soviet state, in contrast, had a clear idea about the future of partisans and survivors, especially of young ones. Party control over the partisan movement was part of the government's attempt to centralize its command over the movement. This effort was reflected first of all in the installation of commissars and Special Departments within detachments. Commissars were assigned to secure partisans' loyalty to state and Party; Special Departments to detect potential spies in the units and to set up intelligence networks both within the partisan units and among the local population.[131] The Party's aim, however, went further and targeted the hearts and minds of those who had been under hostile, fascist influence for a considerable time. The partisans' aim was not only to "make the Germans' life miserable," as Elena Drapkina says.[132] The partisans' mission was also to restore, or produce, local civilians' faith in the Soviet state as the eventual victor of the war and peacemaker, through leaflets, newspapers, and concerts organized by "agitation brigades" within the partisan movement.[133] Propaganda meetings in the villages were one way of distributing this message, and the "Zorin" detachment was asked to participate in the organization of such campaigns.[134]

Education and instruction were also aimed at the units themselves, addressing both the partisans' political commitments and, in the case of teenagers and younger children, their general intellectual development. While Rita Kazhdan describes her individual attempts to keep her mind alert and functioning, younger children were eventually gathered in a makeshift school. Amaliia Iakhontova, sixteen or seventeen years old at the time, acknowledges the efforts of "teachers to take care of the little ones. Whenever possible, they taught them how to read and write."[135] One of the teachers, Anna Sagal'chik, said that Zorin approached her with a request to establish such a school, out of concern that there were a number of children in the unit who were seven and not yet of school age when German troops invaded the country. More than two years into the war, they were nine and ten years old and still did not know a single letter:

> Imagine, to think, in this extremely difficult situation, with all the problems and dangers around us, about the fate of these children. Not to think only about saving their lives, but to enable them to feel more or less like normal people when the war is over and they could enter at least second grade.[136]

Knowing that Sagal'chik had studied at the Pedagogical Institute before the war, the commander asked that she use her day off from sentry duty to start teaching basic skills like reading, writing, and calculating to the children. Of course there were no proper school supplies, but the pupils made do with sticks or coal and birchbark and learned to write.[137]

Teachers, including Anna Sagal'chik, Vika Babirshina, and Dora Solomonova, also told stories or used books that partisans retrieved during requisition missions to read and teach the students history and literature.[138] Vladimir Mordkhilevich's list of books, poems, and songs that he remembers clearly indicates the aim of such instruction; in addition to reading poems and stories about patriotic partisans, teachers taught the students the value of communism and loyalty to Lenin and Stalin.[139] Samuil Volk adds that "there were no grades, there was no lesson plan. They told us whatever was interesting and important, they spoke about what happened at the front, where our troops were, that they were advancing toward us and such things."[140] Alongside the teaching of basic literacy, education aimed to reestablish the youths' trust in the power of the Soviet state to liberate them from Nazi violence and to provide for a bright future. The portrayal of the ongoing war was simultaneously an attempt to write and rewrite history, promoting an account that highlighted the victorious achievements of army and partisans and the patriotic, undivided heroism of civilians. Reestablishing the dominance of Soviet ideology was a strong motive of the Komsomol's leadership to intensify political instruction in the occupied territories and turn the Soviet youth into "real partisans" able to effectively resist German rule.[141] Simultaneously, propaganda materials highlighted children and youth as activists for the Soviet cause, emphasizing their heroism and self-sacrificing participation in the defense of the Soviet Union.[142]

A letter that some youths sent to Stalin clearly articulates these efforts. On May 1, 1944, the detachment celebrated International Labor Day in a festive gathering prepared by the Deputy Commissar A. Mel'tser.[143] Partisans not only acknowledged the holiday but also celebrated the first anniversary of partisan detachment No. 106 and its contribution to the patriotic struggle for the defense of the fatherland.[144] Children received white shirts, made out of parachutes, and red neckerchiefs to mark the foundation of a *pionerskaia druzhina* (Pioneer brigade) and the teenagers' admission into the Soviet Pioneer organization. Two days later, on May 3, a letter was dispatched in which the voice of forty-two Pioneers addressed "our beloved friend and father, our dear Iosif Vissarionovich Stalin."[145] They describe their experience of murder and destruction in "our wonderful Soviet Belorussia that is now temporarily occupied by German bastards." Having endured the "loss of human face and real names," "turned into thieves to avoid starvation," the young were fortunate to "escape and, in lieu of murdered relatives, find new friends with the name partisans." As "Soviet children," they "promise to strive for excellent school grades" and, "together with the adults, retaliate against the enemy for our homeland, the destroyed cities and villages." The list of signatories includes Portnova (maiden name of Sonia Zalesskaia), Mordkhilevich (Vladimir Mordkhilevich), and two Volks (Samuil and his brother). While Mordkhilevich explains that "Zorin wrote the letter," Volk argues that "we even wrote a letter to Stalin, in the name of the Pioneers, that we would take revenge on the fascists for the death of our relatives." Samuil Volk "had forgotten about the letter" until he read about it in the memoir of a fellow partisan, but, he says, "when I read about it I remembered that I had signed it. I didn't remember the text, but I had signed it. Of course that had all been done with the help of adults, the teachers and leadership of the unit."[146] The two men are the only narrators to mention the letter; when I asked her about it, Rita Kazhdan denied having ever heard about it. It is therefore likely that the letter was indeed drawn up by adults, giving the young partisans a language to describe their experience and to express their loyalty to the Soviet state, as Pioneers and patriotic avengers of the destruction of the homeland.

Phrases framing the partisan struggle as a contribution to the heroic and patriotic defense of the Soviet homeland are frequently invoked in speeches given by Zorin, for instance on the importance of resistance against the occupation, more than two years after it began (October 3, 1943), on International Women's Day (March 8, 1944), and on International Labor Day (May 1, 1944).[147] Zorin praised the heroic fulfillment of these tasks, and thus firmly established the heroes as role models. Indeed, the portrayal of different ways to participate in the state's defense and the rescue and protection of civilians features a distinction, most clearly expressed in different forms of reward for women and men. A closer look at the rhetoric of heroism, displayed in both how the partisan leadership is addressed and an internal reward system, reveals that gender played an important role in the social organization of the partisan movement.

In the letter, Stalin was greeted as "friend and father," thus equating his leadership of the state with the role of a patriarch.[148] Anna Sagal'chik, one of the teachers and a twenty-five-year-old woman at the time, noted in passing that members of the family unit used to call Zorin *otets* (father), which reflects a similar recognition of his authority over the community. The symbolic identification of fatherhood with leadership in the context of the family unit allocates to Zorin the ability to make unilateral decisions about the internal functioning of the family (unit) and to require obedience. Furthermore, it draws on a gendered conception of individual roles in the unit, in which adult masculinity justifies leadership, authority, and power over people identified otherwise. A concrete expression of this relationship is the case of Sonia Marshak, who was denied entry to the ranks of combatants in the unit. In a letter to the Interregional Headquarters of the Belorussian Partisan Movement, Marshak complained that upon her arrival in the unit in August 1943, commander Zorin and chief of staff Wertheim ordered her to surrender the pistol she brought with her and which she had used as a rank-and-file partisan in the "Parkhomenko" unit. She refused the order, and Wertheim took the weapon away by force.[149] On the basis of available documents we cannot reconstruct the further repercussions of this conflict; other than a note on Sonia Marshak's transfer to the "Bielski" unit in December 1943 and her return to detachment No. 106 in April 1944, there is no more information about the woman's presence in the detachment.[150] And yet the leadership's refusal of a woman's wish to engage in partisan combat may indicate a persistent conception of the division of labor in which women are not considered fit or able for military combat.

The gendered division of labor was complemented by a hierarchical system of valorization in which the labor assigned and accessible to women had a lower value than that of fighting men. Not only was kitchen duty used as punishment for partisans who fell asleep on guard or failed to fulfill assignments, it was also considered of less merit in the framework of anti-German resistance.[151] On the occasion of two years of struggle against the occupants, a number of partisans were awarded watches, boots, and other goods.[152] Women, standing shoulder to shoulder with male snipers, blasters, doctors, nurses—all praised for their contributions to the defense of the homeland and the rescue of Soviet citizens—received only an honorable mention. Anatol Wertheim received a watch for investigating the shooting of eleven partisans by Polish partisans, the scout F. Raskin 200 rubles for a successful reconnaissance operation.[153] Anna Sagal'chik's day off from sentry duty was canceled so that she could help educate the young, reproducing a pattern of placing the double burden of industrial labor and family work on women familiar from before the war. While everyone was called on to participate in the patriotic struggle, everyone was also assigned a particular position in this endeavor, and a hierarchy was established among these positions: whereas partisan combat and the documentation of its victims received material recognition, women's work in the family unit was acknowledged symbolically. This pattern, in which household, or female, labor remained second rank to heroic, male labor, was familiar from propanda in the early Soviet Union. Women workers were rarely portrayed, and, if at all, as helpers and companions of male workers, but seldom as independent masters of a trade. Female labor, the message was, only played a supporting role, but one that was neglible in comparison to men's work.[154]

The celebration of Soviet holidays, forms of appraisal for partisans' achievements, and schooling reflect attempts to promote values of Soviet patriotism and heroism, and to add meaning to the Soviet citizens' engagement in the partisan movement. Simultaneously, this value system called up the notion of a gendered division of labor. The partisan movement's award system, prioritizing combat and party work, enforced a differentiated acknowledgement and thus discriminated against everyone, female or male, who did not participate in these tasks, including people like Sonia Marshak who were actively denied the opportunity to identify as combatants. Such internal hierarchies reflect a general tendency in military settings, but they also neglect the context in which saving lives is a dangerous mission requiring hard work. The creation of such hierarchies also denies that fieldwork, preparing food, and mending clothes and shoes are essential for civilians and combatants alike, as Yakov Negnevitzki points out: "imagine, they were 2 km from our fighters, they ran a hospital, worked as shoemakers, tailors, there was a school, a mill—and they all worked for several detachments. No fighting unit could have existed without this."[155]

Finally, the emphasis on heroic and vengeful combat against the enemy elided Rita Kazhdan's insecurity about bare survival, and the unease with which children like Vladimir Mordkhilevich may have looked upon further violence, despite feelings of hatred and anger against Germans and collaborators. For others, however, the participation in combat missions provided a channel precisely for such emotions. Samuil Volk and his brother Ziama, Arkadii Teif, Leonid Okon, and many others eagerly joined troops of the regular army when these advanced through Belorussia and liberated the area from Nazi occupation in June 1944. Up to 25,000 orphaned boys were adopted by division commanders or officers. The *synovia polka* (sons of the regiment) helped prepare food for the leadership, worked as messengers between divisions and battalions, or fulfilled other tasks that, for the most part, did not involve the use of weapons. An equal number of orphans lived on navy ships and with partisans throughout the war.[156] Other members of the unit returned to Minsk, facing new challenges related to the destruction of their homes, the loss of all relatives, but first of all to the collapse of Soviet society as it had existed three years before.

Nationality and gender in Jewish family units

A complex of circumstances and relationships within and beyond the unit shaped partisans' struggle for survival. The elements, warfare, scarcity, and conflicts among various nationalities and competing political entities meant that they had to organize shelter, food, and care while engaging in combat or other military operations to disrupt the occupation regime's infrastructure. All the partisans' activities were directed toward the long-term goal of destroying the occupation regime and securing their liberation and future. And all of this was built on mutual assistance and group cohesion; survival demanded a group effort. Collaborative or shared labor contributed to securing food and equipment and supported a collective reaching far beyond the immediate unit. Soviet state propaganda as well as such institutions as the Pioneer organization, the Komsomol, and the Communist Party imparted meaning to these collective efforts. Calling on members to defend the Soviet homeland, save Soviet civilians' lives, and avenge Nazi atrocities, partisans were ordered to engage in specifically assigned tasks, including military missions, fieldwork, and, for children, learning. On the surface, all these elements appear to be of equal value in the partisan movement. And yet, the difficulties that Jews faced in gaining access to the partisans and recognition during and after the war show that the situation was much more complex.

Rita Kazhdan was long silent about her partisan activities during the war; that she feared being stigmatized indicates a fragile relationship between the larger public (including institutions such as veteran's offices) and the partisan movement, which resulted in omissions and distortions in postwar portrayals. For one, former female partisans were frequently dismissed as "fallen women" who had gained access to and protection from partisans by selling their bodies and virtue. However, in the case of the "Zorin" unit, the discrimination targeted not only women, but also included those who were not members of the combat group within the unit. As Leonid Melamed points out, the distinction between fighters and family units, drawn by the leadership during the war, resulted in discriminatory treatment after the war:

> Our detachment was divided in a combat platoon and a family unit. I was part of the combat platoon; therefore I count as a Belorussian partisan and war veteran. There were about a hundred of us. The remaining six hundred were counted as the so-called family unit, they did not receive any benefits. That is of course a failure of the leadership. I don't know why they did that, because there were women and adolescents in all units, even in the Russian ones, and they all counted as partisans. Most of the partisans were people from the villages and brought their families, and no matter whether they were women or children, they were considered partisans, and after the war they were also counted as Belorussian partisans—except for our unit.[157]

Melamed and others argue that the distinction between the combat platoon and the family unit precluded equal recognition for members of partisan detachment No. 106 after the war. Ekaterina Tsirlina's attempts to receive official validation for her work in the underground and family unit serve as a vivid example of this. While it is very likely that anti-Jewish attitudes played a role in enabling the discrimination of individuals, the conflict is also rooted in competing, or exclusive, understandings of what counts as legitimate and valuable resistance against the Nazi regime. A closer look at the meaning of the "Zorin" unit reveals that a combination of sexist and antisemitic stereotypes may be at the root of the exclusion of family units from the memory of the partisan movement and considerations of resistance more generally.

Etymologically, "resistance" describes opposing or withstanding something. In historico-political discourse, specifically, it describes opposition to an invading, occupying, or ruling power, or an organized body of individuals engaged in such opposition.[158] In political and sociological analyses, resistance typically denotes forms of struggle that aim at some kind of progress, unifying a collective to overthrow current conditions based on the idea of a common cause.[159] In other words, resistance is understood to be oppositional and geared toward gaining power. As a whole, the Soviet partisan movement followed a similar mandate; the ultimate objective was to overthrow the Nazi occupation and liberate territory and people from oppression and terror, ensuring survival. Military operations are unquestionably recognized as acts toward this goal. Detachment No. 106 and all efforts to save civilians occupy a complicated space within such a framework. The common cause for the majority of the unit was to survive, and to create the basis that would enable that survival; the labor of the unit's members was determined by quality of life and sociality, not power. The devaluation of members of the family units delegitimizes these efforts as forms of resistance, despite both their function in disrupting the force of a genocidal project and their central function in enabling the other, power-oriented form of resistance.

The term "family unit" is a strong indicator that the distinction between combat and survival is deeply gendered and draws on notions of labor and violence feeding into the creation of social hierarchies. Not everyone who would eventually join detachment No. 106 was part of a family or came with their family. Rather, the name conjures traditional sites of reproduction, of securing survival. The family is traditionally the space where women perform the social services needed for reproduction, of labor power and of the family itself. That the "Zorin" unit, at one point, was home to 280 Jewish women visibly confirmed this image.[160] Where the Soviet partisan movement included between approximately 5 and 9 percent women, detachment No. 106 had a much larger proportion, up to 50 percent.[161] Most of these women were not assigned to combat tasks, but engaged in what could be identified as reproductive labor necessary for hundreds of combatants and others. The name "family unit" thus aptly describes the role of these detachments in enabling survival of the people, the community, and providing for combatants in need of prepared food, medical aid, mended clothes, or weapons. While the safe haven in the form of the family unit was only possible within the framework of the Soviet partisan movement as a whole, it was also essential for it.

Alongside the marginalization of struggle aimed at survival and not at rule, the marginalization of women and Jews in the partisan movement reproduces patterns of the patriarchal organization of labor in which reproductive labor is devalued (unpaid) and made invisible, yet is indispensable for the production of the (wage) laborer.[162] The hierarchy of rewards and punishments within the unit—the use of kitchen duty as a form of punishment for combatants—and postwar policies that denied equal recognition to members of the family units demonstrate the effects of concepts that assign particular kinds of labor, or resistance, different values. Patriarchal authority is thus not only exemplified by the identification of Zorin and Stalin as the "father." It is first of all articulated in combatants and leaders making women do domestic work and having access to women's bodies.[163]

Reports of women being refused by combat units or having abortions and of the punishment of children in search of food remind us that, like many families, the family unit was likely a site of hidden violence against women and children as well as a site of patriarchal authority. It thereby fulfilled a function similar to families and private households, which provide a space for forms of agency denied in public. Here, this denial was produced by the occupation regime; elsewhere it might be an authoritarian society or an oppressive work environment. The exercise of power, or the longing for it, was rerouted into the "private" space of the family unit.

Writing about the family unit reveals the difficulty of portraying the struggle for survival in a way that is cognizant of various forms of labor and the affective dimensions of experience. The challenge resides in the fact that narrators produce few details about this labor and these dimensions. In contrast, narrators equate military engagement with "real" partisanship, and (mostly male) participants in or survivors of combat missions are able to give minute descriptions of events involving, for instance, attacks on police garrisons or blowing up railroads. Drawing largely on biographical interviews in which narrators set their own foci, the limited or absent portrayal of civilian labor is an indicator of internalized patterns of recognition where the normality of labor for survival disappears behind spectacular, extraordinary acts of heroism, which are only possible in exceptional situations such as war.

Survival in the ghetto (and in concentration camps) relied on a "morality of sympathy," on care for one another and the ability to make individual decisions that were not merely a reflex response to the conditions set by the perpetrators. In contrast, national resistance movements, and some of the uprisings in ghettos, were driven by a "morality of principle" in which death acquires value in itself and does not result from individual and free decision but serves an idea, an abstraction.[164] In European societies, the morality of sympathy has often been assigned to women, in conjunction with "the domain of human relations, the private sphere, ordinary virtues," while "the world of work, politics and public affairs, heroic virtues, and the morality of principles" is assigned to men and appreciated more highly than the virtues of the everyday.[165] The way we think about resistance is thus highly gendered and distinguishes between male-identified heroism and daily life behavior, with the latter considered to promote stagnation and attributed to women's sphere of action. Here, the narrators' accounts provide valuable insights into young Soviet Jews' daily struggle and labor to survive that effectively destabilize stereotypes such as that Soviet Jews skirted military service, waiting out the war in hiding or evacuation—an adaptation of old antisemitic imagery of effeminate Jews who do not actively defend their homeland. The dismissal of family units depends on both denying reproductive labor its due recognition and anti-Jewish hostility—in other words, the intersection of sexism and antisemitism.

Overall, the history of the "Zorin" unit highlights that the search for specifically Jewish forms of resistance to Nazi genocide in the Soviet Union needs to account for the larger Soviet context. This context includes complex relationships between different nationalities before the war, their modification or resilience during the war, and Jews' and non-Jews' shared experience of the occupation. Lastly, it must acknowledge the role that Soviet institutions played in supporting both emotional and material survival. Some, especially older Jews, may have been wary of the Soviet leadership's treatment of Jews, grounded in no small part in the long-lasting refusal of the partisan leadership to support ghetto refugees. Younger ones, including Vladimir Mordkhilevich, Samuil Volk, Amaliia Iakhontova, and Sonia Zalesskaia, utilized the school and cultural events in the partisan unit that celebrated Soviet internationalism and patriotism as a means of stabilizing their lives after losing their families and homes.

Conclusion

Soviet Internationalism, Judaism, and the Nazi Genocide in Oral Histories

When Elena Drapkina and her partisan comrades finally united with troops of the regular Soviet army in late June 1944, they knew that liberation from the Nazi regime was near. Nineteen-year-old Elena was so excited that she hugged the first tank commander she encountered and exchanged a valuable piece of equipment with him: "He gave me his watch, and I gave him a little pistol. Then they moved on."[1] To surrender her weapon, the very thing that had provided an important sense of self-protection, Drapkina must have decided that this was, indeed, the long-awaited moment of liberation.

The partisans relocated to Minsk, where their detachment was dissolved. Most males of draft age were integrated into the army and mobilized to drive the German army from Soviet territory. Elena Drapkina and others, mostly women, were demobilized and saw no further combat. Together with Alla Gribok, another partisan from the brigade, Drapkina was assigned to the headquarters of the Belorussian Partisan Movement, where she would work as a secretary. She received housing in a Minsk dormitory and food ration cards reserved for military personnel. In the summer of 1945, Elena Drapkina moved to Leningrad; she lived there with an aunt, her only remaining relative, and began to study dentistry. She also tried, repeatedly, to identify to state authorities the young "unknown"—according to the Minsk Museum of the Great Patriotic War—female member of the Minsk underground brigade who had been hanged by the Germans as her friend, Masha Bruskina. In her frequent attempts to correct the omission, Elena Drapkina (and many others) heard more than once that it is "curious that only one particular people seem to know her." The clear reference to—and slighting of—the Jewish identity of Bruskina, her relatives, and friends worked to undermine the validity of, and indeed the claims to equal Soviet status entailed in, the identification.² Only in 2008 was a new plaque commemorating Bruskina, together with Kirill Trus' and Volodia Shcherbatsevich, revealed in Minsk.³ At that time, Elena Drapkina was deeply engaged in a conversation with herself about her Jewish origins. This topic had emerged in interviews with her when she spoke about her recent interest in Jewish history and customs, indicating a far-reaching reevaluation of her socialization in a secular and Soviet environment.

Frida Ped'ko was much younger and could not rely on ties to former partisans to access housing or food when the war ended. Ped'ko and her sister, who had survived for two and a half years in a shed in the woods near their hometown Slavnoe, found out by chance that Soviet troops had taken the area and that it was safe for them to emerge from their hiding place. The Nastiporenko family allowed them to sleep in their house, but only after the sisters got rid of their clothes and had a thorough bath—Frida and Elena were covered in lice and filth, so much so that both girls had to cut off all their hair. After that, Frida Ped'ko says,

> My god, how light I felt all of a sudden! The long hair with all the lice was gone. Then we took off the rags that we wore, they basically fell to pieces. We threw all of that away and then they gave us new clothes. That was such a joy! We did not need to be afraid any more, nobody would come and shoot us.⁴

Young Frida's greatest wish, to lie down on top of the family's oven, was also fulfilled. Emaciated from living on berries and mushrooms, she was constantly cold and longing for warmth, although it was summer. Soon, her sister Elena began to work at a nearby farmstead where she herded geese to earn some food. Frida helped the Nastiporenko family to work the fields and, in turn, was fed. Meanwhile, an aunt of the two girls heard that two Jewish children had survived the Nazi genocide in Slavnoe and was trying to ascertain who they were. Mania Sirotkina had been evacuated from Leningrad to Chistopol' in the Tatar Soviet Socialist Republic early in the war. Since she worked for a state factory, Sirotkina received permission to travel across the country to search for her relatives. Her journey was quite an accomplishment, considering that the war had not ended yet and most transportation avenues were restricted to military transports. When Sirotkina arrived in Slavnoe, the reunion, Frida Ped'ko remembers, "was happy and sad at the same time: her whole family had been killed."⁵ The aunt took Frida with her, but Elena decided to stay in Belorussia to earn some money by continuing to work for the farmer. By April 1945, aunt Mania and Frida had returned to Leningrad, and her sister Elena joined them there. Frida Ped'ko embarked on a new life, among new people who spoke a different language—Russian, not Belorussian—and largely without a family.

The summer of 1944 brought the end of the occupation, the liberation of Belorussian territories, and thus an end to the fear of being murdered by Germans or collaborators simply for being Jewish. The large-scale displacement of Soviet citizens as well as efforts to rebuild the newly liberated Soviet territories impacted in significant ways how Elena Drapkina, Frida Ped'ko, and other adolescents whose paths this book traces experienced the end of the war.

The search for relatives and the struggle to fulfill basic needs such as housing and food occupied the minds of nearly every Soviet citizen. In Belorussia, at the end of the war, 1,200,000 residential houses in the countryside lay in ruins; 90 percent of urban houses and public buildings were uninhabitable, and only 23 percent of the prewar living space was available for use in Minsk, Gomel', and Mogilev.⁶ Three million people were homeless or lived in makeshift dwellings dug into the soil.⁷ From an economic perspective, the country's development was thrown back decades; 85 percent of the industrial plants were damaged, the economy's capacity had decreased by 95 percent, crop space was nearly halved, and 80 percent of the cattle had been destroyed.⁸ These damages were the result of both the final battles and the German "scorched earth" policy; retreating German troops deliberately destroyed fields, houses, and railroads. This destruction produced famine and homelessness in the immediate postwar period and curtailed economic development for decades to come.

Despite the struggle common to many Soviet citizens in the immediate postwar Soviet Union, Jewish youths continued to experience certain elements of the Great Patriotic War in ways that highlighted the particularity of their experience. First, age and gender continued to determine both access to resources and the types of tasks available or assigned to those who had lost family networks, survived in hiding, or participated in the partisan movement. Second, Jewish youths had to confront the particularity of their wartime trauma; there were a disproportionately large number of orphans among the surviving Jewish youths. Sharing the trauma of war and genocide with many Soviet citizens—an experience that was now increasingly channeled into celebrating victory—provided Jewish youths with a framework to connect with peers and other people, while state institutions offered opportunities, even if insufficient, to rebuild and reintegrate. However, remembering the loss of loved ones, of a life full of hope for a bright future, often set them apart from their peers. Young Jews had lost many relatives and friends because they were Jewish, while other Soviet families had survived unscathed, though many lost male family members who died at the front or were missing. The magnitude of the genocide meant that the search for relatives was often in vain. Third, at the same time, the specificity of Jewish suffering was officially erased, the memory of it dismissed as not constituting an authentic Soviet experience of the Great Patriotic War. Rather, it was subsumed into the overall Soviet war experience, which denied the special targeting of Jews for decades. The tension between assimilation and particularization of national identity, known from the prewar period in a modified form, played out in restrictions on individual and communal Jewish life in postwar Soviet society that, after the experience of genocide, appeared offensive, even to the young generation of Jews who had grown up socialist and secular in the 1930s. This tension, and its release after the breakup of the Soviet Union, was the foil for the interviews I conducted in the early 2000s, several decades after the war. At that moment, many women and men were in the process of re-evaluating their personal history and their sense of self as a Jew and a member of the Soviet (and post-Soviet) society.

This conclusion provides a snapshot of these multiple dimensions of postwar Soviet history and memory based on oral histories with elderly Jewish women and men in the former Soviet Union. The postwar lives of several people introduced in this book show that the nexuses between age and gender, trauma and cohesion, and memory and identity provide crucial frames to assess individual lives beyond the end of the war.

Age, gender, and the military

The women and men who, in advanced age, remember growing up Soviet and surviving the Nazi genocide were still very young when Soviet troops liberated German-occupied areas in June and July of 1944. However, not all youths faced the same challenges. For Frida Ped'ko, who was ten years old, and Elena Drapkina, twenty at the time, returning and adjusting to life in peacetime required different solutions. Whereas, for the moment, people of Frida's age could count on the compassion and support of adults like the Nastiporenkos, Elena Drapkina and her older peers had to earn a living independently. In the end, both would have to build a life largely without the support of family networks, but always in interaction with state policies and the larger public.

The opportunities available to young women and men to rebuild their lives were, in no small part, determined by their gender. The tension between the propaganda of gender equality and the reality of patriarchal authority—which became increasingly apparent during the war and limited women's participation in army and partisan units—persisted. To some extent, the conflict was decided in favor of reestablishing a gender order privileging traditional roles; men should lead and make decisions, and women should provide auxiliary services and become mothers. Elena Drapkina, for instance, worked as a secretary, first in the partisan headquarters and then in the Minsk Ispolkom, the city's executive council. Authorities were looking for, as she remembers, "two educated and reliable young women"; being reliable meant being free from the suspicion of having collaborated with the German occupation regime.[9] Though this suspicion fell upon nearly everyone who had lived in the occupied territories, Elena and Alla Gribok were exculpated because of their participation in the partisan movement. That the Council specified it wanted to hire women for jobs that were likely to be staffed by women anyway might suggest some correlation in their thinking between being a woman and being innocent. Nonetheless, their employment as secretaries marked their exclusion from higher-ranked leadership positions.

Eventually, Elena's aunt persuaded her to enroll in a university. Elena Drapkina notes that she had a hard time readjusting to normal life when she began to take courses in August 1945:

> There were no newspapers after June 1941, when I had my last exams after ninth grade. And in the ghetto, what did I read there—decrees, orders, but there were no papers. To get those, you needed to be in touch with the underground, but I—all my relatives were dead, how could I get any of that? ... Our house had burned down, and there were no books where I lived. In the partisan unit, we had only leaflets, and there was a radio in the staff headquarters, they told us what was going on. But in fact, between 1941 and 1944 I did not read for three years. That, and my memory, I had a very hard time studying.[10]

Nevertheless, Drapkina completed her courses successfully and began to work as a dentist in Leningrad. In 1945, she married Vul'f Drapkin, an officer who died in 1949 from his wartime injuries. Elena Drapkina raised their son on her own until she married again. Nearly ten million, overwhelmingly male, soldiers died in the war; this placed the rebuilding of Soviet society on women's shoulders, as both workers and mothers. Women comprised more than 60 percent of the population aged sixteen and older, and between 1941 and 1950, 92 percent of all new workers in the USSR were female.[11] Elena Drapkina's single motherhood and full-time employment were thus a common experience for women, whether they had been at the front, worked in the rear, or lived under occupation during the war.

Young men who had joined the partisans during the war, and especially those who had lost their families, were regularly folded into the Soviet army. Samuil Volk and his brother, for instance, left the "Zorin" unit upon the detachment's encounter with a regular army division. Volk explains:

> We were on our way to Minsk, and we rested near a big lake. It was still warm and we went swimming. I saw an army battalion, a medical battalion along the lake. One of the officers called on me to come over and he asked me who I was, what my name was, etc. . . . I told him the whole story, and he asked: "Do you want to come with us?" I did, and so we went to ask the commander of our unit. [Zorin] was wounded [i.e., he was not there] and so he spoke to the commissar [Feigelman]. He told the officer that I had a brother. That made him upset and the commissar told him he could take another boy who didn't have siblings. But the officer wanted to think it over and left. I was upset, and two hours later went over to the battalion. He was talking to a woman and introduced me to her. She said, he should take me and Ziama. . . . So we left the next day, heading west.[12]

Samuil's desire to join the army seems understandable in light of his close relationship with his "patron" and fellow partisan Isaak, his excitement about the weapons he had developed during his time with the partisans, and his subscription to the heroic patriotism that infused the pioneers' letter to Stalin. At the same time, the Volk brothers were two among about 25,000 so-called *synovia polka* (sons of the regiment), adolescents who joined the army as scouts or messengers between divisions and battalions. These "sons of the regiment" made a significant contribution to the military struggle.

Perhaps even more to the point, they fulfilled an integrative function for the military formations by standing in for the real or hoped-for children the soldiers had left behind at home. They thus offered a direct and immediate reminder of what the war was about: the liberation of the Soviet population, their families among them, from violence and terror. As in Samuil's case, the adult men who adopted him and his brother regularly referred to their own children when explaining their wish to take care of them.

In 1945, all children within the army were to leave the military and return to liberated Soviet territories. Lev Tseitlin—a senior sergeant in the division and a former high-ranking employee of the Department of Education who had taken Samuil under his wing when he joined the division—took the two brothers to Moscow. After spending a week with Tseitlin's family, the boys were placed in an orphanage. There, they were allotted a place in a school "for the children of fallen officers," which they received only because of Tseitlin's credentials. Following this description, Samuil and Ziama enrolled in one of the Suvorov Military Schools, schools that admitted entrants exclusively from the sons of serving officers or of other ranks who had died during the Great Patriotic War at the hands of Germans.[13] Upon completing high school, Samuil enrolled in a Military Engineering Academy. He explained his choice by saying, "because I was connected to the military anyway, as a former son of the regiment, and in the orphanage there was also military discipline, so it wasn't new to me and I thought I should just continue with the army."[14] Volk remained in the military for several decades and ended his career as a colonel when he retired in 1985 at the age of fifty-five.

Elena Drapkina, Samuil Volk, and others who in some way worked for state institutions, either as partisans turned civil servants or as adolescents who were put on a path toward long-term military service, benefited from these institutions' high standing within Soviet society. As a rule, former partisans and military often received preferential treatment when claiming access to higher education, housing, or leadership positions. This trend was already emerging in the immediate postwar period when military personnel were supplied with housing and food.[15] Women, however, rarely benefited from the honorable memory of the Soviet victory; the omission of their contributions, as described in chapters 5 and 6, often resulted in their forfeiting subsidies granted to war veterans.

Rita Kazhdan, like Frida Ped'ko, could rely on resources available to war veterans to a much smaller extent. She avoided publicizing her partisan activity for fear of humiliation as a prostitute until the late 1980s.[16] Her struggles to make a living in postwar Soviet society began immediately upon liberation. She returned to Minsk, her hometown, in early July 1944 to find it devastated. There, she—together with her brother Grisha and her "partisan sisters," Polia and Sonia Shostok—joined thousands of others looking for food and housing. The four found the Fridman family home destroyed and the Shostok sisters' home occupied by a former member of the police who insulted them, yelling, "you Jewish mug, are you still alive?!"[17] In addition to such humiliations, reported from many survivors in liberated Soviet territories, Rita and her peers had difficulty feeding themselves.[18] After several unsuccessful attempts to find work, Rita ran into a distant relative who ensured her employment in a dining hall, thus enabling her to eat and earn some money. He also enrolled Grisha in an orphanage and invited Rita to stay with him. The house where he stayed, however, "was right there where the ghetto boundary was. For him, that had no meaning, but for me . . . that was the ghetto."[19] Memories of the terror were always present, compounding the material difficulties.

Finally, Rita Kazhdan managed to write a letter to the address her mother had given her right before she was killed. The recipients of the letter, a maternal aunt and uncle, made arrangements for Rita and her brother to move to Moscow in August 1944. When the uncle, a high-ranking functionary in the Soviet Ministry of Energy, met the siblings at the military airport in Minsk, he was surprised that they did not have any luggage. Kazhdan remembers:

> There were these gas masks, and the bags of these masks, I don't know where I got them, if somebody gave them to me or whether I had bought them, but I filled these bags with apples. So we arrived at the airport and met our uncle, and he asked, "do you have any luggage?" I showed him the bags and he asked, "what's in there?"—"Apples." That's how we went to Moscow.[20]

The family was unable to register the children with the authorities or secure food ration cards for them, and the apartment was too small for the growing family. To alleviate these problems, Rita was soon sent to a maternal aunt in Leningrad who had promised to provide for her. After sticking together for three difficult years, the siblings were thus separated for the first time, a moment Rita Kazhdan described as difficult but inevitable.

Rita Kazhdan enrolled in a technical school and later applied to work in an institute for optical analysis. She was hired only after a friend of hers, a party functionary, intervened on her behalf and overturned the personnel department's rejection of her application. Her Jewish nationality, she explained, had been in the way of her employment at an institute that produced equipment for the Soviet space research program. Similar conflicts occurred again when she tried to find a new job after maternity leave.

This brief survey of the postwar biographies of Jewish women and men who survived the Nazi genocide in the German-occupied Soviet Union points to a number of emerging lines of conflict around issues of gender and nationality. Women were, as a rule, excluded from serving in the military and thus had limited access to crucial resources. Gender also proved to be a contentious element of Soviet postwar memory, in which women received little attention, and women's labor—both the forms of reproductive labor that secured survival during the war and literally the work of women in the Soviet wartime industry—was largely ignored. Jews were increasingly marginalized and excluded from access to higher education and certain professions, a development that reflected state-sponsored anti-Jewish discrimination which was, in large part, motivated by regressive attempts at Soviet state building after the war and in the context of the emerging Cold War.

The vignettes thus suggest developing hierarchies within Soviet society and tensions within the memory of wartime experience, an experience that, on the surface, was shared by all Soviet citizens, yet included distinct experiences of violence and survival which were not acknowledged. What is more, they contradicted the values and promises that the then adolescents had learned in prewar Soviet society, where, formally, discrimination based on national identities was outlawed; women were included on an equal footing, if burdened with double expectations; and interpersonal relationships appeared free from national animosity. The war, during which responses to these notions of unity and sameness were called upon to mobilize for the defeat of the Nazi regime, thus marked a significant turning point. Central ideological claims and policies were not only invalidated by the German occupation, but they were also revoked by Soviet society.

Trauma, cohesion, and the in-between

During the war and occupation, the shared experiences of terror and hunger had created a sense of solidarity among Soviet citizens of all national identities. Many Belorussians, for instance, had helped Jewish refugees from the ghettos find shelter and food, guided them to partisan units, or assisted partisans by sending food or relaying important information about German activities. While not all Belorussians came to the aid of their Jewish compatriots, all Jews who survived the Nazi genocide relied on the help of one or more non-Jewish person. The formation of interpersonal networks of support—chiefly within the ghettos, but also in family units—also (re) created a sense of Jewish communality among those threatened by annihilation. The trauma of violence thus produced connections and a sense of group belonging that was imperative for survival. Soviet wartime and postwar propaganda made use of these connections, presenting the war as a universal and collective endeavor to defeat Nazi Germany. The postwar decades, however, revealed fissures in this imagined community of Soviet victors. Personal challenges related to accessing resources or coping with physical and mental conditions stemming from wartime experiences were especially indicative of this instability. To date, there is scant scholarship on the reintegration of young victims of the war into Soviet society, and the following notes indicate a number of issues and questions to be pursued further. The personal stories provide a glimpse into adolescent lives and the role of national identity in determining commemorative practices in the postwar USSR.

Alevtina Kuprikhina was evacuated from her partisan unit in 1943 and placed in an orphanage near Rogachev. Since the city was very close to the front line, the children were evacuated further into the Soviet interior. The whole orphanage settled in Dikhovka, Saratov province, until the end of the war. A teacher then suggested that Alla write to the local authorities in Zhlobin to find out about her relatives. Alevtina Kuprikhina followed that advice and eventually learned that her grandparents had been evacuated to Sverdlovsk, near the Ural mountains. Together with a group of displaced citizens and some soldiers who took pity on her, Alevtina Kuprikhina traveled there. Upon arrival, Alla stole a loaf of bread and was apprehended by Soviet police. When they heard why she was there, they called the grandfather's company and confirmed that Lev Aronovich Igol'nikov worked there. The grandparents were surprised and very happy that she had survived and welcomed her into their home. But the famine that gripped postwar Soviet society made it impossible for her to stay with them. Kuprikhina explains:

> Life was really hard in Sverdlovsk, a loaf of bread cost 500 rubles, they could not feed me. Grandfather was always afraid that I would not have

enough food. He even taught himself how to make shoes, he sold them to a nearby kindergarten. Everybody tried to make it through. And I saw all of this . . . and so I went and searched for the [local child welfare office], and I found them and said, "I used to be in an orphanage. Now I live with my grandparents, but they don't have enough food for themselves, they can't support me. Please take me into an orphanage." And they took me. Right then a transport from a Leningrad orphanage had arrived, after the siege they sent surviving children to other places, and I ended up with this group. We were in a village, 18 km from Sverdlovsk, in Malyi Istok, and I stayed in that orphanage.[21]

In Alevtina Kuprikhina's narrative of her postwar resettlement, in interviews with both the Visual History Archive and me, she is rather pragmatic about the memory of not being able to live with the last remaining members of her family. In contrast, I observed more emotion in her account of the end of the war.

A main stop on the way to Leningrad, where Kuprikhina would stay until we met in 2002, was Berdichev. This Ukrainian town, where 17,000 out of a prewar population of about 23,000 Jews had been murdered, resembled cities and towns all over the formerly occupied territories.[22] It was there that Alevtina Kuprikhina heard about the end of the war in May 1945. Her face showing excitement and her voice shifting toward a celebratory tone, she described the moment: "You can't imagine what happened that day! There were cars and tanks, people threw flowers into the air, people hugged each other, I can't even describe it. I couldn't even believe that the war was over."[23] Elena Drapkina, Frida Ped'ko, Grigorii Erenburg—all of them described how they heard the news of the German capitulation on May 9, 1945, in similarly colorful terms.[24]

The joy over the end of the war, however, was accompanied by mixed feelings. For instance, when Frida Ped'ko and her sister returned to Slavnoe, they visited their former home. Ped'ko said, "the only thing we found, under a pile of rubbish, were four little shot glasses. I still have them. That is all that remained."[25] Here she not only describes the complete destruction of personal property and homes, but even more so the loss of the people who used these glasses. Victory was accomplished, but the losses and the pain could not be undone and tainted the relief of liberation.

Grigorii Erenburg, who returned to Bobruisk with his father in June 1944, described his struggles to adjust to life in peacetime. The commander of his partisan unit intervened on his behalf and secured a spot in the local *tekhnikum*, the technical school. This enrollment secured Grigorii a space in the school's dormitory and access to the dining hall. Erenburg actively participated in Komsomol attempts to identify former collaborators. And yet the wartime experiences had aftereffects. Grigorii Erenburg said, "During the war, I did not grow. But now I started to grow again, and I needed new clothes every other month."[26] In addition, "I was hungry all the time. I remember, once I received my weekly bread ration, we went to the movies and I ate the whole loaf during the screening."[27] Simultaneously, Grigorii Erenburg was in a difficult emotional situation. Gesturing toward his collection of books, he mentioned a sense of indifference toward the world at the end of the war:

> I've always loved books. Although, when I came out of the woods and left the partisans, nothing interested me. I thought this was all nonsense. When I first started going to the movies, I thought, "Good god, what are we watching here? That is all wrong!" But then I decided that I wanted to live. So that passed, and then I started to read again.[28]

He threw himself into his studies, although, like Elena Drapkina, he found them challenging, considering the long-term lapse of schooling caused by the war. As Amaliia Iakhontova pointed out, however, in addition to promising a professional career and thus a way to earn a livelihood, learning also helped to overcome the sense of loss. She went to medical school and "learned like an animal. I was so happy to be away from war and destruction."[29] Studies were a means of escape, turning schools and universities into important sites of overcoming the past and building a future.

For Frida Ped'ko, the Soviet school system was both promising and problematic. It offered her a way to overcome her wartime experiences, and it came with access to a dining hall where she stuffed herself with bread. But problems arose immediately upon enrollment. She had started elementary school in September 1944 and wanted to continue her education in Leningrad. There, other students scrutinized her: "Everybody looked at me with dismay. For one, I was more or less bald [she had been shaved to prevent renewed lice infestations], and I was wearing this coat made out of goat leather that they had given me in Tatarstan." In addition, Frida hesitated to speak up in class, because she did not know Russian and was afraid to speak Belorussian. A teacher who knew Belorussian met with her regularly after class so that she could demonstrate her knowledge; this support was crucial to enabling her to complete the class. Soon, she also found friends, although there remained a distance between them: "They were surprised that I was an orphan, but they also did not want to know the details."[30] Frida was the only person in the class who had lived under German occupation, and for a long time she only spoke to her sister Elena about the war.

Last but not least, Frida suffered from long-term health problems that are likely related to the malnutrition the girls had suffered from while in hiding. Frida lost all her teeth, "probably because we didn't have anything to chew on for so long," and needed dentures at the age of thirteen. After the war she suffered from illnesses of her digestive system. In 2009, at the age of seventy-nine, Frida Ped'ko died of complications related to colon cancer.

Hunger, difficulty in concentrating, struggling to find a purpose in life, poverty, and adjusting to a new environment often posed problems for the adolescents who had survived the German occupation of Belorussia. The destruction of infrastructure and the devastation of the country placed a huge strain on the Soviet state's ability to feed its population. It took several years before enough decent housing was available, especially in the formerly occupied territories.

While in all cases there were pragmatic reasons to do so—family connections, education, employment, and housing—it is noteworthy that many of the survivors left the formerly occupied region and began to build a new life elsewhere.[31] The spatial distance was perhaps productive for this restart, though of course several thousand survivors chose otherwise and stayed in Minsk and elsewhere. While Rita Kazhdan gestured toward the problems she had living with her uncle close to the former ghetto, she and others also regularly went to visit their hometowns, or the places where they had been partisans.[32] Others went "where my family is buried."[33] That memory has important spatial dimensions is evident in the ambiguous relationship these women and men have with Belorussia—a site of memory that both drives them away and serves as an anchor.

Whereas the move away enabled the young women and men to leave behind the sites of destruction, the physical and emotional effects stayed with them. They were all orphans, and although aunts and uncles and state institutions provided new homes and other support, "that was still not the same, that was not my mother's touch," as Frida Ped'ko noted.³⁴ It is here, in the large number of orphans among the surviving Jewish youths who often had lost several generations of relatives, that the aftermath of the Nazi genocide most vividly emerges as a specifically Jewish experience within the Great Patriotic War. This difference in experience, however, was actively shrouded or even negated in the official Soviet war portrayal, a problem that was closely related to postwar Soviet politics more generally. Both the particular experience of Jewish persecution and mass extermination during the war and Soviet postwar nationality policies required survivors to renegotiate personal positionalities and attitudes toward the Jewish community, Jewish nationality, and state institutions. These negotiations emerge powerfully in interviews with elderly Jewish women and men in the former Soviet Union and reveal the complex layers of shifting identity and memory.

Memory, identity, and censorship

Oral history work exposes not only how young Soviet Jews survived the Nazi genocide in occupied Soviet territories, but how the Jewish condition in the Soviet and post-Soviet world shaped memory-making over subsequent postwar decades. Ranging from descriptions of national and religious disidentification in the 1930s to details on the post-Soviet discovery of Judaism, the narratives shed light on how Soviet Jews made a life under challenging conditions that included state policies and other peoples' attitudes. As women and men reflected on their experiences with me, for instance, they often sought to reconcile previous patriotic and internationalist Soviet orientations with newly adopted references to customs and interpretations shaped by traditional Jewish culture. These shifts and contradictions are connected to ongoing social and political transformations within the larger post-Soviet society, and they reflect personal trajectories molded by interactions within Soviet nationality policy, the history and memory of World War II, and notions of private and public. Eventually, these shifts and contradictions tell us something about how narrators "position themselves in the social world," how their narration "fits into a larger schema."³⁵ They show how identity work and memory work are closely entwined when making life in the Soviet Union and its successor states, and in the aftermath of violence.

There are three variations in which Soviet citizenship and Jewish identity are represented and evoked in conjunction with remembering the war past. Some narrators emphasize the need to honor and address Soviet citizens' common experience of World War II, often simultaneously highlighting the role of the Soviet army for the successful end of the war. Other interviewees describe their recent interest in Jewish customs, identifying both commemorative rituals to honor victims of the genocide and everyday customs, such as preparing Jewish meals to evoke family life before the war. A third group of people, which overlaps with the second, describe their recent rapprochement with religious rituals and frameworks and how this helps them to understand their personal experience.

The latter two phenomena are of special interest, given that the overwhelming majority of the narrators recall their formative years as decidedly unreligious and, in most cases, characterized by indifference toward, if not rejection of, Jewish heritage and religion, as described in chapter 2. Growing up in the Soviet Union in the late 1920s and 1930s, the women and men considered their Jewish identity a label that accompanied their Soviet citizenship and that otherwise was present only in the form of an older generation that prayed, ate special food, or encouraged them to learn Hebrew. Overwhelmingly, it played no role in their daily life, relationships with contemporaries, or in participation in social, cultural, and political activities. Internationalism, these accounts suggest, had become a reality, and personal political commitments were directed at the Soviet Union and Stalin.

When German troops entered and occupied Belorussia in 1941, the situation changed. Jews were separated and isolated from the Soviet population, interned in ghettos, forced to work under dehumanizing conditions, and killed. While some locals remained friendly and helped to organize food, clothes, and shelter or facilitate escape routes, others began to articulate and enact antisemitic attitudes ranging from verbal insults or stealing Jewish property to participation in the killings as part of collaborationist police formations.

After the war, verbalizing these experiences was largely out of the question for survivors. The Soviet war portrayal was largely limited to, and directed at, military achievements of the victorious Soviet army, and omitted the targeted extermination of Jews, the confiscation of their property, and the role of collaboration in both.[36] Experiences of loss, damage, or genocide, as well as the question of collaboration, were marginalized. Secondly, state campaigns against "cosmopolitanism" targeted Jewish intellectuals and professionals to a disproportionate degree and instilled fear of further antisemitic assaults among Soviet Jews. Therefore, many decided to keep a low profile and remained silent about war experiences that highlighted the role of their national identity.

Consider Anna Sagal'chik. Born in 1918, she had left her family in Lagoisk to study at the Pedagogical Institute in Minsk, leaving her old parents and life in the shtetl behind. She narrowly escaped the killing of Lagoisk's Jewish population, and endured pogroms and raids in the Minsk ghetto before she managed to reach a partisan unit. After the war, she says, she "told students and parents about being in the partisan unit, but I did not tell them about the pogroms in Lagoisk or Minsk. I was afraid they would say, 'you kikes deserved it,' or something like that."[37] Her fear can be interpreted as a response to state policies and campaigns that demonstrated anti-Jewish hostility. The Soviet regime's treatment of the Jewish Anti-Fascist Committee, the sole body to represent Jewish interests regarding the acknowledgement of the extermination of Jews or the restitution of Jewish property, sent a clear message to Soviet Jews in terms of their ability to discuss the genocide or the collaboration of non-Jewish citizens in robbery and murder. The actor and theater director Salomon Mikhoels, a leading spokesperson for Jewish interests, was murdered in a fabricated car accident, and the committee was closed and most of its members executed.[38] The publication of the *Black Book of Russian Jewry*, a documentation of atrocities against Soviet Jews, was censored.[39] Moreover, fictitious accusations against Stalin's personal doctors—who allegedly tried to kill him in 1952/53 in a campaign known as the *delo vrachei* (doctors' plot)—increased aggressions against Jewish citizens who, like several of the doctors, were suspected to be agents of foreign powers. A number of Soviet citizens and worker brigades wrote letters to the government, condoning the antisemitic campaigns as a necessary means to eliminate internal enemies of the Soviet state. A number of citizens refused to be treated by physicians of Jewish nationality.[40] While she did not experience such rejection, Elena Drapkina noted that she was afraid of such incidents in her dentist office and sought to discuss the matter with more senior colleagues.[41] The aforementioned discriminations against Rita Kazhdan and many other Jews with regard to their professional careers were part of a larger backlash in Soviet society aimed at marginalizing Jewish existence.

It was especially painful for survivors to see how their own experiences, and those of their families, were largely neglected in official commemorations of, and responses to, the Great Patriotic War. Ekaterina Tsirlina's attempts to register as a war veteran on the basis of her membership in a family unit were turned down.[42] Elena Drapkina was humiliated by officials who suggested she was trying to claim the memory of her friend Masha Bruskina as a specifically Jewish accomplishment and thereby undermine the efforts to construct a universal Soviet war memory. Frida Ped'ko was told that "life in the ghetto wasn't that bad" upon submitting paperwork to apply for subsidies.[43] Boris Gal'perin's was shocked when he discovered that high-ranking party functionaries had built dachas on the site of the mass graves in his hometown.[44] The list of indifferent, offensive, and negligent actions which violated the commemoration of the Jewish dead is long. It includes the refusal of Soviet authorities to mark the site of the massacre of 33,771 Jews at Babi Yar, a ravine in Kiev, as much as the inability of Boris Gal'perin or Frida Ped'ko to know that the fate of their relatives and their own is not brushed aside with the stroke of a pen or the shovel of a bulldozer.

Soviet Jews were at once part and not part of the Soviet commemorative community. This ambiguity reflected the tension between competing forms of identification that resulted from both inherently contradictory state policies and processes of secularization and Sovietization among young Soviet Jews in the 1930s. In the prewar decade, the legal categorization as Jewish by nationality was institutionalized with the internal passport but had no meaning for people's self-identification, self-perception, or participation in Soviet society as Soviet persons as propagated by the state. After the war, however, this contradiction between state policies (of identification) and cultural affinities reemerged in the form of a strained relationship between individuals and the state. At that time, the state curtailed attempts by people of Jewish nationality who had survived Nazi occupation and genocide to affirm their Jewish cultural identity or commemorate Jewish victims as Jewish victims.[45] The state preferred a collective Soviet war memory that did not allow for differential remembering along the lines of nationality.

For several decades, therefore, many narrators did not actively or publicly commit to Judaism in the form of religious or cultural practices; being Jewish was again largely tied to a passport entry. With perestroika and the breakdown of the Soviet Union in the mid- to late 1980s, the public discourse on national identity, religion, and the official portrayal of history opened up, and several narrators reported that they had developed an increased interest in their Jewish origin. As other scholars have described, studying Jewish history, taking up specific cultural practices of food preparation, commemoration, and reading Jewish writers' work have emerged as key elements of rediscovering Jewish roots.[46] These processes affect the presentation of personal and collective history. The simultaneous commitment to Soviet internationalism, patriotism, and Judaism shaped interpretations of, and relationships to, the past as they were offered in many interviews and pose questions with regard to memory and identity.

For all interviewees, the anniversary of May 9, 1945, celebrated as Victory Day, continues to be the most important holiday of the year. In that, they follow the commemorative calendar of the state, the Soviet as well as the post-Soviet one. Frida Ped'ko, who survived the extermination of the Jews of Slavnoe, articulates the importance of honoring and recalling Soviet citizens' common experience of World War II. Cognizant of her own struggles to receive social benefits or compensation, she is clear about moments in which she experienced such difficulties alongside non-Jewish neighbors and friends, especially when it comes to the lack of material support given to those who even today suffer from the repercussions of the war: "In any case, Jews did suffer a lot, but everything should be distributed equally ... I understand that Jews suffered and that Germany is responsible for that, but those who suffer within their country, the Russians, they should also be helped."[47]

Samuil Volk's interview with the Visual History Archive reveals a slightly different attitude, indicating an emerging Jewish self-consciousness that is, however, limited to the experience of the Nazi genocide. Volk demonstrates an attempt to simultaneously retain internationalism and military pride and promote national specificity. He grew up removed from religious instruction or Jewish customs, and thus, as he says, "did not pass these traditions on to my daughter either."[48] Working within an association of child survivors of the war in Novosibirsk, however, he explains that he works hard to distinguish the fate of Jewish victims of the Nazi regime, highlighting their nationality as the sole reason for the murder. Resembling a common practice among Soviet war veterans of presenting themselves for special occasions such as holidays in public in uniform, the closing section of the interview shows Volk in his military uniform. A similar claim to sharing the honor accorded to military veterans was brought home to me when I asked Elena Drapkina for permission to take a picture of her. She agreed, but only after she donned a jacket to which she had pinned all medals and orders she had received for her partisan activity, which she regularly wears for celebrations or gatherings at the association of ghetto survivors.

Multiple interviewees related how they commemorate relatives who were killed during the Holocaust. Elena Drapkina and Grigorii Erenburg light a candle at the anniversary of close relatives' deaths, mentioning that they began doing so only a few years ago. Whether consciously or not—no one ever referred to this ritual as such—they resort to the Jewish custom of lighting a yahrzeit candle on the anniversary of the death of a close relative. Frida Ped'ko related that she fasted on March 16, the anniversary of the day her family was shot in Slavnoe. This ritual might be traced back to the fast days in the Jewish religion, when fasting is usually a sign of repentance (as during Yom Kippur), or a way to commemorate the tragedies that have befallen the Jewish people (as during Tisha B'av). It is likely that Elena, Grigorii, and Frida saw their grandparents or other older relatives perform such rituals before Jewish culture in Belorussia was almost entirely destroyed by the Nazi regime. As scholars have said, rituals evoke "past events and former epochs" and contribute to (re)establishing cognitive forms of identity.[49]

The attraction to Jewish customs extends into everyday activities; like other women, Rita Kazhdan delights in cooking Jewish meals, trying to recreate the tastes her family's maid produced in the 1930s, and gathering for the Sabbath with friends. Anna Sagal'chik, who was once a teacher devoted to raising youth in the Soviet spirit, says that she has now "turned into a real Jew" and is reading books by Jewish writers. She added, "unfortunately, I don't know Yiddish, that is a big shame. I don't even know why . . . it just so happened. I did not go to a Jewish school. I can speak Yiddish, but I cannot read it." Asked for a message to future generations, a standard element of the Visual History Archive interviews, Sagal'chik assures the listener that she "would tell her children and grandchildren: Don't forget that you are Jewish. Know your national language. Be an internationalist in spirit, all people are equal, no matter what nationality they are, but one should know their language."[50]

Elena Drapkina takes her interest in Jewish culture further and explores the spiritual dimensions of Judaism to find explanations for her own existence. Initially, Drapkina had presented herself as a Soviet patriot who aimed to participate in the defeat of the occupation and of German soldiers. Her decisions and interpretations appeared to be grounded in a deeply felt commitment to the Soviet state: "I believed in Stalin. Everything for the homeland, for Stalin—forward, that was it." In moments when she had to make important decisions, such as how to organize her escape from the ghetto, she managed to do that on the basis of a confidence in her own abilities and a desire to take revenge. In later interviews, Elena Drapkina told me about her urge to learn about her "own culture": she had taken classes on Jewish history, and she was attending services in the St. Petersburg synagogue. Her attempt to adopt Jewish culture and religion modifies her assessment of her own life. The person who was once deeply committed to the Soviet Union and its materialist worldview now thought that

> Somebody must have saved me; somebody must have averted the dangers from me. You see, there were so many incidents where I was supposed to die, but at the last moment . . . somebody made me draw aside. This is when you start to believe. Earlier, I believed in Stalin . . . but now I think that there must be some Higher Power. I don't know whether this is God or not, but something saved me.[51]

Similarly, Boris Gal'perin, who, as a young boy ran away from his grandfather who tried to introduce him to Judaism and Hebrew, evoked the workings of a higher power. Explaining his attitude toward evaluating other people's behavior, both during and after the war, he argues: "I always say, 'May God be his judge,' but I will never judge . . . I don't have the right to do that. Judging a person . . . there is some Higher Power, and we shouldn't judge people. But I cannot do it, because nobody authorized me to do so."[52] For both former partisans and activists in Komsomol and Party, a metaphysical force has come to replace a formerly recognized worldly entity.

Looking at these tendencies, a shift emerges from avoiding, or being indifferent to, commitments to an ethnically or religiously defined community to becoming Jewish and actively practicing Judaism, or at least using it to make sense of personal history. The vignettes thus pose the question, why do people revive a Jewish heritage and identity at the end of their lives? This question arises especially once we take into account that, according to their own description, for several decades religion or traditional culture did not have any significant meaning for them personally. There are a number of ways to approach this puzzle.

First, scholars have argued that biographical work is a mass phenomenon in post-Soviet Russia. Generally, "biographical work" signifies modes of evaluating one's personal history with the aim of constructing, or reconstructing, a usable and agreeable personal identity.[53] In the cases discussed here, biographical work is conceptualized as a response to a general crisis of identity following the breakdown of the Soviet Union. Very often, the family was the only foothold that remained, and biographical work served to reconstruct the family history and thus to secure its cohesion.[54] The accounts emphasize the significance of family history for people's self-image. In the case at hand, the reactivation of traditional culture is a direct means to re-establish intergenerational bonds with relatives who were killed by the Germans and who were the last to know and practice Jewish religion and culture. The religious grandparents personify one's own Jewish origin; becoming religious, or at least taking an interest in religion and traditional culture, allows for a return to this origin.

For some, religion was the only way to preserve Jewish identity in times of repression and upheaval in Russia and the Soviet Union.[55] This may be true for Jews who grew up before Jewish religious institutions were dismantled and ceased to provide guidance for Jewish everyday life in the mid- to late 1920s. The majority of narrators introduced in this book, however, grew up largely removed from those institutions and customs, witnessing their influence and practice only in their grandparents' homes.

It is significant that, at the time of the interviews, interviewees were at the age their own grandparents were shortly before and during the war. Taking up traditions and religion serves to reestablish intergenerational and communal bonds. This is a complicated process, as knowledge about customs and religion is lost and requires labor. Rather than speaking of "preservation," we should perhaps speak here of a reacquisition and redefinition of Jewish identity, one that is in flux and rooted in several layers of experience. Most clearly and powerfully, Jewish identity was articulated during the Nazi genocide, which destroyed families but produced an ethnically (in Soviet terminology, nationally) defined experiential community.[56] Family units, for instance, coalesced because Jews were persecuted as Jews. Before the war, young Soviet Jews hardly formed a distinct community. The Nazi persecution forced this communality upon them, while also revealing rifts within the Soviet population generally, grounded in antisemitic prejudice and aggression. In that sense, the Nazi genocide was instrumental for the revival of Soviet Jewish collective identity. Experiences such as being denied admission to partisan units or needing to hide being Jewish in Soviet army units, as well as in the emerging collectivity of family units, reinforced this revival of Jewish self-identification, one that was, however, always infused with reminders of belonging to the patriotic and internationalist Soviet society.

Ethnic identities, moreover, became generally, and increasingly, meaningful when the Soviet Union began to fall apart. An effect of, and perhaps one of the reasons for, the Soviet state's breakdown was ethnic revival: ethnic identities became important markers of identification for individuals and the society as a whole. Especially in border and peripheral regions of the USSR, politicians framed social conflicts as ethnic conflicts. People who belonged to an ethnic community took the place of the ideal Soviet citizen who disavowed ethnic belonging.[57] The simultaneous civic efforts to rewrite Soviet history during perestroika opened up a space to question the Soviet portrayal of the war, especially the denial of different experiences along ethnic lines such as the deportations of Crimean Tatars, Chechens, and Latvians, among others, by the Soviet government. Given that the experience of the Nazi genocide for many interviewees was the first time that they were identified by and treated based on their nationality, the coincidence of openings in the discourse on the Great Patriotic War and the permission to positively identify as Jewish and practice national traditions facilitated a change in self-perception and self-representation. The aforementioned strategies to commemorate the loss of relatives helped to position the murder within a specifically Jewish context, a context in which the Jewish population of the occupied territories was singled out for extermination. The recent focus on family memory, rather than, as during Soviet times, on the overall Soviet collective, favors an ethnic perspective. In this, the reevaluation of war memory resembles efforts to use family relationships to make sense of social structures more generally. In addition to the political salience of ethnonationalism, the rise of ethnic identification can be understood as an attempt to extend the family (which was the crucial unit to organize survival in Soviet times and has been even more so since the dissolution of the USSR) to those with whom one claims to have similar "natural" bonds—the ethnic community.[58] In this logic, reconstruction of family and ethnic history overlap, perhaps unconsciously, and are closely intertwined phenomena of individual and social memory that come to fruition in producing oral histories of a whole life experience.

The memories of elderly Jewish women and men, recorded in the late 1990s and early 2000s, of their life in the Soviet Union in general, and of the Nazi genocide in particular, are thus distinctly shaped by the sequence of different life periods and by narrators' ability to compare the different ideological and political regimes that frame these periods. Much of the scholarship on the construction of memory rightly emphasizes the role of ideology and collective discourses in explaining how the past is reinterpreted in light of the present and is shaped by ideology, culture, and social relations.[59] But we must also look to the sequence of distinct periods of experience, which are reinterpreted in hindsight and based on an active comparison of different periods in terms of their impact on the interviewees' lives, to understand how memories and representations of the past are constructed. In the case at hand, the sharp contrast between Soviet policies of internationalism and equality, which were implemented in the 1930s and which shaped the childhood and youth of these Jews, and Nazi racism, which destroyed their society, leads the narrators to a more positive portrayal of the Soviet project than scholarship on Soviet nationality policies toward Jews in the 1930s would suggest. Existing scholarly analyses of those policies emphasize party purges and terror, the violence of collectivization, and antireligious campaigning, and they note antisemitic assaults in factories, farms, and schools. The relational construction of memory—i.e., the reinterpretation of the past based on the comparison of distinct periods such as childhood, war, and postwar reconstruction—makes the effects of prewar Soviet policy appear less drastic and harmful, a phenomenon that can only be understood if we pay attention to the lives of historical subjects as a whole.

For survivors of the Holocaust who remained in the Soviet Union after World War II, the Soviet project of creating an internationalist, patriotic, and solidary body politic remained meaningful and valuable. This becomes clear when we look for both the role of personal experience and ideologies that were influential for individuals at particular moments, but also the social and political framework of commemoration and remembering in trying to understand how representations of the past in oral histories emerge. The struggle to remember suffering and survival, to negotiate frustration about anti-Jewish and sexist hostility with loyalty toward those who helped secure liberation from the Nazi genocide, reflect the complexity of Jewish life in the Soviet Union. By recognizing the impact of both Soviet ideology and the actual, personal experience of socialism and internationalism on the lives and minds of Soviet citizens, together with their breakdown, first with the German invasion and later with the dissolution of the Soviet Union in 1991, we can gain a better understanding of both the Holocaust and Jewish responses in the Soviet Union and of Soviet nationality policies and their effects on individuals.

Memories that speak back

What distinguishes the survival of young Soviet Jews from their peers in other areas of occupied Europe is the role of the partisan units and other Soviet institutions in securing their survival. I do not wish to deny the failures of the Soviet government in protecting Soviet citizens, especially Jewish citizens, against the genocide; there are too many to ignore. But it is important to acknowledge the moments that survivors highlight as turning points during the war and which are, in several instances, rooted in the efforts of the Communist Party and other Soviet institutions to challenge the occupation regime. These efforts may not have been designed to specifically protect Jews from the Holocaust, but they were aimed at liberating the Soviet population, which included people of Jewish nationality, and they were perceived as such. The accounts of survivors, who grew up and were socialized in an environment that promoted secular and Soviet values in the 1930s, are absolutely critical for understanding not only the experience of the Holocaust in the USSR, but how it was and is represented and how individuals responded to those representations in the postwar Soviet Union. The continuity, or reestablishment, of Soviet institutions such as the Party, youth organizations, and the military was a central foothold, both emotionally and materially, for those who had participated and believed in them before the war and who had lost everything during the war.

This insight does not refute the downside of Soviet state institutions' authoritarian nature, which marginalized those who did not participate or had no choice. Nor does it diminish the necessity of critical examinations of the recent and current Russian governments' commemorations of the victorious Soviet army, which are often accompanied by generous subsidies or symbolic honors for war veterans to secure their loyalty and generate an artificial sense of state legitimacy. But, alongside an analysis of how the Nazi genocide unfolded in Belorussia, this perspective may provide some clues to placing it in an analytical framework that is attentive to specific features of its representation in the Soviet Union and to similarities and dissimilarities in the history and memory of the Nazi genocide and World War II in the former Soviet Union and elsewhere.

Browsing the wealth of literature on the Nazi genocide, one question arises: why is there still comparatively little material available on the destruction and struggles of the Jewish population in the German-occupied Soviet territories, compared to other areas in which hundreds of thousands of Jewish girls, boys, women, and men were killed? To understand why it took over five decades for more substantial scholarship on the Nazi genocide of the Soviet Jewish population to develop, within or outside the former USSR, one must take into account the position of survivors of the genocide in Soviet and post-Soviet society and the nature of the genocide.[60]

The historian Zvi Gitelman reminds us that the "general Soviet tendency to ignore or downplay the Holocaust" was facilitated by the fact that

> no country in the West lost as many of its non-Jewish citizens in the war against Nazism as did the USSR, so that the fate of the Jews in France, Holland, Germany, or Belgium stands in sharper contrast to that of their co-nationals or co-religionists than it does in the East.[61]

Official statistics for Soviet war losses arrive at a number of 26.6 million casualties, including 8.7 million military deaths.[62] Belorussia, together with present-day Ukraine, was hit hardest under the German occupation. The republic was occupied for nearly three years and saw continuous military clashes. Fewer than seven million residents of Belorussia survived the war; every third or fourth of a population of 9,200,000 people died between 1941 and 1944.[63] Rebuilding the country after this damage, one could argue, required a sense of community and belonging. In this regard, the Soviet government's choice to focus on universality in commemoration (and the historiography required to build it) was perhaps necessary and even legitimate, as it produced a sense of cohesion and purpose among a deeply divided and fragmented population. Acknowledging the special targeting of the Jewish population might have cast doubt upon the idea of shared victimhood.[64] As problematic as the incorporation of Jewish victims into an overall mass of victims is (because Jews were also killed by other Soviet citizens), in part it reflected the reality of the war of destruction.

In addition to the isolationist and inherently problematic politics of memory in the Soviet Union, the anticommunist attitudes of the Western bloc produced a further impediment to acknowledging Soviet war losses during the Cold War. An image of the USSR, or its population, as a victim (of World War II) was irreconcilable with the then current perception of the Soviet Union as the prime enemy and threat to world capitalism. Such a defensive attitude against concerns for the losses experienced by the population was boosted by the knowledge that many of the victims had been members of the Communist Party or other left-wing groups, making it hard to clearly identify the reason for their persecution by the Nazis. The changing roles of local residents, victims turned perpetrators and vice versa—often the former when it came to the abuse and killing of Jews—complicate the construction of a cohesive and meaningful historical memory.[65]

The nature of the Nazi genocide in the Soviet territories itself plays a major role in the silence surrounding the suffering and survival of Soviet Jews during World War II. Globally, during and immediately after the war the mass murder of the Jews in Europe was not immediately recognized as a phenomenon that warranted special attention. It took well into the 1960s for the international community to attempt a thorough investigation of the history of the Nazi genocide. The 1961 trial against Adolf Eichmann, the manager of mass deportation of Jews to the concentration camps, is generally considered to be a crucial moment for the study of the Holocaust, as the mass murder of European Jewry has become known since then. The trial in Jerusalem brought to international attention the organization of the mass murder, but also painful questions concerning the collaboration of non-German individuals and the failure of the international community to respond to calls for rescue or intervention on behalf of European Jewry.[66] Today, a globalized memory of the Holocaust is part and parcel of political debates and subject to international cooperation securing educational and commemorative efforts.[67] The commitment to preserving this memory often serves as a litmus test for a society's adherence to democratic values and ability to partake in international decision-making. Eastern European countries wishing to accede to European Union membership, for instance, are regularly called upon to investigate Nazi atrocities and local participation.

At the center of Holocaust memory is the systematic extermination of European Jewry, symbolized by the extermination camp at Auschwitz in present-day Poland. Immediately upon arrival, or after varying periods of forced labor under horrific conditions, inmates were gassed with industrialized precision in the "death factories" of this and other camps. The breakdown of all moral and religious norms within the National Socialist regime culminated in these facilities designed for the systematic killing of members of particular social groups. The extermination camps

> offend . . . our common sense . . . by the complete senselessness of a world where punishment persecutes the innocent more than the criminal, where labor does not result and is not intended to result in products, where crimes do not benefit and are not even calculated to benefit their authors.[68]

Being nonutilitarian and antiutilitarian institutions at the same time, these camps signify the unprecedented character of the Nazi genocide.[69] Consequently, the name of Auschwitz acquired metaphorical meaning and evokes the singularity of the genocide.

Yet most Soviet Jews were not deported to concentration or extermination camps. When German troops invaded the Soviet Union in June 1941, they immediately began to round up the male Jewish population, together with known functionaries of the Communist Party, and killed both groups on the spot, mostly at trenches at the outskirts of towns and villages. Beginning in August 1941, women were included in these massacres. During nightly pogroms and organized mass executions, thousands of girls, boys, women, and men were rounded up, led to ditches, and shot.

Is it because of their form—the brutal massacres and killings on the spot, in contrast to the industrialized murder in the camps—that these atrocities have been excluded from the public memory of the Holocaust? Are mass shootings less specific, too similar to other genocides in history? Do they too closely resemble the mode of warfare known from other invasions, that is, armies rounding up civilians and killing them just because they are the "enemy population" or belong to a different ethnicity? Can they not be included in a portrayal of a historical caesura, which is constituted by the industrialized killing of people, because they are too connected to other nationalist or imperialist projects?[70] Can the struggle for survival in the ghettos, in hiding, and in family units not be recognized as equally valorous because it is too mundane, too rooted in or too close to the daily struggle of thousands of people against deprivation, hunger, repression? Is the long-lasting ignorance of the Holocaust in the Soviet Union, and how individuals responded to it, another iteration of a "dilemma [that] emerges partly because our understanding of the Holocaust as a break with the past conflicts with our knowledge of the continuities that are present in these events"?[71] Considering the continuities and similarities between the Nazi genocide of Jews in the Soviet Union, other incidents of mass crimes, and ongoing violence based on people's age, gender, nationality/race, sexuality, or ability is imperative for a critique of, and challenge to, incomplete historiographies and memories of systematic violence such as the Nazi genocide.

Tracking particular individuals, including Elena Drapkina, Rita Kazhdan, Alevtina Kuprikhina, Frida Ped'ko, Sonia Zalesskaia, Grigorii Erenburg, Boris Gal'perin, Mikhail Treister, and Samuil Volk, and framing their stories against a broader historical and cultural backdrop, this book reveals the shift in perspective that Soviet Jewish adolescents had to undergo during and after World War II. These people's narratives show that individual experiences and perceptions of the Nazi genocide were molded by people's socialization and worldview before the war and were further complicated by postwar restrictions on individual lives in the USSR. The stories—recollections of unlikely witnesses to war and genocide, buried under Soviet bureaucracy and state ideology, silenced by Cold War propaganda, and, finally, reshaped by a shifting political terrain after the dissolution of the Soviet Union—speak back not only to systematic murder, but also to ignorant practices of commemoration and historiography. The survivors challenge us to think differently about Jewish identity, the Holocaust, and children and young people's resilience in ghettos and forests in Belorussia.

Notes

Introduction

1. Frida Ped'ko, interviewed by author, St. Petersburg, May 13, 2005.
2. "Tolochinskii raion," in USHMM, RG22.002M, "Selected Records of the Extraordinary State Commission to Investigate German-Fascist Crimes Committed on Soviet Territory, 1941-1945," Sub-group 7021-84 "Belarus, Vitebskaya (Vitebsk) oblast," reel 8, p. 20.
3. Frida Ped'ko, interviewed by author, St. Petersburg, May 13, 2005.
4. Frida Ped'ko, interviewed by author, St. Petersburg, May 27, 2001.
5. Frida Ped'ko, interviewed by author, St. Petersburg, May 13, 2005.
6. Frida Ped'ko, interviewed by author, St. Petersburg, May 13, 2005.
7. Frida Ped'ko, interviewed by author, St. Petersburg, May 13, 2005.
8. This rather limited definition of internationalism reflects the turn away from proletarian internationalism, favoring the unified struggle of workers around the world, to the promotion of multinational brotherhood within the USSR in 1930s Soviet propaganda. See David Brandenberger, "Proletarian Internationalism, 'Soviet Patriotism' and the Rise of Russocentric Etatism During the Stalinist 1930s," *Left History* 6.2 (2000): 80-100; and Gleb J. Albert, "From 'World Soviet' to 'Fatherland of All Proletarians.' Anticipated World Society and Global Thinking in Early Soviet Russia," *InterDisciplines* 1 (2012): 85-119.
9. Komsomol is the acronym for *Kommunisticheskii soiuz molodiozhi* (Communist Union of Youth), the official youth organization of the Communist Party of the Soviet Union, established in 1918.
10. Christian Gerlach, *Kalkulierte Morde: Die deutsche Wirtschafts- und Vernichtungspolitik in Weißrussland 1941–1944* (Hamburg: Hamburger Edition 1999), 683ff.
11. Leonid Smilovitsky, "A Demographic Profile of the Jews in Belorussia from the Pre-war Time to the Post-war Time," *Journal of Genocide Research* 5, no. 1 (2003): 117, 119. Estimates, Smilovitsky points out, range from 245,000 to 1,000,000. See also I. P. Gerasimova, *Vstali my plechom k plechu: Evrei v partizanskom dvizhenii Belorussii, 1941–1944 gg.* (Minsk: Asobnyi Dakh, 2005), 3, 11n1.
12. Zvi Gitelman, "Soviet Jewry before the Holocaust," in *Bitter Legacy: Confronting the Holocaust in the USSR*, ed. Zvi Gitelman (Bloomington and Indianapolis: Indiana University Press, 1997), 11.
13. Wendy Lower, "Facilitating Genocide: Nazi Ghettoization Practices in Occupied Ukraine, 1941–1942," in *Life in the Ghettos during the Holocaust*, ed. Eric J. Sterling (Syracuse, NY: Syracuse University Press, 2005), 133, 137. See also Dan Michman's recent analysis, which underscores the functional proximity of camps and ghettos in the occupied Soviet Union, marking them different solely due to their location, with ghettos being established in urban areas; Dan Michman, *The Emergence of Jewish Ghettos during the Holocaust* (New York: Cambridge University Press, 2011), 121.

14. On young Soviet Jews' increasing distance from traditional Judaism, see for instance Anna Shternshis, *Soviet and Kosher: Jewish Popular Culture in the Soviet Union, 1923–1939* (Bloomington: Indiana University Press, 2006), and Leonid Smilovitskii, "Sovetskaia shkola na idish," in Smilovitskii, *Evrei Belarusi: Iz nashei obshchei istorii, 1905–1953* (Minsk: Arti-Feks, 1999). An in-depth analysis of this trend follows in chapter 2.

15. For a comprehensive discussion of the variegated and complex nature of Jewish assimilation in the 19th century, see Jonathan Frankel and Steven J. Zipperstein (eds.), *Assimilation and Community: The Jews in Nineteenth-Century Europe* (New York: Cambridge University Press, 1992).

16. Among the vast literature on this topic, Joseph Katz, *From Prejudice to Destruction: Anti-Semitism, 1700–1933* (Cambridge, MA: Harvard University Press, 1980) provides a most detailed analysis of the arguments and effects of racial anti-semitism in late-19th and early-20th century Germany.

17. For North American readers, a comparison of nationality to ethnicity or race may be useful, as a racialized concept of descent in which a person's ancestors determine their nationality informs the identification. A concise analysis of Soviet nationality policies and the institutionalization of ethnic heterogeneity is in Rogers Brubaker, "Nationhood and the National Question in the Soviet Union and Post-Soviet Eurasia: An Institutionalist Account," *Theory and Society* 23, no. 1 (1994): 47–48. A more detailed discussion of Soviet nationality policies and their role for Soviet Jews' adolescence follows in chapter 2 of this book.

18. Detailed analyses of the secularization drive are in Anna Shternshis, "Passover in the Soviet Union, 1917–41," *East European Jewish Affairs* 31.1 (2001): 61–76, and Marianne Kamp, "The Wedding Feast: Living the New Uzbek Life in the 1930s," in *Everyday Life in Central Asia*, ed. Jeff Sahadeo and Russell Zanca (Bloomington and Indianapolis: Indiana University Press, 2007), 103–114.

19. The rationale and implications of the internal Soviet passport are explained in Wendy Z. Goldman, "The Internal Soviet Passport: Workers and Free Movement," in *Extending the Borders of Russian History*, ed. Marsha Siefert (Budapest: CEU Press, 2003), 315–331, and David Shearer, "Passports, Identity, and Mass Policing," in *Policing Stalin's Socialism: Repression and Social Order in the Soviet Union, 1924–1953* (New Haven: Yale University Press, 2009), 243–284.

20. On the need to account for a whole life experience and not only the experience of violence in working with survivors of catastrophe, see Catherine Merridale, *Night of Stone: Death and Memory in Twentieth-Century Russia* (New York and London: Viking, 2000), 333, where she argues that "the catastrophe has deep influences, but other experiences [do] too."

21. Foundational to this approach was Maurice Halbwachs, *On Collective Memory* (Chicago: University of Chicago Press, 1992; orig. 1941). Recent scholarship developing a similar framework includes Paul Connerton, *How Societies Remember* (New York: Cambridge University Press, 1989); Jan Assmann, *Das kulturelle Gedächtnis: Schrift, Erinnerung, und politische Identität in frühen Hochkulturen* (Munich: Beck, 1992); Iwona Irwin-Zarecka, *Frames of Remembrance. The Dynamics of Collective Memory* (New Brunswick, NJ and London: Transaction Publishers, 1994); James Wertsch, *Voices of Collective Remembering* (New York: Cambridge University Press, 2002); and Elizabeth Jelin, *State Repression and the Labors of Memory* (Minneapolis: University of Minnesota Press, 2003). Barbara Misztal, *Theories of Social Remembering* (Maidenhead, UK: Open University Press, 2003) provides a comprehensive survey of theories on the topic. My analysis of the sociality of memory is

further inspired by Luisa Passerini, "Work Ideology and Consensus under Italian Fascism" (orig. 1979), in *The Oral History Reader*, 1st Ed., ed. Robert Perks and Alistair Thomson (New York and London: Routledge, 1998), 53–62; Peter Burke, "History as Social Memory," in *Memory, History, Culture and the Mind*, ed. Thomas Butler (New York: Blackwell, 1989), 97–113; and Joan Scott, "The Evidence of Experience," *Critical Inquiry* 17, no. 4 (1991): 773–797.

22. Gabriele Rosenthal, "Die Biographie im Kontext der Familien und Gesellschaftsgeschichte," in *Biographieforschung im Diskurs: Theoretische und methodologische Verknüpfungen*, eds. Bettina Völter, Bettina Dausien, Gabriele Rosenthal, and Helma Lutz (Wiesbaden, Germany: Verlag für Sozialwissenschaften, 2005), 51f.

23. "Hannah Arendt, "Understanding and Politics" (orig. 1954), in *Hannah Arendt, Essays in Understanding, 1930–1954: Formation, Exile, and Totalitarianism*, ed. Jerome Kohn (New York: Schocken, 1994), 319.

24. Arendt, "Understanding and Politics," 320.

25. Deborah Dwork, *Children with a Star: Jewish Youth in Nazi Europe* (New Haven: Yale University Press, 1991). Whereas there are a number of works on the fate of children during the Nazi regime or World War II, either the experience of Soviet children is omitted completely; the situation in the ghettos for Jewish residents is conspicuously absent, whereas a portrayal of Soviet children is included, as in Lynn H. Nicholas' study *Cruel World: The Children of Europe in the Nazi Web* (New York: Knopf, 2005), esp. chap. 11; or the depiction is limited to descriptions of executions and a cursory account of Jewish youth in partisan units, as in Nicholas Stargardt, *Witnesses of War: Children's Lives under the Nazis* (New York: Vintage Books, 2005), 149–152. Patricia Heberer's edition of contemporaneous documents reflecting children's perceptions of the Holocaust includes only a very few sources to address the German-occupied Soviet Union, and of course an analysis of these documents is still to be done; see Patricia Heberer, *Children during the Holocaust* (New York: AltaMira 2012). Leonid Smilovitskii, however, devotes a full chapter to the children in Belorussian ghettos, though his work remains largely inaccessible to non-Russian-speaking audiences; see Leonid Smilovitskii, *Katastrofa evreev v Belorussii, 1941–1944 gg.* (Tel Aviv: Biblioteka Matveia Chernogo, 2000), chap. 3.

26. See, for instance, United States Holocaust Memorial Museum (USHMM), Exhibition "Remember the Children: Daniel's Story." Yad Vashem in Israel has an interactive website, "Children in the Ghetto," which is "about children, written for children;" see Yad Vashem—The Holocaust Martyrs' and Remembrance Authority, "Children in the Ghetto" <http://ghetto.galim.org.il/eng/about/.index.html>, accessed July 7, 2012.

27. Gerlach, *Kalkulierte Morde*; Martin Dean, *Collaboration in the Holocaust: Crimes of the Local Police in Belorussia and Ukraine, 1941–44* (New York: St. Martin's Press, 2000); Wolfgang Curilla, *Die deutsche Ordnungspolizei und der Holocaust im Baltikum und in Weißrussland 1941–1944* (Paderborn, Germany: Schöningh, 2006); Dieter Pohl, *Die Herrschaft der Wehrmacht: Deutsche Militärbesatzung und einheimische Bevölkerung in der Sowjetunion 1941–1944* (Munich: Oldenbourg, 2008); Jörn Hasenclever, *Wehrmacht und Besatzungspolitik in der Sowjetunion: Die Befehlshaber der Rückwärtigen Heeresgebiete 1941–1943* (Paderborn, Germany: Schöningh, 2010). Such material is also the basis for document collections that have been published in formerly occupied areas; see Raisa Chernoglazova, ed., *Tragedia evreev Belorussii (1941–1944 gg.): Sbornik materialov i dokumentov* (Minsk: Izd. E. S. Gal'perin, 1997); Raisa Chernoglazova, ed., *Judenfrei! Svobodno ot Evreev! Istoriia minskogo getto v dokumentakh* (Minsk: Asobny Dakh, 1999); E. G. Ioffe et al., eds., *Kholokost v Belarusi, 1941–1944: Dokumenty i materialy* (Minsk: NARB, 2002).

28. Christoph Dieckmann notes a similar challenge for ghettos in German-occupied Lithuania: Dieckmann, *Deutsche Besatzungspolitik in Litauen*, Vol. 2 (Göttingen, Germany: Wallstein, 2012), 820.

29. Yehuda Bauer, *The Death of the Shtetl* (New Haven: Yale University Press, 2009), 10–12.

30. See Lena Jockusch, *Collect and Record! Jewish Holocaust Documentation in Early Postwar Europe* (New York: Oxford University Press, 2012), and Boaz Cohen, "The Children's Voice: Postwar Collection of Testimonies from Child Survivors of the Holocaust," *Holocaust and Genocide Studies* 21, no. 1 (2007): 73–95. David Boder was the first to systematically conduct interviews with Jewish survivors, but his collection does not include interviews with people who had been interned in German-occupied Soviet territories; see "Voices of the Holocaust," the digital archive of interviews with Holocaust survivors conducted by David Boder in 1946, available at http://voices.iit.edu/david_boder; Donald L. Niewyk, "Introduction," in *Fresh Wounds: Early Narratives of Holocaust Survival*, ed. Donald L. Niewyk (Chapel Hill: University of North Carolina Press, 1998), 6.

31. The records of the Soviet Extraordinary State Commission for Ascertaining and Investigating Crimes by the German-Fascist Invaders and their Accomplices are held at the State Archive of the Russian Federation (GARF); a selection of these records can be accessed in the archives of the US Holocaust Memorial Museum (USHMM), RG-22.002M, "Selected Records of the Extraordinary State Commission to Investigate German-Fascist Crimes Committed on Soviet Territory, 1941-1945."

32. Parts of the collection are accessible in Ilya Ehrenburg and Vasily Grossman, *The Complete Black Book of Russian Jewry*, tr. and ed. David Patterson (New Brunswick: Transaction, 2002), and Joshua Rubenstein and Ilya Altman, eds., *The Unknown Black Book: The Holocaust in the German-Occupied Soviet Territories* (Bloomington and Indianapolis: Indiana University Press, 2008).

33. A rare diary, completed immediately after World War II, is *Kogda slova krichat i plachut: Dnevniki Liali i Berty Bruk*, ed. I. Gerasimova (Minsk: Asobnyi Dakh, 2004).

34. Daniel Romanovsky, "The Holocaust in the Eyes of *Homo Sovieticus*: A Survey Based on Northeastern Belorussia and Northwestern Russia," *Holocaust and Genocide Studies* 13, no. 3 (1999): 357.

35. Joanna Michlic, "The Aftermath and After: Memories of Child Survivors of the Holocaust," in *Lessons and Legacies X: Back to the Sources: Reexamining Perpetrators, Victims, and Bystanders*, ed. Sara R. Horowitz (Evanston, IL: Northwestern University Press, 2012), 142.

36. The most familiar example from other regions is Anne Frank; other memoirs and collections of diaries or testimonies documenting Jewish adolescents' survival in hiding include Maxine B. Rosenberg, *Hiding to Survive: Stories of Jewish Children Rescued from the Holocaust* (New York: Clarion, 1994), and Alexandra Zapruder, *Salvaged Pages: Young Writers' Diaries of the Holocaust* (New Haven: Yale University Press, 2004).

37. By now canonical, the following texts initiated attention to gender as an important category of analysis for Holocaust history: Renate Bridenthal, Atina Grossman, and Marion Kaplan, eds., *When Biology Became Destiny: Women in Weimar and Nazi Germany* (New York: Monthly Review Press, 1984); Esther Katz and Joan Ringelheim, eds., *Proceedings of the Conference: Women Surviving: The Holocaust* (New York: Institute for Research in History, 1983); Joan Ringelheim, "Women and the Holocaust: A Reconsideration of Research," *Signs* 10, no. 4 (1985): 741–761; Claudia Koonz, *Mothers in the Fatherland: Women, the Family, and Nazi Policy* (New York: St.

Martin's Press, 1987); and Carol Rittner and John K. Roth, eds., *Different Voices: Women and the Holocaust* (New York: Paragon House, 1993). Another wave of publications at the end of the 20th century pushed the issue further, including the scrutiny of the category "woman" and expanding the analysis of "gender" as a form of identification and its role in representation: Judith Tydor Baumel, *Double Jeopardy: Gender and the Holocaust* (London: Vallentine Mitchell, 1998); Esther Fuchs, ed., *Women and the Holocaust: Narrative and Representation* (Lanham, MD: University Press of America, 1999); and Elizabeth Baer and Myrna Goldenberg, eds., *Experience and Expression: Women, the Nazis, and the Holocaust* (Detroit: Wayne State University Press, 2003).

38. See, among others, "Minsk Hell," in Rubenstein and Altman, eds., *Unknown Black Book*, 252; "The Recollections of Dr. Tsetsilia Mikhaylovna Shapiro," ibid. 257. See also Solly Ganor, *Das andere Leben: Kindheit im Holocaust* (Frankfurt am Main: Fischer, 1997), 81–82, and Anatoly Podolsky, "The Tragic Fate of Ukrainian Jewish Women under Nazi Occupation," in *Sexual Violence against Jewish Women during the Holocaust*, eds. Sonja M. Hedgepeth and Rochelle G. Saidel (Waltham, MA: Brandeis University Press, 2010), 94–107. It is, for instance, likely that (Jewish) men were also the target of sexual violence in German-occupied Belorussia, acts that may range from forced nudity and sexual torture to rape and sexual enslavement, though little information has as yet been uncovered. Regina Mühlhäuser, *Eroberungen: Sexuelle Gewalttaten und intime Beziehungen deutscher Soldaten in der Sowjetunion* (Hamburg: Hamburger Edition, 2010), 136, cites reports that members of the SS specifically targeted the genitals of young males during beatings, as well as the castration of fifty-six Jewish men in the ghetto of Bauska (Latvia) in July 1941.

39. Ibid. 92, 192. Terror against women and particularly the use of sexual violence have been a staple of military conflicts and war; see, for instance, Paul Preston, *The Spanish Holocaust: Inquisition and Extermination in Twentieth-Century Spain* (New York: W. W. Norton, 2012), especially chap. 2, and Cindy S. Snyder, Wesley J. Gabbard, J. Dean May, and Nihada Zulcic, "On the Battleground of Women's Bodies: Mass Rape in Bosnia-Herzegovina," *Affilia: Journal of Women and Social Work* 21, no. 2 (2006): 184–195.

40. On the symbolic function of sexual violence in wartime, see Ronit Lentin, "Introduction," in *Gender and Catastrophe*, ed. Ronit Lentin (London: Zed, 1997), 2–17; Valerie Smith, "Split Affinities: The Case of Interracial Rape," in *Theorizing Feminism*, eds. Anne C. Herrmann and Abigail J. Stewart (Boulder, CO: Westview Press, 1994), 155–171; and Wendy Bracewell, "Rape in Kosovo: Masculinity and Serbian Nationalism," *Nations and Nationalisms* 6, no. 4 (2000): 563–590.

41. See, for instance, Stefan Lehnstaedt, *Okkupation im Osten: Besatzeralltag in Warschau und Minsk, 1939–1944* (Munich: Oldenbourg, 2010), 244.

42. Cf. Beate Fieseler, "Der Krieg der Frauen: Die ungeschriebene Geschichte," in *Mascha + Nina + Katjuscha: Frauen in der Roten Armee, 1941–1945*, ed. Deutsch-Russisches Museum Berlin Karlshorst (Berlin: Museum Karlshorst, 2002), 11–20.

43. On silence as a form of protection, see Dori Laub, "Bearing Witness or the Vicissitudes of Listening," in *Testimony: Crises of Witnessing in Literature, Psychoanalysis, and History*, by Shoshana Felman and Dori Laub (New York and London: Routledge, 1992), 58.

44. The existence of different spheres of communication in the Soviet Union has been analyzed by many scholars who point to these spheres' reflectivity of legitimate and illegitimate discourse, including Ingrid Oswald and Viktor Voronkov, "The Public-Private Sphere in Soviet and Post-Soviet Society: Perception and Dynamics of 'Public' and 'Private' in Contemporary Russia," *European Societies* 6,

no. 1 (2004): 97–117; Vladimir Shlapentokh, *Public and Private Life of the Soviet People: Changing Values in Post-Stalin Russia* (New York: Oxford University Press, 1989); and various contributions in Jeff Alan Weintraub and Krishan Kumar, eds., *Public and Private in Thought and Practice: Perspectives on a Grand Dichotomy* (Chicago: University of Chicago Press, 1997) and Gabor Tamas Rittersporn, Malte Rolf, and Jan C. Behrends, eds., *Sphären von Öffentlichkeit in Gesellschaften sowjetischen Typs: Zwischen partei-staatlicher Selbstinszenierung und kirchlichen Gegenwelten* (Frankfurt am Main: Lang, 2003).

45. The distinction between eastern and western Belorussia is of utmost importance here, as the establishment of Soviet institutions and ideology in the formerly Polish and newly Soviet territories proceeded very differently and much more quickly than in the rest of the BSSR, where they had been operating since 1922. See Jan Tomasz Gross, "The Sovietization of Western Ukraine and Western Byelorussia," in *Jews in Eastern Poland and the USSR, 1939–46*, eds. Norman Davies and Antony Polonsky (New York: St. Martin's Press, 1991), 60–76.

46. For a comprehensive account of Soviet nationality policies, see Jeremy Smith, *Red Nations: The Nationalities Experience in and after the USSR* (Cambridge: Cambridge University Press, 2013).

47. On this process of biographical work in the post-Soviet context, see Robert Miller, Robin Humphrey, and Elena Zdravomyslova, "Introduction: Biographical Research and Historical Watersheds," in *Biographical Research in Eastern Europe: Altered Lives and Broken Biographies*, eds. Robin Humphrey, Robert Miller, and Elena Zdravomyslova (Aldershot, UK: Ashgate: 2003), 1–26.

48. See Olga Kalacheva and Oksana Karpenko, "Leben im 'Zustand der Wahl'? Die Ambivalenz der ethnischen Identitätsbildung bei russischen Juden," in *Post-sowjetische Ethnizitäten: Ethnische Gemeinden in St. Petersburg und Berlin/Potsdam*, eds. Ingrid Oswald and Viktor Voronkov (Berlin: Berliner Debatte, 1997), 38–54; Zvi Gitelman, "The Reconstruction of Community and Jewish Identity in Russia," *East European Affairs* 24.1 (1999): 35–56; and Viktor Voronkov and Elena Chikadze, "Different Generations of Leningrad Jews in the Context of Public/Private Division: Paradoxes of Ethnicity," in Humphrey et al., *Biographical Research in Eastern Europe*, 239–262.

49. The related concept of positionality is discussed in detail in Floya Anthias, "Where Do I Belong? Narrating Collective Identity and Translocal Positionality," *Ethnicities* 2, no. 4 (2002): 491–514.

50. Publications on the split war memory include Nina Tumarkin, *The Living and the Dead: The Rise and Fall of the Cult of World War II in Russia* (New York: Basic Books, 1994); Sabine Arnold, *Stalingrad im sowjetischen Gedächtnis: Kriegserinnerung und Geschichtsbild im totalitären Staat* (Bochum, Germany: Projekt, 1998); Babette Quinkert, ed., *"Wir sind die Herren dieses Landes": Ursachen, Verlauf und Folgen des deutschen Überfalls auf die Sowjetunion* (Hamburg: VSA, 2002); Mikhail Gabovich, ed., *Pamiat' o voine: 60 let spustia; Rossiia, Germaniia, Evropa* (Moskva: Novoe Literaturnoe Obozrenie, 2005); Catherine Merridale, *Ivan's War: Life and Death in the Red Army, 1939–1945* (New York: Metropolitan Books, 2006); and Mark Edele, *Soviet Veterans of World War II: A Popular Movement in an Authoritarian Society* (New York: Oxford University Press, 2008).

51. Leonid Gol'braikh, interviewed by author, St. Petersburg, May 5, 2001; Boris Gal'perin, interviewed by author, St. Petersburg, May 16, 2001.

52. See Saul Friedländer, "History, Memory, and the Historian: Dilemmas and Responsibilities," *New German Critique* No. 80 (2000): 5, who argues that after massive trauma like war and genocide, coherent and unifying narratives are often essential in order to stabilize the affected society.

53. I borrow here from Gail Hershatter's insightful study of memory in China: Gail Hershatter, *The Gender of Memory: Rural Women and China's Collective Past* (Berkeley: University of California Press, 2011), 30.

54. Veena Das, "Trauma and Testimony: Implications for Political Community," *Anthropological Theory* 3, no. 3 (2003): 299.

55. See the statistics provided by Victor Karady in his comprehensive sociohistorical study of European Jews, Victor Karady, *The Jews of Europe in the Modern Era: A Socio-Historical Outline* (New York and Budapest: CEU Press, 2004), 44–45.

56. W. E. B. Du Bois, "The Strivings of the Negro People," *The Atlantic*, August 1897, 194f.

57. Recent studies on this subject include, among others, John-Paul Himka, "Ukrainian Collaboration in the Extermination of the Jews during the Second World War: Sorting Out the Long-Term and Conjectural Factors," in *The Fate of the European Jews, 1939–1945: Continuity or Contingency?*, ed. Jonathan Frankel (New York: Oxford University Press, 1997), 170–189; Dean, *Collaboration in the Holocaust*; Leonid Rein, "Local Collaboration in the Execution of the 'Final Solution' in Nazi-Occupied Belorussia," in *Holocaust and Genocide Studies* 20.3 (2006): 381–409.

58. Gerlach, *Kalkulierte Morde*, 81; Jürgen Matthäus, "Reibungslos und planmäßig: Die zweite Welle der Judenvernichtung im Generalkommissariat Weißruthenien (1942–1944)," in *Jahrbuch für Antisemitismusforschung* No. 4 (1995), 258f.

59. A nuanced portrayal of non-Jewish reactions to the Nazi genocide is in Karel Berkhoff, *Harvest of Despair: Life and Death in Ukraine under Nazi Rule* (Cambridge, MA: Harvard University Press, 2004), 71ff., 83. For another discussion of the complex relationship between Jews and non-Jews in Ukraine, see, for instance, M. I. Koval, "The Nazi Genocide of the Jews and the Ukrainian Population, 1941–1944," in Gitelman, *Bitter Legacy*, 51–60. The author alludes to the debate about Ukrainian antisemitism when he urges readers not to identify the involvement of Ukrainian police units in pogroms and executions with the attitude of the Ukrainian population as a whole. The police, Koval writes, "constituted only 1 percent of the local population, and it was despised and criticized by people" (ibid. 53).

60. Baumel, *Double Jeopardy*, chap. 4.

61. Melissa Raphael, *The Female Face of God in Auschwitz* (New York: Routledge, 2003), 95.

62. Nancy K. Miller and Jason Tougaw, "Introduction: Extremities," in *Extremities: Trauma, Testimony, and Community*, eds. Nancy Miller and Jason Tougaw (Urbana: University of Illinois Press, 2002), 19; see also other contributions in that volume and my discussion below of Thomas Trezise, "Between History and Psychoanalysis: A Case Study in the Reception of Holocaust Survivor Testimony," *History and Memory* 20, no. 1 (2008): 7–47.

63. Elena E. Nosenko-Shtein, "O kollektivnoi pamiati rossiiskikh evreev na rubezhe vekov (predvaritel'nye nabliudeniia)," *Etnograficheskoie Obozrenie* 6 (2009): 20–29.

64. Nechama Tec, *Defiance: The Bielski Partisans* (New York: Oxford University Press, 1993), 218ff.; Fieseler, "Der Krieg der Frauen." See also the testimonies collected by Svetlana Alexievich, *U voiny ne zhenskoe litso* (Moscow: Palmira, 2004 [orig. 1985]).

65. Fieseler, "Der Krieg der Frauen," 18, and see Sabine Arnold's detailed analysis of the Soviet memorial in Stalingrad, where heroic masculinity is juxtaposed with female calls for action: Arnold, *Stalingrad im sowjetischen Gedächtnis*.

66. My discussion of reproductive labor draws on Frederick Engels, *The Origin of the Family, Private Property and the State* (orig. 1884), ed. Eleanor Burke Leacock

(New York: International Publishers, 1972) and feminist scholarship on the sexual division of labor and women's work, for instance, Mariarosa Dalla Costa and Selma Jones, *The Power of Women and the Subversion of Community* (Richmond, UK: Falling Wall Press, 1972); Angela Y. Davis, "Women and Capitalism: Dialectics of Oppression and Liberation" (orig. 1977), in *The Black Feminist Reader*, eds. Joy James and T. Denean Sharpley-Whiting (Malden, MA: Blackwell, 2000 [1977]), 146–182; and Heidi Hartmann, "The Unhappy Marriage of Marxism and Feminism: Towards a More Progressive Union," *Capital & Class* 3, no. 1 (1979): 1–33.

67. See, for instance, Yehuda Bauer's review of scholarship on Jewish resistance in "Jewish Resistance—Myth or Reality?," in Bauer, *Rethinking the Holocaust* (New Haven and London: Yale University Press, 2001), 120. For recent examples that foreground armed struggle, see Yitzhak Arad, *In the Shadow of the Red Banner* (New York and Jerusalem: Gefen, 2010), and Julie Chervinsky, ed., *Lives of the Great Patriotic War: The Untold Stories of Soviet Jewish Soldiers in the Red Army during World War II* (New York: Blavatnik Archive Foundation, 2011).

68. On the feminist project to validate everyday lives as history through oral history, see Sherna Berger Gluck, "What's So Special about Women?," in *Women's Oral History: The Frontiers Reader*, ed. Susan H. Armitage with Patricia Hart and Karen Weathermon (Lincoln and London: University of Nebraska Press, 2002), 3ff. These analyses draw on the assumption that studying the production and reproduction of life in the mundane and everyday allows us to detect the basic forms of subordination and ways to undermine it; see Nancy Hartsock, "The Feminist Standpoint: Developing the Ground for a Specifically Feminist Historical Materialism," in *Discovering Reality: Feminist Perspectives on Epistemology, Metaphysics, Methodology, and Philosophy of Science*, eds. Sandra Harding and Merrill B. Hintikka (Boston: Reidel), 304.

69. Judith Tydor Baumel, "'You Said the Words You Wanted Me to Hear but I Heard the Words You Couldn't Bring Yourself to Say': Women's First Person Accounts of the Holocaust," *Oral History Review* 27, no. 1 (2000): 21.

70. Hannah Arendt, *The Origins of Totalitarianism* (New York: Harcourt, 1968), 301: "The human being who has lost his place in a community, his political status in the struggle of his time, and the legal personality which makes his actions and part of his destiny a consistent whole, is left with those qualities which usually can become articulate only in the sphere of private life and must remain unqualified, mere existence in all matters of public concern. This mere existence . . . can be adequately dealt with only by the unpredictable hazards of friendship and sympathy . . ."

Chapter 1

1. Alevtina Kuprikhina, interviewed by author, St. Petersburg, September 6, 2002.

2. Ulrike Jureit and Karin Orth, *Überlebensgeschichten: Gespräche mit Überlebenden des KZ Neuengamme* (Hamburg: Dölling & Galitz, 1994), 103.

3. Alevtina Kuprikhina, Interview 49623, Visual History Archive, USC Shoah Foundation Institute, accessed online at USHMM on February 23, 2010.

4. Ronald Grele, "Movement Without an Aim: Methodological and Theoretical Problems in Oral History" (orig. 1975), in Perks and Thompson, eds., *The Oral History Reader*, 44.

5. Alessandro Portelli, *The Order Has Been Carried Out: History, Memory, and Meaning of a Nazi Massacre in Rome* (New York: Palgrave Macmillan, 2003), 16; Sherna Berger Gluck and Daphne Patai, "Introduction," in *Women's Words: The Feminist Practice of Oral History*, eds. Sherna Berger Gluck and Daphne Patai (New York: Routledge, 1991), 2; Sangster, "Telling Our Stories," 93.

6. Film director Steven Spielberg created the foundation after completing the film *Schindler's List* in 1994, with the goal of collecting 50,000 testimonies by survivors. In 2006, the resulting archive became part of the College of Letters, Arts, and Sciences at the University of Southern California, Los Angeles, and was renamed USC Shoah Foundation—The Institute for Visual History and Education.

7. For instance, Tyia Miles writes that to "combine imagination and documentation, envisioning how things might have been" is a useful and familiar approach in studying the lives of Black women in slavery in North America; Tiya Miles, *Ties That Bind: The Story of An Afro-Cherokee Family in Slavery and Freedom* (Berkeley: University of California Press, 2005), 212.

8. Rita Kazhdan, interviewed by author, St. Petersburg, May 12, 2005.

9. I draw here on a discussion I presented in Anika Walke, "Remembering and Recuperation: Memory Work in the Post-Soviet Context," *Zeitgeschichte* 36, no. 2 (2009): 67–87.

10. Portelli, *The Order Has Been Carried Out*, 15f.

11. An early documentation of debates on a revision of Soviet historiography provides Gert Meyer, ed., *Wir brauchen die Wahrheit: Geschichtsdiskussion in der Sowjetunion* (Cologne: Pahl-Rugenstein, 1989). Other works on the divisive Soviet war memory include Tumarkin, *The Living and the Dead*; Sabine Arnold, *Stalingrad im sowjetischen Gedächtnis*; and Gabovich, ed., *Pamiat' o voine*.

12. In 1991 and later years, Germany made agreements with several Eastern European countries on the provision of humanitarian aid for survivors of Nazi persecution. For a detailed account of West German politics of compensation and reparation, see, for instance, Günter Saathoff, "Die politischen Auseinandersetzungen über die Entschädigung von NS-Zwangsarbeit im Deutschen Bundestag—politische und rechtliche Aspekte," in *Entschädigung für NS-Zwangsarbeit: Rechtliche, historische und politische Aspekte*, eds. Klaus Barwig and Günter Saathoff (Baden-Baden, Germany: Nomos, 1998), 49–64.

13. See clause number five of the London Debt Agreement (1953). In 1996, German courts ruled that individuals from East European countries have the right to sue German companies for compensation for forced labor. Among others, the Bonn and Bremen district court denied the deferral of reparations positioned in the London Debt Agreement, referring to the Two Plus Four Agreement (1990) as an effective replacement of the Peace Treaty that was designated as the prerequisite for negotiations about reparations (Herbert Küpper, "Die neuere Rechtsprechung in Sachen NS-Zwangsarbeit," *Kritische Justiz* 31.2 (1998): 249-252).

14. Mario Kessler, "Schuld und Sühne: Reparation und Restitution in der Sowjetischen Besatzungszone," in Kessler, *Die SED und die Juden—zwischen Repression und Toleranz: Politische Entwicklungen bis 1967* (Berlin: Akademie Verlag, 1995), 37–47.

15. See Jeffrey Herf's insightful portrayal of the two Germanys' policies on restitution and memory of the Nazi past, *Divided Memory: The Nazi Past in the Two Germanys* (Cambridge, MA: Harvard University Press, 1997). In German, the history of German reparation or compensation payments is scrutinized in Klaus Barwig and Günter Saathoff, eds., *Entschädigung für NS-Zwangsarbeit*; Dieter Schröder and Rolf Surmann, "Entschädigung im Jahrhunderttakt," *Blätter für deutsche und internationale Politik* 3 (1999): 292–295; and Rolf Surmann, "Kleine Geschichte der 'Wiedergutmachung,'" *Blätter für deutsche und internationale Politik* 5 (1999): 585–594.

16. For this discussion of memory work I draw on Deborah Bird Rose's work on the repercussions and ethical demands for the memory of settler violence in Australia,

where she argues that "[i]f the purpose of violence was to extinguish certain people, knowledges, and perspectives, memory continues to resist violence": Deborah Bird Rose, *Reports from a Wild Country: Ethics for Decolonization* (Sydney: University of New South Wales Press, 2004), 30.

17. Rose, *Reports from a Wild Country*, 24.

18. On the relationality of interviewees between German researchers and victims of Nazi persecution, see Jureit and Orth, *Überlebensgeschichten*, 157f.

19. Anna Isaievna and Roman Borisovich Pudovik, interviewed by author, St. Petersburg, September 4, 2002.

20. In August 2000 the German parliament adopted the Law on the Creation of a Foundation "Remembrance, Responsibility and Future," which regulates financial compensation to former Nazi forced laborers and "to those affected by other injustices from the National Socialist period" (section 2, clause 1; *Federal Law Gazette* I 1263).

21. Elena Drapkina, interviewed by author, St. Petersburg, April 26, 2001.

22. One should note that the hierarchy of criminals is based on experiences, as some interviewees indicate. They report that during the first weeks of the war, soldiers of the Wehrmacht who moved through the areas warned Jewish inhabitants of succeeding SS troops. At any rate, scholars agree that there is sufficient evidence for the participation of troops of the Wehrmacht in mass shootings of Jewish women, men, and children; see, for instance, Christian Gerlach, *Kalkulierte Morde*, 620, and Waitman W. Beorn, *Marching Into Darkness: The Wehrmacht and the Holocaust in Belarus* (Cambridge, MA: Harvard University Press, 2014).

23. See Birgit Schreiber, "'Leaps of Faith': Die 'Krise des Zeugnisgebens' in narrativen Interviews mit einst in Deutschland versteckten jüdischen Kindern," *Zeitschrift für Politische Psychologie* 9.4 (2001): 189–202.

24. Berger Gluck and Patai, "Introduction," 1–3; Portelli, *The Order Has Been Carried Out*, 16.

25. Baumel, "You Said the Words You Wanted Me to Hear," 18, 21.

26. Tec, *Defiance*; Barbara Epstein, *The Minsk Ghetto, 1941–1943: Jewish Resistance and Soviet Internationalism* (Berkeley: University of California Press, 2008); Bauer, *Death of the Shtetl*.

27. Jessica Wiederhorn, "Survivors of the Shoah Visual History Foundation," in *Trauma Research Newsletter* 1 (2000), Hamburg Institute for Social Research, electronic document, <www.traumaresearch.net/focus1/wieder.htm>, accessed March 25, 2011.

28. At present, the digitized archive of more than 52,000 interviews is housed at the University of Southern California and, through an elaborate Internet-based infrastructure, is publicly accessible at fifty-one institutions in eleven countries; see USC Shoah Foundation Institute, "Find an Access Site Near You," USC Shoah Foundation, electronic document available at < http://sfi.usc.edu/locator >, accessed February 8, 2015.

29. See Michael Rothberg and Jared Stark, "After the Witness: A Report from the Twentieth Anniversary Conference of the Fortunoff Video Archive for Holocaust Testimonies at Yale," *History and Memory* 15.1 (2003): 89, and Diane L. Wolf, "Holocaust Testimony: Producing Post-memories, Producing Identities," in *Sociology Confronts the Holocaust: Memories and Identities in Jewish Diasporas*, eds. Judith M. Gerson and Diane L. Wolf (Durham, NC: Duke University Press, 2007), 173. The "Americanization" of Holocaust memory is most strongly criticized in Annette Wieviorka, *The Era of Witness* (Ithaca, NY: Cornell University Press, 2006), 120ff.

30. My account of Visual History Archive practice is based on my own observations and on Wiederhorn, "Survivors of the Shoah Visual History Foundation"; USC Shoah Foundation Institute, "Interview Guidelines," electronic document available at <http://dornsife.usc.edu/vhi/download/USCSFI_Interviewer_Guidelines_1.pdf>, accessed April 1, 2011; and USC Shoah Foundation Institute, "Videographer Guidelines," USC Shoah Foundation Institute, electronic document available at <http://dornsife.usc.edu/vhi/download/USCSFI_Videographer_Guidelines.pdf>, accessed April 1, 2011.

31. Aleksandr Gol'din, Interview 30675, Visual History Archive, USC Shoah Foundation Institute, accessed online at USHMM on March 8, 2010.

32. Henry Greenspan and Sidney Bolkosky, "When Is an Interview an Interview? Notes from Listening to Holocaust Survivors," *poetics today* 27, no. 2 (2006): 439.

33. Wolf, "Holocaust Testimony," 172, 174.

34. Wiederhorn, "Survivors of the Shoah Visual History Foundation."

35. Diana Wolf even quotes a survivor who tried to speak "about today. I wanted to speak about how the war affected me today, but they wouldn't let me": Wolf, "Holocaust Testimony," 172.

36. Portelli, *The Order Has Been Carried Out*, 12f.

37. Arendt refers to the role of storytelling to explicate her concept of understanding (as the discovery of meaning): Hannah Arendt, "Isak Denisen, 1885–1963," in Arendt, *Men in Dark Times*. Ursula Ludz suggested bringing these central concerns of Arendt's oeuvre (understanding and storytelling) together in an attempt to emphasize another of Arendt's concern, the human ability to create: Ursula Ludz, "Einleitung," in *Hannah Arendt: Ich will verstehen; Selbstauskünfte zu Leben und Werk*, ed. Ursula Ludz (Munich: Piper, 2005), 22.

38. Saul Friedlander, "Introduction," in *Probing the Limits of Representation: Nazism and the Final Solution*, ed. Saul Friedlander (Cambridge, MA: Harvard University Press, 1992), 2.

39. The abundance of works addressing the representation of the Nazi genocide since the early 1990s, the majority of them in the North American context, is possibly rooted in the coincidence of two factors. The genocide happened in Europe, far away from the United States, and thus the portrayal of the events in literature, film, and historical narratives is essential in order to bridge the geographical distance. At the same time, the generations of survivors and eyewitnesses, who could provide firsthand descriptions of the event, are slowly passing away, and questions about younger generations' ability to learn about the genocide center around appropriate and meaningful ways of representation. Consequently, many of the inquiries focus on the artistic representation of the past; another cluster examines the psychological effects of traumatic experience on describing and interpreting the genocide. Among these works, some stand out, either because they were first attempts to grapple with the problem, because they included previously marginalized themes within the field, or because they highlight recent accomplishments in the field: James Young, *Writing and Rewriting the Holocaust: Narrative and the Consequences of Interpretation* (Bloomington: Indiana University Press, 1988); Felman and Laub, *Testimony*; Saul Friedlander, ed., *Probing the Limits*; Dominick LaCapra, *Representing the Holocaust: History, Theory, Trauma* (Ithaca, NY: Cornell University Press, 1994); Fuchs, ed., *Women and the Holocaust*; Baer and Goldenberg, eds., *Experience and Expression*; Michael Bernard-Donals and Richard Glejzer, eds., *Witnessing the Disaster: Essays on Representation and the Holocaust* (Madison: University of Wisconsin Press, 2003); and Marianne Hirsch and Irene Kacandes, eds., *Teaching the Representation of the Holocaust* (New York: Modern Language Association of America, 2004).

40. Laub, "Bearing Witness," 57.

41. An influential text advancing this theory is Cathy Caruth, *Unclaimed Experience: Trauma, Narrative, and History* (Baltimore: The Johns Hopkins University Press, 1996). In a similar vein, Shoshana Felman argues that trauma is a truth that continues to escape, is unavailable to, the witness (survivor) of trauma (Shoshana Felman, "Education and Crisis, Or the Vicissitudes of Teaching," in Felman and Laub, *Testimony*, 15). Ruth Leys criticizes the "contemporary literary-critical fascination with the allegedly unrepresentable and unspeakable nature of trauma, especially the trauma of the Holocaust, prominently laid out by Caruth": Ruth Leys, *Trauma: A Genealogy* (Chicago and London: University of Chicago Press, 2000), 16; for the critique of Caruth, see especially chap. 8.

42. Felman, "Education and Crisis," 46; Laub, "Bearing Witness," 57.

43. Merridale, *Night of Stone*, 326.

44. Jureith and Orth, *Überlebensgeschichten*, 171.

45. Thomas Trezise, "Between History and Psychoanalysis," 24.

46. Ruth Klüger, *Von hoher und niedriger Literatur* (Göttingen, Germany: Wallstein, 1996), 36f.

47. Ruth Kluger, *Still Alive: A Holocaust Girlhood Remembered* (New York: The Feminist Press, 2003). The book initially appeared in German: Ruth Klüger, *Weiter leben: Eine Jugend* (Göttingen, Germany: Wallstein, 1992).

48. Klüger, *Von hoher und niedriger Literatur*, 37.

49. USC Shoah Foundation Visual History Archive, "VHA Subject Guide: Countries," University of Southern California Library, electronic document available at <http://libguides.usc.edu/content.php?pid=58585&sid=429353 >, accessed July 7, 2013.

50. I draw here on feminist scholars' insistence on stories as a way to access the lived reality especially of marginalized social groups; see Bettina Aptheker, "Conditions for Work," in Aptheker, *Tapestries of Life: Women's Work, Women's Consciousness, and the Meaning of Daily Experience* (Amherst: University of Massachusetts Press, 1989), 3-36, and Gail Nomura, "Filipina American Journal Writing: Recovering Women's History," in *Asian/Pacific Islander American Women: A Historical Anthology*, eds. Shirley Hue and Gail M. Nomura (New York: New York University Press, 2003), 138-152.

51. This draws on Marianne Hirsch's work on the role of visuals in transmitting the memory of the Holocaust: Marianne Hirsch, "The Generation of Postmemory," *poetics today* 29, no. 1 (2008): 103-128.

Chapter 2

1. Rita Kazhdan, Interview 654, Visual History Archive, USC Shoah Foundation Institute, accessed online at USHMM on January 15, 2010.

2. On the Soviet state's explicit inclusion of young people in political campaigns see, for instance, Lisa Kirschenbaum, *Small Comrades: Revolutionizing Childhood in Soviet Russia, 1917-1932* (New York: RoutledgeFalmer, 2001); and Olga Kucherenko, *Little Soldiers: How Soviet Children Went to War, 1941-1945* (Oxford: Oxford University Press, 2011), Part I.

3. Arkadi Zeltser, "Inter-War Ethnic Relations and Soviet Policy: The Case of Eastern Belorussia," *Yad Vashem Studies* 34 (2006): 87-124. For more general analyses that discuss the prevalence of antisemitism in 1930s Soviet Union, see Zvi Gitelman, *Jewish Nationality and Soviet Politics: The Jewish Sections of the CPSU, 1917-1930* (Princeton: Princeton University Press, 1972); Gitelman, *Century of Ambivalence*; and Benjamin Pinkus, *The Jews of the Soviet Union: The History of a National Minority* (Cambridge, UK: Cambridge University Press, 1988).

4. Anna Shternshis, *Soviet and Kosher: Jewish Popular Culture in the Soviet Union, 1923–1939* (Bloomington and Indianapolis: Indiana University Press, 2006); Elissa Bemporad, *Becoming Soviet Jews: The Bolshevik Experiment in Minsk* (Bloomington and Indianapolis: Indiana University Press, 2013).

5. Shternshis, *Soviet and Kosher*, 185.

6. See, for instance, Stefan Lehnstaedt, review of Barbara Epstein, *The Minsk Ghetto, 1941–1943: Jewish Resistance and Soviet Internationalism* (Berkeley: University of California Press, 2008), *sehepunkte* 11, no. 1 (2011) [15.01.2011], URL: <http://www.sehepunkte.de/2011/01/16085.html>, accessed June 5, 2012, where Lehnstaedt argues that portrayals of interethnic relationships in Belorussia and Nazi-occupied Belorussia with survivors who remained in the Soviet Union will inevitably display pro-Soviet attitudes because those who did experience antisemitism left the Soviet Union.

7. Svetlana Boym, *The Future of Nostalgia* (New York: Basic Books, 2001), 16.

8. Boris Gal'perin, interviewed by author, St. Petersburg, May 16, 2001.

9. Boris Gal'perin, "Boris Mikhailovich Gal'perin" [unpublished autobiography, includes lists, maps, and sketches], St. Petersburg, 2000 (25 pages), copy in author's possession.

10. Anika Walke, Research Diary, St. Petersburg, May 4, 2001.

11. On Shklov, see *The Encyclopedia of Jewish Life before and during the Holocaust*, Vol. 3, ed. Shmuel Spector (New York: New York University Press, 2001), 1170.

12. The Decree "On Abolition of Confessional and National Restrictions," passed by the Provisional Government on March 20, 1917, specified the lifting of restrictions on, among others, settlement, residence, and movement.

13. A concise discussion of the role, functioning, and characteristics of shtetls in the Russian Empire is in Ben-Cion Pinchuk, "The Shtetl: An Ethnic Town in the Russian Empire," *Cahiers du Monde russe* 41, no. 4 (2000): 495–504.

14. Yuri Slezkine, *The Jewish Century* (Princeton: Princeton University Press, 2004), 254.

15. For portrayals of the Russian Revolution, see, among others, Sheila Fitzpatrick, *The Russian Revolution*, 3rd ed. (New York: Oxford University Press, 2008), and S. A. Smith, *The Russian Revolution: A Very Short Introduction* (New York: Oxford University Press, 2002).

16. *Korenizatsiia* is the focus of state campaigns to modify Soviet national cultures in the 1920s, and is variously translated as "indigenization" or "nativization": Peter Kenez, *A History of the Soviet Union from the Beginning to the End* (New York: Cambridge University Press, 1999, 2006), 57; Zeltser, "Inter-War Ethnic Relations and Soviet Policy," 90. For more and recent analyses of this particular aspect of Soviet nationality policy, see Terry Martin, *The Affirmative Action Empire: Nations and Nationalism in the Soviet Union* (Ithaca, NY: Cornell Unversity Press, 2001), and Smith, *Red Nations*, chaps. 3 and 4.

17. The phrase "national in form, socialist in content" is widely used to summarize Joseph Stalin's speech at the Sixteenth Party Congress in 1930, in which he described his ideal of Soviet culture, reiterating principles that he and V. I. Lenin had developed in their theoretization of nations and nationalities; see "Marxism and the National Question" (1913), accessible online at the Marxists Internet Archive, <http://www.marxists.org/reference/archive/stalin/works/1913/03.htm>, accessed June 5, 2012. See also Eric D. Weitz, *A Century of Genocide: Utopias of Race and Nation* (Princeton: Princeton University Press, 2003), 67.

18. Sasha Goluboff, *Jewish Russians: Upheavals in a Moscow Synagogue* (Philadelphia: University of Pennsylvania Press, 2003), 22. These campaigns

affected all religious communities, including the Russian Orthodox Church, and encouraged the establishment of societies promoting atheism; Kenez, *A History of the Soviet Union*, 70-75.

19. Insightful essays on Jewish mass politics in light of economic and political crises in tsarist Russia can be found in Stefani Hoffman and Ezra Mendelsohn, eds., *The Revolution of 1905 and Russia's Jews* (Philadelphia: University of Pennsylvania Press, 2008).

20. Gitelman, *Century of Ambivalence*, 59-74. For more detailed discussions of the history of Jewish social movements in tsarist Russia, see Mendelsohn, *Class Struggle in the Pale: The Formative Years of the Jewish Workers' Movement in Tsarist Russia* (New York: Cambridge University Press, 1970); Walter Laqueur, *A History of Zionism* (New York: Holt, Rinehart and Winston, 1972), chaps. 3 and 6; and Naomi Shepherd, *A Price Below Rubies: Jewish Women as Rebels and Radicals* (London: Weidenfeld and Nicolson, 1993).

21. A detailed account of the Evsektsiia is in Gitelman, *Jewish Nationality and Soviet Politics*.

22. Gitelman, *Century of Ambivalence*, 88-114.

23. Gitelman, *Century of Ambivalence*, 76ff.

24. Slezkine, "The USSR as a Communal Apartment," 416. The role of linguistic unification in the creation of (imagined) national communities has been discussed, among others, by Ernest Gellner, *Nations and Nationalism* (Oxford: Blackwell, 1983), and Benedict Anderson, *Imagined Communities: Reflections on the Origins and Spread of Nationalism* (London: Verso, 1983)

25. Slezkine, "The USSR as a Communal Apartment," 420.

26. Elissa Bemporad, "The Yiddish Experiment in Soviet Minsk," *East European Jewish Affairs* 37, no. 1 (2007): 92.

27. For a detailed account of the history and culture of Birobidzhan, see Robert Weinberg, *Stalin's Forgotten Zion: Birobidzhan and the Making of a Soviet Jewish Homeland; An Illustrated History, 1928-1996* (Berkeley: University of California Press, 1998).

28. Slezkine, "The USSR as a Communal Apartment," 431.

29. Gitelman, *Century of Ambivalence*, 79.

30. Leonid Smilovitskii, "Sovetskaia shkola na idish," in Smilovitskii, *Evrei Belarusi: Iz nashei obshchei istorii, 1905-1953* (Minsk: Arti-Feks, 1999), especially 53.

31. Smilovitskii, "Sovetskaia shkola na idish," 75.

32. On the limitations and failures of the campaigns for literacy and education, see Kenez, *A History of the Soviet Union*, 73.

33. Slezkine, "The USSR as a Communal Apartment," 442ff.

34. Slezkine, "The USSR as a Communal Apartment," 444. On the introduction of the internal passport and the emerging regime of policing movement and residence in the USSR in the 1930s, see Goldman, "The Internal Soviet Passport;" and Shearer, *Policing Stalin's Socialism*, chap. 8.

35. Gitelman, *Century of Ambivalence*, 107-114.

36. Kate Brown, *A Biography of No Place: From Ethnic Borderland to Soviet Heartland* (Cambridge, MA: Harvard University Press, 2005); Lynne Viola, *The Unknown Gulag: The Lost World of Stalin's Special Settlements* (New York: Oxford University Press, 2007); Wendy Goldman, *Inventing the Enemy: Denunciation and Terror in Stalin's Russia* (New York: Cambridge University Press, 2011); *Gulag Voices: Oral Histories of Social Incarceration and Exile*, eds. Jehanne M. Gheith and Katherine R. Jolluck (New York: Palgrave Macmillan, 2011).

37. See Jochen Hellbeck's insightful analysis of Soviet citizens' diaries of the time, which display how they attempted to find a place in the revolutionary

society: *Revolution on My Mind: Writing a Diary under Stalin* (Cambridge, MA: Harvard University Press, 2009).

38. USHMM, RG50.378*0022, Oral History, Belarus Documentation Project, Interview with Yakov Negnevitzki.

39. Kirschenbaum, *Small Comrades*, 5f.

40. Gitelman, *Century of Ambivalence*, 84f, 108–111. Arkady Zeltser argues that especially those aged twenty-four to forty-nine in 1935 left the shtetls, seeking employment in larger cities of Belorussia or the Soviet Union more generally: Arkady Zeltser, "The Belorussian Shtetl in the 1920s and 1930s," in *Revolution, Repression, and Revival: The Soviet Jewish Experience*, eds. Zvi Gitelman and Yaacov Ro'i (Lanham, MD: Rowman & Littlefield, 2007), 93, 95.

41. *The Encyclopedia of Jewish Life before and during the Holocaust* indicates there were 200 Jewish inhabitants on the eve of World War II and points out that the last prewar census (1939) does not provide demographical data for Slavnoe: Spector, ed., *The Encyclopedia of Jewish Life*, Vol. 3, 1198. Lev Fridliand estimates that 30 percent of the residents of his hometown Slavnoe were Jewish, the remaining two-thirds Russians and Belorussians; see Lev Fridliand, Interview 32057, Visual History Archive, USC Shoah Foundation Institute, accessed online at USHMM on March 10, 2010.

42. Liubov Belen'kaia, Interview 30764, Visual History Archive, USC Shoah Foundation Institute, accessed online at USHMM on March 9, 2010. Belen'kaia's first name is transliterated incorrectly in the VHA database.

43. Female relatives introduced in several interviews indicate women's employment in various sectors: Rita Kazhdan, interviewed by author, St. Petersburg, May 24, 2001; Frida Ped'ko, interviewed by author, St. Petersburg, May 27, 2001, and May 13, 2005; Elena Drapkina, interviewed by author, St. Petersburg, April 26, 2001.

44. Michael Paul Sacks, "Women in the Industrial Labor Force," in *Women in Russia*, eds. Dorothy Atkinson, Alexander Dallin, and Gail W. Lapidus (Stanford, CA: Stanford University Press, 1977), 194.

45. Boris Gal'perin, interviewed by author, St. Petersburg, May 16, 2001.

46. Gal'perin, "Boris Mikhailovich Gal'perin," 1. Jewish cooperatives were one form in which the Evsektsiia sought to "productivize the Jewish masses," yet at the same time these colonies attracted Jews who were interested in making a living as farmers and doing so as a community. Beginning in 1928, colonies and cooperatives were collectivized, resulting in increased demands from the state for dues and a dissolution of ethnically distinct cooperatives: Zeltser, "The Belorussian Shtetl in the 1920s and 1930s," 97f.; Gitelman, *Century of Ambivalence*, 94–106. For a comprehensive history of "productivizing" the Jewish population and the role of Jewish agricultural colonies in this campaign, see Jonathan Dekel-Chen, *Farming the Red Land: Jewish Agricultural Colonization and Local Soviet Power, 1924–1941* (New Haven: Yale University Press, 2005).

47. See below, including accounts by Elena Drapkina, Grigorii Erenburg, Alevtina Kuprikhina, and Rita Kazhdan.

48. Boris Gal'perin, interviewed by author, St. Petersburg, May 16, 2001.

49. Boris Gal'perin, interviewed by author, St. Petersburg, May 16, 2001.

50. Galina Slutskaia, Interview 47490, Visual History Archive, USC Shoah Foundation Institute, accessed online at USHMM on March 31, 2010.

51. Liubov Belen'kaia, Interview 30764, Visual History Archive.

52. Frida Ped'ko, interviewed by author, St. Petersburg, May 13, 2005.

53. Boris Gal'perin, interviewed by author, St. Petersburg, May 16, 2001.

54. Frida Ped'ko, interviewed by author, St. Petersburg, May 13, 2005.

55. Alevtina Kuprikhina, Interview 49623, Visual History Archive.

56. Alevtina Kuprikhina, Interview 49623, Visual History Archive; Alevtina Kuprikhina, interviewed by author, St. Petersburg, September 6, 2002.
57. Spector, ed., *The Encyclopedia of Jewish Life*, Vol. 3, 1198, 1086.
58. Between 1917 and 1936, 633 of the 704 synagogues that had been in in Belorussia in 1917 were closed; Leonid Smilovitskii, "Evreiskie religioznye obshchiny v Belarusi, 1939–1953 gg.," in Smilovitskii, *Evrei Belarusi*, 248.
59. Alevtina Kuprikhina, Interview 49623, Visual History Archive.
60. Alevtina Kuprikhina, Interview 49623, Visual History Archive. Included with almost exactly the same wording in Alevtina Kuprikhina, interviewed by author, St. Petersburg, September 6, 2002.
61. Aleksandr Gol'din, Interview 30675, Visual History Archive.
62. Alevtina Kuprikhina, Interview 49623, Visual History Archive.
63. Alevtina Kuprikhina, Interview 49623, Visual History Archive.
64. Spector, ed., *The Encyclopedia of Jewish Life*, Vol. 3, 1198, 1507.
65. Alevtina Kuprikhina, interviewed by author, St. Petersburg, September 6, 2002.
66. Alevtina Kuprikhina, Interview 49623, Visual History Archive.
67. Smilovitskii, "Sovetskaia shkola na idish," 84.
68. Alevtina Kuprikhina, Interview 49623, Visual History Archive.
69. Smilovitskii, "Sovetskaia shkola na idish," 69.
70. Smilovitskii, "Sovetskaia shkola na idish," 69.
71. Grigorii Erenburg, interviewed by author, St. Petersburg, April 25, 2001.
72. Grigorii Erenburg, "Zhizn' kak podarok," in *Kniga zhivykh: Vospominaniia evreev-frontovikov, uznikov getto i kontslagerei, boitsov partizanskikh otriadov, zhitelei blokadnogo Leningrada*, Vol. 2, ed. L. Leibov (St. Petersburg, Akropol', 1995), 103; Grigorii Erenburg, interviewed by author, St. Petersburg, May 19, 2005; Dora Polonskaya, Interview 6936, Visual History Archive, USC Shoah Foundation Institute, accessed online at USHMM on January 20, 2010; Semion Levin, "Na rubezhe vekov," *Mishpokha* 9 (2001), electronic document, <http://mishpoha.org/nomer9/levin.php >, accessed February 8, 2015.
73. Grigorii Erenburg, interviewed by author, St. Petersburg, April 25, 2001.
74. Grigorii Erenburg, interviewed by author, St. Petersburg, April 25, 2001. On the causes of unemployment in the Soviet Union in the 1920s, see Kenez, *A History of the Soviet Union*, 93.
75. Leonid Smilovitskii, "Bobruiskaia sinagoga," in Smilovitskii, *Evrei Belarusi*, 278; *The Encyclopedia of Jewish Life before and during the Holocaust*, Vol. 1, ed. Shmuel Spector (New York: New York University Press, 2001), 160f.
76. Spector, ed., *The Encyclopedia of Jewish Life*, Vol. 1, 160.
77. Grigorii Erenburg, interviewed by author, St. Petersburg, May 19, 2005.
78. Spector, ed., *The Encyclopedia of Jewish Life*, Vol. 1, 159.
79. Sheila Fitzpatrick, "The Great Departure: Rural-Urban Migration in the Soviet Union, 1929–33," *Social Dimensions of Soviet Industrialization*, eds. William G. Rosenberg and Lewis H. Siegelbaum (Bloomington and Indianapolis: Indiana University Press, 1993), 15–40.
80. Zeltser, "Inter-War Ethnic Relations and Soviet Policy," 113; Slezkine, "The USSR as a Communal Apartment," 443–445.
81. Grigorii Erenburg, interviewed by author, St. Petersburg, April 25, 2001.
82. At least one woman of a similar age who lived in Bobruisk at the time reiterates this split between oral skills and literacy in Yiddish/Hebrew: Liudmila Kriuchkova, Interview 50719, Visual History Archive, USC Shoah Foundation Institute, accessed online at USHMM on February 4, 2010.
83. Grigorii Erenburg, interviewed by author, St. Petersburg, April 25, 2001.

84. Grigorii Erenburg, interviewed by author, St. Petersburg, May 19, 2005.
85. Grigorii Erenburg, interviewed by author, St. Petersburg, May 19, 2005.
86. Liudmila Kriuchkova, Interview 50719, Visual History Archive.
87. Shternshis, *Soviet and Kosher*, 12.
88. Grigorii Erenburg, interviewed by author, St. Petersburg, April 25, 2001, and May 19, 2005.
89. Grigorii Erenburg, interviewed by author, St. Petersburg, April 25, 2001.
90. Nikolai Ostrovski, *How the Steel Was Tempered*, transl. R. Prokofieva (Moscow: Foreign Languages Publishing House, 1952 [1934]), 73.
91. Grigorii Erenburg, interviewed by author, St. Petersburg, May 19, 2005.
92. Smilovitskii, "Sovetskaia shkola na idish," 76.
93. *The Encyclopedia of Jewish Life before and during the Holocaust*, Vol. 2, ed. Shmuel Spector (New York: New York University Press, 2001), 826–828.
94. Like Kazhdan and Drapkina, Mikhail Treister, Leonid Okun, and Yakov Negnevitzki report that their parents had taken on leadership positions in factories or local administrations; Mikhail Treister, interviewed by author and Eva Determann, Minsk, March 19, 2003; USHMM, RG50.120*116, Oral History, Israel Documentation Project, Interview with Leonid Okon (Okun); USHMM, RG50.378*022, interview with Yakov Negnevitzki.
95. Rita Kazhdan, interviewed by author, St. Petersburg, May 24, 2001.
96. Elena Drapkina, interviewed by author, St. Petersburg, September 10, 2002.
97. Elena Drapkina, interviewed by author, St. Petersburg, September 10, 2002.
98. Elena Drapkina, Interview 2325, Visual History Archive, USC Shoah Foundation Institute, accessed online at USHMM on January 22, 2010.
99. Tefillin (from Hebrew), also called phylacteries, are a set of small cubic leather boxes that contain scrolls of parchment inscribed with verses from the Torah, worn during weekday morning prayers.
100. Rita Kazhdan, Interview 654, Visual History Archive.
101. Vladimir Mordkhilevich explains that even his father, who had been educated in cheders and studied the Torah and was expected to become a rabbi, had turned to communist ideas and proceeded to support and participate in Soviet institutions; see USHMM, RG50.120*209, Oral History, Israel Documentation Project, Interview with Vladimir Mordkhilevich.
102. Samuil Volk, Interview 43231, Visual History Archive, USC Shoah Foundation Institute, accessed online at USHMM on July 23, 2010.
103. Rita Kazhdan, Interview 654, Visual History Archive.
104. Rita Kazhdan, Interview 654, Visual History Archive.
105. Elena Drapkina, interviewed by author, St. Petersburg, May 18, 2005.
106. Rita Kazhdan, interviewed by author, St. Petersburg, May 12, 2005.
107. Elena Drapkina, interviewed by author, St. Petersburg, May 18, 2005.
108. USHMM, RG50.378*025, Oral History, Belarus Documentation Project, interview with Vera Smirnova; USHMM, RG50.120*209, interview with Vladimir Mordkhilevich; Elena Drapkina, interviewed by author, St. Petersburg, September 10, 2002. Similarly, Amaliia Moiseevna Iakhontova explained that her command of the Belorussian language was stronger than either Yiddish or Russian. Her parents spoke Yiddish to each other when they wanted to hide particular conversations from her: Amaliia Moiseevna Iakhontova (Knurgina), Interview 43211, Visual History Archive, USC Shoah Foundation Institute, accessed online at USHMM on July 20, 2010.
109. Smilovitskii, "Sovetskaia shkola na idish," 84f.

110. Leonid Smilovitskii emphasizes the pragmatism involved in enrolling children in Russian schools, which would enable them to continue their educational careers outside of Belorussia: Smilovitskii, "Sovetskaia shkola na idish," 83.

111. Vera Smirnova, Interview 30334, Visual History Archive, USC Shoah Foundation Institute, accessed online at USHMM on May 18, 2010. See also Rita Kazhdan, interviewed by author, St. Petersburg, May 24, 2001; Elena Drapkina, interviewed by author, St. Petersburg, April 26, 2001, and September 10, 2002; Roza Zelenko, interviewed by author, Minsk, October 20, 2002; USHMM, RG50.120*0116, interview with Leonid Okon; USHMM, RG50.378*025, interview with Vera Smirnova.

112. Elena Drapkina, interviewed by author, St. Petersburg, May 18, 2005.

113. Vera Smirnova, USHMM, RG50.378*025. See also Elena Drapkina, Interview 2325, Visual History Archive; Elena Drapkina, interviewed by author, St. Petersburg, May 18, 2005; USHMM, RG50.120*209, interview with Vladimir Mordkhilevich; Mikhail Treister, Interview 2324, Visual History Archive, USC Shoah Foundation Institute, accessed online at the USHMM on June 25, 2010.

114. Roza Zelenko, interviewed by author, Minsk, October 20, 2002.

115. Elena Drapkina, interviewed by author, St. Petersburg, September 10, 2002.

116. Samuil Volk, Interview 43231, Visual History Archive.

117. For more on the role of Soviet kindergardens and schools in assisting the physical needs of Soviet children, see Kirschenbaum, *Small Comrades*, 94.

118. Kenez, *A History of the Soviet Union*, 114–119.

119. USHMM, RG50.378*022, interview with Yakov Negnevitzki.

120. Clashes at the border with Mongolia threatening to pull the USSR into war with Japan in May 1939 and the Russo-Finnish War in November 1939 surely did not help to quell the dread of war; Kenez, *A History of the Soviet Union*, 131, 133.

121. Amaliia Iakhontova, Interview 43211, Visual History Archive.

122. Elena Drapkina, interviewed by author, St. Petersburg, May 18, 2005; Elena Drapkina, Interview 2325, Visual History Archive.

123. Elena Drapkina, interviewed by author, St. Petersburg, May 18, 2005; Elena Drapkina, Interview 2325, Visual History Archive.

124. Rita Kazhdan, interviewed by author, St. Petersburg, May 24, 2001. See also Anna Krylova, "Stalinist Identity from the Viewpoint of Gender: Rearing a Generation of Professionally Violent Women-Fighters in 1930s Stalinist Russia," *Gender and History* 16, no. 3 (2004): 632.

125. For detailed accounts of the policies and institutions intended to support and utilize the emancipation of women as part of the socialist revolution, see Gail W. Lapidus, *Women in Soviet Society: Equality, Development and Social Change* (Berkeley: University of California Press, 1978); Wendy Z. Goldman, *Women, the State, and Revolution: Soviet Family Policy and Social Life, 1917–1936* (Cambridge, UK: Cambridge University Press, 1993); Elizabeth Wood, *The Baba and the Comrade: Gender and Politics in Revolutionary Russia* (Bloomington and Indianapolis: Indiana University Press, 1997); Thomas G. Schrand, "Soviet 'Civic-Minded Women' in the 1930s: Gender, Class and Industrialization in a Socialist Society," *Journal of Women's History* 11, no. 3 (1999): 126–150; A. Borodina and D. Borodin, "Baba ili tovarishch? Ideal novoi sovetskoi zhenshchiny v 20-kh–30-kh godakh," in *Zhenskie i gendernye issledovaniia v Tverskom gosudarstvennom universitete*, ed. Valentina Uspenskaia (Tver', Russia: Tverskii Gosudarstvennyi Universitet, 2000), 45–51; and Pavla Vesela, "The Hardening of Cement: Russian Women and Modernization," *Feminist Formations* 15, no. 3 (2003): 104–123.

126. USHMM, RG50.378*022, interview with Yakov Negnevitzki.

127. Krylova, "Stalinist Identity from the Viewpoint of Gender," 628, 648.

128. Anna Temkina, *Seksual'naia zhizn' zhenshchiny: Mezhdu podchineniem i svobodoi* (St. Petersburg: Izdatel'stvo Evropeiskogo Universiteta, 2008), 35.

129. For an extended discussion of the role of women's labor for economic transformation and development, see Wendy Z. Goldman, *Woman at the Gates: Gender and Industry in Stalin's Russia* (Cambridge, UK: Cambridge University Press, 2002). On the utilization of women's labor to limit the influx of immigrants from the countryside to industrial centers, keep wages low, and secure reproductive labor for working husbands, see Thomas G. Schrand, "Soviet 'Civic-Minded Women' in the 1930s," 129, and Kenez, *A History of the Soviet Union*, 93f.

130. Elena Drapkina refers here to the song "Esli zavtra voina," composed by Dmitrii and Daniil Pokrass and Vasilii Lebedev-Kumach for the film with the same title, *Esli zavtra voina (If War Comes Tomorrow)*, dir. Efim Dzigan et al. (USSR, 1938).

131. Elena Drapkina, Interview 2325, Visual History Archive. See also Rita Kazhdan, interviewed by author, St. Petersburg, May 24, 2001.

132. Elena Drapkina, interviewed by author, St. Petersburg, May 18, 2005.

133. Shternshis, *Soviet and Kosher*, 12.

134. Samuil Volk, Interview 43231, Visual History Archive.

Chapter 3

1. Sonia Zalesskaia, Interview 30810, Visual History Archive, USC Shoah Foundation Institute, accessed online at USHMM on July 13, 2010.

2. USHMM, RG50.378*025, interview with Vera Smirnova.

3. The exact number of children, Jewish and non-Jewish, who fell victim to the Nazi extermination policy, is hard to establish. Leonid Smilovitskii outlines the difficulty and cites competing data, showing, among others, how children and women were often not included in Soviet statistics of the dead: Smilovitskii, *Katastrofa evreev v Belorussii*, 86–88.

4. Smilovitskii, *Katastrofa evreev v Belorussii*, 89.

5. On the persecution of men, see Smilovitskii, *Katastrofa evreev v Belorussii*, 68; Rita Kazhdan, interviewed by author, St. Petersburg, May 24, 2001; Elena Drapkina, interviewed by author, St. Petersburg, April 26, 2001; Ekaterina Tsirlina, Interview 28012, Visual History Archive, USC Shoah Foundation Institute, accessed online at USHMM on July 13, 2010; USHMM, RG50.120*209, interview with Vladimir Mordkhilevich; see also "The Minsk Ghetto," in *The Complete Black Book of Russian Jewry*, by Ilya Ehrenburg and Vasily Grossman, transl. and ed. David Patterson (New Brunswick, NJ: Transaction Publishers, 2002), 109f., 116; "From the Notes of the Partisan Mikhail Grichanik," in *The Unknown Black Book: The Holocaust in the German-Occupied Soviet Territories*, eds. Joshua Rubenstein and Ilya Altman (Bloomington and Indianapolis: Indiana University Press, 2008), 234f., 237; Yitzhak Arad, *The Holocaust in the Soviet Union* (Lincoln: University of Nebraska Press, 2009), 151f.; and Enta Maizles, "Minsk: Fashistskaia okkupatsia; genotsid," in *Uroki Kholokosta: Istoria i sovremennost'*, ed. Iakov Basin (Minsk: Kovcheg, 2009), 178.

6. To contextualize these experiences, I draw on Hersh Smolar, *The Minsk Ghetto: Soviet Jewish Partisans against the Nazis* (New York: Holocaust Library, 1989); "The Minsk Ghetto," in Ehrenburg and Grossman, *Complete Black Book of Russian Jewry*, 109–155; Uwe Gartenschläger, *Die Stadt Minsk während der deutschen Besetzung* (Düsseldorf: IBB; 2002); Epstein, *The Minsk Ghetto*; and Petra Rentrop, *Tatorte der "Endlösung": Das Ghetto Minsk und die Vernichtungsstätte Maly Trostinez* (Berlin: Metropol, 2011). Christian Gerlach describes the power structures ruling the ghettos in *Kalkulierte Morde*, 656f.

7. Marat Botvinnik, *Pamiatniki genotsida evreev Belarusi* (Minsk: Belaruskaia Navuka, 2000), 13-21.

8. Smolar, *The Minsk Ghetto*, 139. Smolar gives the number of 5,000 victims. Marat Botvinnik cites the number of 150 to 400 Jews who were killed as hostages, Botvinnik, *Pamiatniki genotsida evreev Belarusi*, 19.

9. "Account of the brigade commander of the SS and Maj. Gen. of Police von Gottenberg on the punitive operation against the partisans and peaceful inhabitants under he code name 'Swamp Fever,' conducted in the city and province of Minsk from April 17 to 24, 1943," in USHMM, RG22.001, "Records relating to the Soviet Union under Nazi Occupation, 1941-1945," pp. 101-104.

10. Ainsztein, *Jewish Resistance*, 67; Christopher Browning, *Nazi Policy, Jewish Workers, German Killers* (New York: Cambridge University Press, 2000), 88.

11. Gerlach, *Kalkulierte Morde*, 735.

12. Lower, "Facilitating Genocide," 133, 137.

13. Gerlach, *Kalkulierte Morde*, 527.

14. Smolar, *The Minsk Ghetto*, 61.

15. Leonid Smilovitsky introduces the members of the largely communist underground movement in "Minsk Ghetto: An Issue of Jewish Resistance," *SHVUT* 1-2 (17/18) (1995): 161-182. See also Barbara Epstein's account of the Minsk underground movement and its reliance on relationships that had been established before the war: Epstein, *The Minsk Ghetto*. Detailed first-person accounts of the underground are also provided by Smolar, *The Minsk Ghetto*, and *Arkhiv Khasi Pruslinoi: Minskoe getto, antifashistskoe podpol'e, repatriatsiia detei iz Germanii*, ed. Z. A. Nikodimova (Minsk: I. P. Loginov, 2010).

16. Kenez, *A History of the Soviet Union*, 89-91. Much of the industrial growth was achieved at the expense of peasants, forced laborers caught up in the penal camps of the Gulag, and those suffering from collectivization and famine. However, Robert C. Allen demonstrates that the Soviet economy grew significantly and that the often denounced Five Year Plans were eventually successful in developing industry and raising living standards, especially for the many peasants who moved to the cities, beginning in the 1930s; see Robert C. Allen, *Farm to Factory: A Reinterpretation of the Soviet Industrial Revolution* (Princeton: Princeton University Press, 2009).

17. Minsk: Staryi-Novyi, "Komsomol'skoe ozero," http://minsk-old-new.com/minsk-2858-ru.htm, accessed November 3, 2010.

18. USHMM, RG50.120*116, interview with Leonid Okon; see also USHMM, RG50.378*022, interview with Yakov Negnevitzki.

19. Ekaterina Tsirlina, Interview 28012, Visual History Archive. The draft largely failed, as German troops had advanced toward Minsk and occupied the city faster than the Soviet military was able to prepare and equip the recruits; Maizles, "Minsk," 177.

20. Pesia Aizenshtadt, Interview 29732, Visual History Archive, USC Shoah Foundation Institute, accessed online at USHMM on July 12, 2010.

21. Estimates speak of several hundred children who were separated from their parents when the war began: Smilovitskii, *Katastrofa evreev v Belorussii*, 68; "They Were Dealing in Children," in Rubenstein and Altman, eds., *The Unknown Black Book*, 248; "Minsk Hell: The Recollections of the Teacher Sofia Ozerskaya," in Rubenstein and Altman, eds., *The Unknown Black Book*, 250.

22. Kenez, *A History of the Soviet Union*, 138; Geoffrey Hosking, *The First Socialist Society: A History of the Soviet Union from Within* (Cambridge, MA: Harvard University Press, 1992), 272; Joshua Rubenstein, "The War and the Final Solution on the

Russian Front," in Rubenstein and Altman, eds., *The Unknown Black Book*, 6; Arad, *The Holocaust in the Soviet Union*, 65.

23. Pesia Aizenshtadt, Interview 29732, Visual History Archive; David Taubkin, "Moi gorod, znakomyi do slioz," in *Katastrofa: Poslednie svideteli*, ed. Z. Tsukerman (Moscow: Dom Evreiskoi Knigi, 2008), 256. Taubkin also highlights his shock at the German invasion by recounting his attendance of the military parade on May 1, 1941, where powerful Soviet war technology was displayed.

24. Amaliia Iakhontova, Interview 43211, Visual History Archive; see also Mikhail Treister, "Probleski pamiati," in Tsukerman, ed., *Katastrofa*, 303; Nikodimova, *Arkhiv Khasi Pruslinoi*, 18.

25. USHMM, RG50.378*022, interview with Yakov Negnevitzki; Amaliia Iakhontova, Interview 43211, Visual History Archive; Mikhail Treister, Interview 2324, Visual History Archive.

26. Elena Drapkina, interviewed by author, St. Petersburg, April 26, 2001.

27. Smolar, *The Minsk Ghetto*, 17; Inna Gerasimova, "Evrei v partizanskom dvizhenii Belorussii, 1941–1944: Obshchaia kharakteristika," in Basin, ed., *Uroki Kholokosta*, 138; Epstein, *The Minsk Ghetto*, 77; Rebecca Manley, *To the Tashkent Station: Evacuation and Survival in the Soviet Union at War* (Ithaca, NY: Cornell University Press, 2009), 48.

28. USHMM, RG50.378*022, interview with Yakov Negnevitzki; Pesia Aizenshtadt, Interview 29732, Visual History Archive.

29. Rita Kazhdan, interviewed by author, St. Petersburg, May 24, 2001.

30. Ekaterina Tsirlina, Interview 28012, Visual History Archive; USHMM, RG50.120*209, interview with Vladimir Mordkhilevich. See also "Reminiscences of Albert Lapidus, from Baltimore, a Former Prisoner of the Minsk Ghetto," in USHMM, RG02.174, p. 4; these reminiscences were published, as the first two of a four-part publication, in as: "Nas malo ostalos', nam mnogo dostalos'," *Vestnik* 2(313)–3(314) (2003), available online at http://www.vestnik.com/win/arch03.htm, accessed on November 4, 2010.

31. Other Jews hoped that they would not be targeted by the German aggression because they were not Communists; Pesia Aizenshtadt recalls that, during her flight attempt from Minsk, she stayed with a Jewish family who had matzo displayed on their table. When Pesia asked why they did that, they explained "in case the Germans come, then they see that we are religious and not communists": Pesia Aizenshtadt, Interview 29732, Visual History Archive.

32. Arad, *The Holocaust in the Soviet Union*, 88f.; Aristotle Killis, "'Licence' and Genocide in the East: Reflections on Localised Eliminationist Violence During the First Stages of 'Operation Barbarossa,'" *Studies in Ethnicity and Nationalism* 7, no. 3 (2007): 6–23; specifically on Riga, where 2,500 Jews were killed: Andrej Angrick and Peter Klein, *The 'Final Solution' in Riga: Exploitation and Annihilation, 1941–1944* (New York: Berghahn 2009), 60; on Jedwabne: Jan T. Gross, *Neighbors: The Destruction of the Jewish Community in Jedwabne, Poland* (Princeton: Princeton University Press, 2001).

33. Treister, "Probleski pamiati," 305.

34. Most recently and succinctly, Rentrop, *Tatorte*, 65–76.

35. Dieter Pohl, *Die Herrschaft der Wehrmacht: Deutsche Militärbesatzung und einheimische Bevölkerung in der Sowjetunion 1941–1944* (Munich: Oldenbourg, 2008), 248f.

36. The order to all Jews of Minsk to move into a Jewish quarter was issued on July 19, 1941, demanding that the move be completed by July 24 (Arad, *The Holocaust in the Soviet Union*, 152).

37. Smolar, *The Minsk Ghetto*, 14; USHMM, RG50.378*022, interview with Yakov Negnevitzki; Samuil Volk, Interview 43231, Visual History Archive; Mikhail Treister, Interview 2324, Visual History Archive; Ekaterina Tsirlina, Interview 28012, Visual History Archive. Amaliia Iakhontova, Interview 43211, Visual History Archive, vividly describes the appropriation of Jewish property by non-Jewish residents of the city.

38. Smolar, *The Minsk Ghetto*, 14; USHMM, RG50.378*022, interview with Yakov Negnevitzki; Samuil Volk, Interview 43231, Visual History Archive; Mikhail Treister, Interview 2324, Visual History Archive; Ekaterina Tsirlina, Interview 28012, Visual History Archive.

39. Amaliia Iakhontova, Interview 43211, Visual History Archive.

40. Estimates of the actual number of Jews who entered the ghetto in summer 1941 range from 30,000 to 100,000. Petra Rentrop's calculation, the most recent one available, arrives at a plausible number of 45,000–50,000: Rentrop, *Tatorte*, 114.

41. Smilovitsky, "Minsk Ghetto: An Issue of Jewish Resistance," 66.

42. Oral Testimony of Lisa Gordon, Yad Vashem Archives, YV 4047, p. 5; see also "The Minsk Ghetto," in Ehrenburg and Grossman, *Complete Black Book of Russian Jewry*, 114.

43. Daily Journal of the Police Battalion 322, Sept. 30, 1941, NARB fond 4683, opis 3, delo 936, l. 43–45, published in Raisa Chernoglazova, *Judenfrei! Svobodno ot evreev! Istoriia minskogo getto v dokumentakh* (Minsk: Asobny Dakh, 1999), 163.

44. USHMM, RG50.378*022, interview with Yakov Negnevitzki; Epstein, *The Minsk Ghetto*, 84.

45. Elena Drapkina, interviewed by author, St. Petersburg, April 26, 2001.

46. Treister, "Probleski pamiati," 303.

47. Gerlach, *Kalkulierte Morde*, 576.

48. Epstein, *The Minsk Ghetto*, 90f.

49. USHMM, RG50.120*209, interview with Vladimir Mordkhilevich.

50. Order No. 31 of the Security Police (SiPo) and Security Service (SD) on the Formation of a Judenrat; NARB fond 4683, opis 3, delo 943, l. 88–89, published in Chernoglazova, *Judenfrei*, 33

51. Compare this, for instance, with Deborah Dwork's description of the Vilna and Łódź Judenrat leaders' attempts to distinguish between elderly, young, and people of working and reproductive age, and Sara Bender's account of the Judenrat of Białystok's ghetto compiling a list of people to be "evacuated": Dwork, *Children With a Star*, 178; Sara Bender, *The Jews of Białystok During World War II and the Holocaust* (Waltham, MA: Brandeis University Press, 2008), 110ff.

52. Smolar, *The Minsk Ghetto*, 18, 53.

53. Romanovskii, "Minsk," in Al'tman, ed., *Kholokost*, 591. Ioffe was killed during the pogrom in July 1942, and Zamenshtein was subsequently appointed chair of the council. See also Epstein, *The Minsk Ghetto*, 92ff.; "The Minsk Ghetto," in Ehrenburg and Grossman, *Complete Black Book of Russian Jewry*, 123. Successor committees—again installed by the Germans, who placed recent arrivals from Poland with a known history of criminal activity in leadership positions—were less inclined to fulfill Mushkin's mission. For instance, the leader of the Jewish police, Naum Epstein, who essentially ruled the ghetto after the pogrom in July 1942, actively persecuted members of the underground movement: Romanovskii, "Minsk," in Al'tman, ed., *Kholokost*, 596; Smolar, *The Minsk Ghetto*, 72.

54. USHMM, RG50.378*002, Oral History, Belarus Documentation Project, Interview with Tatyana Samuilovna Gildiner.

55. Gerlach, *Kalkulierte Morde*, 46, 272.

56. Rita Kazhdan, interviewed by author, St. Petersburg, May 24, 2001.
57. Taubkin, "Moi gorod, znakomyi do slioz," 267.
58. Ol'ga Glazebnaia, interviewed by author, Minsk, October 11, 2002; Elena Drapkina, interviewed by author, St. Petersburg, September 10, 2002.
59. Ol'ga Glazebnaia, interviewed by author, Minsk, October 11, 2002.
60. Among others, this situation is described by Rita Kazhdan, interviewed by author, St. Petersburg, May 24, 2001, and May 12, 2005; Elena Drapkina, interviewed by author, St. Petersburg, April 26, 2001, September 10, 2002, and May 18, 2005; Mikhail Treister, Interview 2324, Visual History Archive.
61. Smolar, *The Minsk Ghetto*, 18. David Taubkin adds that his family spent their resources on outfitting a dacha, on the children's education, and on other cultural activities in the prewar decade: Taubkin, "Moi gorod, znakomyi do slioz," 265.
62. Mikhail Treister, Interview 2324, Visual History Archive; Taubkin, "Moi gorod, znakomyi do slioz," 265, 273.
63. On the conditions in the Sonderghetto, see Karl Loesten (Löwenstein), "Aus der Hölle Minsk in das 'Paradies' Theresienstadt," Leo Baeck Institute New York, ME 398.MM50 (published as Karl Loewenstein, "Minsk—Im Lager der deutschen Juden," *Das Parlament (Beilage)*, B. 45/46, November 7, 1956); Heinz Rosenberg, *Jahre des Schreckens . . . und ich blieb übrig, daß ich Dir's ansage* (Göttingen, Germany: Steidl Verlag, 1985); Rentrop, *Tatorte*, chap. 5.
64. Treister, "Probleski pamiati," 310.
65. See Anika Walke, "'It Wasn't That Bad in the Ghetto, Was It?'—Living On in the USSR after the Nazi Genocide," in *Survivors of Nazi Persecution in Europe after the Second World War: Landscapes after Battle*, Vol. 1, ed. Suzanne Bardgett, David Cesarani, Jessica Reinisch, and J. D. Steinert (London: Vallentine Mitchell, 2010), 218–236.
66. Roza Zelenko and Ol'ga Glazebnaia, interviewed by author, Minsk, October 11, 2002.
67. USHMM, RG50.378*025, interview with Vera Smirnova; Mikhail Treister, Interview 2324, Visual History Archive; Mikhail Treister, interviewed by author and Eva Determann, Minsk, March 19, 2003.
68. Amaliia Iakhontova, Interview 43211, Visual History Archive.
69. Sonia Zalesskaia, Interview 30810, Visual History Archive.
70. "Minsk Hell," in Rubenstein and Altman, eds., *The Unknown Black Book*, 251f. A commissar of the German Field Police noted that the local population's attitude toward the murder of Jews was negative and that these unfounded atrocities contributed to anti-German sentiments: App. 1 to Report of Field Police 723 on the attitude of the local population toward executions of Jews, NARB fond 4683, opis 3, delo 962, l. 24, published in Chernoglazova, *Judenfrei*, 167.
71. Rita Kazhdan, interviewed by author, St. Petersburg, May 24, 2001.
72. Karl Löwenstein, a German Jew who was transferred to the Sonderghetto in November 1941, uses the same word to describe the pogrom in the Russian ghetto on March 2, 1942: Loesten, "Aus der Hölle," p. 40.
73. Among others, see Elena Drapkina, interviewed by author, St. Petersburg, April 26, 2001; Roza Zelenko, interviewed by author, Minsk, October 11, 2002; Nikodimova, *Arkhiv*, 23.
74. Lev Pasherstnik, "Pobeg iz getto," in Tsukerman, ed., *Katastrofa*, 245.
75. Mariia Boiko, Interview 32128, Visual History Archive, USC Shoah Foundation Institute, accessed online at USHMM on July 12, 2010.
76. Samuil Volk, Interview 43231, Visual History Archive.

77. Rita Kazhdan, interviewed by author, St. Petersburg, May 24, 2001; USHMM, RG50.378*025, interview with Vera Smirnova; Sonia Zalesskaia, Interview 30810, Visual History Archive.
78. USHMM, RG50.120*116, interview with Leonid Okon.
79. Sonia Zalesskaia, Interview 30810, Visual History Archive. On such relationships, see also Smilovitskii, *Katastrofa evreev v Belorussii*, 72.
80. Deborah Dwork highlights the necessary failure of internal ghetto institutions to care for the incredible number of impoverished and homeless children in other ghettos: Dwork, *Children With a Star*, 201.
81. Grigorii Rozinskii, *Deti Minskogo getto* (Tel Aviv: Krugozor, 2004), 30.
82. Rozinskii, *Deti Minskogo getto*. Similar accounts of the inability of the orphanage to supply children with food are in Samuil Volk, Interview 43231, Visual History Archive; "Reminiscences of Albert Lapidus, from Baltimore," USHMM, RG02.174, p. 27.
83. Sonia Zalesskaia, Interview 30810, Visual History Archive.
84. "They Were Dealing in Children," in Rubenstein and Altman, eds., *The Unknown Black Book*, 248. Vera Smirnova, having been arrested in Minsk while fulfilling a task she had received from a partisan commander, saw many Jewish children imprisoned in the basement of the Minsk Prison, where she was held for interrogation: USHMM, RG50.378*025, interview with Vera Smirnova.
85. Samuil Volk, Interview 43231, Visual History Archive.
86. Samuil Volk, Interview 43231, Visual History Archive.
87. Samuil Volk, Interview 43231, Visual History Archive.
88. Samuil Volk, Interview 43231, Visual History Archive.
89. Roza Zelenko and Ol'ga Glazebnaia, interviewed by author, Minsk, October 11, 2002; USHMM, RG50.378*025, interview with Vera Smirnova; Mikhail Treister, Interview 2324, Visual History Archive; Mikhail Treister, interviewed by author and Eva Determann, Minsk, March 19, 2003.
90. The etymology of the word "malina" is highly disputed. In addition to the Russian reference to rapsberry, others explain it as rooted in the Hebrew word "malon" for shelter; Ephraim G. in *Fresh Wounds: Early Narratives of Holocaust Survival*, ed. Donald L. Niewyk (Chapel Hill: University of North Carolina Press, 1998), 251.
91. Oral Testimony of Sara Goland, Yad Vashem Archives, YV 03.4126, p. 7.
92. Elena Drapkina, interviewed by author, St. Petersburg, April 26, 2001.
93. Solomon Khomikh, "Otvoiovannaia zhizn'," in Tsukerman, ed., *Katastrofa*, 424; Mikhail Treister, Interview 2324, Visual History Archive, USC Shoah Foundation Institute; Maizles, "Minsk," 180.
94. Sonia Zalesskaia, Interview 30810, Visual History Archive.
95. Sonia Zalesskaia, Interview 30810, Visual History Archive; Sonia Zalesskaia, Interview 30810, Visual History Archive; USHMM, RG50.120*209, interview with Vladimir Mordkhilevich.
96. Samuil Volk, Interview 43231, Visual History Archive.
97. Sonia Zalesskaia, Interview 30810, Visual History Archive; USHMM, RG50.378*025, interview with Vera Smirnova; Samuil Volk, Interview 43231, Visual History Archive; USHMM, RG50.120*209, interview with Vladimir Mordkhilevich; Taubkin, "Moi gorod, znakomyi do slioz," 277.
98. Taubkin, "Moi gorod, znakomyi do slioz," 282.
99. Epstein, *The Minsk Ghetto*, esp. 171–180.

100. Smilovitskii, *Katastrofa evreev v Belarusi*, 74.
101. Taubkin, "Moi gorod, znakomyi do slioz," 281.
102. USHMM, RG50.120*209, interview with Vladimir Mordkhilevich; Oral Testimony of Elena Gringauz, Yad Vashem Archives, YV 03.4126, p. 6, 23.
103. See Regina Mühlhäuser, "Between 'Racial Awareness' and Fantasies of Potency: Nazi Sexual Politics in the Occupied Territories of the Soviet Union," in *Brutality and Desire: War and Sexuality in Europe's Twentieth Century*, ed. Dagmar Herzog (New York: Palgrave Macmillan, 2009), 199–203.
104. See *"Dann kam die deutsche Macht:" Weißrussische Kinderhäftlinge in deutschen Konzentrationslagern, 1941–1945*, ed. Projektgruppe Belarus e.V. (Köln: Betrieb für Öffentlichkeit, 1999); Nikodimova, *Arkhiv*, chap. 2; Rozinskii, *Deti*, 10.
105. Elissa Bemporad shows the persistence of the ritual circumcision among Jewish inhabitants of Minsk, including party members and nonmembers, workers and intellectuals, until the early 1930s; Elissa Bemporad, "Behavior Unbecoming a Communist: Jewish Religious Practice in Soviet Minsk," *Jewish Social Studies* 14, no. 2 (2008): 1–31.
106. USHMM, RG50.120*209, interview with Vladimir Mordkhilevich. The names reference Zhilin and Kostylin, the main characters in L. N. Tolstoi's "Kavkazskii plennik" (*Prisoner of the Mountains*).
107. Oral Testimony of Leonid Okun, Yad Vashem Archives, YV 03.6278, p. 8.
108. Samuil Volk, Interview 43231, Visual History Archive.
109. Samuil Volk, Interview 43231, Visual History Archive.
110. Smilovitskii, *Katastrofa evreev v Belorussii*, 68.
111. Reminiscences of Botvinnik-Lup'ian Tsilia Iankelevich about her participation in the Minsk Underground, 1941–44 (Sept. 1, 1963), NARB fond 4386, opis 2, delo 59, p. 2; "The Minsk Ghetto," in Ehrenburg and Grossman, *Complete Black Book of Russian Jewry*, 110–114.
112. Bericht von Xaver Dorsch, Dienststelle Organisation Todt, an Alfred Rosenberg, Reichsminister für die besetzten Ostgebiete, vom 10. Juli 1941, published in *Dokumente des Verbrechens: Aus Akten des Dritten Reiches 1933–1945*, Vol. 3, eds. Helma Kaden and Ludwig Nestler (Berlin: Dietz, 1993), 25ff.
113. "The Minsk Ghetto," in Ehrenburg and Grossman, *Complete Black Book of Russian Jewry*, 110–114; Gerlach, *Kalkulierte Morde*, 509; "Dok. 72: Rafael M. Bromberg beschreibt Masseninternierungen, den Mord an den Juden und die Einrichtung des Gettos in Minsk bis zur Übergabe an die Zivilverwaltung am 1. September 1941," in *Die Verfolgung und Ermordung der europäischen Juden durch das nationalsozialistische Deutschland 1933–1945*, Vol. 7, *Sowjetunion mit annektierten Gebieten I*, eds. Bert Hoppe und Hildrun Glass (Munich: Oldenbourg Verlag, 2011), 275f.
114. "The Minsk Ghetto," in Ehrenburg and Grossman, *Complete Black Book of Russian Jewry*, 110, 116; Maizles, "Minsk," 178.
115. Rita Kazhdan, interviewed by author, St. Petersburg, May 24, 2001; Elena Drapkina, interviewed by author, St. Petersburg, April 26, 2001; Ekaterina Tsirlina, Interview 28012, Visual History Archive; USHMM, RG50.120*209, interview with Vladimir Mordkhilevich. See also "The Minsk Ghetto," in Ehrenburg and Grossman, *Complete Black Book of Russian Jewry*, 109; "From the Notes of the Partisan Mikhail Grichanik," in Rubenstein and Altman, eds., *The Unknown Black Book*, 234f., 237; and Arad, *The Holocaust in the Soviet Union*, 151f.
116. Oral Testimony of Sara Goland, Yad Vashem Archives, YV 03.4126, p. 7; Nikodimova, *Arkhiv*, 19f.

117. Rita Kazhdan, interviewed by author, St. Petersburg, May 24, 2001.
118. Rita Kazhdan, interviewed by author, St. Petersburg, May 24, 2001.
119. Sprats, also known as spratfish or Baltic sprats, are herring-like marine fishes that are often smoked and canned, a popular staple in many Eastern European countries.
120. Rita Kazhdan, interviewed by author, St. Petersburg, May 24, 2001.
121. Mikhail Treister, Interview 2324, Visual History Archive; Mikhail Treister, interviewed by author and Eva Determann, Minsk, March 19, 2003; see also Treister, "Probleski pamiati," 303.
122. Elena Drapkina, interviewed by author, St. Petersburg, April 26, 2001.
123. Rita Kazhdan, interviewed by author, St. Petersburg, May 12, 2005.
124. Mikhail Treister, Interview 2324, Visual History Archive; Mikhail Treister, interviewed by author and Eva Determann, Minsk, March 19, 2003; Ekaterina Tsirlina, interviewed by author, Minsk, October 13, 2002; Ekaterina Tsirlina, Interview 28012, Visual History Archive.
125. The role of women in underground work against the Nazi regime and how they utilized stereotypes about women's passivity to their advantage is the subject of Ingrid Strobl's *Die Angst kam erst danach: Jüdische Frauen im Widerstand in Europa, 1939–1945* (Frankfurt am Main: Fischer, 1998). Chaika Grossman describes the work of females, especially as couriers, in the Białystok ghetto underground in her memoir *The Underground Army: Fighters of the Białystok Ghetto* (New York: Holocaust Library, 1987).
126. Rita Kazhdan, interviewed by author, St. Petersburg, May 24, 2001.
127. Rita Kazhdan, interviewed by author, St. Petersburg, May 24, 2001.
128. Rita Kazhdan, Interview 654, Visual History Archive.
129. Cf. Helene Sinnreich, "The Rape of Jewish Women during the Holocaust," in *Sexual Violence against Jewish Women during the Holocaust*, eds. Sonja M. Hedgepeth and Rochelle G. Saidel (Waltham, MA: Brandeis University Press, 2010), 108.
130. Treister, "Probleski pamiati," 308.
131. "Reminiscences of Albert Lapidus," in USHMM, RG 02.174, p. 26. Likely the scene described here correlates with Karl Löwenstein's report on ghetto commander Rübe's punishment of ten Jewish women who did not wear the yellow patch on their clothes while working in a German arms repairshop (Loesten, "Aus der Hölle," p. 21).
132. Elena Drapkina, interviewed by author, St. Petersburg, April 26, 2001.
133. "Minsk Hell," in Rubenstein and Altman, eds., *The Unknown Black Book*, 252; "The Recollections of Dr. Tsetsilia Mikhaylovna Shapiro," in Rubenstein and Altman, eds., *The Unknown Black Book*, 257; Anatoly Podolsky, "The Tragic Fate of Ukrainian Jewish Women under Nazi Occupation," in Hedgepeth and Saidel, eds., *Sexual Violence against Jewish Women*, 94–107.
134. Oral Testimony of Elena Gringauz, Yad Vashem Archives, YV 03.4126, p. 12.
135. USHMM, RG50.378*006, Oral History, Belarus Documentation Project, interview with Ida Moyseyevina Brion; USHMM, RG50.378*018, Oral History, Belarus Documentation Project, Interview with Genya Moyseyevna Kobrina. See also Regina Mühlhäuser, *Eroberungen: Sexuelle Gewalttaten und intime Beziehungen deutscher Soldaten in der Sowjetunion* (Hamburg: Hamburger Edition, 2010), 128, and Sinnreich, "The Rape of Jewish Women during the Holocaust," on such violence in other ghettos in the occupied Soviet Union.
136. Smolar, *The Minsk Ghetto*, 74.
137. Elena Drapkina, interviewed by author, St. Petersburg, April 26, 2001.

138. Elena Drapkina, interviewed by author, St. Petersburg, April 26, 2001, and September 20, 2002.
139. Elena Drapkina, interviewed by author, St. Petersburg, April 26, 2001.
140. Smolar, *The Minsk Ghetto*, 87.
141. In spring 1943, Gestapo Hauptscharführer Rübe (a.k.a. Ribbe) was deployed to Minsk to prepare the final destruction of the ghetto and its inhabitants, beginning with the destruction of a number of worker columns: Botvinnik, *Pamiatniki genotsida evreev Belarusi*, 19; Smolar, *The Minsk Ghetto*, 120; Rentrop, *Tatorte*, 150, 183, 210.
142. Rita Kazhdan, interviewed by author, St. Petersburg, May 24, 2001.
143. Shagreen is untanned leather that shrinks when dry.
144. USHMM, RG50.378*005, Oral History, Belarus Documentation Project, Interview with Arkady Sergeyevich Teif; Khomikh, "Otvoiovannaia zhizn'," 427.
145. Among others, the following confirm this date, which is now the occasion for an annual commemoration among Jewish survivors and the Jewish community in Minsk: Smolar, *The Minsk Ghetto*, 145; Botvinnik, *Pamiatniki genotsida evreev Belarusi*, 21; "The Minsk Ghetto," in Ehrenburg and Grossman, *Complete Black Book of Russian Jewry*, 138.
146. USHMM, RG-50.378*002, interview with Tatyana Samuilovna Gildiner.
147. Dwork, *Children with a Star*, 193.
148. Smilovitskii, *Katastrofa evreev v Belorussii*, 84. On education targeting Belorussian children, see Nicholas, *Cruel World*, 343.
149. Smilovitskii, *Katastrofa evreev*, 86–88.
150. I draw here on Erving Goffman's discussion of social institutions such as prisons and mental hospitals and their ability to impose role expectations and their fulfillment on their involuntary members (inmates); see Erving Goffman, *Asylums: Essays on the Social Situation of Mental Patients and Other Inmates* (Chicago: Aldine, 1961).
151. Tec, *Resilience and Courage*, 118.
152. On the increased participation of women in the Soviet labor force in the 1930s, see Wendy Z. Goldman, *Women at the Gates: Gender and Industry in Stalin's Russia* (New York: Cambridge University Press, 2002), and Melanie Ilič, *Women Workers in the Soviet Interwar Economy: From "Protection" to "Equality"* (New York: St. Martin's Press, 1999).
153. Joan Ringelheim, "The Split between Gender and the Holocaust," in *Women in the Holocaust*, eds. Dalia Ofer and Leonore J. Weitzman (New Haven: Yale University Press, 1998), 343.
154. Beate Fieseler, "Der Krieg der Frauen: Die ungeschriebene Geschichte," in *Mascha + Nina + Katjuscha: Frauen in der Roten Armee, 1941–1945*, ed. Deutsch-Russisches Museum Berlin Karlshorst (Berlin: Museum Karlshorst, 2002), 11–20.
155. Lev Arkadyev and Ada Dikhtyar, "The Unknown Girl: A Documentary Story," *Yiddish Writers Almanac* 1 (1987): 161–204. See chapter 5 and Conclusion for more details on this subject.
156. Olga Kucherenko, *Little Soldiers: How Soviet Children Went to War, 1941–1945* (Oxford: Oxford University Press, 2011), 5; Oral Testimony of Leonid Okun, Yad Vashem Archives, YV 03.6278, p. 27; Pavel Markovich Rubinchik, conversation with author, St. Petersburg, December 2000; Vladimir Rubezhin, interviewed by author, Minsk, October 2002.
157. Kucherenko, *Little Soldiers*, 4–5.

Chapter 4

1. Amaliia Iakhontova, Interview 43211, Visual History Archive.
2. Amaliia Iakhontova, Interview 43211, Visual History Archive.
3. David Patterson, "Death and Ghetto Death," in *Life in the Ghettos During the Holocaust*, ed. Eric J. Sterling (Syracuse, NY: Syracuse University Press, 2005), 162, 171.
4. Arendt, *Origins*, 447.
5. The Soviet government created the Extraordinary State Commission for the Investigation of Atrocities Committed on Soviet Territory by the German Fascists and Their Accomplices in November 1942. Immediately after Soviet troops had liberated areas in the USSR from the Nazi occupation, the commission began to collect information about the atrocities based on interviews with survivors, eyewitnesses, or perpetrators. Some of the evidence was used in war crimes trials held in Soviet courts, some of it was forwarded to the Nuremberg Trial against Nazi officials, held by the victorious Allied forces, in 1945–1946 (Altman, "The History and Fate of *The Black Book* and *The Unknown Black Book*, " in Rubenstein and Altman, eds., *The Unknown Black Book*, xxx n32).
6. Vera Pogorelaia, Interview 28756, Visual History Archive, USC Shoah Foundation Institute, accessed online at USHMM on March 11, 2010.
7. Giorgio Agamben, *Remnants of Auschwitz* (New York: Zone, 1999), 34.
8. Klüger, *Von hoher und niedriger Literatur*, 43.
9. Tiya Miles discusses inferential inquiry, drawing on both documentation and imagination as an important strategy to account for histories of destruction and violation: Miles, *Ties That Bind*, 212.
10. Saidiya Hartman, *Lose Your Mother: A Journey Along the Atlantic Slave Route* (New York: Farrar, Straus and Giroux, 2007), 16.
11. Boris Gal'perin, "Moi universitety," in *Kniga zhivykh: Vospominaniia evreev-frontovikov, uznikov getto i natsistskikh kontslagerei, boitsov partizanskikh otriadov, zashchitnikov blokadnogo Leningrada*, Vol. 2, eds. I. I. Baburina et al. (Saint Petersburg: Izdatel'stvo Zhurnal 'Neva,' 2004), 324.
12. Gennadii Vinnitsa, "Kholokost v shklovskom raione," in Vinnitsa, *Gorech' i bol'* (Orsha, Belarus: Otdel kul'tury Goretskogo raiispolkoma, 1998), 160; Gennadii Vinnitsa, "Shklov," in Dean, ed., *Encyclopedia*, 1729f.
13. Lower, "Facilitating Genocide," 131.
14. See Al'bert Kaganovich, "Voprosy i zadachi issledovaniia mest prinuditel'nogo soderzhaniia evreev na territorii Belarusi v 1941–1944 gg.," in *Aktual'nye voprosy izucheniia Kholokosta na territorii Belarusi v gody nemetsko-fashistskoi okkupatsii: Sbornik nauchnykh rabot*, ed. Ia. Z. Basin (Minsk: Kovcheg, 2005), electronic document, <http://www.homoliber.org/ru/kg/kg020108.html>, accessed March 8, 2011; and Martin Dean, "Life and Death in the 'Gray Zone' of Jewish Ghettos in Nazi-Occupied Europe: The Unknown, the Ambiguous, and the Disappeared," in *Gray Zones: Ambiguity and Compromise in the Holocaust and Its Aftermath*, eds. Jonathan Petropoulos and John K. Roth (New York: Berghahn Books, 2005), 209.
15. Christian Gerlach, "Deutsche Wirtschaftsinteressen, Besatzungspolitik und der Mord an den Juden in Weißrussland, 1941–1943," in *Nationalsozialistische Vernichtungspolitik 1939–1945: Neue Forschungen und Kontroversen*, ed. Ulrich Herbert (Frankfurt am Main: Fischer, 1998), 279.
16. Gerlach, "Deutsche Wirtschaftsinteressen," 284; Gerlach, *Kalkulierte Morde*, 606.
17. Gennadii Vinnitsa, "Getto tolochinskogo raiona," in Vinnitsa, *Gorech' i bol'*, 133; Daniel Romanovsky, "Slavnoe," in Dean, ed., *Encyclopedia*, 1732f.

18. Frida Ped'ko, interviewed by author, St. Petersburg, May 27, 2001; Vera Pogorelaia, Interview 28756, Visual History Archive; Liubov Belen'kaia, Interview 30764, Visual History Archive.

19. Liubov Belen'kaia, Interview 30764, Visual History Archive.

20. Frida Ped'ko, interviewed by author, St. Petersburg, May 27, 2001; Frida Ped'ko, "Avtobiografiia" (copy in my possession); Judgment of Federal Court, City of St. Petersburg, Kalininskii district, September 3, 2001, # 2-5415 (copy in my possession). On the history of the ghetto in Slavnoe, see Liubov Belen'kaia, Interview 30764, Visual History Archive; Vera Pogorelaia, Interview 28756, Visual History Archive; Vinnitsa, "Getto tolochinskogo raiona," in Vinnitsa, *Slovo pamiati* (Orsha, Belarus: Orshanskaia Tipografia, 1997), 124–127; Vinnitsa, "Getto tolochinskogo raiona," in Vinnitsa, *Gorech' i bol'*, 128–140.

21. Frida Ped'ko, interviewed by author, St. Petersburg, May 13, 2005.

22. Liubov Belen'kaia, Interview 30764, Visual History Archive.

23. "Interview of an eyewitness of the Holocaust, Menukha Boroda, with Dr. Irina P. Gerasimova, director of the Museum for the History and Culture of Belorussian Jews" (no date; video in Russian), available at *Moio mestechko—My Shtetl*, electronic document, http://shtetle.co.il/Shtetls/slavnoe/boroda.html, accessed March 4, 2011.

24. Frida Ped'ko, interviewed by author, St. Petersburg, May 13, 2005.

25. "Tolochinskii raion," in USHMM, RG22.002M, "Selected Records of the Extraordinary State Commission to Investigate German-Fascist Crimes Committed on Soviet Territory, 1941-1945," Sub-group 7021–84 "Belarus, Vitebskaya (Vitebsk) oblast," reel 8, p. 20; Romanovsky, "Slavnoe," in Dean, ed., *Encyclopedia*, 1733.

26. "Tolochinskii raion," in USHMM, RG22.002M, reel 8, pp. 59–60.

27. Sandra Rafman, Joyce Canfield, José Barbas, and Janusz Kaczorowski, "Children's Representations of Parental Loss Due to War," *International Journal of Behavioral Development* 20, no.1 (1997): 164.

28. Hans Keilson, *Sequentielle Traumatisierung bei Kindern: Deskriptiv-klinische und quantifizierend-statistische follow-up Untersuchung zum Schicksal der jüdischen Kriegswaisen in den Niederlanden* (Stuttgart: Enke, 1979); Sarah Moskovitz, "Longitudinal Follow-up of Child Survivors of the Holocaust," *Journal of the American Academy of Child Psychiatry* 24 (1985): 401–407; Judith Kestenberg and Ira Brenner, *The Last Witness: The Child Survivor of the Holocaust* (Washington, DC: American Psychiatric Press, 1996); see also: *Sozialisation und Traumatisierung: Kinder in der Zeit des Nationalsozialismus*, eds. Ute and Wolfgang Benz (Frankfurt am Main: Fischer, 1998). Few scholars explore the lives of orphaned children in ghettos and their reaction to the death of loved ones; see Dina Wardi, *Memorial Candles: Children of the Holocaust* (New York: Routledge, 1994), and Sharon Kangisser Cohen, *Child Survivors of the Holocaust in Israel: Social Dynamics and Post-War Experiences; "Finding Their Voice"* (Brighton, UK: Sussex Academic Press, 2005). For recent studies, see Sharon Kangisser Cohen, "The Experience of the Jewish Family in the Nazi Ghetto: Kovno—A Case Study," *Journal of Family History* 31, no. 3 (2006): 275f.

29. Authors such as Toni Morrison have explored these questions in fictional writing; see Toni Morrison, *Beloved* (1987).

30. Rafman et al., "Children's Representations of Parental Loss," 172f.

31. Anna Temkina, *Seksual'naia zhizn' zhenshchiny*, 35.

32. Frida Ped'ko, interviewed by author, St. Petersburg, May 27, 2001.

33. "Tolochinskii raion," in USHMM, RG22.002M, reel 8, pp. 4, 6. The numbers quoted here may be inaccurate; the website of Tolochin region features numbers of

9,521 people killed and 2,500 deported to forced labor, though there is no source given for these statistics. See http://tolochin.vitebsk-region.gov.by/ru/region/new_3.

34. Patterson, "Death and Ghetto Death," 164.

35. I. P. Gerasimova, "Bobruisk," in Al'tman, ed., *Kholokost*, 91f.

36. Grigorii Erenburg, interviewed by author, St. Petersburg, April 25, 2001. Solly Ganor writes about one such visit and the rape of his aunt in his presence in the ghetto of Kaunas in *Light One Candle: A Survivor's Tale from Lithuania to Jerusalem* (New York: Kodansha International, 1995), 118.

37. "City of Bobruisk, Bobruisk region, and Paricheskiy region: List of names of those who were shot, hung, tortured, or deported to Germany for forced labor," in USHMM, RG.22.002M, "Selected Records of the Extraordinary State Commission to Investigate German-Fascist Crimes Committed on Soviet Territory, 1941-1945," Sub-group 7021-82, "Belarus, Bobruyskaya oblast," reel 24, pp. 10, 11, 26, 32; Botvinnik, *Pamiatniki genotsida evreev Belarusi*, 281; Gerasimova, "Bobruisk," in Al'tman, ed., *Kholokost*, 91f.; Gennadii Vinitsa, "Bobruisk," in Dean, ed., *Encyclopedia*, 1649f.

38. Grigorii Erenburg, interviewed by author, St. Petersburg, April 25, 2001.

39. Grigorii Erenburg, interviewed by author, St. Petersburg, September 2, 2002.

40. Rita Kazhdan, interviewed by author, St. Petersburg, May 12, 2005.

41. Elena Drapkina, interviewed by author, St. Petersburg, April 26, 2001.

42. UHSMM, RG50.378*022, interview with Yakov Negnevitzki.

43. Ilya Ehrenburg, "Hatred," in Ehrenburg, *Russia at War* (London: Hamish Hamilton, 1943), 131. N.b.: Although the writer and the survivor share what at first glance appears to be the same last name, the spelling of each is different. The famous writer Ilya Ehrenburg's name is spelled with an Э in Russian, and in English his name is transliterated as "Ehrenburg" (using the German spelling). The survivor's last name begins, in Russian, with the Russian letter E.

44. *Ogoniok*, Feb. 4, 1942, quoted in David Shneer, *Through Soviet Jewish Eyes: Photography, War, and the Holocaust* (New Brunswick, NJ: Rutgers University Press, 2011), 103.

45. Silke Wenk and Insa Eschebach, "Soziales Gedächtnis und Geschlechterdifferenz: Eine Einführung," in *Gedächtnis und Geschlecht: Deutungsmuster in Darstellungen des nationalsozialistischen Genozids*, eds. Insa Eschebach, Sigrid Jacobeit, and Silke Wenk (Frankfurt am Main: Campus, 2002), 28.

46. Ronit Lentin, "(En)gendering Genocide: Die Feminisierung der Katastrophe," *Zeitschrift für Genozidforschung* 1, no.1 (1999): 76.

47. This correlation has been shown especially with regard to Soviet war posters and analyses of the Soviet war memory: Beate Fieseler, "Der Krieg der Frauen," 18.

48. See chapters 5 and 6 for a detailed discussion of this issue.

49. Grigorii Erenburg, interviewed by author, St. Petersburg, May 19, 2005.

50. "Statement from 17 June, 1942 about the examination of a body of a woman who had been raped and shot," in USHMM, RG22.016: Reports and Investigative Materials Compiled by the Military Commissions of the Red (Soviet) Army Related to the Crimes Committed by the Nazis and Their Collaborators on the Occupied Territories of the Soviet Union and Eastern Europe during WWII, 1942-1945, Box 5, Folder 40: fond 354, opis 5814, delo 118, p. 290.

51. Liubov Belen'kaia, Interview 30764, Visual History Archive; Elena Drapkina, interviewed by author, St. Petersburg, April 26, 2001; Report of an Investigative Commission of the 70. Army, in USHMM, RG22.008M*01*, "Records relating to Auschwitz and other camps from the Central State Archive of the Ministry of Defense,

Podolsk, 1940-1945," fond 233, opis 2374, delo 58, pp. 152-155 (the forensic report on exhumed corpses from several mass graves includes notes on the examination of children's bodies that suggest the children did not die of bullet wounds but as a result of blunt force against their heads).

52. Temma Kaplan, "Acts of Testimony: Reversing the Shame and Gendering the Memory," *Signs* 28, no.1 (2002): 187.

53. Ganor, *Light One Candle*, 119.

54. Gerlach, *Kalkulierte Morde*, 773.

55. "City of Bobruisk, Bobruisk region, and Paricheskiy region: List of names of those who were shot, hung, tortured, or deported to Germany for forced labor," in USHMM, RG22.002M, 7021-82, reel 24, pp.10 (reverse), 11 (reverse), 26, 32, 127; Vinnitsa, "Bobruisk," in Dean, ed., *Encyclopedia*, 1650.

56. Smilovitsky, "Rogachev," in Dean, ed., *Encyclopedia*, 1723.

57. Leonid Smilovitsky, "Zhlobin," in Dean, ed., *Encyclopedia*, 1751.

58. See *Zalozhniki vermakhta: Ozarichi—Lager' smerti; Dokumenty i materialy*, ed. G. D. Knat'ko (Minsk: Natsional'nyi Arkhiv Respubliki Belarus', 1999).

59. "Perechen' partizanov v Belorussii," 15.8.1944, in RGASPI fond 625, opis 1, delo 18, p. 93.

60. A. Zamoiskii, "Rogachev," in Al'tman, ed., *Kholokost*, 861f.; Smilovitsky, "Rogachev," in Dean, ed., *Encyclopedia*, 1723.

61. Alevtina Kuprikhina, Interview 49623, Visual History Archive.

62. Alevtina Kuprikhina, Interview 49623, Visual History Archive.

63. Alevtina Kuprikhina, Interview 49623, Visual History Archive.

64. *Professor Mamlock*, dir. Herbert Rappaport (USSR, 1938).

65. Alevtina Kuprikhina, interviewed by author, St. Petersburg, September 6, 2002.

66. Identical in Alevtina Kuprikhina, Interview 49623, Visual History Archive; Alevtina Kuprikhina, interviewed by author, St. Petersburg, September 6, 2002.

67. Alevtina Kuprikhina, interviewed by author, St. Petersburg, September 6, 2002.

68. "Statement from June, 1944 by residents of Staraya Dubrova, Oktiabriskiy Rayon, Polesskaya Oblast about German crimes," USHMM, RG22.016, Box 5, Folder 32: fond 32, opis 11302, delo 244, p. 82.

69. See *"Dann kam die deutsche Macht:" Weißrussische Kinderhäftlinge in deutschen Konzentrationslagern, 1941-1945*, ed. Projektgruppe Belarus e.V. (Cologne: Betrieb für Öffentlichkeit, 1999).

70. Leonid Smilovitsky/Martin Dean, "Parichi," in Dean, ed., *Encyclopedia*, 1717.

71. "City of Bobruisk, Bobruisk region, and Paricheskiy region: List of names of those who were shot, hung, tortured, or deported to Germany for forced labor," in USHMM, RG22.002M, reel 24, p. 132-135.

72. Maia Levina-Krapina, *Trizhdy rozhdionnaia: Vospominaniia byvshei uznitsy minskogo getto* (Minsk: Emizer Kolaz, 2008), 30-36; conversation with Anastasia Zinov'evna Khurs, Parichi, March 2003.

73. "Statement of Military and Medical Commission, 65th Army, from 4 April, 1944, about thousands of residents in Belorussia being sent to concentration camps in early 1944," in USHMM, RG22.016, Box 5, Folder 38: fond 422, opis 10510, delo 112, p. 12-21; "Testimony from 27 March, 1944 by a 15 year old girl from ZHLOBIN, BELORUSSIA about her experiences in early 1944 at a concentration camp," in USHMM, RG22.016, Box 5, Folder 38: fond 422, opis 10510, delo 112, pp. 98-118. See also Hans-Heinrich Nolte, "Ozarichi," in *Zalozhniki vermachta—Geiseln der Wehrmacht*, eds. G. D. Knatko et al. (Minsk: Natsional'ny Arkhiv Respubliki Belarus, 1999), 269-279.

74. "Statement of Military and Medical Commission, 65th Army, from 4 April, 1944," in USHMM, RG22.016, Box 5, Folder 38: fond 422, opis 10510, delo 112, p. 17.
75. Kelly, *Children's World*, 243; Petrova, "Deti Velikoi Otechestvennoi voiny," 213.
76. Alevtina Kuprikhina, interviewed by author, St. Petersburg, September 6, 2002.
77. Alevtina Kuprikhina, interviewed by author, St. Petersburg, September 6, 2002; also E. Boksitogorskii, "Eio belorusskaia mama," n.d., copy in author's possession.
78. Alevtina Kuprikhina, interviewed by author, St. Petersburg, September 6, 2002.
79. Alevtina Kuprikhina, Interview 49623, Visual History Archive.
80. Alevtina Kuprikhina, Interview 49623, Visual History Archive.
81. Harriet Murav, *Music from a Speeding Train: Jewish Literature in Post-Revolution Russia* (Stanford: Stanford University Press, 2011), 172.
82. Murav, *Music from a Speeding Train*, 176.
83. Frida Ped'ko, interviewed by author, St. Petersburg, May 27, 2001; Frida Ped'ko, "Avtobiografiia."
84. Grigorii Erenburg, interviewed by author, St. Petersburg, September 2, 2002. Erenburg refers to the pictures of executions in Liepaja, Latvia, in December 1941. The images are included in a number of publications on the Holocaust; for examples, see the Yad Vashem Photo Archive, available at http://collections.yadvashem.org/photosarchive/en-us/36449.html, accessed June 6, 2013.
85. Hirsch, "The Generation of Postmemory."
86. M. R. Zezina, "The System of Social Protection for Orphaned Children in the USSR," *Russian Social Science Review* 42, no. 3 (2001): 49–51.
87. The numbers are difficult to establish, especially since statistics often combine the number of prisoners of war with that of missing in action. Rather detailed statistics are available in: *Rossia i SSSR v voinakh XX veka: Poteri vooruzhonnykh sil—Statisticheskoe issledovanie*, ed. G. F. Krivosheev (Moskva: Olimp Press, 2001), 453ff.
88. James Hatley, *Suffering Witness: The Quandary of Responsibility after the Irreparable* (New York: State University of New York Press, 2000), 30f.

Chapter 5

1. Leonid Gol'braikh, interviewed by author, St. Petersburg, May 11, 2005.
2. On the history of the Beshenkovichi ghetto, see most recently "Beshchenkovichi," in Dean, ed., *Encyclopedia*, 1647.
3. Leonid Gol'braikh, interviewed by author, St. Petersburg, May 5, 2001.
4. Leonid Gol'braikh, interviewed by author, St. Petersburg, May 5, 2001.
5. Leonid Gol'braikh, Interview 42481, Visual History Archive, USC Shoah Foundation Institute, accessed online at USHMM on Jan 29, 2010.
6. Leonid Gol'braikh, interviewed by author, St. Petersburg, May 5, 2001.
7. Lev Arkadyev and Ada Dikhtyar, "The Unknown Girl: A Documentary Story," *Yiddish Writers Almanac* 1 (1987): 161–204; Nechama Tec and Daniel Weiss, "Eight Photographs of an Execution," *History of Photography* 23, no. 4 (1999): 322–330; a comprehensive documentation of the conflict is *Izvestnaia "Neizvestnaia": Sbornik materialov*, ed. Iakov Basin (Minsk: 2007), available online at http://mb.s5x.org/homoliber.org/ru/kg/kg010000.html.
8. Mordechai Altshuler, "Jewish Holocaust Commemoration Activity in the USSR under Stalin," *Yad Vashem Studies* 30 (2002): 271–296; Leonid Smilovitskii, "Antisemitism in the Soviet Partisan Movement, 1941–1944: The Case of Belorussia," *Holocaust and Genocide Studies* 20, no. 2 (2006): 207f.
9. Fieseler, "Der Krieg der Frauen," 18. Svetlana Alexievich's attempt to remedy this situation with the publication of *U voiny ne zhenskoe litso* ["The Unwomanly Face of

War," a book consisting of interviews with women who had served in the Soviet Army during World War II, nearly cost her her job; see Alexievich, *U voiny ne zhenskoe litso*.

10. Tec and Weiss, "Eight Photographs," 374.

11. Mordechai Altshuler, "Jewish Warfare and the Participation of Jews in Combat In the Soviet Union as Reflected in Soviet and Western Historiography," in *The Historiography of the Holocaust Period: Proceedings of the Fifth Yad Vashem International Historical Conference*, eds. Yisrael Gutman and Gideon Greif (Jerusalem: Yad Vashem, 1988), 217–239; Smilovitskii, "Antisemitism in the Soviet Partisan Movement." A somewhat different emphasis is developed in Moshe Kaganovich, *Der yidisher onteyl in der partizaner-bavegung fun Sovyet-Rusland* (Rome: Central Historical Commission at the Union of Partisans "Pachach" in Italy, 1948); Arad, *In the Shadow*; Chervinsky, ed., *Lives of the Great Patriotic War*.

12. I borrow here W. E. B. Du Bois's concept of double-consciousness, developed to analyze African-American experience in the post-slavery United States, to grasp the tensions inherent in efforts to survive racial exclusion and in seeing themselves "through the revelation of the other world": Du Bois, "Strivings of the Negro People," 194.

13. Elena Drapkina, interviewed by author, St. Petersburg, September 10, 2002.

14. Arad, *In the Shadow*, 173. More extensively on this topic: Alexei Popov, *Diversanty Stalina* (Moscow: Iauza Eksmo, 2004).

15. Estimates of the number of those who left the ghetto for partisan units in the vicinity of Minsk greatly vary, as do attempts to gauge the number of survivors among these refugees, which often is set at about 50 percent of these refugees. I utilize the latest data available, cited in Romanovskii, "Minsk," in Al'tman, ed., *Kholokost*, 601.

16. While there are several accounts and memoirs describing underground activity in Vilna and Białystok, other than Barbara Epstein's book on the Minsk underground there is no monograph or substantial analysis available, especially for the non-Russian-speaking audience; see Epstein, *The Minsk Ghetto*. Yitzhak Arad and Il'ia Al'tman devote selected chapters of their books on the Holocaust in the USSR to various forms of resistance; see Arad, *The Holocaust in the Soviet Union*, chaps. 35–57, and Il'ia Al'tman, *Zhertvy nenavisty: Kholokost v SSSR, 1941–1945 gg.* (Moscow: Kovcheg, 2002), chap. 4. Kuz'ma Kozak recently put forth a summary of existing research on Belorussia, but his book is based on previous publications and presents little original research; see Kuz'ma Kozak (ed.), *Evreiskoie soprotivlenie natsizmu na territorii Belarusi v gody Velikoi Otechestvennoi voiny 1941–1944 gg.* (Minsk: I. P. Logvinov, 2011).

17. Among others: *Partizanskaia druzhba: Vospominaniia o boevykh delakh partizan-evreev, uchastnikov Velikoi Otechestvennoi voiny* (Moscow: OGIZ, 1948), published in English as *Jewish Partisans: A Documentary of Jewish Resistance in the Soviet Union during World War II*, ed. Jack Porter (Washington, DC: University Press of America, 1982); Ainsztein, *Jewish Resistance in Nazi-occupied Eastern Europe*; Yuri Suhl, *They Fought Back: The Story of Jewish Resistance* (New York: Schocken, 1975); Gutman, *Fighters among the Ruins*. For an overview of such attempts, see Robert Rozett, "Jewish Resistance," in *The Historiography of the Holocaust*, ed. Dan Stone (New York: Palgrave Macmillan, 2004), 341–345.

18. On '*amidah* and associated acts, see Yehuda Bauer, "Jewish Resistance—Myth or Reality?" in Bauer, *Rethinking the Holocaust* (New Haven and London: Yale University Press, 2001), 120; Rozett, "Jewish Resistance," 345.

19. John Klier, "The Holocaust and the Soviet Union," in Stone, ed., *The Historiography of the Holocaust*, 279.

20. Kozak, *Evreiskoie soprotivlenie*, 49ff.

21. Arad, *In the Shadow*, 259.

22. Ainsztain, *Jewish Resistance*, 82, 86ff; Kozak, *Evreiskoe soprotivlenie*, 53ff.; Arad, *In the Shadow*, 233–241.

23. Gerlach, *Kalkulierte Morde*, 744.

24. Inna Gerasimova, "Evrei v partizanskom dvizhenii Belorussii, 1941–1944: Obshchaia kharakteristika," in Basin, ed., *Uroki Kholokosta*, 141f.; Mikhail Strelets, "Uchastie evreev v antigermanskom soprotivlenii na okkupirovannoi territorii Belorussii," in Basin, ed., *Uroki Kholokosta*, 133; Arad, *The Holocaust in the Soviet Union*, 508ff.

25. Arad, *In the Shadow*, 343.

26. Evan Mandsley, *Thunder in the East: The Nazi-Soviet War, 1941–1945* (London: Hodder Arnold, 2005), 86. The maltreatment of Soviet prisoners of war by the Nazi regime is the subject of many scholarly works, for instance Christian Streit, *Keine Kameraden: Die Wehrmacht und die Sowjetischen Kriegsgefangenen, 1941–1945* (Stuttgart, Germany: Deutsche Verlags-Anstalt, 1978); Gerhard Hirschfeld, *The Policies of Genocide: Jews and Soviet Prisoners of War in Nazi Germany* (London: Allan and Unwin, 1986). Timothy Snyder, in his recent book *Bloodlands*, also emphasizes the German treatment of Soviet POWs as a form of mass killing.

27. Slepyan, "The Soviet Partisan Movement and the Holocaust," 4; Arad, *In the Shadow*, 169.

28. Rita Kazhdan, interviewed by author, St. Petersburg, May 24, 2001; Arad, *In the Shadow*, 260.

29. Slepyan, "The Soviet Partisan Movement and the Holocaust," 4.

30. Slepyan, "The Soviet Partisan Movement and the Holocaust," 5. Kulaks, and those accused of being part of this class, were persecuted as class enemies of poorer peasants and the proletariat after 1917.

31. Slepyan, *Stalin's Guerillas*, 113; Arad, *In the Shadow*, 174.

32. A. A. Filimonov, *Partizanskii front v gody Velikoi Otechestvennoi voiny* (Minsk: Navuka i Tekhnika, 1993), 19.

33. Filimonov, *Partizanskii front*, 14f.; Vladimir Antonovich Zolotarev, ed., *Partizanskoe dvizhenie: Po opytu Velikoi Otechestvennoi voiny 1941–1945 gg.* (Moscow: Kuchkovo Pole, 2001), 75ff.

34. Smilovitskii, "Antisemitism in the Soviet Partisan Movement," 211.

35. "Statistical report on partisan units and divisions in Belorussia: Report for General Secretary of the Central Committee of the Communist Party Belorussia, Ponomarenko on the personnel count of the Belorussian partisan movement and results of its disbandment," in RGASPI fond 625, opis 1, delo 18, p. 87.

36. Kliment Efremovich Voroshilov (1881–1969), high-ranking officer and politician in the Soviet Union. Boris Gal'perin likely honored Voroshilov for his role in the Russian Revolution and subsequent military and political posts he occupied. Voroshilov was an early member of the Bolshevik faction of the Russian Social Democratic Labor Party, participated in the October Revolution in 1917, was then a member of the Military Council during the Civil War, from 1921 a member of the Party's Central Committee, People's Commissar for Military and Navy Affairs (1925), People's Commissar for Defense (1934), and Marshal of the Soviet Union (1935).

37. Gal'perin, "Boris Mikhailovich Gal'perin," 4.

38. Boris Gal'perin's written autobiography includes the layout of the kolkhoz and the ghetto, as well as a list of kolkhoz residents as of summer 1941 with short notes on their fates during the war. Most men are identified as "killed near meadow Semenovka."

39. Gal'perin, "Boris Mikhailovich Gal'perin," 2. Other narrators report on life in the ghetto, the separation of the Jewish population into different ghettos, and the series of executions in similar ways; see Sofiia Chernina, Interview 30952, Visual History Archive, USC Shoah Foundation Institute, accessed online at USHMM on April 1, 2010; Aleksandra Shumina, Interview 49152, Visual History Archive, USC Shoah Foundation Institute, accessed online at USHMM on March 16, 2010; and Galina Slutskaia, Interview 47490, Visual History Archive. Aleksandra Rusakovich, a Belorussian woman who lived in nearby Zarech'e, witnessed how Jews from the ghetto in Shklov were assembled and led to an execution site. She subsequently rescued and hid a number of Jewish children who were pushed out of the column by their parents; see Aleksandra Rusakovich, Interview 37012, Visual History Archive, USC Shoah Foundation Institute, accessed online at USHMM on March 31, 2010.

40. Gal'perin, "Boris Mikhailovich Gal'perin" 15; Vinnitsa, "Kholokost v shklovskom raione," in Vinnitsa, *Gorech' i bol'*, 166.

41. Botvinnik, *Pamiatniki genotsida evreev Belarusi*, 290, 292; Vinnitsa, "Shklov," in Dean, ed., *Encyclopedia*, 1729. See also the report of the Extraordinary State Commission to Investigate German-Fascist Crimes Committed on Soviet Territory for the region Shklov, where, for political reasons, the nationality of victims is often not mentioned in final reports, yet lists of residents known to be killed identify the majority of victims as Jewish: "Shklovskiy region," USHMM, RG22.002M, 7021–88, reel 8, pp. 1, 2, 38 for reports and eyewitness accounts, pp. 44, 271a+b, 276a+b, 500a–509b for lists.

42. Galina Slutskaia (born Klebanova) and her mother were in a situation like that of Boris Gal'perin; the five refugees even met each other and decided that splitting up in small groups of two or even going alone (as in the case of Boris) promised a better chance to find shelter; see Galina Slutskaia, Interview 47490, Visual History Archive.

43. Gal'perin, "Boris Mikhailovich Gal'perin," 4.
44. Gal'perin, "Boris Mikhailovich Gal'perin," 7.
45. Arad, *In the Shadow*, 175.
46. Christian Gerlach, "Strukturpolitik durch Terror: Die 'Partisanenbekämpfung,'" in Gerlach, *Kalkulierte Morde*, 859–1054; Arad, *In the Shadow*, 180–183.
47. Gal'perin, "Boris Mikhailovich Gal'perin,"7f.
48. Boris Gal'perin, interviewed by author, St. Petersburg, May 16, 2001.
49. Gal'perin, "Boris Mikhailovich Gal'perin," 1.
50. Gal'perin, "Boris Mikhailovich Gal'perin," 9
51. Gal'perin, "Boris Mikhailovich Gal'perin," 10f.
52. Arad, *In the Shadow*, 179.
53. Gal'perin, "Boris Mikhailovich Gal'perin," 12.
54. Arad, *In the Shadow*, 175.
55. Gal'perin, "Boris Mikhailovich Gal'perin," 13.
56. Gal'perin, "Boris Mikhailovich Gal'perin," 13.
57. Filimonov, *Partizanskii front*, 90; Zolotarev, *Partizanskoe dvizhenie*, 192ff.; Arad, *In the Shadow*, 185f.
58. Gal'perin, "Boris Mikhailovich Gal'perin," 1.
59. Gal'perin, "Boris Mikhailovich Gal'perin," 20.
60. Boris Gal'perin, interviewed by author, St. Petersburg, May 16, 2001.
61. Smilovitskii, "Antisemitism in the Soviet Partisan Movement," 221f.
62. Boris Gal'perin, interviewed by author, St. Petersburg, May 16, 2001.
63. Gal'perin, "Boris Mikhailovich Gal'perin," 10.

64. In early 1943, the Soviet government ordered the evacuation of children within partisan units to the Russian rear, supplying airplanes for the transfer where possible or requesting that senior partisans accompany them across the frontline; N. K. Petrova, "Deti Velikoi Otechestvennoi voiny," in *Vtoraia mirovaia voina v detskikh "ramkakh pamiati": Sbornik nauchnykh statei*, ed. A. Iu. Rozhkova (Krasnodar, Russia: Ekoinvest, 2010), 223; Alevtina Kuprikhina, interviewed by author, St. Petersburg, September 6, 2002.

65. Gal'perin, "Boris Mikhailovich Gal'perin," 12.

66. Boris Gal'perin, interviewed by author, St. Petersburg, May 16, 2001.

67. Gal'perin, "Boris Mikhailovich Gal'perin," 20.

68. From the title of a poem that Boris Gal'perin's wrote about the killing of children during the Nazi genocide: Gal'perin, "Boris Mikhailovich Gal'perin," 43.

69. A numerical tally of the losses continues to be difficult, yet Leonid Smilovitskii's comparison between the censuses of 1939 and 1959 indicates dramatic losses of, for instance, 59 percent (Mogilev province, including Shklov, Gal'perin's home) or 62 percent (Vitebsk provice, including Slavnoe, Ped'ko's home) of the Jewish population (Smilovitskii, *Katastrofa evreev v Belorussii*, 31).

70. Zolotarev, ed., *Partizanskoe dvizhenie*, 351.

71. Eric Weitz, "The Heroic Man and the Ever-Changing Woman: Gender and Politics in European Communism, 1917-1950," in *Gender and Class in Modern Europe*, ed. Laura L. Frader and Sonya O. Rose (Ithaca and London: Cornell University Press, 1996), 329.

72. Gal'perin, "Boris Mikhailovich Gal'perin," 22.

73. Gal'perin, "Boris Mikhailovich Gal'perin," 22.

74. Irina V. Rebrova, "Zhenskaia povsednevnost' v ekstremal'noi situatsii: Po materialam ustnykh i pis'mennykh vospominanii zhenshchin o Velikoi Otechestvennoi voine," in *Rossiiskaia povsednevnost' v zerkale gendernykh otnoshenii: Sbornik statei*, ed. Natalia L. Pushkareva (Moscow: Novoe Literaturnoe Obozrenie, 2013), 605, 614.

75. Rebrova, "Zhenskaia povsednevnost' v ekstremal'noi situatsii," 608f.

76. For more details on BGTO, see chapter 2.

77. Elena Drapkina, interviewed by author, St. Petersburg, April 26, 2001.

78. Elena Drapkina, interviewed by author, St. Petersburg, April 26, 2001.

79. Elena Drapkina, interviewed by author, St. Petersburg, September 10, 2002.

80. Elena Drapkina, interviewed by author, St. Petersburg, April 26, 2001.

81. "Brief information on the history of the organization of partisan units, brigades, and groups," in RGASPI fond 625, fond 1, delo 108, p. 703.

82. Archival certificate, issued by the National Archive of the Republic of Belarus to Elena Askarevna Drapkina (Levina) on August 18, 1998.

83. "Proposals for decrees of the Central Partisan Staff, prepared by the Central Committee of the Komsomol, plans for the work of the Special Departments, and reports by the Central Committee of the Komsomol on shortcomings within the partisan movement, on the assignment of regional Komsomol secretaries to partisan units, on the participation of women in the partisan movement, and on the activization of Komsomol organizations in the rear of the enemy," in RGASPI, fond 69, opis 1, delo 1060, p. 4.

84. "Proposals for decrees of the Central Partisan Staff," p. 5

85. "Proposals for decrees of the Central Partisan Staff," p. 22.

86. Anna Krylova, *Soviet Women in Combat: A History of Violence on the Eastern Front* (New York: Cambridge University Press, 2010), 110.

87. "Proposals for decrees of the Central Partisan Staff," p. 17; Andrea Moll-Sawatzki, "Freiwillig an die Front? Junge Frauen zwischen Motivation und Mobilisierung," in Deutsch-Russiches Museum, ed., *Mascha+Nina+Katjuscha*, 24.

88. Elena Drapkina, interviewed by author, St. Petersburg, April 26, 2001.
89. Arad, *In the Shadow*, 177.
90. Elena Drapkina, interviewed by author, St. Petersburg, April 26, 2001.
91. Elena Drapkina, interviewed by author, St. Petersburg, April 26, 2001.
92. Claudia Freytag, "Kriegsbeute 'Flintenweib': Rotarmistinnen in deutscher Gefangenschaft," in Deutsch-Russisches Museum, ed., *Mascha + Nina + Katiuscha*, 32–36.
93. Elena Drapkina, interviewed by author, St. Petersburg, April 26, 2001.
94. "Reports by the Political Department of the Central Staff of the Partisan Movement on the state of party-political work and military activity in the partisan units, on the leadership in Gomel"s underground organization, on the distribution of leaflets, on German atrocities," in RGASPI, fond 69, opis 1, delo 1090, p. 6 (reverse).
95. "Reports by the Political Department of the Central Staff," pp. 6 (reverse), 7. See also Tec, *Defiance*, 216–238; Chiari, *Alltag hinter der Front*, 256; Slepyan, *Stalin's Guerillas*, 194ff., 202ff.
96. "Reports by the Political Department of the Central Staff," p. 7.
97. "Plans, memoranda and reports from the Central Party Committees Belorussia, Ukraine, and Estonia, the Regional Party Committees Vitebsk and Smolensk, and local partisan staff on the status of the partisan movement, on the number and membership of Party and Komsomol organizations in partisan units, on their activity, and on the work and material supplies of print shops in the partisan movement," in RGASPI, fond 69, opis 1, delo 1059, p. 52.
98. Elena Drapkina, interviewed by author, St. Petersburg, April 26, 2001; "Brief information," in RGASPI fond 625, opis 1, delo 108, p. 704.
99. Elena Drapkina, interviewed by author, St. Petersburg, April 26, 2001.
100. Zolotarev, ed., *Partizanskoe dvizhenie*, 355.
101. Slepyan, *Stalin's Guerillas*, 51, 188ff.
102. See the competing assessments in Slepyan, *Stalin's Guerillas*; Arad, *The Holocaust in the Soviet Union*; and Bogdan Musial, *Sowjetische Partisanen 1941–1944: Mythos und Wirklichkeit* (Paderborn, Germany: Ferdinand Schöningh, 2009). For more details on German antipartisan warfare, see Gerlach, *Kalkulierte Morde*, 859–1054, and Ben Shepherd, *War in the Wild East: The German Army and Soviet Partisans* (Cambridge, MA: Harvard University Press, 2004).
103. Filimonov, *Partizanskii front*, 49; Arad, *In the Shadow*, 175.
104. Zolotarev, ed., *Partizanskoe dvizhenie*, 134f.
105. "Zentralinformation I/1e: "Entwicklung der Partisanenbewegung vom Zeitpunkt des Beginns der Reichswerbung an bis heute (1.7.1942 bis 30.4.1943)," NARB fond 370, opis 1, delo 386a, pp. 24–35.
106. Arad, *In the Shadow*, 184
107. For an exemplary German description of such an operation, see the final report of the Höherer SS- und Polizeiführer für das Ostland, Friedrich Jeckeln, on Operation Sumpffieber (Swamp Fever) in 1942: "Account of the supreme commander of the SS and police of the State Commissariat 'Ostland' on the punitive operation against partisans and peaceful inhabitants under the code name 'Swamp Fever,'" November 6, 1942, in USHMM, RG22.001, p. 19.
108. Peter Klein, "Zwischen den Fronten: Die Zivilbevölkerung Weißrusslands und der Krieg der Wehrmacht gegen die Partisanen," in Quinkert, ed., *"Wir sind die Herren dieses Landes,"* 102.
109. Gerlach, *Kalkulierte Morde*, 955.
110. "Report of the Agricultural Representative of Vileyka district to the general commissar of White Russia," June 12, 1943, in USHMM, RG22.001: "Records relating

to the Soviet Union under Nazi Occupation, 1941–1945," p. 23. A similar commission was part of Operation Hermann in summer 1943; see Bogdan Musial, ed., *Sowjetische Partisanen in Weißrußland: Innenansichten aus dem Gebiet Baranovici; Eine Dokumentation* (Munich: Oldenbourg, 2004), 129, fn 27.

111. Zolotarev, ed., *Partizanskoe dvizhenie*, 208ff.

112. Elena Drapkina, interviewed by author, St. Petersburg, April 26, 2001.

113. Marianne Hirsch and Valerie Smith, "Feminism and Cultural Memory: An Introduction," *Signs* 28, no. 1 (2002): 6.

114. Smilovitskii, "Antisemitism in the Soviet Partisan Movement," 207; Bernd Bonwetsch, "Der 'Große Vaterländische Krieg': Vom öffentlichen Schweigen unter Stalin zum Heldenkult unter Breschnew," in Quinkert, ed.,*"Wir sind die Herren dieses Landes,"* 168. For a comprehensive account of Soviet war memory, see Tumarkin, *The Living and the Dead*; Mikhail Gabovich, ed., *Pamiat' o voine 60 let spustia*; and Beate Fieseler and Jörg Ganzenmüller, eds., *Kriegsbilder: Mediale Repräsentationen des "Großen Vaterländischen Krieges"* (Essen, Germany: Klartext, 2010).

115. Soviet women who had participated in the defense of the state against German occupation thereby shared the fate of, for instance, women guerilla fighters in post-independence Zimbabwe, who were also stigmatized as "prostitutes" and denied full citizenship rights as well as benefits for combat veterans: Tanya Lyons, *Guns and Guerilla Girls: Women in the Zimbabwean National Liberation Struggle* (Trenton, NJ: Africa World Press, 2004), 213ff.

116. Moll-Sawatzki, "Freiwillig an die Front?," 26.

117. Sabine Arnold provides a substantial analysis of the memorial, tracing the process of its installation from the first drafts to the final product: Arnold, *Stalingrad im sowjetischen Gedächtnis*.

118. Ronit Lentin, "Introduction: (En)Gendering Genocides," in Lentin, ed., *Gender and Catastrophe* (London and New York: Zed Books, 1997), 2–17.

119. In other words, "[w]omen are ... construed as the symbolic bearers of the nation, but are denied any direct relation to national agency," whereas "men are 'contiguous with each other and with the nation as a whole'": Anne McClintock, "Family Feuds: Gender, Nationalism and the Family," *Feminist Review* 44 (1993): 62.

120. On sexual violence, shame, and memory, see Ringelheim, "Women and the Holocaust: A Reconsideration of Research," and Kaplan, "Acts of Testimony"; on the role of cultural discourses for gendered memory and silence, see Hirsch and Smith, "Feminism and Cultural Memory," among others.

121. Fieseler, "Krieg der Frauen," 18.

122. Pascale Rachel Bos, "Women and the Holocaust: Analyzing Gender Difference," in Baer and Goldenberg, eds., *Experience and Expression: Women, the Nazis, and the Holocaust* (Detroit: Wayne State University Press), 33.

123. Oswald and Voronkov, "The Public-Private Sphere," 100.

124. Natal'ia Kozlova, *Sovietskie liudi: Stseny iz istorii* (Moscow: Evropa, 2005), 274.

125. Smilovitskii, "Antisemitism in the Soviet Partisan Movement," 207.

126. Robert Miller, Robin Humphrey, and Elena Zdravomyslova, "Introduction: Biographical Research and Historical Watersheds," in *Biographical Research in Eastern Europe: Altered Lives and Broken Biographies*, eds. Robin Humphrey, Robert Miller, and Elena Zdravomyslova (Aldershot, UK: Ashgate, 2002), 18.

127. Oswald and Voronkov, "The Public-Private Sphere," 109.

128. Kamala Visveswaran, "Betrayal: An Analysis in Three Acts," in *Fictions of a Feminist Ethnography* (Minneapolis: University of Minnesota Press, 1994), 49.

129. Deborah A. Field, *Private Life and Communist Morality in Khrushchev's Russia* (New York: Peter Lang, 2007).

130. Temkina, *Seksual'naia zhizn' zhenshchiny*, 35.

131. See Hershatter, *The Gender of Memory*, 234, on the inability to apprehend subjectivity independent of a deeply ingrained language of official history, especially in the context of highly ideologized projects of state building.

132. Du Bois, "Strivings of the Negro People," 194.

133. Du Bois, quoted in Michael Rothberg, "W. E. B. Du Bois in Warsaw: Holocaust Memory and the Color Line, 1949–1952," *Yale Journal of Criticism* 14, no. 1 (2001): 172.

134. I am borrowing here from Rothberg, "W. E. B. Du Bois in Warsaw," 186.

135. W. E. B. Du Bois, "The Negro and the Warsaw Ghetto," in *The Oxford W. E. B. Du Bois Reader*, ed. Eric J Sundquist (New York: Oxford University Press, 1996), 471.

136. Katherine Borland, "'That's Not What I Said': Interpretive Conflict in Oral Narrative Research," in Gluck and Patai, eds., *Women's Words*, 64.

Chapter 6

1. Amaliia Iakhontova, Interview 43211, Visual History Archive.

2. Zorin's first name is cited variously as Semion, Sholem, or Shalom in different publications. In the service of consistency, I chose to use Shalom throughout my discussion, thus following most interviewees' practice and also the most recent publication describing Zorin's role in the partisan movement; see "Zorin," in Al'tman, ed., *Kholokost*, 337.

3. Rita Kazhdan, interviewed by author, St. Petersburg, May 24, 2001.

4. Rita Kazhdan, interviewed by author, St. Petersburg, May 24, 2001.

5. For a discussion of female Red Army soldiers and the postwar treatment of Soviet partisans, see Fieseler, "Der Krieg der Frauen," and Mark Edele, *Soviet Veterans of World War II: A Popular Movement in an Authoritarian Society* (New York: Oxford University Press, 2008), 73f.

6. Prikaz 070 of March 25, 1944, in "Report on partisan unit #106 in Ivenetskiy Rayon. 1943," in USHMM, Accession 1996.A.0196, "Holocaust related records from various European archives collected by the Yad Vashem, 1939–1960," "Copies of selected documents from the National Archives, Minsk, Belarus," M-41/89 (3500-4-277), reel 11, p. 47. The original report is archived in the National Archives, Minsk, Belarus (NARB), fond 3500, opis 4, delo 277. Below identified as "Report on partisan unit #106."

7. S. Shveibish, "Evreiskii semeinyi partizanskii otriad Sh. Zorina," *Vestnik Evreiskogo Universiteta v Moskve* 3 (13), 1996: 92.

8. "Brief information on the history of the organization of partisan units, brigades, and groups," 1944, in RGASPI fond 625, opis 1, delo 108, p. 22. Tuvia (Anatolii) Bielski's detachment, then named after Kalinin, had the same status; see "Brief information on the history," p. 73.

9. I. A. Al'tman, "Semeinye lageria," in Al'tman, ed., *Kholokost*, 897.

10. Al'tman, "Semeinye lageria"; Smilovitskii, *Katastrofa evreev v Belorussii*, 125–127. In a brief mention of family camps as important spaces of survival, Yisrael Gutman estimates that up to 10,000 Jews survived the war in such camps: Yisrael Gutman, *Fighters Among the Ruins: The Story of Jewish Heroism During World War II* (Washington, DC: B'nai B'rith Books, 1988), 207.

11. Cf. "Documents on the Executive Committee's refusal to recognize Tsirlina E. I. as a member of the Minsk Party Underground (questionnaire, testimonies, rulings

of the GorKom et al.)," National Archives Belarus (NARB), Minsk, fond 4386, opis 2, delo 165. The folder contains multiple requests by Ekaterina Tsirlina to grant her the status of war veteran, personal autobiographies, and witness affidavits describing her participation in the Minsk ghetto underground. Included are official notifications denying her requests. Finally, in 1989 she was awarded veteran status, thus gaining access to benefits, but first of all, moral recognition. See also Ekaterina Tsirlina, interviewed by author, Minsk, October 13, 2002.

12. "Documents on the Executive Committee's refusal to recognize Tsirlina E. I.," NARB fond 4386, opis 2, delo 165, pp. 25-26.

13. See Shveibish, "Evreiskii semeinyi partizanskii otriad Sh. Zorina," 92. Shveibish refers to the book *Partizanskie formirovaniia v Belorussii v gody Velikoi Otechestvennoi voiny: Kratkie svedeniia ob organizatsionnoi strukture partizanskikh soedinenii, brigad (polkov), otriadov (batalionov) i ikh lichnom sostave,* ed. A. L. Manaenkov (Minsk: Belarus, 1983).

14. "Data on headcount in the Jewish family detachment, January 1944," in "Report on partisan unit #106," p. 109. Important legible data revealed in this sheet include: all 556 members are Jewish, 12 partisans are members of the CP(B) or candidates for membership in the Party, 59 are Komsomol'tsy, 129 are between 20 and 30 years old, 97 between 31 and 40, and 39 are over 40.

15. "Report on partisan unit #106," pp. 1-13. Similar orders follow throughout the document.

16. Davis, "Women and Capitalism," 163; Hartmann, "The Unhappy Marriage," 18. Whereas Davis and other scholars build their analysis of the sexual division of labor grounded in an interrogation of capitalist economy, the main thrust of their analyses is valid for socialist societies as well, see Davis, "Women and Capitalism," 174.

17. The study of the Holocaust is only one example of such tendencies. Until the early 1980s, different experiences of victims and survivors of the Nazi genocide rooted in their gender or sexual identity were hardly subject to inquiry, and some scholars still resist such approaches as distracting. See Lisa Pine, "Gender and the Family," in Stone, ed., *The Historiography of the Holocaust,* 364, and Elizabeth R. Baer and Myrna Goldenberg, "Introduction: Experience and Expression: Women and the Holocaust," in Baer and Goldenberg, eds., *Experience and Expression,* esp. xxvii. Examples of publications that fail to include or address the perspective of women or gendered experience are Raul Hilberg, *The Destruction of the European Jews* (New York: Holmes & Meier, 1985); John K. Roth and Michael Berenbaum, eds., *Holocaust: Religious and Philosophical Implications* (New York: Paragon House, 1989); and I. A. Al'tman, *Kholokost i evreiskoe soprotivlenie na okkupirovannoi territorii SSSR* (Moscow: Kaleidoskop, 2002).

18. My work with first-person narratives, including interviews and written accounts, has greatly benefited from Nechama Tec's detailed description of the partisan unit led by Tuvia Bielski (Tec, *Defiance*). I also look to Inna Gerasimova's, Leonid Smilovitsky's, and Kenneth Slepyan's portrayals of Jewish and Soviet partisans, which, to a great extent, utilize archival records to substantiate their discussion: Gerasimova, "Evrei v partizanskom dvizhenii Belorussii," 137-143; Kenneth Slepyan, "The Soviet Partisan Movement and the Holocaust," *Holocaust and Genocide Studies* 14, no. 1 (2000): 1-27; Kenneth Slepyan, *Stalin's Guerillas: Soviet Partisans in World War II* (Lawrence: University of Kansas Press, 2006); Smilovitskii, "Glava II: Soprotivlenie politike genotsida," in Smilovitskii, *Katastrofa evreev v Belorussii;* Leonid Smilovitskii, "Antisemitism in the Soviet Partisan Movement."

19. Polya Shostak, Interview 20969, Visual History Archive, USC Shoah Foundation Institute, accessed online at USHMM on June 23, 2010.

20. An account in an early publication about Jews in the Soviet partisan movement highlights the increased danger for Jews who tried to conceal their identity during their escape, a disguise that was in some cases interpreted as a cover-up for espionage. See Gregory Linkov ("Batya"), "Women Spies," in *Jewish Partisans: A Documentary of Jewish Resistance in the Soviet Union during World War II*, ed. Jack Porter (Washington, DC: University Press of America, 1982), 164–167. "Women Spies" is a translation of Grigorii Matveevich Lin'kov, *Voina v tylu vraga* (Moscow: Sovetskii pisatel', 1947), Part 3, chap. 15.

21. Shostak's account may well refer to an incident reported by Hersh Smolar. Smolar recounts how a partisan of the "Zhukov" brigade had found the bodies of twenty Jewish women, undoubtedly killed by Soviet partisans after they had crossed the River Neman to reach partisan territory. A representative of the Central Staff of the Belorussian Partisan Movement, Tsaryuk, explained that the execution was a response to a warning they had received that the Gestapo had sent a group of women to poison Soviet partisans (Smolar, *The Minsk Ghetto*, 128).

22. The order reads as follows: "Confidential. To all partisan brigades and units in Belorussia. German intelligence organized a dummy center of the partisan movement in Minsk to uncover the location of partisan detachments, plant traitors, and disseminate false directives in order to liquidate partisan units. Partisan units of the Minsk region uncovered this center. There is evidence for the existence of a second center sending out directives and individuals and thus attempts to establish contacts with partisan units. I DECREE: To prevent the infiltration of units by the enemy's intelligence, units are forbidden to enter into contact with any underground representatives from Minsk or to release information about partisan detachments' disposition, strength, armament, or their activities. Potential recruits are to be meticulously checked and whoever arouses suspicion must be detained," quoted from the Russian in Gerasimova, "Evrei v partizanskom dvizhenii Belorussii," 140; a paraphrased and partial translation is provided by Smilovitskii, "Antisemitism in the Soviet Partisan Movement," 217f.

23. Smilovitskii, "Antisemitism in the Soviet Partisan Movement," 140.

24. Gerasimova, "Evrei v partizanskom dvizhenii Belorussii," 140; Treister, "Probleski pamiati," 332.

25. Inna Gerasimova's quote from Ponomarenko's "Report on the development of the partisan movement" (July 1941) may count as proof of the former. In this report, Ponomarenko questions Jewish preparedness and ability to resist: "One must emphasize the kolkhoz members' extraordinary fearlessness, steadfastness, and uncompromising attitude toward the enemy, in contrast to certain parts of the urban service class, who don't think about anything other than protecting their own skin. This, of course, is to be explained by the large Jewish stratum in the cities. They were gripped by animal fear of Hitler, and instead of fighting, they ran away" (author's translation from: Gerasimova, "Evrei v partizanskom dvizhenii Belorussii," 140).

26. See Leonid Smilovitskii's account of several incidents in Soviet partisan units that involved attacks on Jewish partisans or highlighted the leadership's unwillingness to intervene against antisemitic prejudice and violence (Smilovitskii, "Antisemitism in the Soviet Partisan Movement," 211–225).

27. Gerasimova, "Evrei v partizanskom dvizhenii Belorussii," 141f.; Mikhail Strelets, "Uchastie evreev v antigermanskom soprotivlenii na okkupirovannoi territorii Belorussii," 133; Arad, *The Holocaust in the Soviet Union*, 508ff.

28. Accounts of how partisan detachment No. 106, commonly referred to as the "Zorin" unit, was established vary. Some say it was solely the result of Shalom Zorin's

attempt to create a safe haven for ghetto refugees; others credit Semion Ganzenko, the commander of the "Budionny" brigade, with establishing it and assigning Zorin the task of implementation; and others ascribe its existence to Stalin's good intentions or pragmatic nature. Available sources indicate that elements of all three contributed to the detachment's formation and impacted its internal organization.

29. "Report on partisan unit #106," p. 46; L. Arkin, "Semen Zorin, komandir evreiskogo partizanskogo otriada No. 106 v Moskve," article submitted to *Einikayt* on October 13, 1944, in USHMM, RG22.028M: "Archives of the Jewish Anti-Fascist Committee," from the State Archives of the Russian Federation (GARF), reel 34, fond 8114, opis 1, delo 79, pp. 25–34; Anatol Wertheim, "With Zorin in the Family Camp," in *Minsk Yizkor Book—Minsk, Jewish Mother City: Memorial Anthology (translation of Minsk, ir va-em)*, Vol. 2, ed. Shlomo Even-Shushan (Jerusalem: Irgun yots'e Minsk u-venoteha be-Yisra'el, 1975), 392–395; Smolar, *The Minsk Ghetto*, 117; "The Minsk Ghetto," in Ehrenburg and Grossman, 135; Gerasimova, "Evrei v partizanskom dvizhenii Belorussii," 142; Smilovitskii, *Katastrofa evreev v Belorussii*, 120; Strelets, "Uchastie evreev v antigermanskom soprotivlenii," 133; Epstein, *The Minsk Ghetto*, 23; "Zorin," in Al'tman, ed., *Kholokost*, 337; "Minsk," in Al'tman, ed., *Kholokost*, 599.

30. Tec, *Defiance*; *Defiance* (film), directed by Edward Zwick (US 2008).

31. For the development of Bielski's unit, and this turning point in particular, see Tec, *Defiance*, 132, 176.

32. USHMM, RG50.120*116, interview with Leonid Okon.

33. "The Minsk Ghetto," in Ehrenburg and Grossman, 132–138; Smolar, *The Minsk Ghetto*, 139; Botvinnik, *Pamiatniki genotsida evreev Belarusi*, 19; see also chapter 3 of this book.

34. Smolar, *The Minsk Ghetto*, 117ff.

35. Leonid Melamed, Interview 29418, Visual History Archive, USC Shoah Foundation Institute, accessed online at USHMM on July 14, 2010.

36. Mikhail Treister, Interview 2324, Visual History Archive; see also Treister, "Probleski pamiati," 334; Sholom Kaplan, Interview 4950, Visual History Archive, USC Shoah Foundation Institute, accessed online at USHMM on June 24, 2010.

37. Arad, *The Holocaust in the Soviet Union*, 328.

38. Rita Kazhdan, interviewed by author, St. Petersburg, May 24, 2001.

39. Rita Kazhdan, interviewed by author, St. Petersburg, May 24, 2001.

40. Samuil Volk, Interview 43231, Visual History Archive.

41. Smolar, *The Minsk Ghetto*, 121.

42. Indeed, Rita Kazhdan referred me to Mikhail Treister for my research, and Samuil Volk and Amaliia Iakhontova speak about their postwar friendship and choice to take up residence in the same city in the interview with the Visual History Archive.

43. Amaliia Iakhontova, Interview 43211, Visual History Archive.

44. Rita Kazhdan, interviewed by author, St. Petersburg, May 24, 2001; Sholom Kaplan, Interview 4950, Visual History Archive; Mikhail Treister, Interview 2324, Visual History Archive.

45. Zoia Oboz, Interview 29477, Visual History Archive, USC Shoah Foundation Institute, accessed online at USHMM on July 21, 2010.

46. See Shveibish, "Evreiskii semeinyi partizanskii otriad Sh. Zorina," 95.

47. Klein, "Zwischen den Fronten," 84.

48. See Gerlach, *Kalkulierte Morde*, 744.

49. See Musial, ed., *Sowjetische Partisanen in Weißrußland*, 129.

50. USHMM, RG50.120*209, interview with Vladimir Mordkhilevich.

51. See chapter 5 on antipartisan warfare.

52. Gerlach, *Kalkulierte Morde*, 955. On the Nazi regime's use of forced laborers from occupied countries, see Ulrich Herbert, *Fremdarbeiter: Politik und Praxis des "Ausländer-Einsatzes" in der Kriegswirtschaft des Dritten Reiches* (Berlin and Bonn: Dietz, 1985).

53. Tec, *Defiance*, 159. Bogdan Musial reproduces the report of a Soviet partisan commander that denies such an order and highlights various units' achievements in killing German soldiers or blowing up their vehicles; see Musial, *Sowjetische Partisanen in Weißrußland*, 131. Given the propagandistic purpose of such reports, I do not entirely question this portrayal. Indeed, Nechame Tec's account of how the Bielski partisans and neighboring detachments addressed what she calls "the big hunt" indicate that there were partisans trying to stop attackers in various ways. From the perspective of members of detachment No. 106, however, the order to seek protection makes all the more sense and, if not issued in reality, serves as a rationalization and justification of their commander's decision.

54. Samuil Volk, Interview 43231, Visual History Archive; see also Tec, *Defiance*, 160.

55. Amaliia Iakhontova, Interview 43211, Visual History Archive; similar USHMM, RG50.120*209, interview with Vladimir Mordkhilevich.

56. On July 10, 1943, three days before the blockade began, the detachment consisted of 270 unarmed members and 45 armed combatants; see "Report on partisan unit #106," p. 46b.

57. A. Idin, "Vstrecha s rukovoditeliami evreiskogo natsionalnogo partizanskogo otriada v Evreiskom antifashistskom komitete," article submitted to *Einikayt* on September 11, 1944, in USHMM, RG22.028M, "Archives of the Jewish Anti-Fascist Committee," reel 35, fond 8114, opis 1, delo 80, p. 320.

58. USHMM, RG50.378*022, interview with Yakov Negnevitzki.

59. "Combat report by P. Kalinin (Belorussian Staff of the Partisan Movement) and Briukhanov (Head of Combat Department in BSPM) P. Ponomarenko (Central Staff of the Partisan Movement)," 27.8.1943, in RGASPI, fond 69, opis 1, delo 148, p. 33.

60. Anna Sagal'chik, Interview 27830, Visual History Archive, USC Shoah Foundation Institute, accessed online at USHMM on July 22, 2010; "Report on partisan unit #106," p. 47; "Combat report by P. Kalinin and Briukhanov," in RGASPI, fond 69, opis 1, delo 148, p. 34f.; Smolar, *The Minsk Ghetto*, 140.

61. "A meeting in Minsk: Accounts of Tamara Gershakovich, Captain Lifshitz, and Sofia Disner; Recorded by L. Katzovich," in Rubenstein and Altman, eds., 260.

62. Smolar, *The Minsk Ghetto*, 123; Musial, *Sowjetische Partisanen in Weißrußland*, 131.

63. Khomikh, "Otvoiovannaia zhizn'," 433.

64. "Statement from 9 July, 1944 about the murder of 14 people, whose names are given, in STAROYE SELO, ZASLAVSKIY Rayon, MINSKAYA Oblast," in USHMM RG22.016: Reports and Investigative Materials Compiled by the Military Commissions of the Red (Soviet) Army Related to the Crimes Committed by the Nazis and Their Collaborators on the Occupied Territories of the Soviet Union and Eastern Europe during WWII, 1942–1945, Box 5, F. 35, p. 310.

65. Leonid Melamed, Interview 29418, Visual History Archive.

66. Prikaz 042 of August 30, 1943, in "Report on partisan unit #106," pp. 27b/28.

67. Prikaz 022 of August 16, 1943, in "Report on partisan unit #106," p. 14.

68. Orders from Dubov, Central Staff Headquarter, 17.8.1943 and 22.3.1943, in "Report on partisan unit #106," pp. 96, 104.

69. Prikaz 023 of August 20, 1943, in "Report on partisan unit #106," pp. 14b, 15. Vladimir Mordkhilevich states that mostly women were assigned to work in the fields; see USHMM, RG50.120*209, interview with Vladimir Mordkhilevich.

70. USHMM, RG50.120*116, interview with Leonid Okon.

71. Rita Kazhdan, interviewed by author, St. Petersburg, May 24, 2001.

72. USHMM, RG50.378*005, interview with Arkady Sergeyevich Teif. See also Arad, *In the Shadow*, 178, on the problematic practice of confiscating foodstuffs from local residents.

73. Such endorsements came in the form of decrees by the Central Staff that assigned specific villages in the partisans' area of deployment for food requisitions. See, for instance, "Report on partisan unit #106," pp. 104, 110, 112, 117b, 190. The practice of Soviet partisans of requisitioning food and supplies from local residents is often the basis for criticism and condemnation of the movement as a whole, essentially accusing it of criminal treatment of the Soviet population. The practice does require critical investigation, but it must not be used to deny that the responsibility for scarcity and war was with the German Nazi regime. One recent and problematic attempt to portray the Soviet partisan movement as a band of criminals is Bogdan Musial, *Sowjetische Partisanen 1941–1944: Mythos und Wirklichkeit* (Paderborn, Germany: Ferdinand Schöningh, 2009).

74. Mikhail Treister, Interview 2324, Visual History Archive.

75. Prikaz 072 of April 13, 1944, in "Report on partisan unit #106," p. 48; Treister, "Probleski pamiati," 343.

76. Rita Kazhdan, interviewed by author, St. Petersburg, May 24, 2001. The lack of salt is mentioned by several interviewees, including USHMM, RG50.378*005, interview with Arkady Sergeyevich Teif; USHMM, RG50.120*209, interview with Vladimir Mordkhilevich.

77. Zoia Oboz, Interview 29477, Visual History Archive.

78. Anna Sagal'chik, Interview 27830, Visual History Archive; Rita Kazhdan, interviewed by author, St. Petersburg, May 24, 2001; Sonia Zalesskaia, Interview 30810, Visual History Archive.

79. On September 9, 1943, the commander of the detachment "Suvorov" asked to have twenty poods of grain processed in the mill; the "Parkhomenko" unit confirmed receipt of flour, see "Report on partisan unit #106," p. 94, 99; Rita Kazhdan, interviewed by author, St. Petersburg, May 24, 2001.

80. "Report on partisan unit #106," p. 158, 174, 99, 25, 25b.

81. "Report on partisan unit #106," pp. 14b, 15, 27b, 28; Smolar, *The Minsk Ghetto*, 129.

82. Request by General Mayor Platon to units in the area "to support 'Zorin' unit with grain, as their situation is extremely hard," in "Report on partisan unit #106," p. 139. Includes a note by General Suvorov: "In response to Platon's order to support 'Zorin' unit, several units of the 'Zhukov' brigade are sending supplies."

83. "Report on partisan unit #106," p. 191. A sergeant mayor (name illegible, seal of unit illegible) responds to a request for help: "In response to your request for permission to retrieve food in my brigade's area of operation. I suggest you wait a little. Due to the increased German-fascist mobilization, the local population is currently very agitated. I will get back to you once the situation has calmed down."

84. Smolar, *The Minsk Ghetto*, 129.

85. USHMM, RG50.120*116, interview with Leonid Okon.

86. "Report on partisan unit #106," p. 68 (a tailor is requested by the Budionny unit), p. 74 (the barber Peker is sent to the "Ryzhak" unit), p. 149 (the unit "Mstitel'" requires a shoemaker), p. 149 (commander Sapov of the unit "Mstitel'" requests the services of a locksmith who can repair locks and rifles), p. 154 (request of a commander to send a typist, Sonia Mindel, who has worked in unit Soviet BSSR

previously, asking that her child stay behind for the time being), p. 162 (note from the chief of staff, Tretiakov, to Zorin, explaining partisan Mindel's long absence from detachment No. 106 for repairs of typewriter and subsequent illness), p. 172 (request from "Voronov" unit to send a mechanic for two days who can repair the unit's typewriter), p. 177 (request by chief of staff of the "Suvorov" brigade to send a typist 3.4.1944), p. 142 (confirmation of Zorin to commander of the "Zhukov" brigade to send the typist Tatarina for work at the Staff HQ for two weeks, Jan. 14, 1944).

87. "Report on partisan unit #106," p. 174 (note by Zorin to General Platon, explaining that the shoemaker Okun is indispensable, as he does not manage to keep up with the work in his own unit; furthermore, there should be more skilled shoemakers available in the "Bielski" unit).

88. "Report on partisan unit #106," p. 71 (request of December [day illegible], 1943, from Lieutenant Samodakhov to send surgeon for treatment of a partisan who was critically wounded in a battle with members of the Polish White Guard), p. 72 (request by the Interregional Central Staff Headquarter of the Partisan Movement, Dec. 18, 1943), p. 140 (note by Staff Headquarters of "Stalin" brigade to commander Zorin of Jan. [date unintelligible], 1944, thanking him for the provision of medical staff and explaining that Dr. Rita Iakovlevna is to remain with the staff headquarters), p. 166 (request by Head Doctor 1st rank [name illegible] of the "Dzherzhinski" brigade to treat a partisan in the "Zorin" detachment, March 6, 1944).

89. Prikaz 029 of September 14, 1943, ordering Head Nurse Dorfman to ensure standards of hygiene, in "Report on partisan unit #106," p. 18.

90. USHMM, RG50.120*209, interview with Vladimir Mordkhilevich.

91. Samuil Volk, Interview 43231, Visual History Archive. Volk used the Russian word "negr" in his statement, which could be translated in various ways, including "blackamoor," "coon," or "black." In light of Volk's upbringing in the formally internationalist Soviet context, I chose "negro" to indicate the problematic, even if well meant and not offensive, terminology that haunts Soviet and post-Soviet discourse.

92. Mikhail Treister, Interview 2324, Visual History Archive.

93. Several requests by the leadership of detachment No. 106 indicate that the medical services provided for the partisan movement relied on such exchanges; see "Report on partisan unit #106," pp. 178, 183.

94. Prikaz 058: New courses for emergency medical aid were offered, partisans born in 1923, 1924, and 1925 were encouraged to enroll; Feb. 3, 1944, "Report on partisan unit #106," pp. 39b, 40.

95. None of the requests cited here indicate Livshits's first name, but an entry for Shalom Zorin in the recently published encyclopedia for the Holocaust in the USSR gives her full name: "Zorin," Al'tman, ed., *Kholokost*, 337.

96. "Report on partisan unit #106," p. 164 (request by Headquarters of Belorussian Partisan Movement for Baranovichi region to send Dr. Livshits (gynecologist) for two days for treatment of the sick wife of the "Kotovskii" unit's commander), p. 150 (explanation for the need to have Dr. Livshits's help, or her instruments, for performing an abortion, [name, date, and unit unintelligible]), p. 143 (request by deputy commander of "Bielski" unit, Gordon, to send Dr. Livshits with her special tools, as a female partisan's life is in danger [no date visible]).

97. "Report on partisan unit #106," p. 79 (request by chief of staff, "Dzherzhinski" unit, "Stalin" brigade, to send the gynecologist with all necessary instruments on Dec. 4, 1943, Dec. 4, 1943), p. 83 (Request of chief of staff, "Dzherzhinksi" unit, "Stalin" brigade, to Zorin, to lend the tools for abortion for one day, Dec. 2, 1943).

98. "Report on partisan unit #106," p. 65 (Dec. 22 1943), p. 66 (Dec. 22, 1943), p. 78 (no date), p. 141 (Jan. 8, 1944), p. 144 (Jan. 10, 1944), p. 152 (no date), p. 161 (Feb. 10, 1944), p. 167 (March 7, 1944), p. 185 (April 20, 1944).

99. See chapter 5 on this subject.

100. The Russian encyclopedia of the Holocaust in the USSR celebrates women's engagement in these areas as a continuation of traditional positions and a way to recreate normalcy: I. A. Al'tman, T. G. Vershitskaia, "Zhenshchiny," in Al'tman, ed., *Kholokost*, 311.

101. See chapter 5 of this book.

102. Slepyan, *Stalin's Guerillas*, 205.

103. Samuil Volk, Interview 43231, Visual History Archive.

104. Zoia Oboz, Interview 29477, Visual History Archive.

105. Amaliia Iakhontova, Interview 43211, Visual History Archive.

106. Rita Kazhdan, interviewed by author, St. Petersburg, May 24, 2001.

107. J.V. Stalin, "Radio Broadcast, July 3, 1941," available online at https://www.marxists.org/reference/archive/stalin/works/1941/07/03.htm, accessed February 24, 2015. See also Geoffrey Hosking, *The First Socialist Society*, 272.

108. Mikhail Treister, Interview 2324, Visual History Archive; Treister, "Probleski pamiati," 340.

109. Treister, "Probleski pamiati," 342f.

110. Mikhail Treister, Interview 2324, Visual History Archive.

111. USHMM, RG50.120*209, interview withVladimir Mordkhilevich. Arkadii Teif also describes the group of youngsters gathering around the kitchen, always hoping for an extra bite here and there; see USHMM, RG50.378*005, interview with Arkady Sergeyevich Teif.

112. Samuil Volk, Interview 43231, Visual History Archive.

113. Arad, *The Holocaust in the Soviet Union*, 509.

114. Rita Kazhdan, interviewed by author, St. Petersburg, May 12, 2005. Kazhdan here echoes a description of Sagal'chik; see Anna Sagal'chik, Interview 27830, Visual History Archive.

115. Leonid Melamed, Interview 29418, Visual History Archive.

116. USHMM, RG50.378*005, interview with Arkady Sergeyevich Teif. Like other narrators, Teif places the event he describes in September 1943; other records, however, indicate that he is referring to an incident in November of that year.

117. Anatol Wertheim, Chief of Staff of detachment No. 106 was tasked to investigate the murder; his reports largely confirms the narratives of Treister, Volk, Teif, Negnevitzki, and Kazhdan: Prikaz 050, Report by Anatol Wertheim, Chief of Staff, Dec. 8, 1943, in "Report on partisan unit #106," pp. 32b–36. Prikaz 051, Dec. 8, 1943, "Report on partisan unit #106," p. 47; Tec, *Defiance*, 213.

118. Cf. Arad, *In the Shadow*, 191ff.

119. "Report on partisan unit #106," p. 47b; Revekka Gringauz, Interview 38136, Visual History Archive, USC Shoah Foundation Institute, accessed online at USHMM on July 14, 2010; Sofia Libo, Interview 28024, Visual History Archive, USC Shoah Foundation Institute, accessed online at USHMM on July 21, 2010; USHMM, RG50.120*116, interview with Leonid Okon; USHMM, RG50.120*209, interview with Vladimir Mordkhilevich; Rita Kazhdan, interviewed by author, St. Petersburg, May 24, 2001.

120. "Report on partisan unit #106," p. 47b.

121. USHMM, RG50.120*116, interview with Leonid Okon.

122. USHMM, RG50.120*116, interview with Leonid Okon.

123. USHMM, RG50.120*209, interview with Vladimir Mordkhilevich.

124. USHMM, RG50.120*209, interview with Vladimir Mordkhilevich.
125. USHMM, RG50.120*116, interview with Leonid Okon.
126. USHMM, RG50.120*116, interview with Leonid Okon.
127. Zoia Oboz, Interview 29477, Visual History Archive.
128. USHMM, RG50.120*209, interview with Vladimir Mordkhilevich.
129. Chiari, *Alltag hinter der Front*, 263–269; Slepyan, "The Soviet Partisan Movement and the Holocaust," 7f.
130. Rita Kazhdan, interviewed by author, St. Petersburg, May 12, 2005.
131. See Slepyan, *Stalin's Guerillas*, 248.
132. Elena Drapkina, interviewed by author, St. Petersburg, April 26, 2001.
133. For an exemplary account of propaganda activities, see "Reports by Central Staff of the Partisan Movement to Central Committee of the Komsomol, Head Command, Soviet Narodnykh Komissarov et al.," in RGASPI, fond 69, opis 1, delo 25, p. 40ff.
134. Request by Sidorok, Deputy Secretary of the Ivenetsk Regional Committee of the Communist Party, to organize meetings in villages to discuss the "historic victories of the Red Army" and the need to support their campaigns, March 1944, in "Report on partisan unit #106," p. 15.
135. Amaliia Iakhontova, Interview 43211, Visual History Archive; similarly Ekaterina Tsirlina, Interview 28012, Visual History Archive,.
136. Anna Sagal'chik, Interview 27830, Visual History Archive.
137. See Sonia Zalesskaia, Interview 30810, Visual History Archive; Mikhail Treister, Interview 2324, Visual History Archive; Anna Sagal'chik, Interview 27830, Visual History Archive.
138. Vladimir Mordkhilevich, USHMM, RG50.120*209.
139. Vladimir Mordkhilevich, USHMM, RG50.120*209.
140. Samuil Volk, Interview 43231, Visual History Archive; similarly USHMM, RG50.120*209, interview with Vladimir Mordkhilevich.
141. Slepyan, *Stalin's Guerillas*, 193.
142. Kelly, *Childrens's World*, 115ff.
143. Prikaz 078 ordering A. Meltser to organize festivities to celebrate International Labor Day, in "Report on partisan unit #106," p. 50b. See also Tec, *Defiance*, 274f.
144. Prikaz 080, May 1, 1944, in "Report on partisan unit #106," pp. 52b–54b.
145. S. Persov, "Zamechatel'nyi dokument," article submitted to *Einikayt* on June 7, 1944, in USHMM, RG22.028M, "Archives of the Jewish Anti-Fascist Committee," reel 76, fond 8114, opis 1, delo 168, pp. 403–414b. The article about the letter includes its text.
146. Samuil Volk, Interview 43231, Visual History Archive.
147. "Report on partisan unit #106," pp. 21b–24 (Prikaz 036, October 3, 1943), pp. 45b–46b (Prikaz 069, March 8, 1944), pp. 52b–54b (Prikaz 080, May 1, 1944).
148. On the historical congruity between male heads of households and the state as proprietor of property and rights, and hence authority, see Frederick Engels, *The Origin of the Family, Private Property and the State*, ed. Eleanor Burke Leacock (New York: International Publishers, 1972). Feminist scholars, including Carol Pateman and Catharine MacKinnon, have developed this concept further to critique the state as purveyor and mediator of male dominance. A critical discussion, including an overview of this scholarship, is in Wendy Brown, "Finding the Man in the State," *Feminist Studies* 18, no. 1 (1992): 7–34.
149. "Report on partisan unit #106," pp. 105–105b.

150. "Report on partisan unit #106," p. 37; p. 56b. See also Shveibish, "Evreiskii semeinyi partizanskii otriad Sh. Zorina," 107.
151. USHMM, RG50.120*116, interview with Leonid Okon.
152. "Report on partisan unit #106," pp. 23–24.
153. "Report on partisan unit #106," p. 32; p. 30b.
154. Weitz, "The Heroic Man and the Ever-Changing Woman," 329.
155. USHMM, RG50.378*022, interview with Yakov Negnevitzki.
156. Petrova, "Deti Velikoi Otechestvennoi voiny," 223.
157. Leonid Melamed, Interview 29418, Visual History Archive.
158. "Resistance," *Oxford Dictionaries*, Oxford University Press, http://oxforddictionaries.com/definition/american_english/resistance, accessed August 25, 2012.
159. Bettina Aptheker, "'Get Over This Hurdle Because There's Another One Coming': Women's Resistance and Everyday Life," in Aptheker, *Tapestries of Life*, 170, 173.
160. Data on headcount in the Jewish family detachment, January 1944, in "Report on partisan unit #106," p. 109.
161. Tec, *Defiance*, 218; Slepyan, *Stalin's Guerillas*, 195.
162. Mariarosa Dalla Costa and Selma Jones, "Women and the Subversion of the Community," in Dalla Costa and Jones, *The Power of Women and the Subversion of Community* (Richmond, UK: The Falling Wall Press, 1972), 28.
163. See Hartmann, "The Unhappy Marriage," 14, for an analysis of such patriarchal setups.
164. Tzvetan Todorov, *Facing the Extreme: Moral Life in the Concentration Camps* (New York: Metropolitan Books, 1996), 7.
165. Ibid. 293f. See also Aptheker, "Get Over This Hurdle," 173, on the dailiness of women's work as a form of resistance against social pressures and productive of long-term social change.

Conclusion

1. Elena Drapkina, interviewed by author, St. Petersburg, April 26, 2001.
2. Elena Drapkina, interviewed by author, St. Petersburg, April 26, 2001; see also a round table discussion in Minsk in 1992, where a representative of the Belorussian Academy of Sciences continued to locate specific interest in Masha Bruskina's identification among Jewish journalists: "'Kak zvali neizvestnuiu?' Stenogramma 'kruglovo stola', Minsk, 23.10.1992," in Basin, ed., *Izvestnaia "neizvestnaia,"* http://www.homoliber.org/ru/kg/kg010001.html, accessed July 14, 2013.
3. Arkadii Brzhovskii, "Oni byli pervymi," *Belarus' Segodnia*, July 11, 2008, http://pda.sb.by/post/87303/, accessed August 24, 2009.
4. Frida Ped'ko, interviewed by author, St. Petersburg, May 13, 2005.
5. Frida Ped'ko, interviewed by author, St. Petersburg, May 13, 2005.
6. Leonid Smilovitskii, "Bor'ba evreev Belorussii za vozvrat svoego imushchestvo i zhilishch v pervoe poslevoennoe desiatiletie, 1944–1954 gg.," in *Belarus' u XX stahoddzi*, ed. V. I. Andreev, ed. (Minsk: Vodolei, 2002), 167f., available online at http://mb.s5x.org/homoliber.org/ru/xx/xx010120.html, accessed January 30, 2015.
7. Gerlach, *Kalkulierte Morde*, 11.
8. Gerlach, *Kalkulierte Morde*, 11.
9. See also Arkadyev and Dikhtyar, "The Unknown Girl," 201.
10. Elena Drapkina, interviewed by author, St. Petersburg, April 26, 2001.
11. See Greta Bucher, "Struggling to Survive: Soviet Women in the Postwar Years," *Journal of Women's History* 12, no. 1 (2000): 139.
12. Samuil Volk, Interview 43231, Visual History Archive.

13. Hosking, *The First Socialist Society*, 292.
14. Samuil Volk, Interview 43231, Visual History Archive.
15. Edele, *Soviet War Veterans*, 133, 195f; Manley, *To the Tashkent Station*, 260ff.
16. See chapter 6.
17. Rita Kazhdan, interviewed by author, St. Petersburg, May 24, 2001.
18. See the letters by Jewish survivors to the Jewish Anti-Fascist Committee describing antisemitic assaults by civilians and lack of support from state authorities, quoted in Smilovitski, "Bor'ba evreev Belorussii," 170.
19. Smilovitski, "Bor'ba evreev Belorussii," 170.
20. Rita Kazhdan, interviewed by author, St. Petersburg, May 24, 2001.
21. Alevtina Kuprikhina, Interview 49623, Visual History Archive; Alevtina Kuprikhina, interviewed by author, St. Petersburg, September 6, 2002.
22. "Berdichev," in Dean, ed., *Encyclopedia*,
23. Alevtina Kuprikhina, interviewed by author, St. Petersburg, September 6, 2002.
24. Many European countries and the U.S. commemorate Victory Day on May 8. However, the German military surrender in May 1945 became effective when it was May 9 Moscow Time, so that many European countries east of Germany mark the Day of Liberation on May 9.
25. Frida Ped'ko, interviewed by author, St. Petersburg, May 27, 2001.
26. Grigorii Erenburg, interviewed by author, St. Petersburg, May 19, 2005.
27. Grigorii Erenburg, interviewed by author, St. Petersburg, April 25, 2001.
28. Grigorii Erenburg, interviewed by author, St. Petersburg, April 25, 2001.
29. Amaliia Iakhontova, Interview 43211, Visual History Archive.
30. Frida Ped'ko, interviewed by author, St. Petersburg, May 13, 2005.
31. Romanovsky, "The Holocaust in the Eyes of the *Homo Sovieticus*," 376.
32. Rita Kazhdan, interviewed by author, St. Petersburg, May 24, 2001.
33. Elena Drapkina, interviewed by author, St. Petersburg, April 26, 2001.
34. Frida Ped'ko, interviewed by author, St. Petersburg, May 13, 2005.
35. Abrams, *Oral History Theory*, 53.
36. Il'ia Al'tman, "Memoralizatsia Kholokosta v Rossii: Istoria, sovremennost', perspektivy," in Gabovich, ed., *60 let spustia*, 509–530.
37. Anna Sagal'chik, Interview 27830, Visual History Archive.
38. A comprehensive documentation of the destruction of the JAFC, including official documents, can be found in Shimon Redlich and Ilya Altman, eds., *War, Holocaust, and Stalinism: A Documented Study of the Jewish Anti-Fascist Committee in the USSR* (Luxembourg: Harwood, 1995). See also Arno Lustiger, *Rotbuch: Stalin und die Juden; Die tragische Geschichte des Jüdischen Antifaschistischen Komitees und der sowjetischen Juden* (Berlin: Aufbau, 1998), and Joshua Rubenstein and Vladimir P. Naumov, eds., *Stalin's Secret Pogrom: The Postwar Inquisition of the Jewish Anti-Fascist Committee* (New Haven: Yale University Press, 2001).
39. See Ilya Altman, "The History and Fate of *The Black Book* and *The Unknown Black Book*." Sasha Charnyj documents a further incident of censorship in the USSR in the 1960s, describing how the publication of a book that discusses the 1943 uprising in the ghetto of Warsaw in the USSR was hindered; see Charnyi, "Sovietskii gosudarstvennyi antisemitizm v tsenzure nachala 60-kh godov (na primere sud'by knigi B. Marka 'Vosstanie v varshavskom getto')," *Vestnik Evreiskogo Universiteta v Moskve* 2, no. 15 (1997): 76–81.
40. See A. Lokshin, "'Delo vrachei': Otkliki trudiashchikhsia," *Vestnik Evreiskogo Universiteta v Moskve* 1(5) (1994): 52–62.
41. Elena Drapkina, interviewed by author, April 2001, St. Petersburg.

42. See chapter 6.

43. Frida Ped'ko, interviewed by author, St. Petersburg, May 13, 2005; see also Walke, "'It Wasn't That Bad in the Ghetto, Was It?'"

44. Boris Gal'perin, interviewed by author, St. Petersburg, May 16, 2001.

45. Altshuler, "Jewish Holocaust Commemoration Activity';" Frank Grüner, "Jüdischer Glaube und religiöse Praxis unter dem stalinistischen Regime in der Sowjetunion während der Kriegs- und Nachkriegsjahre," *Jahrbücher für Geschichte Osteuropas* N.F. 52, no. 4 (2004): 534-556.

46. See Olga Kalacheva and Oksana Karpenko, "Leben im 'Zustand der Wahl'? Die Ambivalenz der ethnischen Identitätsbildung bei russischen Juden," in *Post-sowjetische Ethnizitäten: Ethnische Gemeinden in St. Petersburg und Berlin/Potsdam*, eds. Ingrid Oswald and Viktor Voronkov (Berlin: Berliner Debatte, 1997), 38-54; Zvi Gitelman, "The Reconstruction of Community and Jewish Identity in Russia," *East European Affairs* 24.1 (1999): 35-56; Viktor Voronkov and Elena Chikadze, "Different Generations of Leningrad Jews in the Context of Public/Private Division: Paradoxes of Ethnicity," in *Biographical Research in Eastern Europe: Altered Lives and Broken Biographies*, eds. Robert Miller, Robin Humphrey, and Elena Zdravomyslova, 239-262; and Elena E. Nosenko-Shtein, "O kollektivnoi pamiati rossiiskikh evreev na rubezhe vekov (predvaritel'nye nabliudeniia)," *Etnograficheskoie Obozrenie* 6 (2009): 20-29.

47. Frida Ped'ko, interviewed by author, May 2005, St. Petersburg.

48. Samuil Volk, Interview 43231, Visual History Archive.

49. Frances Pine, Deema Kaneff, and Haldis Haukanes, "Memory, Politics and Religion: A Perspective on Europe," in *Memory, Politics and Religion: The Past Meets the Present in Europe*, ed. Frances Pine (Münster, Germany: Lit, 2004), 6.

50. Anna Sagal'chik, Interview 27830, Visual History Archive.

51. Elena Drapkina, interviewed by author, May 2005, St. Petersburg.

52. Boris Gal'perin, interviewed by author, May 2001, St. Petersburg.

53. Cf. Richard Sennett, *The Corrosion of Character: The Personal Consequences of Work in the New Capitalism* (New York: Norton 1998); Margret Kraul and Winfried Marotzki, "Bildung und biographische Arbeit: Eine Einleitung," in *Biographische Arbeit*, ed. Margret Kraul (Opladen: Leske+Budrich 2002), 7-21.

54. Miller et al., "Introduction: Biographical Research and Historical Watersheds," 15.

55. Valery Chervyakov, Zvi Gitelman, and Vladimir Shapiro, "Religion and Ethnicity: Judaism in the Ethnic Consciousness of Contemporary Russian Jews," *Ethnic and Racial Studies* 20, no. 2 (1997): 282.

56. See also Elena E. Nosenko-Shtein, "O kollektivnoi pamiati."

57. Ingrid Oswald and Viktor Voronkov "Einleitung," in Ingrid Oswald and Viktor Voronkov, eds., *Post-sowjetische Ethnizitäten*, 8.

58. Detlev Claussen, "Das Verschwinden des Sozialismus: Zur ethnonationalistischen Auflösung des Sowjetsystems," *Hannoversche Schriften 2: Kritik des Ethnonationalismus*, eds. Detlev Claussen, Oskar Negt, and Michael Werz (Frankfurt am Main: Neue Kritik, 2000), 16-41.

59. Luisa Passerini's work on working-class memories of Italian fascism and, more to the point of this article, Daria Khubova and Irina Sherbakova and other scholars' work on the construction of Gulag memory in the former Soviet Union provide strong and insightful examples of this approach; see Passerini, "Work Ideology and Consensus under Italian Fascism," and Daria Khubova et al., "After Glasnost: Oral History in the Soviet Union," in *Memory and Totalitarianism*, ed. Luisa Passerini, 3rd ed. (New York: Oxford University Press, 2009), 89-102; see also Introduction.

60. For example Arad, *The Holocaust in the Soviet Union*; Ray Brandon and Wendy Lower, eds., *The Shoah in Ukraine: History, Testimony, Memorialization* (Bloomington and Indianapolis: Indiana University Press, 2010); Norman Davies and Antony Polonsky, eds., *Jews in Eastern Poland and the USSR, 1939-46* (Basingstoke, UK: Macmillan, 1991); Lucjan Dobroszycki and Jeffrey S. Gurock, eds., *The Holocaust in the Soviet Union: Studies and Sources on the Destruction of the Jews in the Nazi-Occupied Territories of the USSR, 1941-1945* (Armonk, NY: M. E. Sharpe, 1993); Andrew Ezergailis, *The Holocaust in Latvia, 1941-1944: The Missing Center* (Riga and Washington: The Historical Institute of Latvia/USHMM, 1996); Wendy Lower, *Nazi Empire-Building and the Holocaust in Ukraine* (Chapel Hill: University of North Carolina Press, 2007); Rubenstein and Altman, eds., *The Unknown Black Book*; Timothy Snyder, *Bloodlands: Europe Between Hitler and Stalin* (New York: Basic Books, 2010); and Anton Weiss-Wendt, *Murder Without Hatred: Estonians and the Holocaust* (Syracuse, NY: Syracuse University Press, 2010). In Russian, recent publications include Vinnitsa, *Slovo pamiati*; Vinnitsa, *Gorech' i bol'*; Botvinnik, *Pamiatniki genotsida evreev Belarusi*; Il'ia Al'tman, ed., *Kholokost—soprotivlenie—vozrozhdenie*; Smilovitskii, *Katastrofa evreev v Belorussii*; and Al'tman, *Zhertvy nenavisti*. Chernoglazova, ed., *Tragedia evreev Belorussii*; Chernoglazova, ed., *Judenfrei! Svobodno ot evreev!*; Ioffe et al., eds., *Kholokost v Belarusi, 1941-1944*; for first-person accounts, see L. Leibov, ed., *Kniga zhivykh*, Vol. 1; L. A. Aizenshtat, ed., *Kniga zhivykh*, Vol. 2; ... *Na perekriostkakh sudeb: Iz vospominanii byvshikh uznikov getto i pravednikov narodov mira*, eds. O. M. Arkadyeva et al. (Minsk: Chetyrie Chetverti, 2001); Tsukerman, ed., *Katastrofa: Poslednie svideteli*.

61. Zvi Gitelman, "Politics and the Historiography of the Holocaust in the Soviet Union," in *Bitter Legacy*, ed. Zvi Gitelman (Bloomington and Indianapolis: Indiana University Press, 1997), 14, 18.

62. A discussion of these numbers is in Michael Ellman and S. Maksudov, "Soviet Deaths in the Great Patriotic War: A Note," *Europe-Asia Studies* 46.4 (1994): 671-680.

63. Aleksei Litvin, "K voprosu o kolichestve liudskikh poter' Belarusi v gody Velikoi Otechestvennoi voiny (1941-1945 gg.)," in Andreev, ed., *Belarus' v XX stahoddzi*, 127-138.

64. Tumarkin, *The Living and the Dead*, 50

65. Adam Hochschild. "Tug of War: Timothy Snyder Looks East," review of *Bloodlands: Europe Between Hitler and Stalin*, by Timothy Snyder, *Harper's Magazine*, February 2011, 81f. Hochschild refers here to the lack of knowledge of and interest in this particular part of European history, but I think the general tendency he describes can be observed elsewhere too: "We Americans prefer historical characters who can be separated into heroes and villains, but in Eastern Europe that distinction is often hard to make."

66. See Peter Novick's detailed account of how the Holocaust became a topic of interest in the United States; Peter Novick, *The Holocaust in American Life* (Boston: Houghton Mifflin, 1999).

67. A milestone for these efforts was the Stockholm International Forum on the Holocaust in 2000; the declaration of the forum is available at http://www.holocaustremembrance.com/about-us/stockholm-declaration.

68. Hannah Arendt, "Social Science Techniques and the Study of Concentration Camps," in *Essays in Understanding, 1930-1954*, ed. Jerome Kohn (New York: Harcourt, 1994), 241.

69. Arendt, "Social Science Techniques and the Study of Concentration Camps," 233.

70. In the above-quoted essay, Arendt attempted to outline the difference between the "comprehensible" and the "incomprehensible" (the extermination camps) and

explicitly identifies the "establishment of ghettos in Eastern Europe and the concentration of all Jews in them during the first years" as "hardly surprising": "All this appeared hideous and criminal but entirely rational" (Arendt, "Social Science," 235). Arendt does not mention the massacres within and close to these ghettos, perhaps because she was not aware of their extent at the time of her writing in 1950. It is, therefore, hard to tell whether she would place them in the realm of the comprehensible or the incomprehensible.

71. Joan Ringelheim, "Genocide and Gender: A Split Memory," in *Gender and Catastrophe*, ed. Ronit Lentin (London: Zed Books, 1997), 22.

Sources

I. Interviews cited

Interviews by the author, interviews in author's possession
Drapkina, Elena. Interviewed by author. St. Petersburg. April 26, 2001.
Drapkina, Elena. Interviewed by author. St. Petersburg. September 10, 2002.
Drapkina, Elena. Interviewed by author. St. Petersburg. May 18, 2005.
Erenburg, Grigorii. Interviewed by author. St. Petersburg. April 25, 2001.
Erenburg, Grigorii. Interviewed by author. St. Petersburg. September 2, 2002.
Erenburg, Grigorii. Interviewed by author. St. Petersburg. May 19, 2005.
Gal'perin, Boris. Interviewed by author. St. Petersburg. May 16, 2001.
Glazebnaia, Ol'ga. Interviewed by author. Minsk. October 11, 2002.
Gol'braikh, Leonid. Interviewed by author. St. Petersburg. May 5, 2001.
Gol'braikh, Leonid. Interviewed by author. St. Petersburg. May 11, 2005.
Kazhdan, Rita. Interviewed by author. St. Petersburg. May 24, 2001.
Kazhdan, Rita. Interviewed by author. St. Petersburg. May 12, 2005.
Kuprikhina, Alevtina. Interviewed by author. St. Petersburg. September 6, 2002.
Ped'ko, Frida. Interviewed by author. St. Petersburg. May 27, 2001.
Ped'ko, Frida. Interviewed by author. St. Petersburg. May 13, 2005.
Treister, Mikhail. Interviewed by author and Eva Determann. Minsk. March 19, 2003.
Tsirlina, Ekaterina. Interviewed by author. Minsk. October 13, 2002.
Zelenko, Roza. Interviewed by author. Minsk. October 11, 2002.
Zelenko, Roza. Interviewed by author. Minsk. October 20, 2002.

Testimonies of the Visual History Archive—USC Shoah Foundation Institute, Los Angeles, CA, USA
Aizenshtadt, Pesia. Interview 29732. Visual History Archive. USC Shoah Foundation Institute. Accessed online at USHMM on July 12, 2010.
Belen'kaia, Liubov. Interview 30764. Visual History Archive. USC Shoah Foundation Institute. Accessed online at USHMM on March 9, 2010.
Boiko, Mariia. Interview 32128. Visual History Archive. USC Shoah Foundation Institute. Accessed online at USHMM on July 12, 2010.
Chernina, Sofiia. Interview 30952. Visual History Archive. USC Shoah Foundation Institute. Accessed online at USHMM on April 1, 2010.
Drapkina, Elena. Interview 2325. Visual History Archive. USC Shoah Foundation Institute. Accessed online at USHMM on January 22, 2010.
Fridliand, Lev. Interview 32057. Visual History Archive. USC Shoah Foundation Institute. Accessed online at USHMM on March 10, 2010.
Gol'braikh, Leonid. Interview 42481. Visual History Archive. USC Shoah Foundation Institute. Accessed online at USHMM on Jan 29, 2010.
Gol'din, Aleksandr. Interview 30675. Visual History Archive. USC Shoah Foundation Institute. Accessed online at USHMM on March 8, 2010.

Gringauz, Revekka. Interview 38136. Visual History Archive. USC Shoah Foundation Institute. Accessed online at USHMM on July 14, 2010.
Iakhontova (Khurgina), Amaliia Moiseevna. Interview 43211, Visual History Archive. USC Shoah Foundation Institute. Accessed online at USHMM on July 20, 2010.
Kaplan, Sholom. Interview 4950. Visual History Archive. USC Shoah Foundation Institute. Accessed online at USHMM on June 24, 2010.
Kazhdan, Rita. Interview 654. Visual History Archive. USC Shoah Foundation Institute. Accessed online at USHMM on January 15, 2010.
Kriuchkova, Liudmila. Interview 50719. Visual History Archive. USC Shoah Foundation Institute. Accessed online at USHMM on February 4, 2010.
Kuprikhina, Alevtina. Interview 49623. Visual History Archive. USC Shoah Foundation Institute. Accessed online at USHMM on February 23, 2010.
Libo, Sofia. Interview 28024. Visual History Archive. USC Shoah Foundation Institute. Accessed online at USHMM on July 21, 2010.
Melamed, Leonid. Interview 29418.Visual History Archive. USC Shoah Foundation Institute. Accessed online at USHMM on July 14, 2010.
Oboz, Zoia. Interview 29477. Visual History Archive. USC Shoah Foundation Institute. Accessed online at USHMM on July 21, 2010.
Pogorelaia, Vera. Interview 28756. Visual History Archive. USC Shoah Foundation Institute. Accessed online at USHMM on March 11, 2010.
Polonskaya, Dora. Interview 6936. Visual History Archive. USC Shoah Foundation Institute. Accessed online at USHMM on January 20, 2010.
Rusakovich, Aleksandra. Interview 37012. Visual History Archive. USC Shoah Foundation Institute. Accessed online at USHMM on March 31, 2010.
Sagal'chik, Anna. Interview 27830. Visual History Archive. USC Shoah Foundation Institute. Accessed online at USHMM on July 22, 2010.
Shostak, Polya. Interview 20969. Visual History Archive. USC Shoah Foundation Institute. Accessed online at USHMM on June 23, 2010.
Shumina, Aleksandra. Interview 49152. Visual History Archive. USC Shoah Foundation Institute. Accessed online at USHMM on March 16, 2010.
Slutskaia, Galina. Interview 47490. Visual History Archive. USC Shoah Foundation Institute. Accessed online at USHMM on March 31, 2010.
Smirnova, Vera. Interview 30334. Visual History Archive. USC Shoah Foundation Institute. Accessed online at USHMM on May 18, 2010.
Treister, Mikhail. Interview 2324. Visual History Archive. USC Shoah Foundation Institute. Accessed online at the USHMM on June 25, 2010.
Tsirlina, Ekaterina. Interview 28012. Visual History Archive. USC Shoah Foundation Institute. Accessed online at USHMM on July 13, 2010.
Volk, Samuil. Interview 43231. Visual History Archive. USC Shoah Foundation Institute. Accessed online at USHMM on July 23, 2010.
Zalesskaia, Sonia. Interview 30810. Visual History Archive. USC Shoah Foundation Institute. Accessed online at USHMM on July 13, 2010.

Interviews conducted by the United States Holocaust Memorial Museum—Oral History Branch, Washington, DC, USA

RG50.120*116. Oral History, Israel Documentation Project. Interview with Leonid Okon (Okun).
RG50.120*209. Oral History, Israel Documentation Project. Interview with Vladimir Mordkhilevich.

RG50.378*002. Oral History, Belarus Documentation Project. Interview with Tatyana Samuilovna Gildiner.
RG50.378*005. Oral History, Belarus Documentation Project. Interview with Arkady Sergeyevich Teif.
RG50.378*006. Oral History, Belarus Documentation Project. interview with Ida Moyseyevina Brion.
RG50.378*018. Oral History, Belarus Documentation Project. Interview with Genya Moyseyevna Kobrina.
RG50.378*022. Oral History, Belarus Documentation Project. Interview with Yakov Negnevitzki.
RG50.378*025. Oral History, Belarus Documentation Project. Interview with Vera Vladimirovna Smirnova.

Oral Testimonies conducted for the Yad Vashem—The Holocaust Martyrs' and Remembrance Authority, Jerusalem, Israel
Oral Testimony of Lisa Gordon, Yad Vashem Archives, YV 4047.
Oral Testimony of Sara Goland, Yad Vashem Archives, YV 03.4126.
Oral Testimony of Elena Gringauz, Yad Vashem Archives, YV 03.4126.
Oral Testimony of Leonid Okun, Yad Vashem Archives, YV 03.6278.

II. Interview-related materials

Boroda, Menukha. "Interview of an eyewitness of the Holocaust. Menukha Boroda, with Dr. Irina P. Gerasimova, director of the Museum for the History and Culture of Belorussian Jews." No date; video in Russian. *Moio mestechko—My Shtetl.* http://shtetle.co.il/Shtetls/slavnoe/boroda.html.
Gal'perin, Boris Mikhailovich. "Boris Mikhailovich Gal'perin." Unpublished autobiography, includes lists, maps, and sketches. St. Petersburg, 2000. Copy in author's possession.
Ped'ko, Frida. "Avtobiografiia." St. Petersburg 2001. Copy in author's possession.

III. Archival sources

Leo Baeck Institute, New York, USA
ME 398.MM50. Karl Loesten (Löwenstein), "Aus der Hölle Minsk in das 'Paradies' Theresienstadt."

National Archives Belarus (NARB) Minsk, Republic of Belarus
Fond 4386. "Tsentral'nyi Komitet KP(b)B."
Fond 370. "Generalkommissariat Weißruthenien."

Russian Archive for Social and Political History (RGASPI), Moscow, Russia
Fond 69. "Tsentral'nyi shtab partizanskogo dvizheniia pri stavke Verkhovnogo Glavkomandovaniia (TsShPD), 1942–1944."
Fond 625. "Ponomarenko Panteleimon Kondrat'evich (1902–1984)."

United States Holocaust Memorial Museum (USHMM), Washington, DC, USA
Accession 1996.A.0169. "Holocaust related records from European archives collected by Yad Vashem, 1939–1960."

Record Group 22.001. "Records relating to the Soviet Union under Nazi Occupation, 1941–1945."

Record Group 22.002M. "Selected Records of the Extraordinary State Commission to Investigate German-Fascist Crimes Committed on Soviet Territory from the USSR."

Record Group 02.174. "Reminiscences of Albert Lapidus, from Baltimore, a former prisoner of the Minsk ghetto."

Record Group 22.008M*01*. "Records relating to Auschwitz and other camps from the Central State Archive of the Ministry of Defense, Podolsk, 1940-1945."

Record Group 22.016. "Reports and Investigative Materials Compiled by the Military Commissions of the Red (Soviet) Army Related to the Crimes Committed by the Nazis and Their Collaborators on the Occupied Territories of the Soviet Union and Eastern Europe during WWII, 1942–1945."

Record Group 22.028M. "Archives of the Jewish Anti-Fascist Committee."

IV. Bibliography

Abrams, Lynn. *Oral History Theory*. London and New York: Routledge, 2010.

Agamben, Giorgio. *Remnants of Auschwitz*. New York: Zone, 1999.

Ainsztein, Reuben. *Jewish Resistance in Nazi-Occupied Eastern Europe*. London: Elek Books, 1974.

Aizenshtat, L. A., ed. *Kniga zhivykh: Vospominaniia evreev-frontovikov, uznikov getto i kontslagerei, boitsov partizanskikh otriadov, zhitelei blokadnogo Leningrada*. Vol. 2. Saint Petersburg: Akropol', 2004.

Albert, Gleb J. "From 'World Soviet' to 'Fatherland of All Proletarians.' Anticipated World Society and Global Thinking in Early Soviet Russia." *InterDisciplines* 1 (2012): 85–119.

Alexievich, Svetlana. *U voiny ne zhenskoe litso* (Moscow: Palmira, 2004 [orig. 1985]).

Allen, Robert C. *Farm to Factory: A Reinterpretation of the Soviet Industrial Revolution*. Princeton: Princeton University Press, 2009.

Althusser, Louis. "Ideology and Ideological State Apparatuses: Notes towards an Investigation" (orig. 1971). In *Lenin and Philosophy and Other Essays*. Translated by Ben Brewster. New York: Monthly Review Press, 2001.

Altshuler, Mordechai. "Jewish Warfare and the Participation of Jews in Combat In the Soviet Union as Reflected in Soviet and Western Historiography." In Yisrael Gutman and Gideon Greif, eds., *The Historiography of the Holocaust Period: Proceedings of the Fifth Yad Vashem International Historical Conference*, 217–239. Jerusalem: Yad Vashem, 1988.

——. "Jewish Holocaust Commemoration Activity in the USSR under Stalin." *Yad Vashem Studies* 30 (2002): 271–296.

Al'tman, Il'ia. *Evrei v Velikoi Otechestvennoi voine: Vklad v pobedu; Katalog vystavki*. Moscow: Nauchno-prosvetitel'nyi tsentr "Kholokost," 1995.

——. *Zhertvy nenavisti: Kholokost v SSSR 1941–1945 gg*. Moscow: Kovcheg, 2002.

——. "Memorializatsiia Kholokosta v Rossii: Istoria, sovremennost', perspektivy." In Mikhail Gabovich, ed., *Pamiat' o voine: 60 let spustia; Rossiia, Germaniia, Evropa*, 2nd ed., 509–530. Moscow: Novoe Literaturnoe Obozrenie, 2005.

Al'tman, Il'ia, ed. *Kholokost na territorii SSSR: Entsiklopediia*. Moscow: ROSSPEN, 2009.

Al'tman, Il'ia et al., eds. *Kholokost—soprotivlenie—vozrozhdenie: Evreiskii narod v gody Vtoroi mirovoi voiny i poslevoennyi period 1939–1948*. Moscow: Fond Kholokost, 2000.

Altman, Ilya. "The History and Fate of *The Black Book* and *The Unknown Black Book.*" In Joshua Rubenstein and Ilya Altman, eds., *The Unknown Black Book: The Holocaust in the German-Occupied Soviet Territories*, xix–xxxix. Bloomington and Indianapolis: Indiana University Press, 2008.

Anderson, Benedict. *Imagined Communities: Reflections on the Origins and Spread of Nationalism.* London: Verso, 1983.

Angrick, Andrej, and Peter Klein. *The "Final Solution" in Riga: Exploitation and Annihilation, 1941–1944.* New York: Berghahn 2009.

Anthias, Floya. "Where Do I Belong? Narrating Collective Identity and Translocal Positionality." *Ethnicities* 2, no. 4 (2002): 491–514.

Aptheker, Bettina. *Tapestries of Life: Women's Work, Women's Consciousness, and the Meaning of Daily Experience.* Amherst: University of Massachusetts Press, 1989.

Arad, Yitzhak. "The Destruction of the Jews in German-Occupied Territories of the Soviet Union." In Joshua Rubenstein and Ilya Altman, eds., *The Unknown Black Book*, xiii–xvii. Bloomington and Indianapolis: Indiana University Press, 2008.

———. "The Holocaust of Soviet Jewry in the Occupied Territory of the Soviet Union." *Yad Vashem Studies* 21 (1991): 1–47.

———. *The Holocaust in the Soviet Union.* Lincoln: University of Nebraska Press, 2009.

———. *In the Shadow of the Red Banner.* New York and Jerusalem: Gefen, 2010.

Arad, Itzhak, and T. Pavlova, eds. *Neizvestnaia Chornaya kniga.* Jerusalem: Yad Vashem, and Moscow: State Archive of the Russian Federation, 1993.

Arendt, Hannah. "Social Science Techniques and the Study of Concentration Camps" (orig. 1950). In Jerome Kohn, ed. *Hannah Arendt: Essays in Understanding, 1930–1954*, 232–247. New York: Harcourt, 1994.

———. "Understanding and Politics" (orig. 1954). In Jerome Kohn, ed. *Hannah Arendt: Essays In Understanding, 1930–1954*, 307–327. New York: Harcourt, 1994.

———. *The Origins of Totalitarianism.* New York: Harcourt, 1968.

———. *Men in Dark Times.* New York: Harcourt, 1968.

Arkadyev, Lev, and Ada Dikhtyar. "The Unknown Girl: A Documentary Story." *Yiddish Writers Almanac* 1 (1987): 161–204.

Arkadyeva, O. M., et al., eds. . . . *Na perekriostkakh sudeb: Iz vospominanii byvshikh uznikov getto i pravednikov narodov mira.* Minsk: Chetyrie Chetverti, 2001.

Arnold, Sabine. *Stalingrad im sowjetischen Gedächtnis: Kriegserinnerung und Geschichtsbild im totalitären Staat.* Bochum, Germany: Projekt-Verlag, 1998.

Assmann, Jan. *Das kulturelle Gedächtnis: Schrift, Erinnerung, und politische Identität in frühen Hochkulturen.* Munich: Beck, 1992.

Baer, Elizabeth, and Myrna Goldenberg, eds. *Experience and Expression: Women, the Nazis, and the Holocaust.* Detroit: Wayne State University Press, 2003.

Barwig, Klaus, Günter Saathoff et al., eds. *Entschädigung für NS-Zwangsarbeit: Rechtliche, historische und politische Aspekte.* Baden-Baden, Germany: Nomos, 1998.

Basin, Iakov, ed. *Izvestnaia "neizvestnaia": Sbornik materialov.* Minsk: IBB, 2007.

Bauer, Yehuda. *Rethinking the Holocaust.* New Haven and London: Yale University Press, 2001.

———. *The Death of the Shtetl.* New Haven: Yale University Press, 2009.

Bauer, Yehuda, with Nili Keren. *A History of the Holocaust.* New York: Watts, 1982.

Baumel, Judith Tydor. *Double Jeopardy: Gender and the Holocaust.* London: Vallentine Mitchell, 1998.

———. "'You Said the Words You Wanted Me to Hear but I Heard the Words You Couldn't Bring Yourself to Say': Women's First Person Accounts of the Holocaust." *Oral History Review* 27, no.1 (2000): 17–56.

Bemporad, Elissa. *Becoming Soviet Jews: The Bolshevik Experiment in Minsk.* Bloomington and Indianapolis: Indiana University Press, 2013.
——. "Behavior Unbecoming a Communist: Jewish Religious Practice in Soviet Minsk." *Jewish Social Studies* 14, no. 2 (2008): 1–31.
——. "The Yiddish Experiment in Soviet Minsk." *East European Jewish Affairs* 37, no. 1 (2007): 91–107.
Bender, Sara. *The Jews of Białystok during World War II and the Holocaust.* Waltham, MA: Brandeis University Press, 2008.
Benz, Ute, and Wolfgang Benz, eds. *Sozialisation und Traumatisierung: Kinder in der Zeit des Nationalsozialismus.* Frankfurt am Main: Fischer, 1998.
Berg, Mary. *The Diary of Mary Berg: Growing up in the Warsaw Ghetto.* Oxford: Oneworld, 2006.
Bergen, Doris. *War and Genocide: A Concise History of the Holocaust.* Lanham, MD: Rowman & Littlefield, 2009.
Berkhoff, Karel. *Harvest of Despair: Life and Death in Ukraine under Nazi Rule.* Cambridge, MA: Harvard University Press, 2004.
Berkner, Sergei. *Zhizn' i bor'ba belostokskogo getto.* Moscow: Rossiiskaia Biblioteka Kholokosta, 2001.
Bernard-Donals, Michael, and Richard Glejzer, eds. *Witnessing the Disaster: Essays on Representation and the Holocaust.* Madison: University of Wisconsin Press, 2003.
Bonwetsch, Bernd. "Der 'Große Vaterländische Krieg': Vom öffentlichen Schweigen unter Stalin zum Heldenkult unter Breschnew." In Babette Quinkert, ed., *"Wir sind die Herren dieses Landes": Ursachen, Verlauf und Folgen des deutschen Überfalls auf die Sowjetunion,* 166–187. Hamburg: VSA, 2002.
Borland, Katherine. "'That's Not What I Said': Interpretive Conflict in Oral Narrative Research." In Sherna Berger Gluck and Daphne Patai, eds. *Women's Words: The Feminist Practice of Oral History,* 63–76. New York: Routledge, 1991.
Borodina, A., and D. Borodin. "Baba ili tovarishch? Ideal novoi sovetskoi zhenshchiny v 20-kh–30-kh godakh." In V. I. Uspenskaia, ed., *Zhenskie i gendernye issledovaniia v Tverskom gosudarstvennom universitete,* 45–51. Tver', Russia: Gosudarstvennyi Universitet, 2000. http://tvergenderstudies.ru/44. Accessed online July 7, 2013.
Bos, Pascale Rachel. "Women and the Holocaust: Analyzing Gender Difference." In Elizabeth Baer and Myrna Goldenberg, eds., *Experience and Expression: Women, the Nazis, and the Holocaust,* 23–52. Detroit: Wayne State University Press, 2003.
Botvinnik, Marat. *Pamiatniki genotsida evreev Belarusi.* Minsk: Belaruskaia Navuka, 2000.
Boym, Svetlana. *The Future of Nostalgia.* New York: Basic Books, 2001.
Bracewell, Wendy. "Rape in Kosovo: Masculinity and Serbian Nationalism." *Nations and Nationalisms* 6, no. 4 (2000): 563–590.
Brandenberger, David. "Proletarian Internationalism, 'Soviet Patriotism' and the Rise of Russocentric Etatism During the Stalinist 1930s." *Left History* 6, no. 2 (2000): 80–100.
Brandon, Ray, and Wendy Lower, eds. *The Shoah in Ukraine: History, Testimony, Memorialization.* Bloomington and Indianapolis: Indiana University Press, 2010.
Bridenthal, Renate, Atina Grossman, and Marion Kaplan, eds. *When Biology Became Destiny: Women in Weimar and Nazi Germany.* New York: Monthly Review Press, 1984.
Brown, Kate. *A Biography of No Place: From Ethnic Borderland to Soviet Heartland.* Cambridge, MA: Harvard University Press, 2005.

Brown, Wendy. "Finding the Man in the State." *Feminist Studies* 18, no. 1 (1992): 7–34.
Browning, Christopher. *Nazi Policy, Jewish Workers, German Killers.* New York: Cambridge University Press, 2000.
Brubaker, Rogers. "Nationhood and the National Question in the Soviet Union and Post-Soviet Eurasia: An Institutionalist Account." *Theory and Society* 23, no. 1 (1994): 47–78.
Bucher, Greta. "Struggling to Survive: Soviet Women in the Postwar Years." *Journal of Women's History* 12, no. 1 (2000): 137–159.
Burke, Peter. "History as Social Memory." In Thomas Butler, ed., *Memory, History, Culture and the Mind*, 97–113. New York: Blackwell, 1989.
Caruth, Cathy. *Unclaimed Experience: Trauma, Narrative, and History.* Baltimore: The Johns Hopkins University Press, 1996.
Charnyi, Sasha. "Sovietskii gosudarstvennyi antisemitizm v tsenzure nachala 60-kh godov (na primere sud'by knigi B. Marka 'Vosstanie v varshavskom getto.'" *Vestnik Evreiskogo Universiteta v Moskve* 2, no. 15 (1997): 76–81.
Chernoglazova, Raisa, ed. *Tragediia evreev Belorussii (1941–1944 gg.): Sbornik materialov i dokumentov.* Minsk: Izd. E. S. Gal'perin, 1997.
———, ed. *Judenfrei! Svobodno ot evreev! Istoriia minskogo getto v dokumentakh.* Minsk: Asobny Dakh, 1999.
Chervinsky, Julie, ed. *Lives of the Great Patriotic War: The Untold Stories of Soviet Jewish Soldiers in the Red Army during World War II.* New York: Blavatnik Archive Foundation, 2011.
Chervyakov, Valery, Zvi Gitelman, and Vladimir Shapiro. "Religion and Ethnicity: Judaism in the Ethnic Consciousness of Contemporary Russian Jews." *Ethnic and Racial Studies* 20, no. 2 (1997): 280–305.
Chiari, Bernhard. *Alltag hinter der Front: Besatzung, Kollaboration und Widerstand in Weißrussland, 1941–1944.* Düsseldorf, Germany: Droste, 1998.
Cholawsky, Shalom. *The Jews of Bielorussia during World War II.* Amsterdam: Harwood, 1998.
Claussen, Detlev. "Das Verschwinden des Sozialismus: Zur ethnonationalistischen Auflösung des Sowjetsystems." In Detlev Claussen, Oskar Negt, and Michael Werz, eds. *Hannoversche Schriften 2: Kritik des Ethnonationalismus*, 16–41. Frankfurt am Main: Neue Kritik, 2000.
Cohen, Boaz. "The Children's Voice: Postwar Collection of Testimonies from Child Survivors of the Holocaust." *Holocaust and Genocide Studies* 21, no. 1 (2007): 73–95.
Cole, Tim. "Ghettoization." In Dan Stone, ed., *The Historiography of the Holocaust*, 65–87. New York: Palgrave Macmillan, 2006.
Connerton, Paul. *How Societies Remember.* New York: Cambridge University Press, 1989.
Curilla, Wolfgang. *Die deutsche Ordnungspolizei und der Holocaust im Baltikum und in Weißrussland 1941–1944.* Paderborn, Germany: Ferdinand Schöningh, 2006.
Czerniakow, Adam. *The Warsaw Diary of Adam Czerniakow: Prelude to Doom.* Edited by Raul Hilberg et al. Chicago: Ivan R. Dee, 1999.
Dalla Costa, Mariarosa, and Selma Jones. *The Power of Women and the Subversion of Community.* Richmond, UK: Falling Wall Press, 1972.
Das, Veena. "Trauma and Testimony: Implications for Political Community." *Anthropological Theory* 3, no. 3 (2003): 293–307.
Davies, Norman, and Antony Polonsky, eds. *Jews in Eastern Poland and the USSR, 1939–46.* Basingstoke, UK: Macmillan, 1991.

Davis, Angela Y. "Women and Capitalism: Dialectics of Oppression and Liberation" (orig. 1977). In Joy James and T. Denean Sharpley-Whiting, eds., *The Black Feminist Reader*, 146–182. Malden, MA: Blackwell, 2000.

Dean, Martin. *Collaboration in the Holocaust: Crimes of the Local Police in Belorussia and Ukraine, 1941–44*. New York: St. Martin's Press, 2000.

———. "Life and Death in the 'Gray Zone' of Jewish Ghettos in Nazi-Occupied Europe: The Unknown, the Ambiguous, and the Disappeared." In Jonathan Petropoulous and John K. Roth, eds., *Gray Zones: Ambiguity and Compromise in the Holocaust and Its Aftermath*, 205–221. New York: Berghahn Books 2005.

Dean, Martin, ed. *Encyclopedia of Camps and Ghettos 1933–1945*. Vol. 2, *Ghettos in German-Occupied Eastern Europe*. Bloomington and Indianapolis: Indiana University Press in association with the United States Holocaust Memorial Museum, 2011.

Dieckmann, Christoph. *Deutsche Besatzungspolitik in Litauen*. 2 vols. Göttingen, Germany: Wallstein, 2012.

Dekel-Chen, Jonathan. *Farming the Red Land: Jewish Agricultural Colonization and Local Soviet Power, 1924–1941*. New Haven: Yale University Press, 2005.

Dobroszycki, Lucjan, and Jeffrey S. Gurock, eds. *The Holocaust in the Soviet Union: Studies and Sources on the Destruction of the Jews in the Nazi-Occupied Territories of the USSR, 1941–1945*. Armonk, NY: M. E. Sharpe, 1993.

Du Bois, W. E. B. "The Strivings of the Negro People." *The Atlantic*, August 1897, 194–198.

———, "The Negro and the Warsaw Ghetto." In Eric J. Sundquist, ed., *The Oxford W. E. B. Du Bois Reader*, 469–473. New York: Oxford University Press, 1996.

Dwork, Deborah. *Children with a Star: Jewish Youth in Nazi Europe*. New Haven: Yale University Press, 1991.

Edele, Mark. *Soviet Veterans of World War II: A Popular Movement in an Authoritarian Society*. New York: Oxford University Press, 2008.

Ehrenburg, Ilya. *Russia at War*. Translated by Gerard Shelley. London: Hamish Hamilton, 1943.

Ehrenburg, Ilya, and Vasily Grossman. *The Complete Black Book of Russian Jewry*. Translated and edited by David Patterson. New Brunswick, NJ and London: Transaction Publishers, 2002.

Ellman, Michael, and S. Maksudov. "Soviet Deaths in the Great Patriotic War: A Note." *Europe-Asia Studies* 46, no. 4 (1994): 671–680.

Engels, Frederick. *The Origin of the Family, Private Property and the State*. Edited by Eleanor Burke Leacock. New York: International Publishers, 1972 (orig. 1884).

Epstein, Barbara. *The Minsk Ghetto, 1941–1943: Jewish Resistance and Soviet Internationalism*. Berkeley: University of California Press, 2008.

Erenburg, Grigorii. "Zhizn' kak podarok." In L. Leibov, ed., *Kniga zhivykh: Vospominaniia evreev-frontovikov, uznikov getto i kontslagerei, boitsov partizanskikh otriadov, zhitelei blokadnogo Leningrada*, Vol. 1, 102–108. Saint Petersburg: Akropol', 1995.

Ezergailis, Andrew. *The Holocaust in Latvia, 1941–1944: The Missing Center*. Riga and Washington: Historical Institute of Latvia/USHMM, 1996.

Felman, Shoshana, and Dori Laub. *Testimony: Crises of Witnessing in Literature, Psychoanalysis and History*. New York: Routledge, 1991.

Field, Deborah A. *Private Life and Communist Morality in Khrushchev's Russia*. New York: Peter Lang, 2007.

Fieseler, Beate. "Der Krieg der Frauen: Die ungeschriebene Geschichte." In Deutsch-Russisches Museum Berlin Karlshorst, ed., *Mascha + Nina +*

Katjuscha: Frauen in der Roten Armee 1941–1945. Katalog zur Ausstellung 15.11.2002 – 23.2.2003, 11–20. Berlin: Museum Karlshorst, 2002.
Fieseler, Beate, and Jörg Ganzenmüller, eds. Kriegsbilder: Mediale Repräsentationen des "Großen Vaterländischen Krieges." Essen, Germany: Klartext, 2010.
Filimonov, A. A. Partizanskii front v gody Velikoi Otechestvennoi voiny. Minsk: Navuka i Tekhnika, 1993.
Fitzpatrick, Sheila. The Russian Revolution. 3rd ed. New York: Oxford University Press, 2008.
Flaschka, Monika. "Race, Rape and Gender in Nazi-Occupied Territories." PhD diss., Kent State University, 2009.
Frankel, Jonathan, and Steven J. Zipperstein, eds. Assimilation and Community: The Jews in Nineteenth-Century Europe. New York: Cambridge University Press, 1992.
Freytag, Claudia. "Kriegsbeute 'Flintenweib': Rotarmistinnen in deutscher Gefangenschaft." In Deutsch-Russisches Museum, ed., Mascha + Nina + Katjuscha: Frauen in der Roten Armee 1941–1945. Katalog zur Ausstellung 15.11.2002 – 23.2.2003, 32–36. Berlin: Museum Karlshorst, 2002.
Friedländer, Saul. "History, Memory, and the Historian: Dilemmas and Responsibilities." New German Critique No. 80 (2000): 3–15.
Friedländer, Saul, ed. Probing the Limits of Representation: Nazism and the Final Solution. Cambridge, MA: Harvard University Press, 1992.
Fuchs, Esther, ed. Women and the Holocaust: Narrative and Representation. Lanham, MD: University Press of America, 1999.
Gabovich, Mikhail, ed. Pamiat' o voine: 60 let spustia; Rossiia, Germaniia, Evropa. 2nd ed. Moscow: Novoe Literaturnoe Obozrenie, 2005.
Gal'perin, Boris. "Moi universitety." In I. I. Baburina et al., eds., Kniga zhivykh: Vospominaniia evreev-frontovikov, uznikov getto i natsistskikh kontslagerei, boitsov partizanskikh otriadov, zashchitnikov blokadnogo Leningrada, Vol. 2, 324–338. Saint Petersburg: Izdatel'stvo zhurnal 'Neva,' 2004.
Ganor, Solly. Light One Candle: A Survivor's Tale from Lithuania to Jerusalem. New York: Kodansha International, 1995.
Gartenschläger, Uwe. Die Stadt Minsk während der deutschen Besetzung. Düsseldorf, Germany: IBB, 2002.
Gellner, Ernest. Nations and Nationalism. Oxford: Blackwell, 1983.
Gerasimova, Inna. "Evrei v partizanskom dvizhenii Belorussii, 1941–1944: Obshchaia kharakteristika." In Iakov Z. Basin, ed., Uroki Kholokosta: Istoriia i sovremennost', 137–141. Minsk: Kovcheg, 2009.
Gerlach, Christian. "Deutsche Wirtschaftsinteressen, Besatzungspolitik und der Mord an den Juden in Weißrussland, 1941–1943." In Ulrich Herbert, ed., Nationalsozialistische Vernichtungspolitik 1939–1945: Neue Forschungen und Kontroversen, 263–292. Frankfurt am Main: Fischer, 1998.
———. Kalkulierte Morde: Die deutsche Wirtschafts- und Vernichtungspolitik in Weißrussland, 1941–1944. Hamburg: Hamburger Edition, 1999.
Gheith, Jehanne M., and Katherine R. Jolluck, eds. Gulag Voices: Oral Histories of Social Incarceration and Exile. New York: Palgrave Macmillan, 2011.
Gitelman, Zvi. Jewish Nationality and Soviet Politics: The Jewish Sections of the CPSU, 1917–1930. Princeton: Princeton University Press, 1972.
———. Century of Ambivalence: The Jews of Russia and the Soviet Union, 1881 to the Present. Bloomington and Indianapolis: University of Indiana Press, 1988.
———. "Politics and the Historiography of the Holocaust in the Soviet Union." In Zvi Gitelman, ed., Bitter Legacy: Confronting the Holocaust in the USSR, 14–42. Bloomington and Indianapolis: Indiana University Press, 1997.

———. "Soviet Jewry before the Holocaust." In Zvi Gitelman, ed., *Bitter Legacy: Confronting the Holocaust in the USSR*, 1–13. Bloomington and Indianapolis: Indiana University Press, 1997.

———. "The Reconstruction of Community and Jewish Identity in Russia" *East European Affairs* 24, no. 1 (1999): 35–56.

Gitelman, Zvi, ed. *Bitter Legacy: Confronting the Holocaust in the USSR*. Bloomington and Indianapolis: Indiana University Press, 1997.

Gluck, Sherna Berger, and Daphne Patai. "Introduction." In Sherna Berger Gluck and Daphne Patai, eds., *Women's Words: The Feminist Practice of Oral History*, 1–3. New York: Routledge, 1991.

Gluck, Sherna Berger. "What's So Special about Women?." In Susan H. Armitage with Patricia Hart and Karen Weathermon, eds., *Women's Oral History: The Frontiers Reader*, 3–26. Lincoln and London: University of Nebraska Press, 2002.

Goffman, Erving. *Asylums: Essays on the Social Situation of Mental Patients and Other Inmates*. Chicago: Aldine, 1961.

Goldenberg, Myrna "Different Horrors, Same Hell: Women Remembering the Holocaust." In Roger Gottlieb, ed., *Thinking the Unthinkable: Meanings of the Holocaust*, 150–166. New York: Paulist Press, 1990.

Goldman, Wendy Z. *Women, the State, and Revolution: Soviet Family Policy and Social Life, 1917–1936*. Cambridge, MA: Cambridge University Press, 1993.

———. "The Internal Soviet Passport: Workers and Free Movement." In Marsha Siefert, ed., *Extending the Borders of Russian History*, 315–331. Budapest: CEU Press, 2003.

———. *Inventing the Enemy: Denunciation and Terror in Stalin's Russia*. New York: Cambridge University Press, 2011.

———. *Woman at the Gates: Gender and Industry in Stalin's Russia*. Cambridge, MA: Cambridge University Press, 2002.

Goluboff, Sasha *Jewish Russians: Upheavals in a Moscow Synagogue*. Philadelphia: University of Pennsylvania Press, 2003.

Gordon, Avery. *Ghostly Matters: Haunting and the Sociological Imagination*. Minneapolis: University of Minnesota Press, 2004 (orig. 1997).

Greenspan, Henry, and Sidney Bolkosky. "When Is an Interview an Interview? Notes from Listening to Holocaust Survivors." *poetics today* 27, no. 2 (2006): 431–449.

Grele, Ronald. "Movement without an Aim: Methodological and Theoretical Problems in Oral History" (orig. 1975). In Robert Perks and Alistair Thomson, eds., *The Oral History Reader*, 1st ed., 38–52. New York and London: Routledge, 1998.

Gringauz, Samuel. "The Ghetto as an Experiment of Jewish Social Organization (Three Years of the Kovno Ghetto)." *Jewish Social Studies* 11, no. 1 (1949): 3–20.

———. "Some Methodological Problems in the Study of the Ghetto." *Jewish Social Studies* 12, no. 1 (1950): 66–72.

Gross, Jan Tomasz. "The Sovietization of Western Ukraine and Western Byelorussia" In Norman Davies and Antony Polonsky, eds., *Jews in Eastern Poland and the USSR, 1939–46*, 60–76. New York: St. Martin's Press, 1991.

———. *Neighbors: The Destruction of the Jewish Community in Jedwabne, Poland*. Princeton: Princeton University Press, 2001.

Grossman, Chaika *The Underground Army: Fighters of the Białystok Ghetto*. New York: Holocaust Library, 1987.

Grossman, Wassili, and Ilja Ehrenburg. *Das Schwarzbuch: Der Genozid an den sowjetischen Juden*. Edited by Arno Lustiger. Hamburg: Rowohlt, 1994.

Grüner, Frank. "Jüdischer Glaube und religiöse Praxis unter dem stalinistischen Regime in der Sowjetunion während der Kriegs- und Nachkriegsjahre." *Jahrbücher für Geschichte Osteuropas* N.F. 52, no. 4 (2004): 534-556.
Gutman, Israel. *Fighters among the Ruins: The Story of Jewish Heroism During World War II*. New York: B'nai B'rith Books, 1988.
Halbwachs, Maurice. *Das Gedächtnis und seine sozialen Bedingungen*. Frankfurt am Main: Suhrkamp, 1985.
Haraway, Donna. *When Species Meet*. Minneapolis: University of Minnesota Press 2008.
Hartman, Saidiya. *Lose Your Mother: A Journey Along the Atlantic Slave Route*. New York: Farrar, Straus and Giroux, 2007.
Hartmann, Heidi. "The Unhappy Marriage of Marxism and Feminism: Towards a More Progressive Union." *Capital & Class* 3, no. 1 (1979): 1-33.
Hartsock, Nancy. "The Feminist Standpoint: Developing the Ground for a Specifically Feminist Historical Materialism." In Sandra Harding and Merrill B. Hintikka, eds., *Discovering Reality: Feminist Perspectives on Epistemology, Metaphysics, Methodology, and Philosophy of Science*, 283-310. Boston: Reidel, 1983.
Hasenclever, Jörn. *Wehrmacht und Besatzungspolitik in der Sowjetunion: Die Befehlshaber der rückwärtigen Heeresgebiete 1941-1943*. Paderborn, Germany: Ferdinand Schöningh, 2010.
Hatley, James. *Suffering Witness: The Quandary of Responsibility after the Irreparable*. New York: State University of New York Press, 2000.
Heberer, Patricia. *Children during the Holocaust*. New York: AltaMira 2012.
Hedgepeth, Sonia M. and Rochelle G. Saidel, eds. *Sexual Violence against Jewish Women during the Holocaust*. Lebanon, NH: Brandeis University Press, 2010.
Hellbeck, Jochen. *Revolution on My Mind: Writing a Diary Under Stalin*. Cambridge, MA: Harvard University Press, 2009.
Herbert, Ulrich. *Fremdarbeiter: Politik und Praxis des "Ausländer-Einsatzes" in der Kriegswirtschaft des Dritten Reiches*. Berlin and Bonn: Dietz, 1985.
———. *Arbeit, Volkstum, Weltanschauung: Über Fremde und Deutsche im 20. Jahrhundert*. Frankfurt am Main: Fischer, 1995.
Herf, Jeffrey. *Divided Memory: The Nazi Past in the Two Germanys*. Cambridge, MA: Harvard University Press, 1997.
Hershatter, Gail. *The Gender of Memory: Rural Women and China's Collective Past*. Berkeley: University of California Press, 2011.
Himka, John-Paul. "Ukrainian Collaboration in the Extermination of the Jews during the Second World War: Sorting Out the Long-Term and Conjectural Factors." In Jonathan Frankel, ed., *The Fate of the European Jews, 1939-1945: Continuity or Contingency?*, 170-189. New York: Oxford University Press, 1997.
Hirsch, Marianne. "The Generation of Postmemory." *poetics today* 29, no. 1 (2008): 103-128.
Hirsch, Marianne, and Irene Kacandes, eds. *Teaching the Representation of the Holocaust*. New York: Modern Language Association of America, 2004.
Hirsch, Marianne, and Valerie Smith. "Feminism and Cultural Memory: An Introduction." *Signs* 28, no. 1 (2002): 1-19.
Hirschfeld, Gerhard. *The Policies of Genocide: Jews and Soviet Prisoners of War in Nazi Germany*. London: Allan and Unwin, 1986.
Hochschild, Adam. "Tug of War: Timothy Snyder Looks East." Review of *Bloodlands: Europe Between Hitler and Stalin*, by Timothy Snyder. *Harper's Magazine*, February 2011, 79-82.

Hoffman, Stefani, and Ezra Mendelsohn, eds. *The Revolution of 1905 and Russia's Jews.* Philadelphia: University of Pennsylvania Press, 2008.

Hoppe, Bert, and Hildrun Glass, eds. *Die Verfolgung und Ermordung der europäischen Juden durch das nationalsozialistische Deutschland 1933–1945.* Bd. 7, *Sowjetunion mit annektierten Gebieten I.* Munich: Oldenbourg, 2011.

Hosking, Geoffrey. *The First Socialist Society: A History of the Soviet Union from Within.* Cambridge, MA: Harvard University Press, 1992.

Ilič, Melanie. *Women Workers in the Soviet Interwar Economy: From "Protection" to "Equality."* New York: St. Martin's Press, 1999.

Ioffe, E. G. et al., eds. *Kholokost v Belarusi, 1941–1944: Dokumenty i materialy.* Minsk: NARB, 2002.

Irwin-Zarecka, Iwona. *Frames of Remembrance: The Dynamics of Collective Memory.* New Brunswick and London: Transaction, 1994.

Jelin, Elizabeth. *State Repression and the Labors of Memory.* Minneapolis: University of Minnesota Press, 2003.

Jockusch, Lena. *Collect and Record! Jewish Holocaust Documentation in Early Postwar Europe.* New York: Oxford University Press, 2012.

Jureit, Ulrike, and Karin Orth. *Überlebensgeschichten: Gespräche mit Überlebenden des KZ Neuengamme.* Hamburg: Dölling & Galitz, 1994.

Kaden, Helma, and Ludwig Nestler, eds. *Dokumente des Verbrechens: Aus Akten des Dritten Reiches 1933–1945*, Vol. 3. Berlin: Dietz, 1993.

Kagan, Jack. *Surviving the Holocaust with the Russian Jewish Partisans.* Portland, OR: Vallentine Mitchell, 1998.

Kaganovich, Al'bert. "Voprosy i zadachi issledovaniia mest prinuditel'nogo soderzhaniia evreev na territorii Belarusi v 1941–1944 gg." In Iakov Z. Basin, ed., *Aktual'nye voprosy izucheniia Kholokosta na territorii Belarusi v gody nemetsko-fashistskoi okkupatsii: Sbornik nauchnykh rabot.* Minsk: Kovcheg, 2005. http://www.homoliber.org/ru/kg/kg020108.html. Accessed March 8, 2011.

Kaganovich, Moshe. *Der Yidisher onteyl in der partizaner-bavegung fun Sovyet-Rusland.* Rome: Central Historical Commission at the Union of Partisans "Pachach" in Italy, 1948.

Kalacheva, Ol'ga, and Oksana Karpenko, "Leben im 'Zustand der Wahl'? Die Ambivalenz der ethnischen Identitätsbildung bei russischen Juden." In Ingrid Oswald and Viktor Voronkov, eds., *Post-sowjetische Ethnizitäten: Ethnische Gemeinden in St. Petersburg und Berlin/Potsdam*, 38–54. Berlin: Berliner Debatte, 1997.

Kamp, Marianne. "*The Wedding Feast*: Living the New Uzbek Life in the 1930s." In Jeff Sahadeo and Russell Zanca, eds. *Everyday Life in Central Asia*, 103–114. Bloomington and Indianapolis: Indiana University Press, 2007.

Kangisser Cohen, Sharon. *Child Survivors of the Holocaust in Israel: Social Dynamics and Post-War Experiences: "Finding Their Voice."* Brighton, UK: Sussex Academic Press, 2005.

———. "The Experience of the Jewish Family in the Nazi Ghetto: Kovno—A Case Study." *Journal of Family History* 31, no. 3 (2006): 267–288.

Kaplan, Chaim Aron. *Scroll of Agony: The Warsaw Diary of Chaim A. Kaplan.* Edited by Abraham I. Katsh. Bloomington and Indianapolis: Indiana University Press, 1999.

Kaplan, Temma. "Acts of Testimony: Reversing the Shame and Gendering the Memory." *Signs* 28, no. 1 (2002): 179–199.

Karady, Victor. *The Jews of Europe in the Modern Era: A Socio-Historical Outline.* New York and Budapest: CEU Press, 2004.

Kassow, Samuel. *Who Will Write Our History? Emanuel Ringelblum, the Warsaw Ghetto, and the Oyneg Shabes Archive*. Bloomington and Indianapolis: Indiana University Press, 2007.
Katz, Esther, and Joan Ringelheim, eds. *Proceedings of the Conference: Women Surviving: The Holocaust*. New York: Institute for Research in History, 1983.
Katz, Joseph. *From Prejudice to Destruction: Anti-Semitism, 1700–1933*. Cambridge, UK: Harvard University Press, 1980.
Keilson, Hans. *Sequentielle Traumatisierung bei Kindern: Deskriptiv-klinische und quantifizierend-statistische follow-up Untersuchung zum Schicksal der jüdischen Kriegswaisen in den Niederlanden*. Stuttgart, Germany: Enke, 1979.
Kelly, Catriona. *Children's World: Growing up in Russia, 1890–1991*. New Haven and London: Yale University Press, 2007.
Kenez, Peter. *A History of the Soviet Union from the Beginning to the End*. New York: Cambridge University Press, 1999, 2006.
Kessler, Mario. *Die SED und die Juden—zwischen Repression und Toleranz: Politische Entwicklungen bis 1967*. Berlin: Akademie Verlag, 1995.
Kestenberg, Judith, and Ira Brenner. *The Last Witness: The Child Survivor of the Holocaust*. Washington, DC: American Psychiatric Press, 1996.
Khomikh, Solomon. "Otvoiovannaia zhizn'." In Z. Tsukerman, ed., *Katastrofa: Poslednie svideteli*, 422–439. Moscow: Dom Evreiskoi Knigi, 2008.
Khubova, Daria, Andreu Ivankiev, and Tonia Sharova. "After Glasnost: Oral History in the Soviet Union." In Luisa Passerini, ed., *Memory and Totalitarianism*, 3rd ed., 89–102. New York: Oxford University Press, 2009.
Killis, Aristotle. "'Licence' and Genocide in the East: Reflections on Localised Eliminationist Violence During the First Stages of 'Operation Barbarossa'." *Studies in Ethnicity and Nationalism* 7, no. 3 (2007): 6–23.
Kirschenbaum, Lisa. *Small Comrades: Revolutionizing Childhood in Soviet Russia, 1917–1932*. New York: RoutledgeFalmer, 2001.
Klein, Peter. "Zwischen den Fronten: Die Zivilbevölkerung Weißrusslands und der Krieg der Wehrmacht gegen die Partisanen." In Babette Quinkert, ed., *"Wir sind die Herren dieses Landes": Ursachen, Verlauf und Folgen des deutschen Überfalls auf die Sowjetunion*, 82–103. Hamburg: VSA, 2002.
Klier, John. "The Holocaust and the Soviet Union." In Dan Stone, ed., *The Historiography of the Holocaust*, 276–295. Basingstoke, UK: Palgrave, 2004.
Kluger, Ruth. *Still Alive: A Holocaust Girlhood Remembered*. New York: The Feminist Press, 2003.
Klüger, Ruth. *Weiter leben: Eine Jugend*. Göttingen, Germany: Wallstein, 1992.
———. *Von hoher und niedriger Literatur*. Göttingen, Germany: Wallstein, 1996.
Knat'ko, G. D., ed., *Zalozhniki Vermakhta: Ozarichi—Lager' smerti. Dokumenty i materialy*. Minsk: Natsional'nyi Arkhiv Respubliki Belarus', 1999.
Koonz, Claudia. *Mothers in the Fatherland: Women, the Family, and Nazi Policy*. New York: St. Martin's Press, 1987.
Koval, M. I. "The Nazi Genocide of the Jews and the Ukrainian Population, 1941–1944." In Zvi Gitelman, ed., *Bitter Legacy: Confronting the Holocaust in the USSR*, 51–60. Bloomington and Indianapolis: Indiana University Press, 1997.
Kozlova, Natal'ia. *Sovietskie liudi: Stseny iz istorii*. Moscow: Evropa, 2005.
Kozak, Kuz'ma, ed., *Evreiskoie soprotivlenie natsizmu na territorii Belarusi v gody Velikoi Otechestvennoi voiny 1941–1944 gg*. Minsk: I. P. Logvinov, 2011.
Krasnoperko, Anna. *Briefe meiner Erinnerung*. Villigst, Germany: Haus Villigst, 1991.

Kraul, Margret, and Winfried Marotzki. "Bildung und biographische Arbeit—Eine Einleitung." In Margret Kraul, ed., *Biographische Arbeit*, 7–21. Opladen, Germany: Leske+Budrich 2002.

Krausnick, Helmut, and Hans-Heinrich Wilhelm. *Die Truppe des Weltanschauungskrieges: Die Einsatzgruppen der Sicherheitspolizei und des SD 1938–1942*. Stuttgart, Germany: Deutsche Verlags-Anstalt, 1981.

Krivosheev, G. F. ed. *Rossiia i SSSR v voinakh XX veka: Poteri vooruzhonnykh sil—Statisticheskoe issledovanie*. Moscow: Olimp Press, 2001. http://lib.ru/MEMUARY/1939-1945/KRIWOSHEEW/poteri.txt. Accessed online July 7, 2013.

Kruk, Herman. *Togbukh fun Vilner Geto*. Edited by Mordekhai Bernshtain. New York: YIVO, 1961.

Krylova, Anna. "Stalinist Identity from the Viewpoint of Gender: Rearing a Generation of Professionally Violent Women-Fighters in 1930s Stalinist Russia." *Gender and History* 16, no. 3 (2004): 626–653.

———. *Soviet Women in Combat: A History of Violence on the Eastern Front*. New York: Cambridge University Press, 2010.

Kucherenko, Olga. *Little Soldiers: How Soviet Children Went to War, 1941–1945*. Oxford: Oxford University Press, 2011.

Küpper, Herbert. "Die neuere Rechtsprechung in Sachen NS-Zwangsarbeit." *Kritische Justiz* 31, no. 2 (1998): 246–254.

LaCapra, Dominick. *History in Transit: Experience, Identity, Critical Theory*. Ithaca, NY and London: Cornell University Press, 2004.

———. *Representing the Holocaust: History, Theory, Trauma*. Ithaca, NY: Cornell University Press, 1994.

———. *Writing History, Writing Trauma*. Baltimore: The Johns Hopkins University Press, 2001.

Langer, Lawrence. *Holocaust Testimony: The Ruins of Memory*. New Haven: Yale University Press, 1991.

Lapidus, Albert. "Nas malo ostalos', nam mnogo dostalos'." *Vestnik* 2(313)–3(314) (2003). http://www.vestnik.com/win/arch03.htm. Accessed November 4, 2010.

Lapidus, Gail W. *Women in Soviet Society: Equality, Development and Social Change*. Berkeley: University of California Press, 1978.

Laqueur, Walter. *A History of Zionism*. New York: Holt, Rinehart and Winston, 1972.

Lehnstaedt, Stefan. *Okkupation im Osten: Besatzeralltag in Warschau und Minsk*. Munich: Oldenburg, 2010.

———. Review of *The Minsk Ghetto, 1941–1943: Jewish Resistance and Soviet Internationalism*, by Barbara Epstein. *sehepunkte* 11, no. 1 (2011) [15.01.2011]. http://www.sehepunkte.de/2011/01/16085.html. Accessed June 5, 2012.

Leibov, L., ed. *Kniga zhivykh: Vospominaniia evreev-frontovikov, uznikov getto i kontslagerei, boitsov partizanskikh otriadov, zhitelei blokadnogo Leningrada*. Vol. 1. Sankt-Petersburg: Akropol', 1995.

Lentin, Ronit. "(En)gendering Genocide: Die Feminisierung der Katastrophe." *Zeitschrift für Genozidforschung* 1, no.1 (1999): 70–89.

———. "Introduction." In Ronit Lentin, ed., *Gender and Catastrophe*, 2–17. London: Zed, 1997.

Levin, Semion. "Na rubezhe vekov." *Mishpokha* 9 (2001). http://mishpoha.org/nomer9/levin.php, accessed February 8, 2015.

Levina-Krapina, Maia. *Trizhdy rozhdionnaia: Vospominaniia byvshei uznitsy minskogo getto*. Minsk: Emizer Kolaz, 2008.

Leys, Ruth. *Trauma: A Genealogy*. Chicago and London: University of Chicago Press, 2000.

Linkov, Gregory ("Batya"). "Women Spies." In Jack Porter, ed., *Jewish Partisans: A Documentary of Jewish Resistance in the Soviet Union during World War II*, 164–167. Washington, DC: University Press of America, 1982.

Lin'kov, Grigorii Matveevich. *Voina v tylu vraga*. Moscow: Sovetskii pisatel', 1947. Available online at http://www.litmir.me/bd/?b=187521. Accessed February 23, 2015.

Litvin, Aleksei. "K voprosu o kolichestve liudskikh poter' Belarusi v gody Velikoi Otechestvennoi voiny (1941–1945 gg.)." In V. I. Andreev, ed., *Belarus' v XX stahoddzi*, 127–138. Minsk: Vodolei, 2002.

Loewenstein, Karl. "Minsk—Im Lager der deutschen Juden." *Das Parlament (Beilage)*. B. 45/46. November 7, 1956.

Lokshin, A. "'Delo vrachei': Otkliki trudiashchikhsia." *Vestnik Evreiskogo Universiteta v Moskve* 1(5) (1994): 52–62.

Lower, Wendy. "Facilitating Genocide: Nazi Ghettoization Practices in Occupied Ukraine, 1941–1942." In Eric J. Sterling, ed., *Life in the Ghettos During the Holocaust*, 120–144. Syracuse, NY: Syracuse University Press, 2005.

——. *Nazi Empire-Building and the Holocaust in Ukraine*. Chapel Hill: University of North Carolina Press, 2007.

Ludz, Ursula. "Einleitung." In Ursula Ludz, ed., *Hannah Arendt: Ich will verstehen. Selbstauskünfte zu Leben und Werk*, 7–26. Munich: Piper, 2005.

Lustiger, Arno. *Rotbuch: Stalin und die Juden; Die tragische Geschichte des Jüdischen Antifaschistischen Komitees und der sowjetischen Juden*. Berlin: Aufbau, 1998.

Lyons, Tanya. *Guns and Guerilla Girls: Women in the Zimbabwean National Liberation Struggle*. Trenton, NJ: Africa World Press, 2004.

Maizles, Enta. "Minsk: Fashistskaia okkupatsiia; Genotsid." In Iakov Basin, ed., *Uroki Kholokosta: Istoriia i sovremennost'*, 177–181. Minsk: Kovcheg, 2009.

Manaenkov, A. L. *Partizanskie formirovaniia v Belorussii v gody Velikoi Otechestvennoi voiny: Kratkie svedeniia ob organizatsionnoi strukture partizanskikh soedinenii, brigad (polkov), otriadov (batalionov) i ikh lichnom sostave*. Minsk: Belarus, 1983.

Mandsley, Evan. *Thunder in the East: The Nazi-Soviet War, 1941–1945*. London: Hodder Arnold, 2005.

Martin, Terry. *The Affirmative Action Empire: Nations and Nationalism in the Soviet Union*. Ithaca, NY: Cornell Unversity Press, 2001.

Marx, Karl. "Economic and Philosophical Manuscripts of 1844: Estranged Labour." In Robert C. Tucker, ed., *The Marx-Engels Reader*, 66–125. New York: Norton, 1978.

Matthäus, Jürgen. "Reibungslos und planmäßig: Die zweite Welle der Judenvernichtung im Generalkommissariat Weißruthenien (1942–1944)." *Jahrbuch für Antisemitismusforschung* No. 4 (1995), 224–274.

McClintock, Anne. "Family Feuds: Gender, Nationalism and the Family." *Feminist Review* no. 44 (1993): 61–80.

Mendelsohn, Ezra. *Class Struggle in the Pale: The Formative Years of the Jewish Workers Movement in Tsarist Russia*. Cambridge, UK: Cambridge University Press, 1970.

Merridale, Catherine. "The Collective Mind: Trauma and Shell-Shock in Twentieth Century Russia." *Journal of Contemporary History* 35, no. 1 (2000): 39–55.

——. *Night of Stone: Death and Memory in Twentieth-Century Russia*. New York and London: Viking, 2000.

——. *Ivan's War: Life and Death in the Red Army, 1939–1945*. New York: Metropolitan Books, 2006.

Meyer, Gert, ed. *Wir brauchen die Wahrheit: Geschichtsdiskussion in der Scwjetunion*. Cologne: Pahl-Rugenstein, 1989.

Michlic, Joanna. "The Aftermath and After: Memories of Child Survivors of the Holocaust." In Sara R. Horowitz, ed., *Lessons and Legacies X: Back to the Sources: Reexamining Perpetrators, Victims, and Bystanders*, 141–189. Evanston, IL: Northwestern University Press, 2012.

Michman, Dan. *The Emergence of Jewish Ghettos during the Holocaust*. New York: Cambridge University Press, 2011.

Miles, Tiya. *Ties That Bind: The Story of an Afro-Cherokee Family in Slavery and Freedom*. Berkeley: University of California Press, 2005.

Miller, Nancy K., and Jason Tougaw. "Introduction: Extremities." In Nancy Miller and Jason Tougaw, eds., *Extremities: Trauma, Testimony, and Community*, 1–24. Urbana: University of Illinois Press, 2002.

Miller, Robert, ed. *Biographical Research Methods*. 4 vols. London: Sage, 2005.

Miller, Robert, Robin Humphrey, and Elena Zdravomyslova. "Introduction: Biographical Research and Historical Watersheds." In Robin Humphrey, Robert Miller, and Elena Zdravomyslova, eds., *Biographical Research in Eastern Europe: Altered Lives and Broken Biographies*, 1–26. Aldershot, UK: Ashgate, 2003.

Minsk: Staryi-Novyi. "Komsomol'skoe ozero." http://minsk-old-new.com/minsk-2858-ru.htm.

Misztal, Barbara. *Theories of Social Remembering*. Maidenhead, UK: Open University Press, 2003.

Moll-Sawatzki, Andrea. "Freiwillig an die Front? Junge Frauen zwischen Motivation und Mobilisierung." In Deutsch-Russisches Museum Berlin Karlshorst, ed., *Mascha + Nina + Katjuscha: Frauen in der Roten Armee 1941–1945. Katalog zur Ausstellung 15.11.2002 – 23.2.2003*, 21–27. Berlin: Museum Karlshorst, 2002.

Morrison, Toni. *Beloved*. New York: Knopf, 1987.

Moskovitz, Sarah. "Longitudinal Follow-up of Child Survivors of the Holocaust." *Journal of the American Academy of Child Psychiatry* 24 (1985): 401–407.

Mühlhäuser, Regina. "Between 'Racial Awareness' and Fantasies of Potency: Nazi Sexual Politics in the Occupied Territories of the Soviet Union." In Dagmar Herzog, ed., *Brutality and Desire: War and Sexuality in Europe's Twentieth Century*, 199–203. New York: Palgrave Macmillan, 2009.

——. *Eroberungen: Sexuelle Gewalttaten und intime Beziehungen deutscher Soldaten in der Sowjetunion*. Hamburg: Hamburger Edition, 2010.

Murav, Harriet. *Music from a Speeding Train: Jewish Literature in Post-Revolution Russia*. Stanford: Stanford University Press, 2011.

Musial, Bogdan, ed. *Sowjetische Partisanen in Weißrußland: Innenansichten aus dem Gebiet Baranovici; Eine Dokumentation*. Munich: Oldenbourg, 2004.

Musial, Bogdan. *Sowjetische Partisanen 1941–1944: Mythos und Wirklichkeit*. Paderborn, Germany: Ferdinand Schöningh, 2009.

Nicholas, Lynn H. *Cruel World: The Children of Europe in the Nazi Web*. New York: Knopf, 2005.

Nikodimova, Z. A., ed., *Arkhiv Khasi Pruslinoi: Minskoe getto, antifashistskoe podpol'e, repatriatsiia detei iz Germanii*. Minsk: I. P. Loginov, 2010.

Niewyk, Donald L. ed. *Fresh Wounds: Early Narratives of Holocaust Survival*. Chapel Hill: University of North Carolina Press, 1998.

Nolte, Hans-Heinrich. "Ozarichi." In G. D. Knat'ko et al., eds., *Zalozhniki Vermakhta—Geiseln der Wehrmacht*, 269–279. Minsk: Natsional'ny Arkhiv Respubliki Belarus', 1999.

Nomura, Gail. "Filipina American Journal Writing: Recovering Women's History." In Shirley Hue and Gail M. Nomura, eds., *Asian/Pacific Islander American Women: A Historical Anthology*, 138–152. New York: New York University Press, 2003.
Nosenko-Shtein, Elena E. "O kollektivnoi pamiati rossiiskikh evreev na rubezhe vekov (predvaritel'nye nabliudeniia)." *Etnograficheskoie Obozrenie* 6 (2009): 20–29.
Novick, Peter. *The Holocaust in American Life*. Boston: Houghton Mifflin, 1999.
Ofer, Dalia. "Everyday Life of Jews under Nazi Occupation: Methodological Issues." *Holocaust and Genocide Studies* 9, no. 1 (1995): 42–69.
Ostrovski, Nikolai. *How the Steel Was Tempered*. Translated by R. Prokofieva. Moscow: Foreign Languages Publishing House, 1952 (orig. 1934).
Oswald, Ingrid, and Viktor Voronkov. "Einleitung." In Ingrid Oswald and Viktor Voronkov, eds., *Post-sowjetische Ethnizitäten: Ethnische Gemeinden in St. Petersburg und Berlin/Potsdam*, 7–37. Berlin: Berliner Debatte, 1997.
——. "The Public-Private Sphere in Soviet and Post-Soviet Society: Perception and Dynamics of 'Public' and 'Private' in Contemporary Russia." *European Societies* 6, no. 1 (2004): 97–117.
Partizanskaia druzhba: Vospominaniia o boevykh delakh partizan-evreev, uchastnikov Velikoi Otechestvennoi voiny. Moscow: OGIZ, 1948.
Pasherstnik, Lev. "Pobeg iz getto." In Z. Tsukerman, ed., *Katastrofa: Poslednie svideteli*, 245–252. Moscow: Dom Evreiskoi Knigi, 2008.
Passerini, Luisa. "Work Ideology and Consensus under Italian Fascism" (orig. 1979). In Robert Perks and Alistair Thomson, eds., *The Oral History Reader*, 1st ed., 53–62. New York and London: Routledge, 1998.
Patai, Daphne. "U.S. Academics and Third World Women: Is Ethical Research Possible?" In Sherna Berger Gluck and Daphne Patai, eds. *Women's Words: The Feminist Practice of Oral History*, 137–154. New York: Routledge, 1991.
Patterson, David. "Death and Ghetto Death." Eric J. Sterling, ed., *Life in the Ghettos during the Holocaust*, 160–171. Syracuse, NY: Syracuse University Press, 2005.
Petrenko, Vasilii. *Do i posle Osventsima*. Moscow: Rossiiskaia Biblioteka Kholokosta, 2000.
Petrova, N. K. "Deti Velikoi Otechestvennoi voiny." In A. Iu. Rozhkova, ed., *Vtoraia mirovaia voina v detskikh "ramkakh pamiati": Sbornik nauchnykh statei*, 210–228. Krasnodar, Russia: Ekoinvest, 2010.
Pinchuk, Ben-Cion. "The Shtetl: An Ethnic Town in the Russian Empire." *Cahiers du Monde russe* 41, no. 4 (2000): 495–504.
Pine, Frances, Deema Kaneff, and Haldis Haukanes. "Memory, Politics and Religion: A Perspective on Europe." In Frances Pine, ed., *Memory, Politics and Religion: The Past Meets the Present in Europe*, 1–30, Münster, Germany: Lit, 2004.
Pine, Lisa. "Gender and the Family." In Dan Stone, ed., *The Historiography of the Holocaust*, 364–382. New York: Palgrave Macmillan, 2004.
Pinkus, Benjamin. *The Jews of the Soviet Union: The History of a National Minority*. Cambridge, UK: Cambridge University Press, 1988.
Platt, Kristin. "Gedächtnis, Erinnerung, Verarbeitung: Spuren traumatischer Erfahrung in lebensgeschichtlichen Interviews." *BIOS* 11, no. 2 (1998): 242–262.
Plotkin, Andrei. *Podvigov ne sovershal*. Moscow: Rossiiskaia Biblioteka Kholokosta, 2000.
Podolsky, Anatoly. "The Tragic Fate of Ukrainian Jewish Women under Nazi Occupation." In Sonja M. Hedgepeth and Rochelle G. Saidel, eds., *Sexual Violence against Jewish Women during the Holocaust*, 94–107. Waltham, MA: Brandeis University Press, 2010.

Pohl, Dieter. *Die Herrschaft der Wehrmacht: Deutsche Militärbesatzung und einheimische Bevölkerung in der Sowjetunion 1941–1944.* Munich: Oldenbourg, 2008.

Popov, Alexei. *Diversanty Stalina.* Moscow: Iauza Eksmo, 2004.

Portelli, Alessandro. *The Order Has Been Carried Out: History, Memory, and Meaning of a Nazi Massacre in Rome.* New York: Palgrave Macmillan, 2003.

Porter, Jack Nusan. *Jewish Partisans: A Documentary of Jewish Resistance in the Soviet Union During World War II.* Washington, DC: University Press of America, 1982.

Preston, Paul. *The Spanish Holocaust: Inquisition and Extermination in Twentieth-Century Spain.* New York: W. W. Norton, 2012.

Projektgruppe Belarus, ed. *"Dann kam die deutsche Macht": Weißrussische Kinderhäftlinge in deutschen Konzentrationslagern, 1941–1945.* Cologne: Betrieb für Öffentlichkeit, 1999.

———. *Existiert das Ghetto noch? Weißrussland: Jüdisches Überleben gegen nationalsozialistische Herrschaft.* Berlin and Hamburg: Assoziation A, 2003.

Quinkert, Babette, ed. *"Wir sind die Herren dieses Landes": Ursachen, Verlauf und Folgen des deutschen Überfalls auf die Sowjetunion.* Hamburg: VSA, 2002.

Rafman, Sandra, Joyce Canfield, José Barbas, and Janusz Kaczorowski. "Children's Representations of Parental Loss due to War." *International Journal of Behavioral Development* 20, no.1 (1997): 163–177.

Raphael, Melissa. *The Female Face of God in Auschwitz.* New York: Routlegde, 2003.

Reading, Anna. *The Social Inheritance of the Holocaust: Gender, Culture, and Memory.* New York: Palgrave Macmillan, 2002.

Rebrova, Irina V. "Zhenskaia povsednevnost' v ekstremal'noi situatsii: Po materialiam ustnykh i pis'mennykh vospominanii zhenshchin o Velikoi Otechestvennoi voine." In Natalia L. Pushkareva, ed., *Rossiiskaia povsednevnost' v zerkale gendernykh otnoshenii,* 605–630. Moscow: Novoe Literaturnoe Obozrenie, 2013.

Redlich, Shimon. "Evreiskii antifashistskii komitet v SSSR i antisemitskaia politika sovetskikh vlastei v poslevoennye gody." In Al'tman, Il'ia, et al., eds., *Kholokost—soprotivlenie—vozrozhdenie: Evreiskii narod v gody VOV i poslevoennyi period 1939–1948,* 213–261. Moscow: Fond Kholokost, 2000.

Redlich, Shimon, and Ilya Altman, eds. *War, Holocaust, and Stalinism: A Documented Study of the Jewish Anti-Fascist Committee in the USSR.* Luxembourg: Harwood, 1995.

Rein, Leonid. "Local Collaboration in the Execution of the "Final Solution" in Nazi-Occupied Belorussia." *Holocaust and Genocide Studies* 20, no. 3 (2006): 381–409.

Rentrop, Petra. *Tatorte der "Endlösung": Das Ghetto Minsk und die Vernichtungsstätte Maly Trostinez.* Berlin: Metropol, 2011.

Ringelheim, Joan. "Genocide and Gender: A Split Memory." Ronit Lentin, ed., *Gender and Catastrophe,* 18–34. London: Zed Books, 1997.

———. "The Split between Gender and the Holocaust." In Dalia Ofer and Leonore J. Weitzman, eds., *Women in the Holocaust,* 340–350. New Haven: Yale University Press, 1998.

———. "Women and the Holocaust: A Reconsideration of Research." *Signs* 10, no. 4 (1985): 741–61.

Rittersporn, Gabor Tamas, Malte Rolf, and Jan C. Behrends, eds. *Sphären von Öffentlichkeit in Gesellschaften sowjetischen Typs: Zwischen partei-staatlicher Selbstinszenierung und kirchlichen Gegenwelten.* Frankfurt am Main: Lang, 2003.

Rittner, Carol and John K. Roth, eds. *Different Voices: Women and the Holocaust.* New York: Paragon House, 1993.

Rolnikaite, Maria. *Mein Tagebuch*. Berlin (GDR): Union Verlag, 1967.
Romanovsky, Daniel. "The Holocaust in the Eyes of *Homo Sovieticus*: A Survey Based on Northeastern Belorussia and Northwestern Russia." *Holocaust and Genocide Studies* 13, no. 3 (1999): 355–387.
Rose, Deborah Bird. *Reports from a Wild Country: Ethics for Decolonisation*. Sydney: University of New South Wales Press, 2004.
Rosenberg, Heinz. *Jahre des Schreckens. ... und ich blieb übrig, daß ich Dir's ansage*. Göttingen, Germany: Steidl Verlag, 1985.
Rosenberg, Maxine B. *Hiding to Survive: Stories of Jewish Children Rescued from the Holocaust*. New York: Clarion, 1994.
Rosenthal, Gabriele. *Erlebte und erzählte Lebensgeschichte: Gestalt und Struktur biographischer Selbstbeschreibungen*. Frankfurt am Main: Campus, 1995.
———. "Die Biographie im Kontext der Familien und Gesellschaftsgeschichte." In Bettina Völter et al., eds., *Biographieforschung im Diskurs*, 46–64. Wiesbaden, Germany: Verlag für Sozialwissenschaften, 2005.
Rosenthal, Gabriele, and Wolfram Fischer-Rosenthal. "Warum Biographieanalyse und wie man sie macht." *Zeitschrift für Sozialisationsforschung und Erziehungssoziologie* 17, no. 4 (1997): 405–427.
Rothberg, Michael. "W. E. B. Du Bois in Warsaw: Holocaust Memory and the Color Line, 1949–1952." *Yale Journal of Criticism* 14, no. 1 (2001): 169–189.
Roth, John K., and Michael Berenbaum, eds. *Holocaust: Religious and Philosophical Implications*. New York: Paragon House, 1989.
Rothberg, Michael, and Jared Stark. "After the Witness: A Report from the Twentieth Anniversary Conference of the Fortunoff Video Archive for Holocaust Testimonies at Yale." *History and Memory* 15, no. 1 (2003): 85–96.
Rozett, Robert. "Jewish Resistance." In Dan Stone, ed., *The Historiography of the Holocaust*, 341–363. New York: Palgrave Macmillan, 2004.
Rozinskii, Grigorii. *Deti Minskogo getto*. Tel Aviv: Krugozor, 2004.
Rubenstein, Joshua, and Ilya Altman, eds. *The Unknown Black Book: The Holocaust in the German-Occupied Soviet Territories*. Bloomington and Indianapolis: Indiana University Press, 2008.
Rubenstein, Joshua, and Vladimir P. Naumov, eds. *Stalin's Secret Pogrom: The Postwar Inquisition of the Jewish Anti-Fascist Committee*. New Haven: Yale University Press, 2001.
Rudashevski, Yitskhok. *The Diary of the Vilna Ghetto, June 1941–April 1943*. Edited by Percy Matenko. Tel Aviv: Ghetto Fighters' House, 1973.
Saathoff, Günter. "Die politischen Auseinandersetzungen über die Entschädigung von NS-Zwangsarbeit im Deutschen Bundestag—politische und rechtliche Aspekte." In Klaus Barwig and Günter Saathoff, eds., *Entschädigung für NS-Zwangsarbeit: Rechtliche, historische und politische Aspekte*, 49–64. Baden-Baden, Germany: Nomos, 1998.
Sacks, Michael Paul. "Women in the Industrial Labor Force." In Dorothy Atkinson, Alexander Dallin, and Gail W. Lapidus, eds., *Women in Russia*, 189–204. Stanford: Stanford University Press, 1977.
Sangster, Joan. "Telling Our Stories: Feminist Debates and the Use of Oral History." In Robert Perks and Alistair Thomson, eds., *The Oral History Reader*, 1st ed., 87–100. New York and London: Routledge, 1998.
Santner, Eric L. "History beyond the Pleasure Principle." In Saul Friedlander, ed., *Probing the Limits of Representation: Nazism and the "Final Solution,"* 143–154. Cambridge, MA: Harvard University Press, 1992.

Schrand, Thomas G. "Soviet 'Civic-Minded Women' in the 1930s: Gender, Class and Industrialization in a Socialist Society." *Journal of Women's History* 11, no. 3 (1999): 126-150.
Schreiber, Birgit. "'Leaps of Faith': Die 'Krise des Zeugnisgebens' in narrativen Interviews mit einst in Deutschland versteckten jüdischen Kindern." *Zeitschrift für Politische Psychologie* 9, no. 4 (2001): 189-202.
Schröder, Dieter, and Rolf Surmann. "Entschädigung im Jahrhunderttakt." *Blätter für deutsche und internationale Politik* 3 (1999): 292-295.
Scott, Joan W. "The Evidence of Experience." *Critical Inquiry* 17, no. 4 (1991): 773-797.
——. *Gender and the Politics of History*. Rev. ed. New York: Columbia University Press, 1999.
Schulman, Faye. *A Partisan's Memoir: Woman of the Holocaust*. Toronto, ON: Second Story Press, 1995.
Schuster, Bernard (Berl). *I Will Die Tomorrow, But Not Today*. Edited by Feitche Schuster; translated by Max Rosenfeld. Rochester, NY: Winterman Ink, 2002.
Seidman, Hillel. *The Warsaw Ghetto Diaries*. Southfield, MI: Targum Press, 1997.
Sennett, Richard. *The Corrosion of Character: The Personal Consequences of Work in the New Capitalism*. New York: Norton 1998.
Shearer, David. *Policing Stalin's Socialism: Repression and Social Order in the Soviet Union, 1924-1953*. New Haven: Yale University Press, 2009.
Shepherd, Ben. *War in the Wild East: The German Army and Soviet Partisans*. Cambridge, MA: Harvard University Press, 2004.
Shepherd, Naomi. *A Price Below Rubies: Jewish Women as Rebels and Radicals*. London: Weidenfeld and Nicolson, 1993.
Shlapentokh, Vladimir. *Public and Private Life of the Soviet People: Changing Values in Post-Stalin Russia*. New York: Oxford University Press, 1989.
Shneer, David. *Through Soviet Jewish Eyes: Photography, War, and the Holocaust*. New Brunswick, NJ: Rutgers University Press, 2011.
Shternshis, Anna. "Passover in the Soviet Union, 1917-1941." *East European Jewish Affairs* 31, no. 1 (2001): 61-76.
——. *Soviet and Kosher: Jewish Popular Culture in the Soviet Union, 1923-1939*. Bloomington and Indianapolis: Indiana University Press, 2006.
Shveibish, S. "Evreiskii semeinyi partizanskii otriad Sh. Zorina." *Vestnik Evreiskogo Universiteta v Moskve* 3 (13), 1996: 88-109.
Sierakowiak, Dawid. *Five Notebooks from the Łódź Ghetto*. Translated by Kamil Turowski. New York: Oxford University Press, 1996.
Sinnreich, Helene. "The Rape of Jewish Women during the Holocaust." In Sonja M. Hedgepeth and Rochelle G. Saidel, eds., *Sexual Violence against Jewish Women during the Holocaust*, 108-123. Waltham, MA: Brandeis University Press, 2010.
Slepyan, Kenneth. "The Soviet Partisan Movement and the Holocaust." *Holocaust and Genocide Studies* 14, no. 1 (2000): 1-27.
——. *Stalin's Guerillas: Soviet Partisans in World War II*. Lawrence: University of Kansas Press, 2006.
Slezkine, Yuri. "The USSR as a Communal Apartment, or How a Socialist State Promoted Ethnic Particularism." *Slavic Review* 53, no. 2 (1994): 414-452.
——. *The Jewish Century*. Princeton: Princeton University Press, 2004.
Smilovitskii, Leonid. *Evrei Belarusi: Iz nashei obshchei istorii, 1905-1953*. Minsk: Arti-Feks, 1999.
——. *Katastrofa evreev v Belorussii, 1941-1944 gg*. Tel Aviv: Biblioteka Matveia Chernogo, 2000.

———. "Bor'ba evreev Belorussii za vozvrat svoego imushchestvo i zhilishch v pervoie poslevoennoe desiatiletie, 1944–1954 gg." In V. I. Andreev, ed., *Belarus' u XX stahoddzi*, Vol. 1, 168–178. Minsk: Vodolei, 2002. Available online at http://mb.s5x.org/homoliber.org/ru/xx/xx010120.html. Accessed January 30, 2015.

———. "Antisemitism in the Soviet Partisan Movement, 1941–1944: The Case of Belorussia." *Holocaust and Genocide Studies* 20, no. 2 (2006): 207–234.

Smilovitsky, Leonid. "Minsk Ghetto: An Issue of Jewish Resistance." *SHVUT* 1–2 (17/18) (1995): 161–182.

———. "A Demographic Profile of the Jews in Belorussia from the Pre-war Time to the Post-war Time." *Journal of Genocide Research* 5, no. 1 (2003): 117–129.

Smith, S. A. *The Russian Revolution: A Very Short Introduction*. New York: Oxford University Press, 2002.

Smith, Theresa, and Thomas Oleszczuk. *No Asylum: State Psychiatric Repression in the Former U.S.S.R.* New York: New York University Press, 1996.

Smith, Valerie. "Split Affinities: The Case of Interracial Rape." In Anne C. Herrmann and Abigail J. Stewart, eds., *Theorizing Feminism*, 155–171. Boulder, CO: Westview Press, 1994.

Smolar, Hersh. *The Minsk Ghetto: Soviet Jewish Partisans against the Nazis*. New York: Holocaust Library, 1989.

Snyder, Cindy S., Wesley J. Gabbard, J. Dean May, and Nihada Zulcic. "On the Battleground of Women's Bodies: Mass Rape in Bosnia-Herzegovina." *Affilia: Journal of Women and Social Work* 21, no. 2 (2006): 184–195.

Snyder, Timothy. *Bloodlands: Europe Between Hitler and Stalin*. New York: Basic Books, 2010.

Soiuz Evreev-Invalidov i Veteranov Voiny, ed. *Ia vspominaiu: Vospominaniia evreev-veteranov Velikoi Otechestvennoi voiny*. Moscow: SEIV, 1994.

Spector, Shmuel, ed. *The Encyclopedia of Jewish Life before and during the Holocaust*. 3 vols. New York: New York University Press, 2001.

Stalin, J. V. "Marxism and the National Question" (orig. 1913). *Marxists Internet Archive*. http://www.marxists.org/reference/archive/stalin/works/1913/03.htm. Accessed July 7, 2013.

———. "Radio Broadcast. July 3, 1941." *Marxists Internet Archive*. https://www.marxists.org/reference/archive/stalin/works/1941/07/03.htm. Accessed February 24, 2015.

Stargardt, Nicholas. *Witnesses of War: Children's Lives under the Nazis*. New York: Vintage Books, 2005.

Sterling, Dorothy, ed. *We Are Your Sisters: Black Women in the Nineteenth Century*. New York and London: Norton, 1984.

Streit, Christian. *Keine Kameraden: Die Wehrmacht und die Sowjetischen Kriegsgefangenen, 1941–1945*. Stuttgart, Germany: Deutsche Verlags-Anstalt, 1978.

Strelets, Mikhail. "Uchastie evreev v antigermanskom soprotivlenii na okkupirovannoi territorii Belorussii." In Iakov Z. Basin, ed., *Uroki Kholokosta*, 131–136. Minsk: Kovcheg, 2004.

Strobl, Ingrid. *Die Angst kam erst danach: Jüdische Frauen im Widerstand in Europa, 1939–1945*. Frankfurt am Main: Fischer, 1998.

Suhl, Yuri. *They Fought Back: The Story of Jewish Resistance*. New York: Schocken, 1975.

Surmann, Rolf. "Kleine Geschichte der 'Wiedergutmachung.'" *Blätter für deutsche und internationale Politik* 5 (1999): 585–594.

Taubkin, David. "Moi gorod, znakomyi do slioz." In Z. Tsukerman, ed., *Katastrofa: Poslednie svideteli*, 253–292. Moscow: Dom Evreiskoi Knigi, 2008.

Tec, Nechama. *Defiance: The Bielski Partisans.* New York: Oxford University Press, 1993.

——. *Resilience and Courage: Women, Men, and the Holocaust.* New Haven: Yale University Press, 2003.

Tec, Nechama, and Daniel Weiss. "Eight Photographs of an Execution." *History of Photography* 23, no. 4 (1999): 322–330.

Temkina, Anna. *Seksual'naia zhizn' zhenshchiny: Mezhdu podchineniem i svobodoi.* Saint Petersburg: Izdatel'stvo Evropeiskogo Universiteta, 2008.

Thomson, Alistair. "Four Paradigm Transformations in Oral History." *Oral History Review* 34, no. 1 (2007): 49–70.

Todorov, Tzvetan. *Facing the Extreme: Moral Life in the Concentration Camps.* New York: Metropolitan Books, 1996.

Treister, Mikhail. "Probleski pamiati." In Z. Tsukerman, ed., *Katastrofa: Poslednie svideteli,* 303–344. Moscow: Dom Evreiskoi Knigi, 2008.

Trezise, Thomas. "Between History and Psychoanalysis: A Case Study in the Reception of Holocaust Survivor Testimony." *History and Memory* 20, no. 1 (2008): 7–47.

Trunk, Isaiah. *Judenrat: The Jewish Councils in Eastern Europe under Nazi Occupation.* New York: Macmillan, 1972.

Tsukerman, Z., ed. *Katastrofa: Poslednie svideteli; Vtoraia kniga vospominanii.* Moscow: Dom Evreiskoi Knigi, 2008.

Tumarkin, Nina. *The Living and the Dead: The Rise and Fall of the Cult of World War II in Russia.* New York: Basic Books, 1994.

USC Shoah Foundation Institute Visual History Archive. "Find an Access Site Near You." USC Shoah Foundation. http://sfi.usc.edu/locator. Accessed February 8, 2015.

——. "Interview Guidelines." *USC Shoah Foundation Institute.* http://dornsife.usc.edu/vhi/download/USCSFI_Interviewer_Guidelines_1.pdf Accessed April 1, 2011.

——. "VHA Subject Guide: Countries." University of Southern California Library. http://libguides.usc.edu/content.php?pid=58585&sid=429353. Accessed July 7, 2013.

——. "Videographer Guidelines." USC Shoah Foundation Institute. http://dornsife.usc.edu/vhi/download/USCSFI_Videographer_Guidelines.pdf. Accessed April 1, 2011.

Ushakin, Sergei. "'Nam eto bol'iu dyshat'? O travme, pamiati i soobshchestvakh." In Sergei Ushakin and Elena Trubina, eds., *Travma: Punkty; Sbornik statei,* 5–45. Moscow: Novoe Literaturnoe Obozrenie, 2009.

Vesela, Pavla. "The Hardening of Cement: Russian Women and Modernization." *Feminist Formations* 15, no. 3 (2003): 104–123.

Vinnitsa, Gennadii. *Slovo pamiati.* Orsha, Belarus: Orshanskaia Tipografia, 1997.

——. *Gorech' i bol'.* Orsha, Belarus: Otdel kul'tury Goretskogo raiispolkoma, 1998.

Viola, Lynne. *The Unknown Gulag: The Lost World of Stalin's Special Settlements.* New York: Oxford University Press, 2007.

Voronkov, Viktor, and Elena Chikadze. "Different Generations of Leningrad Jews in the Context of Public/Private Division: Paradoxes of Ethnicity." In Robin Humphrey, Robert Miller, and Elena Zdravomyslova, eds., *Biographical Research in Eastern Europe: Altered Lives and Broken Biographies,* 239–262. Aldershot, UK: Ashgate, 2003.

Walke, Anika. *Jüdische Partisaninnen: Der verschwiegene Widerstand in der Sowjetunion.* Berlin: Karl Dietz Verlag, 2007.

——. "Remembering and Recuperation: Memory Work in the Post-Soviet Context." *Zeitgeschichte* 36, no. 2 (2009): 67–87.
——. "'It Wasn't That Bad in the Ghetto, Was It?'—Living On in the USSR after the Nazi Genocide." In Suzanne Bardgett, David Cesarani, Jessica Reinisch, and J. D. Steinert, eds., *Survivors of Nazi Persecution in Europe after the Second World War: Landscapes after Battle*, Vol. 1, 218–236. London: Vallentine Mitchell, 2010.
——. "Pamiat', gender i molchanie: Ustnaia istoriia v (post-) sovetskoi Rossii i prizrachnaia gran' mezhdu privatnym i publichnym." *Laboratorium: Zhurnal Sotsial'nykh Issledovanii* 1 (2011): 72–95.
Wardi, Dina. *Memorial Candles: Children of the Holocaust*. New York: Routledge, 1994.
Wenk, Silke, and Insa Eschebach. "Soziales Gedächtnis und Geschlechterdifferenz: Eine Einführung." In Insa Eschebach, Sigrid Jacobeit, and Silke Wenk, eds., *Gedächtnis und Geschlecht: Deutungsmuster in Darstellungen des nationalsozialistischen Genozids*, 13–40. Frankfurt am Main: Campus, 2002.
Weinberg, Robert. *Stalin's Forgotten Zion: Birobidzhan and the Making of a Soviet Jewish Homeland; An Illustrated History, 1928–1996*. Berkeley: University of California Press, 1998.
Weintraub, Jeff Alan, and Krishan Kumar, eds. *Public and Private in Thought and Practice: Perspectives on a Grand Dichotomy*. Chicago: University of Chicago Press, 1997.
Weiss-Wendt, Anton. *Murder Without Hatred: Estonians and the Holocaust* Syracuse, NY: Syracuse University Press, 2010.
Weitz, Eric D. *A Century of Genocide: Utopias of Race and Nation*. Princeton: Princeton University Press, 2003.
——. "The Heroic Man and the Ever-Changing Woman: Gender and Politics in European Communism, 1917–1950." In Laura L. Frader and Sonya O. Rose, eds., *Gender and Class in Modern Europe*, 311–352. Ithaca and London: Cornell University Press, 1996.
Wertheim, Anatol. "With Zorin in the Family Camp." In Shlomo Even-Shushan, ed., *Minsk Yizkor Book—Minsk, Jewish Mother City: Memorial Anthology* (translation of *Minsk, ir va-em*), Vol. 2, 392–395. Jerusalem: Irgun yots'e Minsk u-venoteha be-Yisra'el, 1975. http://www.jewishgen.org/yizkor/minsk/min2_392.html. Accessed January 28, 2015.
Wertsch, James. *Voices of Collective Remembering*. New York: Cambridge University Press, 2002.
Whitehead, Anne. *Memory*. London and New York: Routledge, 2009.
Wiederhorn, Jessica. "Survivors of the Shoah Visual History Foundation." *Trauma ResearchNewsletter* 1 (2000). www.traumaresearch.net/focus1/wieder.htm. Accessed March 25, 2011.
Wieviorka, Annette. *The Era of Witness*. Ithaca, NY: Cornell University Press, 2006.
Wolf, Diane L. "Holocaust Testimony: Producing Post-memories, Producing Identities." In Judith M. Gerson and Diane L. Wolf, eds., *Sociology Confronts the Holocaust: Memories and Identities in Jewish Diasporas*, 154–175. Durham, NC: Duke University Press, 2007.
Wood, Elizabeth. *The Baba and the Comrade: Gender and Politics in Revolutionary Russia*. Bloomington and Indianapolis: Indiana University Press, 1997.
Young, James. *Writing and Rewriting the Holocaust: Narrative and the Consequences of Interpretation*. Bloomington and Indianapolis: Indiana University Press, 1988.

Zapruder, Alexandra. *Salvaged Pages: Young Writers' Diaries of the Holocaust*. New Haven: Yale University Press, 2004.

Zeltser, Arkadi. "Inter-War Ethnic Relations and Soviet Policy: The Case of Eastern Belorussia." *Yad Vashem Studies* 34 (2006): 87–124.

Zeltser, Arkady. "The Belorussian Shtetl in the 1920s and 1930s." In Zvi Gitelman and Yaacov Ro'I. Lanham, eds., *Revolution, Repression, and Revival*, 91–111. Lanham, MD: Rowman & Littlefield, 2007.

Zezina, M. R. "The System of Social Protection for Orphaned Children in the USSR." *Russian Social Science Review* 42, no. 3 (2001): 49–51.

Zipfel, Gaby. "'Blood, Sperm, and Tears': Sexuelle Gewalt in Kriegen." *Mittelweg 36* 10, no. 5 (2001): 3–20.

Zolotarev, Vladimir Antonovich, ed., *Partizanskoe dvizhenie: Po opytu Velikoi Otechestvennoi voiny 1941–1945 gg*. Moscow: Kuchovoe Pole, 2001.

Zuker-Bujanowska, Liliana. *Liliana's Journal: Warsaw 1939–1945*. New York: Dial Press, 1980.

Index

abortion, 154, 161, 183–84, 201
Abram Abramovich (Fridman family friend), 174
The Adventures of Pinocchio (Collodi), 89
agency, 20, 112, 113, 201
Aizenshtadt, Pesia, 72, 73, 253n31
Aktion 1005, 104, 119
Allen, Robert C., 252n16
Andersen, Hans Christian, 59–60
Andrichenko, Leonid Vasilevich (Leonid Gol'braikh), 131–32
Ania (Polia Shostak's friend), 169
antisemitism
    as Nazi collaboration, 16–17, 180
    partisan movement and, 132–34, 145–46, 168, 169–170, 199–200
    Polish partisans and, 189
    in postwar Soviet Union, 202, 219–220
    in Soviet society, 74–75, 82
Arendt, Hannah, 6, 32, 104, 283–84n70
Arkadii Teif, 175–76, 189, 198
Armenia, 42–43
Arnold Sabine, 270n114
Association of Former Prisoners of Ghettos and Concentration Camps, vii, 24
Atlas, Hirsh, 170, 188

Babi Yar, 220
Babirshina, Vika, 194
Belarus (Republic of Belarus), xv, 56
Belen'kaia, Liubov, 44, 46, 47, 110
Belorussian Partisan Movement
    antisemitism in, 132–34, 145–46, 168, 169–170, 199–200
    children in, 1–2, 185–87
    combat units in, 136, 166
    double consciousness and, 157–163
    Gomel' and, 120
    Jews in, 132–141, 143–47
    medical specialists in, 182–83
    Operation Hermann and, 177
    origins and organization of, 139–140, 143
    Polish partisans and, 189
    railroad war and, 145
    as shelter for ghetto refugees, 136–38
    Soviet Army and, 204
    Soviet state and, 192–98
    Stalin and, 19–20, 140, 150
    Staroe Selo as contact site for, 169, 175–76, 179, 182
    supply units in, 181
    support for, 122–23
    survival of Jews and, 227
    women and girls in, 147–48, 150–56, 158–59, 164–65, 204
    See also family units (*semeinye otriady*); Zorin family unit
Bemporad, Elissa, 257n105
Bender, Sara, 254n51
Berdichev, 214
Beshenkovichi, 131
BGTO (Bud' Gotov k Trudu i Oborone SSSR, Be Ready for Labor and Defense of the USSR), 61, 73, 149
Bialystok, 138
Bielski, Tuvia, 170, 171
Bielski unit (detachment), 171, 196, 271n8, 274n31, 275n53
biographical work, 160, 224
biological warfare, 124
Birobidzhan (Jewish Autonomous Region), 42
Black Book of Russian Jewry, 8–9, 219
Bobruisk, 48, 52, 113–15, 119
Boder, David, 236n30
Boiko, Maria/Mariia, 83, 166–67
Bolshoe Zarechie, 142
Boroda, Menukha, 110

Botvinnik, Tsilia, 94–95
Boym, Svetlana, 39
Bruskina, Masha, 101, 133–34, 204–5, 220

censorship, 219
Charnyj, Sasha, 281n39
cheders, 44
Cherniak, Liova, 189
Chernis, Ester, 85
Chernyshov, Vasilii (General Platon), 171, 179
children and young people
  in ghettos, 9–11
  in Minsk ghetto, 70–71, 84–90, 92–93, 99–102
  partisan movement and, 1–2, 185–87
  Pioneers and, 40, 43–44
  portrayal of, 7–10
  in postwar Soviet Union, 206–17
  religious and cultural traditions and, 38, 41, 44–55, 77–79, 147
  in Russian district, 81–82, 85, 92
  See also education; individual witnesses
circumcision, 38, 89
Collodi, Carlo, 89
combat units, 136, 166
commemoration, 27, 104–5, 221–22
communality, 16–22, 212–17
compensations, 2, 24, 26, 28, 29

Daimler Benz, 93
delo vrachei (doctors' plot), 219
Derechin, 138
Dieckmann, Christoph, 236n28
Disna, 138
double-consciousness, 15–16, 157–163
Drapkin, Vul'f, 209
Drapkina, Elena (born Levina)
  antisemitism and, 219
  BGTO and, 61
  Bruskina and, 133, 204–5, 220
  death and, 116
  education and, 58–59
  escape from ghetto, 98–99, 136
  German attack and, 72, 73
  interviews with, 221–22
  language and, 63
  in *maliny*, 87
  in Minsk ghetto, 68, 77, 84, 93, 94, 97

  as partisan, 135, 148–150, 151–57, 159, 161, 162–63, 193, 204
  as Pioneer, 59–60, 62–63
  in postwar Soviet Union, 207–9, 215
  religious and cultural traditions and, 57, 58–59, 63, 222–23
Druia, 138
Du Bois, W.E.B., 15–16, 161–62, 265n12
dushegubki (gas vans), 69
Dwork, Deborah, 254n51, 256n80

East Germany, 26–27
education
  in postwar Soviet Union, 210–12, 215–16
  Soviet nationality policies and, 38, 41–42, 45–46, 50, 53, 58–61
  in Zorin family unit, 193–95
Ehrenburg, Ilya, 117
Eichmann, Adolf, 229
Einikayt (Soviet Yiddish newspaper), 172
Einsatzgruppen, 75, 99, 116, 119, 124, 131, 139
Einsatzkommando, 110, 131, 142
Ekaterina II, Tsarina of Russia, 40
Der Emes (Jewish cooperative), 45
emigration, 15
The Encyclopedia of Jewish Life before and during the Holocaust (Spector), 247n41
Epstein, Barbara, 265n16
Epstein, Naum, 254n53
Erenburg, Boris Davidovich, 51
Erenburg, Grigorii
  death and, 129
  education and, 53
  in ghetto, 108, 113–15
  interviews with, 115–16
  language and, 53
  as partisan, 118, 135, 139
  as Pioneer, 54–55
  in postwar Soviet Union, 215
  religious and cultural traditions and, 51–55, 222
  unsuccessful search for family by, 115–16, 117–19, 127
Evsektsiia, 41, 43

Extraordinary State Commission for the Investigation of Atrocities Committed on Soviet Territory, 8, 105, 106, 119, 124

family units (*semeinye otriady*)
  communality in, 17–19
  interethnic solidarity and, 13–14
  recognition of, 166, 199–203
  retaliation and, 188
  as shelter for ghetto refugees, 165–66
  See also Zorin family unit
fasting, 222
Felman, Shoshana, 244n41
Fieseler, Beate, 101
For a Just Cause (Grossman), 128
Frank, Anne, 236n36
Fridliand, Lev, 247n41
Fridliand, Margolia, 44, 46
Fridman, Abram, 57, 74, 91–92
Fridman, Grigorii
  education and, 57
  escape from ghetto, 174–75
  escape from Minsk, 74
  in Minsk ghetto, 92, 95–96
  in postwar Soviet Union, 211
  in Zorin family unit, 179, 180, 185
Fridman, Rita Abramovna. *See* Kazhdan, Rita Abramovna (born Fridman)
Fridman, Rozaliia, 57, 61, 92
Friedländer, Saul, 238n52
Friedman, Sarra, 96

Gaidar, Arkadii, 59–60
Gal'perin, Boris Mikhailovich
  antisemitism and, 220
  education and, 107
  in ghetto, 107, 108, 141–42
  interviews with, 39–40
  language and, 45
  as partisan, 135, 139, 142–49, 152
  as Pioneer, 40, 43–44
  religious and cultural traditions and, 44–46, 47, 223
Gal'perina, Esfir Zakharovna, 45–46, 142, 148
Gantsevichi, 138
Ganzenko, Semion, 170–71, 273–74n28
Garak, Frants Ivanovich, 155
gas vans (*dushegubki*), 69

Generalplan Ost (Master Plan East), 79
Gerasimova, Inna, 272n18, 273n25
Gertsevna, Rakhil', 51
ghettos
  in Belorussia, 70, 104–8, 113–15
  as sites of mass murder, 4, 68, 108, 121, 131
  in Ukraine, 70
  violence and hunger in, 141–42
  See also compensations; Minsk ghetto
Gil'chik, Lev, 138, 170
Gildiner, Tatiana Samuilovna, 79, 99–100
Gindin, Boris, 138, 170
girls. *See* women and girls
Gitelman, Zvi, 228
glasnost (openness), 25–26
Glazebnaia, Ol'ga, 80, 81
Glazebnaia, Varvara, 81
Glubokoe, 138
Goffman, Erving, 259n150
Gol'braikh, Leonid, 131–32, 134, 139
Gol'din, Aleksandr, 49–50
Gomel', 120
Gribok, Alla, 204, 208
Gringauz, Elena, 89
Grossman, Vasily, 128
Gubinskaia, Marusia, 59, 74, 79
Gurskii (partisan commander), 143

Hebrew (language), 41–42, 45, 53
Hellbeck, Jochen, 246–47n37
heroism, 60, 135, 137, 146–47, 196, 202
Hershatter, Gail, 239n53
Himmler, Heinrich, 70
Hirsch, Marianne, 35
Hitler, Adolf, 70
Hochschild, Adam, 283n65
Holocaust scholarship, 30–36
How the Steel Was Tempered (Ostrovskii), 54, 59–60

Iakhontova (Khurgina), Amaliia Moiseevna
  on antisemitism, 82, 170
  death and, 103–4, 127, 130
  education of, 215
  escape from ghetto, 175–76
  on establishment of Minsk ghetto, 76

Iakhontova (Khurgina), Amaliia
    Moiseevna (*Cont.*)
  German attack and, 72
  language and, 249n108
  in Minsk ghetto, 103–4
  as Pioneer, 61
  in postwar Soviet Union, 215
  S. Volk and, 274n42
  in Zorin family unit, 164, 166–67, 178, 185, 193
Iakovlevna, Rita, 277n88
Ianka (Fridman family's neighbor), 174–75
Iarotskii, S.A., 143
Igol'nikov, Lev Aronovich, 50, 213
Igol'nikov, Solomon, 49
illiteracy, 41
interethnic solidarity, 3, 13–14, 16–17, 53, 90, 226
internationalism, 3, 6–7, 37, 226
Ioffe, Moisei, 79
Iron Curtain, 25–27
Isaak (partisan), 185, 209
Iskra (Jewish kolkhoz), 45

Jewish Anti-Fascist Committee, 219
Jewish communities
  assimilation and, 4–5
  in postwar Soviet Union, 217–227
  religious and cultural traditions and, 38, 41, 44–55, 77–79, 147, 218–19, 220–25
  Soviet nationality policies and, 37–39, 40–42
Jewish schools, 42, 43, 50, 59
Judenrat (Jewish Council), 78–79, 94, 97–98

Kamenets, 138
Kaplan, Shalom, 175–76
Kaplinsky, Hirsh, 138, 170
Kazhdan, Rita Abramovna (born Fridman)
  on antisemitism, 75
  antisemitism and, 219
  death and, 116
  education of, 57–58, 211–12
  escape from ghetto, 99, 174–75
  escape from Minsk, 74
  interviews with, 25
  language and, 37, 58
  in Minsk ghetto, 68, 79, 82–83, 84, 91–93, 95, 100, 101
  in postwar Soviet Union, 210–12, 216
  religious and cultural traditions and, 57, 59, 222
  Treister, 274n42
  on women in partisan units, 164–65, 199
  in Zorin family unit, 166–67, 177, 179, 180–81, 183, 185, 188–89, 192–93, 195, 198
Kenneth Slepyan, 272n18
Khubova, Daria, 282n59
Klebanova, Sarra, 46–47
Kletsk, 138
Kliment Efremovich Voroshilov, 266n36
Klitskii, 154
Klüger, Ruth, 34, 106
Kobrin, 138
kolkhozes (collective farms), 40, 45
Komsomol (Communist Party's youth organization), 3, 146, 151
Komsomolskoe Ozero (Komsomol Lake), 71–72
Kopyl', 138
korenizatsiia (indigenization, nativization), 41
kosher slaughtering, 38
Kosmodemianskaia, Zoia, 102, 152
Koval, M.I., 239n59
Kozak, Kuz'ma, 265n16
Kriuchkova, Liudmila, 53
Kube, Wilhelm, 174
Kuiko, Elena, 131
Kuiko, Foma, 131
Kulish, Maria, 175–76
Kulish family, 179
Kuprikhina, Alevtina (Alla)
  death and, 129
  education and, 50
  end of war and, 213–14
  German occupation and, 119, 120–23, 125–27
  in ghetto, 108
  interviews with, 23–24, 32, 48–49
  language and, 50
  in partisan units, 135
  religious and cultural traditions and, 49–51

language, 37–38, 41–42, 58–59, 78
Lapidus, Albert, 96
Lapidus, Israel, 138, 170
Lehnstaedt, Stefan, 245n6
Lenia (Samuil Volk's friend), 90
Lenin, V.I., 194, 245n17
Leva (Samuil Volk's friend), 86
Levin, Abram, 96
Levina, Elena Askarevna. *See* Drapkina, Elena (born Levina)
Leys, Ruth, 244n41
Liakhovichi, 138
Lianders, Ania, 93
Life and Fate (Grossman), 128
Liova (Samuil Volk's friend), 90
Livshits, Rozaliia, 182, 183, 277n96
London Debt Agreement (1953), 241n13
Löwenstein, Karl, 258n131

MacKinnon, Catharine, 279n148
Makhover, Lev, 142
Malina (maliny) (hiding place), 86-7, 256n90
Maloe Zarechie, 142
Marshak, Sonia, 196, 197
McClintock, Anne, 270n116
Melamed, Leonid, 173, 175–76, 179, 189, 199
Mel'tser, A., 195
memory and memory work, 6, 25–30, 32–36, 105–6, 217–227
Merridale, Catherine, 33
Michman, Dan, 233n13
Mikhailov, Nikolai, 150–51
Miles, Tyia, 241n7, 260n9
Mindel, Sonia, 276–77n86
Minsk
    German attack and, 65, 72–74
    Komsomol Lake and, 71–72
    maliny in, 86
    Russian district in, 81–82, 85, 92
    Soviet nationality policies and, 55–56, 147
Minsk ghetto
    children in, 70–71, 84–90, 92–93, 99–102
    domestic labor in, 67–69
    escapes from, 98–99, 172–77
    establishment of, 75–77, 107

    foreign Jews in, 80–81
    Judenrat in, 78–79
    killings in, 69–70, 82–83, 90–92, 95–96, 97–98, 103–5
    lack of food in, 79–81
    in oral history, 99–102
    partisan units as shelter for refugees from, 136–38, 164–69, 170–71, 172–74, 179
    religious and cultural traditions in, 77–79
    sexual violence in, 69, 96–97, 101
    underground movement in, 71, 94–95, 132–34
    women and girls in, 67–69, 89, 91–93, 100–101
    work and, 93–95
Mir, 138
Mordkhilevich, Vladimir
    escape from ghetto, 175–76
    in Minsk ghetto, 78, 89
    as Pioneer, 59–60
    religious and cultural traditions and, 78, 249n101
    in Zorin family unit, 177, 133, 187, 190–92, 194, 195, 198
Mushkin, Ilya, 78–79, 85
Musial, Bogdan, 275n53

Nastiporenko family, 1, 205
Negnevitzki, Yakov
    death and, 116
    Komsomol Lake and, 72
    parents of, 249n94
    as Pioneer, 61
    on Soviet nationality policies, 43
    on women in Soviet society, 62
    in Zorin family unit, 178, 198
Nesvizh, 138
Nicholas, Lynn H., 235n25
nostalgia, 39
Novogrudok, 138
Nuremberg Laws (1935), 64

Oboz, Zoia, 175–76, 181, 185, 191
Okon (Okun), Leonid
    on Komsomol Lake, 72
    in Minsk ghetto, 84
    parents of, 249n94
    in Zorin family unit, 171, 180, 182, 183, 190, 191, 198

Oktia (Elena Drapkina's friend), 98
Operation Cottbus, 156–57
Operation Hermann, 177–79, 270n108
oral history
  asmemorywork, 25–30, 32–36
  challenges in, 23–25
  Holocaust scholarship and, 30–36
  importance of, 104–7, 217
  as sources, 127–29
  See also Survivors of the Shoah Visual History Archive (VHA)
Orlovskii, Kirill, 138, 170
orphanages, 125
OSOAVIAKhIM (Obshchestvo sodeistviia oborone i aviatsionno-khimicheskomu stroitel'stvu, Society for Promotion of Defense, Aviation, and Chemical Development), 61–2.
Ostrovskii, Nikolai, 54, 59–60
otriady (units), 143

Pale of Settlement, 3–4, 40, 51, 107
Parfimchuk, Lidiia, 93
Parichi, 123–24
Parkhomenko combat unit, 171, 196
partisan movement. *See* Belorussian Partisan Movement
partisan unit No. 106, 136, 165–66, 171, 182, 195, 199–200. *See also* Zorin family unit
partizanskie raiony (partisan zones), 156
Passerini, Luisa, 282n59
passports, 43
Pateman, Carol, 279n148
Patricia Heberer, 235n25
patriotism, 37, 226
Ped'ko, Elena, 1–2, 109, 113
Ped'ko, Frida
  antisemitism and, 220
  commemoration and, 221
  death and, 1–3, 5–6, 109–13, 127, 128–29
  education of, 215–16
  in ghetto, 108
  in postwar Soviet Union, 2–3, 205, 207–8, 214, 215–17
  religious and cultural traditions and, 47–48, 222
  Soviet Army and, 125

Pekhman-Khurgina, Anna Borisovna, 73
perestroika (restructuring), 25–26, 225
Pioneers
  partisan movement and, 195
  Soviet nationality policies and, 40, 43–44, 54–55, 59–61
  summer camps and, 60
Plaszow Zehnerschaft, 18
Pogorelaia, Vera, 105
Polish partisans, 189
Ponomarenko, Panteleimon, 140, 150, 170
Portelli, Alessandro, 32
Portnova, Nekhama, 84
Professor Mamlock (film), 122
Proniagin, Pavel, 138, 170
psychoanalytical practices, 33–34
Pudovik, Roman, 28

Rapoport, Nathan, 162
Raskin, F., 197
Red Army, 145
rel'sovaia voina (railroad war), 145
Rentrop, Petra, 254n40
resistance, 137–38, 168–69, 200
Rivkin, Mr., 49
Rivkina, Riva, 49
Rodina-mat' (Mother Homeland), 158
Rogachev, 48, 49–50, 119–120
Rose, Deborah Bird, 241–42n16
Rübe (ghetto commander), 96–97
Rudnia, 179
Rusakovich, Aleksandra, 267n39
Ryzhkovichi, 40, 44–45, 107, 142, 147

Safonov, Gennadii, 170
Sagal'chik, Anna, 193–94, 196, 197, 219, 222
sanctuary of silence, 12
Scheimer, Willi, 93
Schindler's List (film), 241n6
Schlegelhofer, Karl, 76
semeinye otriady. *See* family units (*semeinye otriady*)
sexual violence
  abortions and, 183–84
  in Minsk ghetto, 69, 96–97, 101

partisan movement and, 20, 153–54, 159
power and, 10–12
Sharkovshchina, 138
Shchedrin, 51–52, 147
Shcherbatsevich, Volodia, 133, 205
Sherbakova, Irina, 282n59
Shoah Visual History Foundation, 23–4, 29, 241n6. *See also* Survivors of the Shoah Visual History Archive (VHA)
Shklov, 107, 142
Shostak, Polia, 169, 185, 211
Shostak, Sonia, 185, 211
shtetls, 40, 44, 51, 147, 245n13
Sirotkina, Mania, 205
Sirotkina, Maria Iosifovna, 47, 109
Skirmontovo, 179
slavery, 16, 112, 162, 241n7, 265n12
Slavnoe, 1, 47–48, 109–11, 127, 147
Slonim, 138
Slutskaia, Galina (born Klebanova), 46–47, 267n42
Smilovitskii, Leonid, 235n25, 250n110, 251n3, 268n69, 272n18, 273n26
Smirnova, Vera Vladimirovna, 59, 68, 82, 84, 256n84
Smolar, Hersh, 273n21
The Snow Queen (Andersen), 59–60
Soboleva, Raisa, vii–viii
soedineniia (partisan formations), 143
Sol'nikov, Mikhail, 132
Solomonova, Dora, 194
Sonderghetto, 80–81
Soviet Army, 106, 118, 125, 151, 204
Soviet nationality policy
education and, 38, 41–42, 45–46, 50, 53, 58–61
language and, 37–38, 41–42, 58–59
Pioneers and, 40, 43–44, 54–55, 59–61
portrayal of, 37–39
religious and cultural traditions and, 38, 40–41, 44–59, 63–66, 147
Soviet Union
glasnost and *perestroika* in, 25–26
Iron Curtain and, 25–27
militarization in, 61–63
treatment of Jews in, 12–13
Spielberg, Steven, 30

Stalin, Joseph
doctors' plot and, 219
German attack and, 72
partisan movement and, 19–20, 140, 150, 194–96
on Soviet culture and values, 185, 245n17
Staraia Dubrova, 123
Stargardt, Nicholas, 235n25
Staroe Selo, 169, 175–76, 179, 182
Stasevich, Piotr I., 1, 111, 113
Stockholm International Forum on the Holocaust (2000), 283n67
supply units, 181
Survivors of the Shoah Visual History Archive (VHA), 23–24, 30–32, 34–35, 48–49, 116, 125–26. *See also* Shoah Visual History Foundation
synagogues, 44
synovia polka (sons of the regiment), 198

Taubkin, David, 79, 80, 89, 255n61
Tec, Nechama, 272n18, 275n53
Terebeinoe, 179
testimonies, 30–32
Timchuk, I.M., 150
Timur and His Team (Gaidar), 59–60
trauma, 16, 33–4, 206–7, 212–17
Treister, Mikhail
on antisemitism, 75, 170
German attack and, 73
as guide for ghetto refugees, 173–74, 175
R. Kazhdan and, 274n42
in Minsk ghetto, 68, 80, 81, 82, 84, 93–95, 96, 101
parents of, 249n94
as Pioneer, 59
in Zorin family unit, 166–67, 180, 186, 191
Trezise, Thomas, 33–34
Tristsenetskaia, Anastasia Ustinovna, 122–23, 125–26
Trus', Kirill, 133, 205
Tseitlin, Lev, 210
Tsirlina, Ekaterina, 72, 94–95, 166, 199, 220
Tsukerman, Lilia, 80
typhus, 124

Ukraine, 17, 42–43, 70, 228
United States Holocaust Memorial Museum, 24
Utiosov, Leonid, 186

VHA. See Survivors of the Shoah Visual History Archive (VHA)
Victory Day, 125, 221
Vlasov Army, 144
Volk, Folia, 58
Volk, Revekka, 58
Volk, Samuil
  death and, 127
  education of, 60, 210
  escape from ghetto, 175–76
  German attack and, 65
  Iakhontova and, 274n42
  in Minsk ghetto, 68, 84, 85–86, 87–88, 89–90
  in postwar Soviet Union, 209–10
  religious and cultural traditions and, 58, 221
  in Zorin family unit, 166–67, 178, 183, 185, 187, 194, 195, 198, 209
Volk, Ziama
  education of, 210
  escape from ghetto, 175–76
  in Minsk ghetto, 87–88, 90
  in postwar Soviet Union, 209–10
  in Zorin family unit, 185, 195, 198

Warsaw ghetto uprising, 70, 162
Wertheim, Anatol, 197
West Germany, 26–27
Wolf, Diana, 243n35
Wolf, Konrad, 122
women and girls
  abortions and, 154, 161, 183–84, 201
  domestic labor and, 20, 45–46, 67–69, 134
  education and, 45–46
  militarization and, 61–63
  in Minsk ghetto, 67–69, 89, 91–93, 100–101
  in partisan units, 134, 147–48, 150–56, 158–59, 164–65, 184, 199, 204
  Plaszow Zehnerschaft and, 18
  in postwar Soviet Union, 207–12

recognition of, 101–2, 132–35, 147–48, 204–5
sexual violence and, 10–12, 20, 69, 96–97, 153–54, 159
Soviet Army and, 151
Soviet nationality policies and, 37–38, 42, 44
See also individual witnesses

Yad Vashem Archive, 24
Yiddish
  in Minsk ghetto, 78
  in Shchedrin, 51
  Soviet nationality policies and, 37, 41–42, 50, 53, 59, 63
Yisrael Gutman, 271n10
Young Pioneer Organization of the USSR. See Pioneers

Zalesskaia, Sonia
  antisemitism and, 82
  escape from ghetto, 175–76
  in Minsk ghetto, 68, 84, 85, 89, 90
  move to the ghetto, 67
  in Zorin family unit, 166–67, 195
Zamenshtein (first name unknown), 79
Zelenko, Roza, 60, 80, 81
Zeltser, Arkady, 247n40
Zemlianka, 123, 185–6
Zhlobin, 50, 120, 124
Zhulega, Nadezhda Alekseevna, 123
Zima (Fridman family's neighbor), 174–75
Zimbabwe, 270n112
Zorin, Shalom
  discipline and, 167
  as father, 196
  formation of the unit and, 170–72
  last attack on the unit and, 190
  letter to Stalin and, 195
  medical specialists and, 182
  orders by, 181
  schooling and, 193–94
  speeches by, 195–96
  Treister and, 186
  unit as shelter for ghetto refugees and, 164
Zorin family unit
  communality in, 17–18
  discipline in, 167, 190–91

education and instruction in, 193–95
end of war and, 209
formation and evolution of, 170–72
gender roles in, 196–97, 198–203
hunger in, 180–81, 190–91
last attack on, 190
locations for, xix
medical specialists in, 182–83
Operation Hermann and, 177–79
"real partisans" in, 187–192
recognition of, 166–68, 200–203
as shelter for ghetto refugees and Jewish family unit, 136, 164–69, 170–71, 172–74, 179
as supply unit, 181
symbolic familial relationships in, 184–87, 196
tasks and military assignments in, 179–184
trip to, 172–77
See also partisan unit No. 106

THE OXFORD ORAL HISTORY SERIES

J. Todd Moye (University of North Texas)
Kathryn Nasstrom (University of San Francisco)
Robert Perks (The British Library),
Series Editors

Donald A. Ritchie,
Senior Advisor

Approaching an Auschwitz Survivor: Holocaust Testimony and Its Transformations Edited by Jürgen Matthäus

Singing Out: An Oral History of America's Folk Music Revivals David K. Dunaway and Molly Beer

Freedom Flyers: The Tuskegee Airmen of World War II J. Todd Moye

Launching the War on Poverty: An Oral History, Second Edition Michael L. Gillette

The Firm: The Inside Story of the Stasi Gary Bruce

The Wonder of Their Voices: The 1946 Holocaust Interviews of David Boder Alan Rosen

They Say in Harlan County: An Oral History Alessandro Portelli

The Oxford Handbook of Oral History Edited by Donald A. Ritchie

Habits of Change: An Oral History of American Nuns Carole Garibaldi Rogers

Soviet Baby Boomers: An Oral History of Russia's Cold War Generation Donald J. Raleigh

Bodies of Evidence: The Practice of Queer Oral History Edited by Nan Alamilla Boyd and Horacio N. Roque Ramírez

Lady Bird Johnson: An Oral History Michael L. Gillette

Dedicated to God: An Oral History of Cloistered Nuns Abbie Reese

Listening on the Edge: Oral History in the Aftermath of Crisis Edited by Mark Cave and Stephen M. Sloan

Chinese Comfort Women: Testimonies from Imperial Japan's Sex Slaves Peipei Qiu, with Su Zhiliang and Chen Lifei

Doing Oral History, Third Edition Donald A. Ritchie

A Guide to Oral History and the Law, Second Edition John A. Neuenschwander